An Illustrated History of Modern Europe
1789–1974
New Edition

An Illustrated History of Modern Britain
by Denis Richards, MA
and J. W. Hunt, MA

A HISTORY OF BRITAIN
GENERAL EDITOR
DENIS RICHARDS, MA

Medieval Britain
Denis Richards, MA and A. D. Ellis, MA

Britain under the Tudors and Stuarts
Denis Richards, MA

Britain 1714–1851
Denis Richards, MA and Anthony Quick, MA

Britain 1851–1945
Denis Richards, MA and Anthony Quick, MA

Twentieth-Century Britain
Denis Richards, MA and Anthony Quick, MA

An Illustrated History of Modern Europe 1789–1974
New Edition

Denis Richards MA
Formerly Principal of Morley College and
Longman Fellow, University of Sussex

Longman

Longman Group Limited
London
Associated companies, branches and representatives
throughout the world

First published 1938
New editions 1939, 1940, 1943, 1950
Sixth edition 1977
Second impression 1978

ISBN 0 582 34106 X

Printed in Hong Kong
by Sheck Wah Tong Printing Press Ltd

Contents

Maps

Acknowledgements

For permission to reproduce photographs we are grateful to the following: Collection of Bayerische National Museum, Munich. Photo by courtesy of the George Eastman House, New York, page 197; The Bettmann Archive, page 265; Bibliotheque Nationale, Paris, page 39; Österreichische National-bibliothek, page 110; Birmingham Public Libraries, page 56; British Museum, pages 113, 183, 213 and 248; Photographie Bulloz, pages 24, 28, 34 (right) and 52; Camera Press, pages 274, 337, 357 (Photo by Inter Nationes); Comune di Milano. Collection Bertarelli, page 134; cartoon on page 360 from Paul Flora *Zeitvertreib* (c). Diogenes Verlag AG Zurich 1969; cartoon on page 304 from *Simplicissimus* Ed. E. Roth. © Karl Arnold Erben, München; Fototeca Servizio Informazioni, Rome, page 310 (left); Musée Carnavalet. Photo: Giraudon, Paris, page 21; Photo-Hachette, pages 11 and 59 (right); Imperial War Museum, pages 163, 264, 267, 268, 310 (right) and 333; Illustrated London News, pages 189, 198 and 292; Fried Krupp GMBH, Essen, pages 203 and 206; Keystone Press Agency, page 355; cartoons by David Low by arrangement with the Trustees and the London Evening Standard, pages 321, 325, 334, 340, 342, 344 and 348; Mansell Collection, pages 18, 30, 34 (left), 59 (left), 71, 153, 195, 199, 211 and 336; Marconi Co Ltd., Chelmsford, page 208; Museo del Prado, Madrid, page 51; Popperfoto, page 273; Punch Publications Ltd, pages 83, 88, 90, 93, 95, 100, 115, 128, 131, 136, 138, 145, 147, 148, 149, 151, 161, 171, 172, 173, 186, 216, 219, 229, 240, 242, 244, 246, 261 and 278; Radio Times Hulton Picture Library, pages 54, 117, 125, 177, 237, 279, 288, 302 and 305 (right); H. Roger-Viollet, page 200; Photo: Science Museum, London, pages 7 and 191; Bildarchiv Preussischer Kulturbesitz, Berlin (c), pages 106, 193, 224, 258 and 270. Time Life Picture Agency © Time Inc 1976. Photo: John Dominis; Ullstein Bilderdienst, page 305 (left); USIS, pages 330 and 350; The Wallace Collection. Crown (c), page 17; John Webb FRPS, page 112.

Preface to the Sixth Edition

When this book was originally written in 1938 its proportions were framed to meet common requirements at that time. The treatment of events from 1871 to 1918 was less full than for the period 1789 to 1871, and the chapter dealing with 1919 to 1938 was included more for general interest than serious study. In the second, third and fourth editions minor changes brought the story up to 1939, and in the fifth edition a new chapter dealt with 1939 to 1945. In this sixth edition the period 1871 to 1945 is now by extensive additions treated at roughly the same length as the period 1789 to 1871, and a new final chapter provides, more briefly, a survey of the years 1945–74. In addition there is a new introductory chapter describing Europe in the 1780s, and some separate treatment of economic developments. Large numbers of new illustrations have been added, the whole text revised, and the format redesigned on more modern and more generous lines. It is hoped that these changes, though inevitably resulting in a larger and more expensive book, will also result in a more useful one for current needs.

In my original preface I explained that the story had been 'kept fairly strictly to the internal history and the interplay of the (continental) great Powers', and that it had also been kept very largely 'to the path of politics and economics'. This still remains true of the new version. Within the space available, I have not felt it wise to include a general cultural history of the period as well.

I should like to repeat my thanks to the friends (notably Miss Margaret Hunt and Mr J.W. Hunt) who helped me when the book was first written, and to express my warmest gratitude to Mrs Elizabeth Hennessy, Mrs Judith Iltis and Mrs Pamela Johnson for their help in connection with the new edition.

D.R.
Autumn 1974

INTRODUCTION
The French Revolution –
Starting-Point of the Modern Age?

'Ancient', 'Medieval' and 'Modern,' as names for periods of history, are of course merely convenient labels. In themselves they have no fixed meaning or hard-and-fast limits. When we talk of 'the end of the Middle Ages' or 'the beginning of Modern Times', we are thinking in purely Western terms – the Chinese have other ideas – and we are usually thinking of the great complex of changes which occurred around the fifteenth and sixteenth centuries AD. Among these changes we think especially of the Renaissance (or increased study of classical art and learning) and the Reformation, which split the Catholic church and created Protestantism. We think, too, of the discovery of the New World and the sea-routes from Europe to the Far East, of the invention or development of printing and of weapons using gunpowder, of the great extension of trade and the rise of a wealthy merchant class. And we think of the enlarged, powerful states built up by kings strong enough to clamp down on feudal independence – states which in a few cases, such as England and France, could already be described as national.

These changes were so important that they soon became regarded as marking the end of one epoch, from then on called the Middle Ages, and the beginning of another – the Modern Age. Most historians have found it convenient to use these terms ever since. But time has gone on, and in the past two hundred years the world has seen more changes, and much greater ones, than in the previous two thousand. So we should have a very good case if we pleaded for a fresh definition of the Modern Age. We might argue that it should be taken as beginning with the scientific movement of the seventeenth century, or with revolutionary democracy in the late eighteenth or with steam-power, railways and industrialisation in the nineteenth, or with mass motoring, flight and world wars in the twentieth. We could even say, quite rightly, that the placing of the first men on the moon in 1970 opened up such fresh vistas for mankind that it heralded the dawn of a new age – Modern Times!

All this means that where we believe the modern era to begin depends not only on the facts but on habit. It also implies that human history is a continuous process, chopped up into sections only for purposes of study. If we are doing this chopping up, we usually find that a single event is not a satisfactory division in itself. We can see, however, that from time to time a whole series of events or developments brings about really profound change. At such moments we may feel that mankind is moving into a new age, and that we can draw a useful historical dividing line.

In this sense, if we look not for 'the starting-point of the modern age' but for 'one of the main starting points of what can reasonably be regarded as the modern age', we shall certainly find this in the great French Revolution. It is with an account of the French Revolution that this book accordingly opens. But the French Revolution did not, of course, come unheralded out of the blue. Many of its ideas were to be found in the works of writers earlier in the eighteenth century, and as a revolution proclaiming democratic principles it was anticipated by the American Revolution of 1775–83 – the war of independence successfully waged by Britain's 'old thirteen' colonies in North America against the government of George III.

The French Revolution in fact was only one of a number of developments which made the succeeding period very different from the preceding one. Outwardly, it probably altered men's lives less than that other so-called revolution, of a more gradual and peaceful kind, which began in Britain in the eighteenth century: the Industrial Revolution, with its growth of machinery, factories and towns. But the system of government under which men live, and their citizen rights, which is what the French Revolution was largely about, may be just as important to human progress as an increased supply of material things, which was the achievement of the Industrial Revolution. At any rate the two revolutions together helped to transform the largely agricultural Europe of the eighteenth century, dominated by the aristocracy, into the highly industrialised Europe of today, dominated by the common man – or his declared representatives.

Some of the importance of the French Revolution lies in the way its battles went echoing on in France throughout the nineteenth century. As late as 1905–6, French politics were still being fought around issues, such as the relations of Church and State, which had divided Frenchmen as far back as the 1790s. But much of its importance also lies in the Revolution's impact on the rest of Europe and the world. In one way or another, but mostly by inspiring revolution or by direct conquest, the French revolutionaries and their heir Napoleon Bonaparte affected almost the whole of Europe. South America, too, became profoundly influenced, as did part of the West Indies. Almost everywhere the struggles continued long after the Revolution itself into the second half of the nineteenth century. On all sides popular or liberal movements strove to overthrow aristocratic governments, and aristocratic governments strove to suppress popular or liberal movements.

In much the same way, we witness today the effects of a later and still more radical Revolution – the seizure of power by the Bolsheviks, or communists, in Russia in 1917. More than half a century later, people are still fighting or struggling along the battle-lines laid down by the Russian Revolution.

CHAPTER I
Europe on the Eve of the French Revolution

Europe on the eve of the French Revolution was more varied than it is nowadays, though it had no division as rigid as the Soviet's present-day 'Iron Curtain'. In general, western Europe was very advanced compared with eastern Europe. The two states at the eastern extremities – the Russian and the Ottoman Empires – were undoubtedly the most backward of all.

In the north the most important power was Sweden. During the seventeenth and eighteenth centuries Sweden had made many conquests but by the 1780s had largely exhausted herself and given up her continental ambitions. She still, however, held Finland and some territory in Germany. Her monarchy was fairly strong, having recently managed to bring the Swedish parliament and nobility under control. Her peasants were free, unlike those in eastern Europe, who were mostly serfs bound to the land on which they worked.

The second strongest country in the north was Denmark, which controlled Norway and had a large navy. Her monarchy was still autocratic, and many of her peasants were still serfs – though those of Norway were not. The Scandinavian lands as a whole played an important trading role in Europe, especially in the supply of naval stores, furs, fish, grain and minerals. Trade apart, their influence beyond the Baltic was now small.

In the east lay the vast undeveloped lands of the Russian Empire, then as now only partly in Europe. It had steadily grown from the fortress and trading centre of Moscow. In the course of the fourteenth and fifteenth centuries the rulers of Moscovy, supported by the Orthodox Church to which the Russian peoples belonged, had freed themselves from the earlier Mongol invaders of Russia and taken over neighbouring territories. By the sixteenth century the duke or prince of Moscovy had become king or Tsar (a Slavonic form of 'Caesar'), and his realm stretched from the Arctic to the Caspian and across the Urals into Siberia. It was the task of Tsar Peter the Great in the early eighteenth century to give this kingdom a westward thrust by winning an outlet to the Baltic, and by establishing at the head of the Gulf of Finland a new capital, St Petersburg. Peter, who took the additional title of Emperor, also gave Russian institutions (including the nobility) a dose of compulsory westernisation. His main object seems to have been to make Russia's government, industry and armed forces strong enough to hold their own against the West. Of course, he could barely scratch the surface of his huge country, but Peter nevertheless succeeded in making it one of the great European powers.

Catherine the Great (1762–96) – and the 'Enlightenment'

Russia's ruler when the French Revolution broke out was the Empress Catherine II, the 'Great'. Like Peter, she believed in modernisation. A German by birth, she was a true product of 'the Enlightenment', the movement in eighteenth-century Europe which criticised superstition and the blind forces of tradition and pleaded instead for reforms inspired by human reason. But although Catherine made improvements in Russian law and institutions and encouraged knowledge of western culture, Russia remained a complete autocracy: the Tsars' power was absolute. In at least one respect Catherine set her country back. To keep the nobles loyal to the throne she gave them large grants of Crown lands and estates in her newly acquired territories. The result was to extend serfdom to many areas where it was previously unknown.

Whatever her limitations as a reformer, Catherine was certainly a worthy successor to Peter the Great as an empire-builder. Catherine extended Russia southwards to the Black Sea and into the Crimea by warring against the remaining Tartar tribesmen and their supporters the Ottoman Turks. By joint action with Prussia and Austria she dismembered a large part of Poland and came off with the lion's share of the spoils.

The Ottoman Empire

Russia's neighbour to the south was the great Moslem power, the Ottoman or Turkish Empire whose Sultan reigned at Constantinople. This empire had reached its zenith in the seventeenth century, when for the second time the Turkish forces threatened Vienna The flood of Turkish success had been stemmed, and Hungary freed, but the Turks still held power over the Christian peoples of south-east Europe: the Serbs, Wallachians, Bulgars, Greeks and others. Because of this difference in religion between governors and governed, the Turks never formed a real state out of all this territory; they were there merely as occupiers. Their rule was generally light – except when taxes were unpaid or resistance offered. Massacres and atrocities then quickly became the order of the day.

In addition to the Balkan countries, the Ottoman Empire included most of Asia Minor, the Levant and North Africa. All the local rulers, whether Muslims in Algiers, Egypt and Syria, or Greeks as was often the case in the European provinces, enjoyed a good deal of independence. In fact by the late eighteenth century the Ottoman Empire was ripe for breaking up. At all times, Russia and Austria were ready to speed up the breaking.

The Hapsburg territories

In south-east Europe, the Ottoman Empire's northern neighbour was the kingdom of Hungary. This had come under the rule of the House of Hapsburg, whose power stretched out from their capital, Vienna, in their ancestral duchy of Austria. There was no one name given to all the Hapsburg possessions, which, besides Austria and Hungary, included Bohemia and Moravia (now part of Czecho-Slovakia), Galicia (now part of Poland), the Hungarian dependency of Croatia (now part of Yugoslavia), territory in northern Italy, and the southern or Austrian Netherlands (now Belgium). Over all these lands stood the head of the House of Hapsburg, who was also by custom elected the Emperor of what was officially called 'The Holy Roman Empire of the German Nation'. The Holy Roman Empire, by the eighteenth century more usually known as the Empire, was a loose grouping of more than 300 states covering modern Germany and some areas beyond. Both as the Emperor and as the ruler of Austria and other Germanic lands, the head of the Hapsburgs had a big stake in what we call Germany, but most of his territory was not German at all. Inhabited by many different nationali-

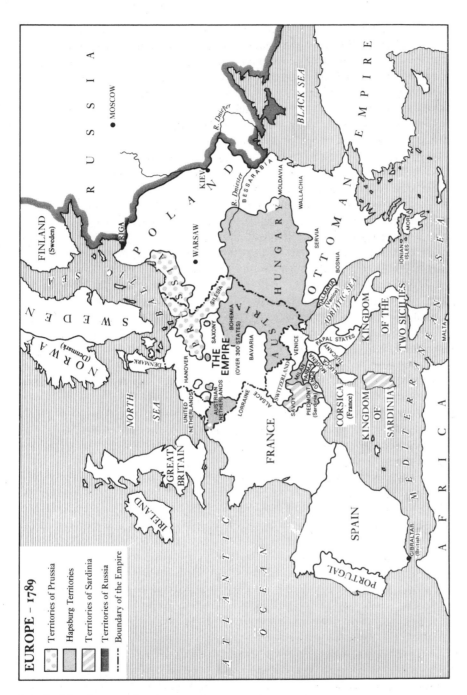

EUROPE – 1789

Legend:
- Territories of Prussia
- Hapsburg Territories
- Territories of Sardinia
- Territories of Russia
- Boundary of the Empire

ties, the Hapsburg realms became known as the Austrian Empire in 1804 and as Austria-Hungary in 1867. Outside Italy and the Netherlands they were largely agricultural, and in central Europe Germans usually ran the bigger towns.[1]

---

[1] Until 1867 the Hapsburg state will normally be referred to in this book, for the sake of convenience, as Austria.

Joseph II – an 'enlightened despot'

The Hapsburg ruler and Emperor when the French Revolution broke out was Joseph II. Like Catherine II of Russia, he was a disciple of 'the Enlightenment' and aimed to rule as an enlightened despot. Some of his reforms were admirable, such as his greater religious toleration and the ending of serfdom on his hereditary lands. But his relentless energy, his determination to enforce economies and increase state revenue, his interference with local customs and his attempts to secure uniformity, for example, by making the German language compulsory for official purposes, gradually created overwhelming opposition. Finally he had to withdraw most of his reforms, and he died in 1790 bitterly conscious of his failures.

Holy Roman Empire

The Holy Roman Empire, of which the ruler of Austria was traditionally elected head, was described by Voltaire during the eighteenth century as 'neither holy, nor Roman, nor an empire'. The Emperor in fact was largely a figurehead, and though there was a Diet, or assembly of rulers of the different states, it had very limited authority. Nearly all the real power rested with the state rulers themselves. Only the greatest of these states, however – the nine whose rulers elected the Emperor – counted for much in European politics. Among these nine, Bavaria, Saxony and Hanover (whose Elector was also king of Great Britain and Ireland) were all important; but the outstanding state, apart from the territories directly under the Emperor himself, was the kingdom of Prussia. Its creators, the Hohenzollern Electors of Brandenburg, had begun by building up a strong army and a military tradition. Their successor Frederick II – Frederick the Great – an 'enlightened despot' who died just before the French Revolution, used these assets to extend the Prussian kingdom still further, mainly at the expense of Austria and Poland.

Prussia

Poland

To her great misfortune, Poland by the mid-eighteenth century had three very powerful neighbours – Prussia, Austria and Russia. At the beginning of the century she had been a large kingdom extending far beyond strictly Polish areas. Her peculiar institutions, however, made it hard for her to remain a great power – institutions such as an elective monarchy (which encouraged outside powers to back rival candidates) and the 'liberum veto', or free veto, by which any member of the Polish Diet could block a proposed measure by his single vote. This privilege made it easy for foreign powers, by bribing a few individuals, to paralyse Polish action whenever they chose. Notorious for the anarchic behaviour of the nobles who dominated the country, and who until 1778 had the power of life and death over their serfs, Poland became less and less able to withstand her three big neighbours. In 1772, on Prussia's suggestion, the three surrounding powers settled their own differences by agreeing to rob Poland, whom they stripped of a third of her territory and a half of her population. Within a little more than twenty years, they were to gobble up all the rest.

Italy

No single authority as yet ruled the whole of Italy. The Italian peninsula, though sharing a common language and literature, was still a conglomeration of kingdoms, duchies and republics. It had long suffered from internal warfare, often brought about by outside rulers eager to acquire Italian territory. By the late eighteenth century the most important state in the south was the kingdom of Naples and Sicily ('the two Sicilies') ruled by a member of the Spanish branch of the Bourbon family. Naples was a great city, but most of Sicily was desperately poor. In the centre of the peninsula lay the States of the Church, under the sovereignty of the Pope. They contained only two big cities – Rome and Bologna – and were noted

Kingdom of Naples and Sicily

States of the Church

mainly for poverty, backwardness, and malaria. In the north of Italy the rising power was Piedmont, with the fast-growing city of Turin as its capital. It was ruled by the House of Savoy, whose territory also included the island of Sardinia – which gave its name to this whole northern kingdom. Among other important states were the duchies of Modena, Parma, and Tuscany in central Italy, and the great trading republic of Venice in the north-east. The rulers of all these states, though sometimes of foreign origin – Tuscany, for instance, was ruled by the younger brother of the Hapsburg Emperor – at least lived in the State concerned. Most of Lombardy, including its greatest city Milan, however, came directly under an outside power. It had become a Hapsburg possession early in the eighteenth century, and was ruled – and usually ruled well – by local Italians under an Austrian viceroy. Socially, Italy was almost as diverse as she was politically. Cities of great prosperity and artistic magnificence existed side by side with areas of appalling poverty.

Kingdom of Sardinia

Hapsburg rule over Lombardy

Italy was only a 'geographical expression', incapable of united action. Spain, on the contrary, was a great power, though not as dominant as she had been earlier. Her decline, which had set in under her later Hapsburg monarchs during the seventeenth century, had been halted under her new Bourbon kings in the eighteenth, and she was still the ruler of a great empire. Early on the scene in Atlantic exploration, she held vast tracts of Central America from California and Texas downwards, most of South America except Brazil, and several of the West Indian islands, besides other outposts in the Philippines.

Spain

Spain had been strong in her religious, and to some extent in her national, unity, though the latter was marred by the resentment of Catalonians, Aragonese and Basques against the supremacy of Castile. The foundation of Spain's wealth had been gold and silver from the New World, but this had also brought problems. Such cheaply acquired riches, which could easily buy goods in the world markets, discouraged manufacture and even enterprising agriculture at home. Spain thus combined great wealth with terrible rural poverty, and intellectually she suffered from the Church's stranglehold on independent thinking, exerted through the Inquisition. In foreign policy, the Spanish kings preserved a steady alliance with their fellow Bourbons in France, and this helped Spain to stand up to British enmity. Britain was determined to break down Spain's monopoly of trade with the Spanish colonies and she had already partly succeeded. Several times in the eighteenth century the British and the Spanish fought each other. During the Seven Years War of 1756–63 victory had gone to Britain; but the most recent bout of fighting, when the Spanish helped the Americans during their War of Independence, had ended in favour of Spain.

Hostilities with Britain

Spain's neighbour Portugal had survived a period of Spanish annexation and regained her independence in 1640. She still owned a large colonial empire, including Brazil, but had lost most of her eastern possessions to the more enterprising Dutch. As with Spain, her imports of gold discouraged industrial development, and despite efforts at modernisation during the 1750s–70s she remained one of the poorest and most backward countries of Europe. This did not stop her spending enormous sums on the construction of churches. She retained much of her empire largely because of the naval strength of Britain, with whom she maintained a constant alliance. This alliance was based on commerce as well as politics. By the Methuen Treaties of 1703, Portuguese wines were imported by Britain at much lower customs rates than French wines, in return for similar concessions to English

Portugal

woollen exports to Portugal. Our ancestors' heavy consumption of port wine, and tendency to gout among the upper classes, was one result of this agreement.

Adjoining France to the north-east were the Netherlands, which since the seventeenth century had been sharply divided. The southern Netherlands, with Brussels as its capital and Antwerp on the Scheldt as its great inland port, had remained under Spanish – and hence Catholic – domination during the seventeenth century, and had come under the Austrian Hapsburgs in the early years of the eighteenth. Austrian rule was light, and during the eighteenth century the Austrian Netherlands increased rapidly in population and developed a prosperous agriculture. Commercial growth was difficult, however, because the Dutch, who controlled the mouth of the Scheldt, refused to admit international trade up the river to Antwerp. They were entitled to do this by long-standing treaties secured after their successful wars against Spain and France.

The Austrian Netherlands

North of the Austrian Netherlands was the territory of the Dutch – the state which since 1579 had called itself the United Provinces of the Netherlands. These were the seven mainly Protestant provinces which had successfully kept up the revolt against Philip II of Spain, and had had their independence finally recognised in 1648. In alliance with England the Dutch had since then fought off the attacks of Louis XIV's France, and had grown extremely rich. Though they were great improvers in agriculture, commerce was their life's blood, and to protect it and their independence they had built up powerful naval forces. These in turn enabled them to maintain a great colonial empire, won mainly in the Far East at the expense of Portugal.

The United Provinces (Holland)

More recently, however, during the American War of Independence, the Dutch and the British had been in conflict, with the Dutch ending up as the losers. By the 1780s it was becoming clear that the strain of repeated wars and internal strife was sapping the Provinces' strength. The internal quarrels arose partly from the desire of the greatest province, Holland, and its chief town, Amsterdam, to dominate the rest, and partly from the system of government. The United Provinces were, apart from Switzerland, the only republic of much size in Europe. Their supreme authority was their States General, or Parliament. Each province also had its own parliament, and begrudged surrendering powers to the central authority. In times of crisis, however, exceptional powers were given in each province to an official known as the *Stadholder*, and by the mid-eighteenth century the House of Orange had managed to secure this office and the commandership of the forces on an hereditary basis in all the provinces. This pull towards monarchy was strongly resisted by the ardent republicans, but finally succeeded when the kingdom of the Netherlands was established in 1815 after the defeat of Napoleon.

Decline of Dutch power

Spain, Savoy and Piedmont, the Empire and the Austrian Netherlands were not France's only neighbours. There was also the Swiss Confederation, which had won independence from the Hapsburgs in the fifteenth century and acknowledgment of this in the seventeenth. Though little more than a permanent alliance of tiny states, it held together by compromise and a fairly tolerant outlook, for some of the cantons were Protestant and others Catholic; between them they spoke three main languages as well as local dialects. Protected by its mountains, Switzerland had a number of profitable activities including agriculture, banking, textile manufacture, mining and the making of clocks, watches and toys. A republic without a nobility and with a prosperous citizenry, it was more 'democratic' than any other country in Europe. But some cantons, such as Bern, reserved important privileges to a small number of their inhabitants, and these cantons were often in violent disagreement with the others.

Great Britain

None of France's neighbours by land gave her as much trouble as her neighbour across the water – Great Britain. Though small, Britain was extremely strong. She was unified with one king and parliament for the whole of England, Scotland and Wales (and from 1801 Ireland), and she was widely envied for her 'freedom'. This meant, not that she was a democracy, but that she had some popular elements in

– her 'freedom'

A ROTARY STEAM ENGINE

During the late eighteenth and early nineteenth centuries the introduction of steam-power began to transform industry in Britain – the pioneer country of the Industrial Revolution (see p. 8). Watt's steam engine patented in 1769, though a great improvement on earlier engines, was, like them, largely limited in use to pumping, since it was based directly on the up-and-down motion of a piston in a cylinder. In 1781 Watt put forward several ideas for converting this motion into rotary action, and the Boulton & Watt engine shown above utilised the most practical of these. In this engine, the pressure in the cylinder is applied, by a system of moving beams, cranks and cogs, to a large fly-wheel which can then drive many kinds of machinery.

her constitution, and that she lived under the rule of established laws which protected her people from arbitrary actions on the part of their rulers. One of the largest areas in Europe without internal customs barriers, and long blessed by peace within her own borders, she had become a leader in world commerce. She also had a powerful navy to protect her trade and her territories. In conflict with the French she had won a great empire in India and Canada during the mid-eighteenth century, but had later suffered the humiliating loss of her original colonies – the 'old thirteen', which had recently (1783) gained their independence as the United States of America.

– her Industrial Revolution

To great commercial and naval strength Britain had added, during the second half of the eighteenth century, strength of a newer kind. Not only was her agriculture, following the enclosure of many of the old open fields, progressing at a pace almost unrivalled elsewhere in Europe, but mechanised industry was also appearing. In the coke-smelting process for the production of iron, and in machinery for spinning cotton, Britain was leading the world along new paths. With James Watt's perfection of a steam-engine (*c.* 1774) and its application to produce rotary movement (*c.* 1781) the Industrial Revolution was fairly launched. This development, as yet largely confined to the production of coal, iron and cotton textiles, would proceed until the life and face of the world were transformed by the growth of machinery, factories, railways, towns and population. At the moment, however, it was a process almost entirely (apart from some beginnings in France) confined to Britain. It gave her an economic strength which was soon to prove greater than that of any other power.

France

Finally, rich in the size and fertility of her countryside and the skill of her urban craftsmen, there was France. For more than a century, since the early days of Louis XIV, France had been the undisputed leader of European civilisation. It was from France, more than from any other country, that European society drew its ideas, its fashions, its codes of polite behaviour. It was French that was the second language of the European aristocracies – unless, as was the case in several countries, they spoke it as their first. Under a line of kings which with its branches had continued for 800 years. France seemed to possess a stability, a wealth and a culture far beyond that of most other lands. Yet it was in France that revolution now erupted, and gathered such force that the 'Establishment' of the day was overturned and its leaders were butchered. And it was from France that, as we shall see, this ferment spread until conflict engulfed the greater part of Europe.

CHAPTER 2
The Causes of the French Revolution

The French Revolution was not the event of a single month or year. In its most novel, violent, or revolutionary aspects, it lasted from 1789 to the rise of Napoleon; but just as its effects carried forward into the nineteenth and twentieth centuries, so its origins stretched back into the seventeenth and eighteenth centuries.

The system of government: the *Ancien Régime*

The prime cause was the existing system of government: the practices of what was afterwards called the *Ancien Régime* – the Old Regime. Indeed, these practices can hardly be called a system, for in general they came nearer to chaos. So chaotic were the legal arrangements that in 1789 there still existed 360 different feudal codes of law in different parts of France. In one town alone there were twenty-nine feudal courts! In taxation the chaos was such that when a geographer in 1789 tried to draw a map showing the customs dues of the various districts, he had to give it up as too complicated to attempt. A boat bearing wine from the south of France to Paris, for example, paid over forty tolls and lost a fortnight in the process. In other fields of administration matters were no better; the government tried to regulate affairs in over 40,000 townships and struggled hopelessly against overwhelming arrears of business. One parish, for instance, which petitioned for a government loan to repair its leaking church roof, waited over ten years for an answer. In spite of all this utter inefficiency two principles stood out. Nearly all power in national matters was in the hands of the King and his personal advisers; and the main burdens of taxation were borne by the classes least able to support them.

1. Bewildering local variations

In the magnificent palace of Versailles, remote from contact with any but the nobility, the upper clergy and his officials, Louis XVI strove to control the destinies of France. There were several royal Councils, a royal Controller of Finances, royal deputies in the provinces known as Intendants, royal officials everywhere through whom the King governed – but the system rested primarily on Louis himself, for his word was virtually law. 'The State', Louis XIV had said, with vanity but with accuracy, 'is – myself'. Louis XVI was later on to remark, concerning a disputed issue, 'The thing is legal because I wish it.'

2. Complete royal power:-

Such a statement sums up the whole nature of the government of the *Ancien Régime*. The mass of the people had no share in government, and even the rising middle classes had very little; for though there remained some of the old medieval institutions in which the wealthier burgesses played a part, these had either lost the habit of opposing the King or else had themselves become largely aristocratic.

Decline of *États* and *parlements*

Institutions which had lost the habit of opposition included many of the assemblies known as *États* (States or Estates), which still met in some of the provinces, and which were supposed to represent the local community in its three estates, or orders, of clergy (First Estate), nobility (Second Estate) and others (Third Estate). And as for the *États-Généraux*, or States-General, the assembly of the three estates which was supposed to represent the whole realm, this existed only as a memory. It had last been called in 1614!

The *parlement* of Paris

There were, however, still twelve provincial *parlements*, or legal corporations which acted as courts of justice and could theoretically disregard the royal wishes in reaching their decisions. Above all, there was the *parlement* of Paris, which also had the task of registering the King's edicts as laws, and claimed that its consent was necessary before this could properly be done. In point of fact, however, those members of the Paris *parlement* who were not nobles of the older sort (the nobility of the sword) had become nobles of a newer and lesser kind, appropriate to magistrates and officials – the nobility of the robe. They were a privileged group, normally content to go along with the King while he respected their privileges. When he did not, as in the years 1787–88, their opposition began the sequence of events which led to revolution.

In sum, during the seventeenth and eighteenth centuries the will of the sovereign had become virtually the law – so much so, that any critic of the government or opponent of some favoured noble was liable to be arrested quite arbitrarily on the issue of a royal writ known as a *lettre de cachet* (sealed letter). He could then find himself flung into prison without a trial or even an accusation of having committed any particular crime. Some 150,000 of these writs were issued in the reign of Louis XV, and another 14,000 under Louis XVI. By no means all of these concerned cases which actually affected the government. Many were issued on the request of nobles wishing to discipline their sons or prevent an 'unsuitable' marriage.

Lettres de cachet

3. Privileged position of nobles and clergy

As allies and buttresses in this system of royal power, the Crown had the clergy and the nobility – the First and Second Estates. Together the first two Estates numbered some 300,000 out of a population of around 25 million. Yet the *Ancien Régime* in France worked almost wholly to their profit. They owned about three-fifths of the land; many of the nobility were gathered round Louis at Versailles in useless attendance and did not work; the higher clergy drew princely rents and shared the general characteristics of the nobility. The lower clergy, however, such as the parish priests, were poorly paid and had plenty to do. Often they received less than a hundredth of a bishop's income, and their sympathies consequently lay not with their superiors but with the Third Estate. Extraordinary privileges were possessed by the nobility and clergy, the most outstanding being exemption from the main weight of taxation. The nobles were relieved of many taxes and paid others lightly. The clergy made only a 'free gift'.

4. Unprivileged position of peasant

The financial burden of the peasant, on the other hand, was crushing. Not only did he pay several taxes to the King – notably the twentieth (*vingtième*) of his income which most nobles paid, a land tax (*taille*), and a poll tax (*capitation*), but in addition he paid a tithe of the produce of his land to the Church, a *gabelle* (or salt-tax – and everyone over seven years of age had to buy 7 lb. of salt a year), a customs-duty if he took his goods through a village, and a money-due to the local lord when his grapes went to the lord's wine-press or his corn to the lord's mill (and usually they had to go). By a system of game-laws he had to be the powerless witness of

EXPLICATION DE L'ALLEGORIE.

le Tiers-Etat fouffrent feul le poids du Royaume fous lequel il flechit, un Noble, au lieu de le foulager, pefe de fus en l'appuyant, le Prebre femble vouloir aider a foutenir ce fardeau mais du bout du doigt.

THE BURDEN OF THE THIRD ESTATE
French satirical cartoon of 1789. The peasant shoulders the whole burden, while the noble presses on it to increase the weight and the priest supports it merely with one finger.

game or its hunters destroying his crops; he alone of all classes was not exempt from militia service. As if these burdens were insufficient, he was often liable to forced labour on the roads or public buildings (*corvée*). It is little wonder that the peasantry, taxed more and more heavily as the expenses of the French government mounted in the eighteenth century, and in many cases seeing their superiors living in the greatest luxury, were becoming ripe for revolt. Some 10,000 of them were annually imprisoned, 2,000 condemned to the galleys, and several hundred executed for offences against the salt laws alone.

Yet it was not so much from the peasantry as from the more prosperous members of the Third Estate – the educated section of lawyers and doctors especially – that the drive towards revolution came. Though not suffering the economic burdens of the peasant, these men resented their exclusion from official positions at the head of the army, the navy, and the diplomatic service. They resented not being able to criticise openly a ridiculous system of government. They resented the lack of religious freedom. If a Protestant service was discovered, the pastor might be

5. Grievances of educated bourgeoisie

hanged and the congregation all sent to the galleys. They resented the liability of the Third Estate to suffer torture, breaking on the wheel, and forms of mutilation which were spared nobles and clergy. Above all, they felt themselves unfairly excluded from all share in government. 'What is the Third Estate?' wrote one of their leaders in 1789. 'Everything. What has it been hitherto in our form of government? Nothing. What does it want? To become Something.' It is not surprising that almost all the revolutionary leaders came from this class.

II: The influence of the Philosophers

There was a further reason, apart from their actual grievances, to account for the leadership of the reform movement by the bourgeoisie. It was, of course, they, rather than the peasants or the urban poor, who enjoyed the possessions and self-confidence necessary to direct a revolution; but, above all, it was they who had the political education. This they had found in the works of certain French writers or philosophers (*Philosophes*) of the eighteenth century. In the first place there was

Voltaire (1694–1778)

Francois-Marie Arouet, who later called himself Voltaire. Famous all over Europe as a historian, a populariser of science, a tragic dramatist, and a poet, he was also an unsparing critic of existing institutions, and especially of the Church. He himself had known the inside of the Bastille, the great prison of Paris, and what a *lettre de cachet* could mean. Over certain flagrant miscarriages of justice he fought for years to secure the reversal of the verdict and the rehabilitation of the honour of the wronged man. He became at once the most admired and the most feared man of Europe while the very classes he criticised, nobility and royalty, competed for the honour of entertaining him. Only his great enemy, the Church, could never forgive him for his criticism – and his deism. The friend of the two most unscrupulous monarchs of the eighteenth century, Frederick the Great of Prussia and Catherine of Russia, he was equally willing to hold up a monarch to admiration for 'enlightened' intentions and to ridicule for unenlightened achievements. With four estates on the borders of France and Switzerland he could speed from one to the other when officials were on his track. Only at the end of his life could he come safely to Paris to see his last play produced, and then the populace thronged to welcome the man who had fought injustice so long and so bravely. But Voltaire knew humanity. 'Ah', he said, 'they'd come in just the same crowds to see me executed.' Yet with all his devastating satire and his wit, and for all his campaigns against religious persecution, antiquated and unfair taxation, and torture, he had nothing positive to suggest to replace the monarchy. He was no democrat. 'I had rather', he remarked, 'be ruled by one lion than by a hundred rats.' His contribution, great though it was, was negative, not positive.

The Encyclopaedists (1751–72)

Together with Voltaire may be mentioned the work of the Encyclopaedists, led by Denis Diderot. They set out to compile an encyclopaedia which would be an account of all existing knowledge. As it went on its articles on political and religious subjects gave increasing offence to the authorities – indeed, no faithful account of contemporary knowledge could be given which did not demonstrate the folly and injustice of many existing claims and practices in Church and State. Among the earlier contributors were some by a group often known as the Economists. They advocated the abolition of all taxation except that on land (which would be paid mainly by the clergy and nobility); but for a general scheme of government, they too had no other solution than enlightened despotism.

Montesquieu (1689–1755)

A more positive contribution was made by the Baron de Montesquieu, who saw the importance of geographical conditions. After experimentally freezing a

figure 1ᵉʳ

A DIAGRAM FROM 'L'ENCYCLOPÉDIE'

A landmark in the eighteenth-century 'Enlightenment', L'Encyclopédie set out to summarise human knowledge, and in so doing often criticised existing beliefs and institutions – especially religious ones. Most of its articles, however, were purely factual. The diagram above illustrates an article on canal-building and the use of locks to link stretches on different levels – a Renaissance invention which made possible the construction of long-distance canals.

tongue, and observing that the taste-papillae were smaller and less sensitive in the cold than the heat, he concluded that people in hot climates would feel things more passionately than those in cold or temperate regions, and would be less able to keep themselves under control. So a strict despotism, he thought, would be best suited for them, while northern Europeans might be trusted with an element of democracy. Visiting England, he found the model he sought. In his chief book, *De l'Esprit des Lois* (which ran through twenty-two editions in eighteen months), he held up the English constitution, with its parliament, its independent judges, and its constitutional king as worthy of imitation by France. He was especially keen on the idea of these various parts of the government acting as checks on each other, thus helping to preserve the liberty of the individual. His influence, both on the French and American revolutionary leaders, was profound.

But the 'philosopher' who, more than all others, provided a positive creed was

Rousseau (1712–1778)

Jean-Jacques Rousseau. His stormy life, in the course of which he was driven out both from his native city of Geneva and from his adopted France, typified the spirit of revolt. A poet and a musician who had written a successful opera, he turned to politics and preached the equality of men. In his greatest political work, *Du Contrat Social*, he seeks a justification for the fact that man, though 'born free, is everywhere in chains' (i.e. is everywhere subject to government). This justification he can find only if the ideas and desires of the people are really carried out by the government – or, as he puts it, if the General Will is sovereign. Only in this way is liberty retained, and equality realised. Obviously, however, the General Will is much less likely to be carried out in a monarchy than in a democracy. In fact, he wanted a direct democracy, where all men actually decide issues, not a representative democracy, like that of Britain, where other people are elected to decide them. 'The English people', he wrote, 'is free only during the election of its MPs. As soon as they are elected, it is a slave, it is nothing.' He suggested dividing a large state into a number of small direct democracies, and the binding of these into a federation. But it was the spirit of democracy, rather than the details, which affected the revolutionary leaders. Catching from Rousseau also a strong vein of emotion and love of nature, the revolutionary leaders developed the passion and violence needed for a revolution. Rousseau thus not only supplied the main doctrine – the Sovereignty of the People, the Supremacy of the General Will – but also helped to create the emotional spirit which made people ready to rebel.

III: Example of the American Revolution

The philosophers, then, supplied much of the theory which underlay the Revolution, even though all the ones mentioned above were dead before the Revolution broke out. It was America, however, which supplied the main practical example. In 1776 the 'old thirteen' British Colonies, already in revolt, issued their Declaration of Independence, and by 1783 they had secured their freedom as the United States of America. From 1778 France, anxious to obtain revenge for the loss of her colonies in Canada and India during the Seven Years War (1756–63), willingly helped the Americans against Britain, and enjoyed her most successful war of the century. She little thought of the consequences. French soldiers who had served in America poured back to France full of American democratic ideas. They had helped to free a nation whose only real grievance was not that the British taxed them, but that they might tax them! An extra tea-duty of threepence, the sole tax still payable by Americans to Britain in 1776, broke up the British Empire. When the French compared this with the overwhelming burdens of their own peasantry, it rapidly became apparent that if the Americans were justified in revolting against the British, the French were far more justified in revolting against the French. The Americans rebelled not so much against misgovernment as for the sake of self-government; the French, with the additional spur of misgovernment, were not slow to learn the lesson. It was no accident that one of the earliest leaders of the French Revolution was the Marquis de Lafayette, returned six years before from the War of Independence.

IV: Bankruptcy of the French Crown

But the influence of the American Revolution did not end there: perhaps even more important, the cost of the war to France meant the last straw on the already cracking back of her finances. All the century the situation had been getting worse. The enormous luxury of the French court under Louis XIV and XV (and under Louis XVI, too, although he was by comparison very economical, and had only 2,000 horses and 200 carriages in the royal stables, while his Queen, Marie Antoinette, managed with only 500 servants and four pairs of shoes a week) alone accounted for one-twelfth of the whole revenue of the government. The ridiculously inefficient system of taxation (by which the nobles and clergy escaped extremely lightly, while the peasantry, owning about a third of the land, paid practically everything) had nothing to commend it. By 1785 even the nobles and clergy were beginning to see that the situation was impossible. Further, the cost of tax-collection, sometimes done by selling the right of collection to the highest bidder, who made what he could, swallowed an absurd proportion of the taxes. The salt-tax, for example, brought in 60 million livres but cost twenty million to collect, and about 50,000 troops and agents had to be used to suppress smuggling. Above all, the constant wars for over a century and the ruinous loss of most of the French Empire in the Seven Years War had made continuous borrowing necessary, and had piled up an enormous amount of debt. Each year about one-half of the royal income had to be set aside to pay interest on debts – and even then the monarchy had already defaulted five times in the eighteenth century by reducing interest or repudiating debt. When on top of this chaotic and dangerous situation the government of Louis XVI joined in the War of American Independence and spent 2,000 million livres on helping to bring about the defeat of Britain, it also brought about its own bankruptcy.

The last straw – War of American Independence

The financial situation was now desperate. Already two Controllers-General with reforming ideas, first the great Intendant and economist Turgot, then the Genevan financier Jacques Necker, had attempted remedies which might have staved off disaster, only to come up against the rock-like obstacle of old-established privileges. Now a new Controller-General, the former Intendant Calonne, came to the same conclusion as Turgot and Necker – that nothing could be done to restore the national finances while the nobles and clergy remained exempt from the bulk of taxation. To help break down this exemption, in particular by a new land tax falling on all landowners, Calonne advised the King to call an Assembly of Notables – nobles, clergy, officials and others – to be selected by the Crown.

Calonne attempts reforms, 1787

The Notables met in 1787, but, not surprisingly, failed to approve all Calonne's desired reforms. Equal failure then followed the efforts of Calonne's successor, Archbishop Brienne, both to have his own proposed measures registered by the Paris *parlement* and then to suspend the *parlements* altogether. At least, however, the cry of reform was now in the air, and in both the Notables and the Paris *parlement* voices were raised to demand that, if great changes were contemplated, the proper body to advise on them was the long defunct States-General. In desperation, Brienne clutched at this straw. Hoping to destroy by this means the most flagrant exemptions of the privileged classes, he advised the King to call the States-General. He had aroused such opposition that the King could no longer retain him; but his successor, the recalled Necker, confirmed Brienne's advice, and suggested an earlier date for the meeting. So it was decided that the States-General should meet again, in May 1789, after a lapse of 175 years. Minister and Monarch little thought that their device for ending bankruptcy would begin revolution.

Brienne and Necker advise calling States-General, 1788

It was natural, of course, though it surprised the government, that the calling of the States-General, and the official request for lists (*cahiers*) of grievances which preceded it, should open the flood-gates of criticism. But the outcome depended on how the demands of the Third Estate were to be handled by the

V: Character of Louis XVI –

King; and unfortunately for France, Louis XVI was a King in name and in power, but not in character. Full of the best intentions – he had rapidly appointed as Controller-General first one outstanding reformer, Turgot, then another, Necker – he could never be relied on to carry out those intentions consistently: he had dismissed Turgot and Necker with equal promptitude. At every stage in the Revolution he was to encourage reform and then to draw back. Such inconsistency was to bring its almost inevitable reward: it is not usually the strong, brutal rulers of this earth who lose their thrones but the inconsistent, well-intentioned ones. 'When you can keep together a number of oiled ivory balls', one of his relatives said of Louis, 'you may do something with the King.' Mildly interested in reform, more interested in his kingship, but most interested in hunting, Louis XVI ·was to hesitate, to play for time, to yield and to deny, till the forces which he had released caught him up in their torrential current and swept him and the monarchy to destruction.

Louis was also unfortunate in his advisers. Necker lacked firmness, and the one great man who was later to try to save the King, Mirabeau, died at a critical moment. For the most part, in fact, Louis was under the fatal influence of his wife,

– and Marie Antoinette

Marie Antoinette. Extremely unpopular among the French as the representative of the hated Austrian alliance which had led to the disastrous Seven Years War and the loss of colonies, she was nick-named with contempt '*l'Autrichienne*' – the Austrian woman. Ignorant of the need for reform, unsympathetic to her people's needs and incapable of grasping the political situation, she poisoned Louis' mind first against Turgot and then against Necker, and everywhere advised a fatal firmness at precisely the wrong moments. 'The King', said Mirabeau, 'has only one man about him, his wife.' France's destiny rested with a King who was too weak-minded to be stable and a Queen who was too strong-minded to be sensible.

VI: High prices, famine, cold and mobs

Finally, among the many factors leading to the Revolution must be mentioned the rise in prices which had taken place during the eighteenth century, and which had not been accompanied by any corresponding increase in wages. All over Europe, thanks largely to improved medical knowledge, the population was increasing, even if most of it lived in wretched conditions; and this increase, coming at a time when there was little mass manufacture or scientific agriculture, brought a keen demand for scarce goods and food and so helped to cause higher prices. It has been calculated that between 1730 and 1789 grain prices in France rose by about sixty per cent, whereas wages rose only by twenty-two per cent. The result was widespread poverty at the lower end of society, sharpened in the countryside by the fact that landlords, to counteract the declining value of some of their fixed dues, began to exploit their privileges more vigorously than ever.

To complete this deteriorating situation the weather of 1788 was disastrous. It ruined the harvest, raised corn to a famine price, and caused widespread starvation. This calamity was to be followed by the desperately severe winter of early 1789, when all the great rivers of France were frozen and even the port of Marseille in the extreme south was blocked with ice. The result was an even greater distress than usual. A commercial treaty with Britain in 1786, admitting British manufactured goods at cheap rates in return for corresponding concessions on French wine, had already caused much industrial suffering. In some towns as many as half the workmen were unemployed. It had long been the custom, in certain parts of France, for the rural poor to seek work in towns during the winter.

MARIE ANTOINETTE AT VERSAILLES
From a portrait (date and artist uncertain) in the Wallace Collection. The portrait-head of the flower vase is that of her husband, Louis XVI.

Now hordes of people gathered in Paris and the other great towns from the surrounding countryside, hoping to find food and shelter in urban conditions. So came into being the characteristic Paris mob of the Revolution – idle, desperate, ready to cheer on the most extreme measures, and destined to sway the fortunes of events on more than one vital occasion.

All the material for a great combustion was now present. An outworn, inefficient, unfair, and bankrupt system of government; a strong body of reforming opinion created by the philosophers; the successful example of the Americans; a weak king and an unpopular queen; widespread economic distress; and a desperate mob of exceptional size in Paris. It needed only a spark to set it all alight, to turn the smoulderings of 1787–89 into a fire. On 5th May 1789, the States-General met.

CHAPTER 3
The French Revolution: Reform and the Restriction of the Monarchy, 1789–92

The cahiers de doléances

The government of Louis XVI had summoned the States-General to meet at Versailles. In preparation for this, it had asked for *cahiers* or lists of grievances. It got over 60,000 of them. From every part of France the Third Estate sent up similar

THE MEETING OF THE STATES GENERAL AT VERSAILLES
From a French engraving of 1789.

demands: reform of taxation (with abolition of the privileges of the First and Second Estates as the first step), a settled constitution with a regular parliament and no *lettres de cachet*, and the abolition of all feudal rights and dues. Naturally this last demand came most strongly from the rural areas. The remark of the men of one district, 'How happy we should be if the feudal system were destroyed!', expresses perfectly the main trend of the peasants' requests.

It might have been thought that Louis and Necker would examine these grievances, draw up a programme of reforms, and present it to the assembly which was meeting after so long a time. But that was not Louis' way. Instead of placing himself at the head of the reform movement, he immediately made reform more difficult by expecting the three Estates to begin by deliberating separately, as they had done in the medieval past. The effect of this would be that reform measures, voted on by the Estates separately, would almost inevitably be defeated by two Estates to one (First and Second v. Third Estate). On the other hand, if all met as one assembly, the fact that the Third Estate had been allowed, as a special new concession by the Crown, to have twice as many representatives as either of the other orders would mean that reform measures could be carried. It would require only a very few of the poorer clergy to support the Third Estate, and the latter would have a clear majority. It was thus essential to the cause of reform that the Estates should meet as one, and not three, assemblies. Louis had seemed to recognise this by granting the Third Estate double representation, and now, typically, he changed course. Until such time as the Estates should propose agreed schemes for joint sessions, he insisted on separate meetings.

Thwarted in this way and irritated by the absence of any positive lead in Necker's opening speech, the Third Estate soon lost its carefree loyal enthusiasm. The opposition to the Crown was at first led by the Comte de Mirabeau. He was a violent and dissolute, but able and fearless nobleman, who had been rejected as a representative by his own order.[1] 'A mad dog, am I?', he had said when he offered himself for election to the Third Estate; 'but elect me, and despotism and privilege will die of my bite.' Under Mirabeau's guidance the Third Estate refused to accept the policy of separatism. Instead it voted to call itself the 'National Assembly' and invited the other Estates to join this body. Some of the parish priests had already come over to the Third Estate and now the majority of the clergy voted to follow suit. Two or three days later Louis ordered the hall where the National Assembly was meeting to be closed for alterations and the Third Estate took the worst possible interpretation of the King's action. Immediately they adjourned to an indoor tennis court nearby, and there they solemnly swore that they would never separate until a constitution was firmly established.

Called next to a special royal session to hear Louis' proposed reforms and his decision to retain separate meetings except for certain purposes, the Third Estate afterwards refused to follow the nobles and clergy in obeying the royal order to retire. Mirabeau put it precisely to a nobleman who acted as messenger for the King: 'Tell your master that nothing but bayonets will drive us from here'. ('If they come we buzz off quick', he is reported to have added in an undertone to a friend.') But they did not come. The vacillating Louis left the Third Estate

Meeting of the States, May, 1789

Tennis Court Oath

---

[1] Mirabeau's behaviour as a young man had been so scandalous that his father had secured a *lettre de cachet* for his imprisonment.

National Assembly,
June 1789

undisturbed; soon a majority of the clergy and some of the nobles joined them; and on 27th June 1789, the three Estates amalgamated officially by the King's command. The joy was universal and there were cries of 'the Revolution is over'. These rejoicings, it soon became clear, were premature.

Paris Commune and
National Guard

Meanwhile events were moving rapidly elsewhere. The increasing hunger of the Paris mobs and the massing of troops by Louis led to a state of uneasiness. Crimes of violence, particularly robbery of farms in the countryside, became frequent. The government could keep no order, and the nation became gripped by fear. As a measure of self-defence the Parisian electors at the end of June set up a committee in the Hôtel de Ville and planned a voluntary militia, later known as the National Guard. From the press, now entirely neglecting the feeble orders of the government, there poured a flood of revolutionary pamphlets and journals, while in open spaces such as the gardens of the Palais Royal young orators and journalists like Camille Desmoulins (who was soon to start a brilliant political newspaper) fired the mob by their intoxicating eloquence. Then on 11th July came the dismissal of Necker from his post of Controller. It seemed that Louis had followed the Queen's advice and rid himself of the only reformer in his court.

Storming of the
Bastille, 14 July 1789

The result of all this was an uprising of the Paris crowds, urged on by Desmoulins and others. Large numbers of citizens rushed to seek weapons to defend themselves, if necessary, against Louis' troops, who were massing in the suburbs. Mobs raided the gunsmiths' shops and surrounded the Hôtel de Ville, clamouring for arms. There the committee of electors found itself in a quandary. To prevent mob rule, it hastily completed its scheme for a citizen militia, but at the same time it found itself forced to hand out its stock of arms to the crowd. With these, on the morning of 14th July, a mob moved on to the great military depot and hospital, Les Invalides, where they found and seized some 30,000 muskets. And from Les Invalides a group several hundred strong swept on to the great fortress-prison of Paris, the Bastille, which was known to contain large quantities of gunpowder.

It is unlikely that the crowd at first intended to storm this hated fortress, in which so many victims of *lettres de cachet* had been confined. Their idea seems to have been to demand the handing-over of the gunpowder, and the dismantling of the fortress's great guns, which could have been used against the Paris population. But the threatening demeanour of the mob as they forced their way into the outer courtyard, and finally their violence as they seized and lowered the drawbridge to the inner court, caused the Governor to order his garrison to open fire. Soon there were nearly 200 killed or wounded among the intruders, who would doubtless have been driven out had not some mutinous French troops seized cannons from Les Invalides and trained them on the main gate of the Bastille's inner citadel. This action proved decisive. The irresolute Governor gave the order to surrender and the mob poured into the inner fortress. There they found a grand total of seven prisoners: four forgers, two madmen, and a notorious rake. Typically of the French Revolution, some of the crowd massacred several of the captive garrison, and tore out their hearts and bowels. Later the Governor too was murdered, and his head paraded round Paris on a pike. Throughout France and throughout most of Europe, this day's work was hailed as heroic. The Bastille, supreme symbol of French royal despotism, had fallen; and before long, the 14th July would become a great national French holiday.

The rebels were now in command of Paris. The committee at the Hôtel de

THE TAKING OF THE BASTILLE, 14th JULY 1789.
From a French engraving of 1789.

Ville became a regular town government, or Commune, with a mayor at its head.
The brave and chivalrous Marquis de Lafayette, who had learned his liberal
politics in America and had been elected Vice-President of the National Assembly,
was installed as commander of the National Guard. Accepting these measures,
the mob was soon quieted, and those who were anxious for more disorder were
suppressed by Lafayette and the Guard. It remained to secure Louis' approval
of accomplished facts. He had little alternative. He reinstated Necker, withdrew
his troops from the Paris suburbs, and on 17th July he came to Paris, escorted by
fifty members of the Assembly. There he had to recognise the new municipal
government of Paris and the National Guard, and to wear in his hat the Guard's

Louis comes to Paris,
17 July 1789

tricolore cockade – the emblem of the Revolution. Its colours, suggested by Lafayette, were the old Paris municipal ones of red and blue, with the white of the monarchy between. Risings of this kind were by no means confined to Paris. In the provinces there was a rush to storm the 'forty thousand Bastilles' (the feudal castles) and burn the manorial records. Everywhere towns organised committees of electors into Communes and set up self-government on the Parisian model.

Disorder in the provinces

Abolition of feudal privileges, August 1789

Soon there occurred one of the most remarkable happenings in history. It took place on 4th August in the Assembly at Versailles. To damp down the riots in the provinces a large group of deputies had secretly resolved to support the peasants' demands and to try to sway the Assembly towards this policy. A nobleman suddenly rose to propose the abolition of all feudal rights and dues. Others followed, and the atmosphere became emotional. Noble after noble arose, amid scenes of weeping and embracing, to approve the surrender of his own privileges. A frenzy of self-sacrifice set in (and naturally others got sacrificed in the process), and by eight o'clock next morning the Assembly had passed thirty proposals designed to alter the whole fabric of French law. Equality of taxation and of legal punishment among the three orders, admission of all to public office, freedom of worship, abolition of the tithe, the right to be free from feudal dues in return for a money payment – these were some of the principles approved that night, and worked out in detail during the following week. The final decree began with the ringing words 'The National Assembly destroys the feudal system in its entirety'. No consent to all this, however, had as yet been wrung from the Monarch.

One result of these changes, when they at length took effect, should not be overlooked. The night of 4th August and its aftermath, it later became clear, gave the peasants almost all they wanted from the Revolution. As time went on and extremism and violence grew, the peasants turned naturally to a leader who would guarantee their newly won rights. They were not democrats, and they happily accepted Napoleon later because he seemed to make secure for them their chief gains from the Revolution.

Declaration of the Rights of Man

The Assembly next concentrated on approving a suitable preface to the Constitution it was devising to replace the royal despotism. Lafayette was mainly responsible for the drawing-up of this preface, which was called 'The Declaration of the Rights of Man and Citizen'. It was in vain that a realist like Mirabeau urged that in such a time of anarchy people needed to be reminded not of their rights but of their duties. Many of the members of the Assembly, in their idealistic and inexperienced way, imagined that the mere statement of the principles guiding the Revolution would be almost sufficient to free mankind from its whole load of past oppression. At all events, the document that was produced seemed designed not for the France of 1789 alone but for all times and all peoples. Men were by nature equal; the people were sovereign, and must share in the making of law, which was the expression of the General Will; liberty of person and speech were sacred rights; rebellion against injustice a holy duty. A statement of democratic principles so complete naturally led to great expectations which in the nature of facts at the time it was simply impossible to fulfil. As one person remarked: 'It was not wise to lead men up to the top of the mountain and show them a promised land which was afterwards to be refused them.' Also, as became clearer later, the framers of the Declaration were interested only in political, not economic, equality: property was another one of their 'sacred rights'. Nevertheless their document, in effect, 'sounded the death knell of the old Régime in Europe'.

It was not long before the Paris mob took a hand again. Feeling was already becoming inflamed against Louis because he refused to accept the Declaration and the nobles' and clergy's sacrifices of 4th August; and when the Assembly showed itself willing to allow him power to hold up proposed laws for six years, indignation mounted higher still. On top of this there was ever-increasing famine and unemployment, and then the news that the King had called the loyal Flanders regiment to Versailles. There the officers were greeted by their colleagues of the Royal Bodyguard with a banquet at which the *tricolore* was insulted. This brought matters to a head. Who supplied the leadership for the next move is uncertain, but probably it came from an alliance of the extremists in the Assembly and in the Paris Commune. At all events, the decision was taken – for such an event can hardly have been accidental – to stage a women's march to Versailles to press the people's grievances. Women were chosen rather than men because the effect would be greater, and their hunger-cries shriller, but in the event a number of men, some painted and petticoated, swelled the throng. Hearing of the March, thousands of citizens, including many members of the National Guard, gathered outside the Hôtel de Ville in Paris. Eventually the Commune ordered Lafayette to set off after the marchers with several thousand of the National Guard. His task was to prevent disorder and if possible bring the King from Versailles to the capital.

'March of the Women', October 1789

Meanwhile at Versailles, Louis was recalled from his usual pastime of hunting, and he agreed to see a deputation of the women. He promised special food supplies for Paris; and later he also decided to meet the renewed request of the Assembly that he should accept the decrees of 4th August and the Declaration of the Rights of Man. When Lafayette appeared, the harassed King also agreed that the National Guard, instead of the Flanders regiment, should be entrusted with the defence of Versailles. While Lafayette was asleep that night, however, some of the mob broke into the palace. They calmed down only when Louis agreed to return with them to Paris. So around noon the next day the whole royal family – 'the baker, the baker's wife, and the baker's son', as the song went – set off for Paris escorted by a motley column of the National Guard, disarmed bodyguards, deputies, food waggons, and mob. The journey took nine hours, and then for two hours more Louis had to listen to speeches at the Hôtel de Ville, before he and his family at length reached the royal palace of the Tuileries. And there they were as good as prisoners.

Louis escorted to Paris, 6 October 1789

Ten days later the Assembly decreed that it would follow the King to Paris. The whole episode was thus very important. As on 14th July, mob action had proved decisive. Neither the Paris Commune nor Lafayette, it was now clear, could control the forces they had helped to set in motion. In Paris, both King and Assembly would soon be at the mercy of mob forces. Already the transactions of the Assembly were public, and outside speakers were even permitted to address the deputies. Soon it would become a mob fashion to attend the debates, to cheer the most revolutionary speakers and boo and hiss and jeer at the rest – even to waylay them afterwards. The whole effect would eventually be to make moderate deputies stay away, and to leave matters more and more in the hands of the extremists.

The Assembly follows

Soon the Assembly took another decisive step in the progress of the Revolution. Desperate for revenue after the abolition of so many taxes, it turned to the vast

THE PRESS: 'PATIENCE, MY LORD, YOUR TURN IS COMING'
A French satirical cartoon of 1790, symbolising the confiscation of church land and the surrender of clerical privileges.

The financial problem: issue of *assignats*

property of the Church. With the strong support of Mirabeau, a measure was passed to nationalise Church estates and put them up to public auction. To secure funds before the public's gold came in, interest-bearing bonds known as *assignats* were issued to creditors of the government, and before long these *assignats* were declared to be a form of general currency. The Assembly, in other words, had gone in for paper-money. Unfortunately paper-money, while unavoidable in modern life, presents a standing temptation to financially embarrassed governments: they print off far more of it than the nature of its backing (whether gold or land) warrants. Not surprisingly, an *assignat* which started by being worth 100 francs in 1790 degenerated, particularly after the outbreak of war in 1792, until by 1797 it had become worth about a *sou* – a halfpenny.

Civil Constitution of the Clergy, July 1790

If the State confiscated the Church's land, it obviously had to take on most of the Church's financial obligations, including the payment of the clergy. In July 1790 the Assembly passed the radical Civil Constitution of the Clergy. By this the State undertook, among other things, responsibility for paying the clergy, who were thus turned into state officials, with bishops and parish priests appointed by a form of election. Though the Pope was still recognised as the head of the Church, he was allowed no power at all in France by this scheme. Louis, a good Catholic, accepted it only with the utmost reluctance; but when, as he had feared, the Pope in April 1791 solemnly condemned the whole measure, his remorse knew no bounds. From this point must be dated two important developments. From then on, the Revolution was rejected by most of the Church leaders, and by some of the strongly religious regions in the west. And from then on, Louis was resolved to halt the Revolution by seeking aid from abroad.

At last Louis decided to flee to eastern France, where he would be well placed to find loyal French troops and to receive help from his Austrian brother-in-law, the Emperor Leopold. From this area, at the head of an army including foreigners and *émigré* French nobles, he could return to dictate terms to the Assembly. It was a fatal plan, however, to rely on forces from outside, and it was one from which Mirabeau, who had come to better terms with the court and was doing his best to keep the Revolution within reasonable bounds, would certainly have dissuaded him. But Mirabeau, elected President of the Assembly in January 1791, had died only four months later, with the despairing realisation that the monarchy was doomed. 'I carry with me', he is reported to have said, 'the last rags of the monarchy.' Bereft of Mirabeau's wise advice, Louis proceeded on his own rash course. At night, disguised as a valet, he escaped from Paris by coach with Marie Antoinette and his family; but the escort and post-horse arrangements went wrong, news outstripped his slow rate of progress, and at Varennes, a little town a few miles from the frontier, some carts placed across a bridge by revolutionaries ended his hopes. At the Hôtel de Ville in Paris, Lafayette, who had taken charge, issued orders for the return of the fugitives. It was a terrible journey for them. Exposed to every form of insult, they were brought back, humiliated by ruffians who despite the bodyguard poked their heads through the coach windows to spit in the Queen's face, and appalled by the alternate jeers and stony silence of the crowds. It is said that during the four-day ordeal Marie Antoinette's hair turned completely white. So the blaze of popularity which had at first surrounded the good-natured, 'reforming' King was finally extinguished. 'At Varennes the monarchy had died. All that Paris had to do, a year later, was to bury it.'

Death of Mirabeau, April 1791

Louis' flight to Varennes, June 1791

The result of this disastrous episode was the growth of a republican movement. Mirabeau was dead, and Lafayette lost his great popularity when in July he ordered the Guard to fire on a mob in the Champ de Mars who were demanding the King's abdication. The leadership of affairs drifted into the hands of the politicians who were making their name by their eloquence in the political clubs. The most important of these new and fast-growing societies was the Jacobin Club, so-called because its parent branch met in the disused convent of St. Jacques in Paris. Within two or three years of its formation, it affiliated over 400 branch clubs in the provinces. Its key role can be seen from the fact that the history of the control of the Jacobin Club till 1794 is in a sense the history of the Revolution. Originally including all shades of reforming opinion, it gradually became confined to extremists as these secured approval for their policies. On the question now of limited monarchy or republic, the extremists drove out one group of moderates, who formed the Feuillant Club devoted to constitutional monarchy.

Movement for a republic: the Clubs

At this stage, however, the Jacobins were not yet all so extreme as the members of a much smaller institution, the Cordelier Club, which was confined to Paris. The Jacobins were mainly middle class; the Cordeliers, though their chief strength too was in radicals of the professional classes, also included working men. The Cordelier Club had from the start been extremely democratic, and it now became the main forum of republicanism.

The National Assembly, in the main an upper-middle-class body, had by now

Work of the
National Assembly

become unpopular with the poor in the towns. These lowest ranks of society had as yet gained neither the vote nor a higher standard of living. Indeed the Assembly, to keep the poor in their place and to encourage freedom of commerce, had recently passed laws banning trade unions and strikes, two of the great weapons of working-class advancement in later times.

On top of this the Assembly was becoming weary from its own immense labours. In two years of ceaseless activity it had swept aside the tradition of separate Estates, framed the Declaration of the Rights of Man, abolished tithes and feudal rights, ended the tax privileges of nobles and clergy, banished most of the religious orders, and completely reorganised the Church. It had also revolutionised local government by discarding the old units of the royal administration (including the historic provinces – Normandy, Brittany and the rest) and the old royal officials (including the powerful Intendants). Instead it had organised France into eighty-three new Départements. Each of these was divided into six or seven Districts, and each District was sub-divided into eight or nine Cantons; and in every Département and District arrangements were made for locally-elected councils and executive officers. In none of the new divisions, however, did the Assembly allow much power to the representative of the central government. The idea was to have only a minimum of control from above; and to this end the Assembly left quite large powers to the lowest units in the scale – the communes, or municipalities, which also had elected councils and officers. All this local reorganisation was a great work in itself; and most of it was to survive all changes of government in France until our own times.

New constitution

With all this work behind it, the Assembly was now anxious to complete the constitution, secure its acceptance by the King, and then make way for the new body to be elected under the fresh scheme of government. At last, in September 1791, the complete constitution was duly accepted by the helpless Louis, and Paris again celebrated 'the end of the Revolution'. Unfortunately, however, the constitution was far from perfect. The new assembly, usually known as the Legislative Assembly, was to be the dominant partner, but on paper at least the King was still to have considerable powers. This was quite unacceptable to the republicans, even though the King's wishes could be thwarted by the financial hold of the Assembly. As for the vote, this was to be restricted to those who paid a certain sum in taxes, another point which annoyed the extremists. The really vital defect, however, concerned the communes, of which there were some 40,000 varying from villages to large towns. These communes were to be almost entirely self-governing: the central government had reserved very little control over them. As the Ambassador of the United States of America remarked of the new constitution: 'the Almighty Himself could not have made it work unless He created a new species of man'.

Lastly, as though to increase the difficulty of operating the new arrangements, the members of the National (or Constituent) Assembly declared themselves ineligible for election to the new Legislative Assembly. They had already in 1789 debarred members from serving as ministers of the Crown, and they now extended this prohibition to the Assembly to come. These measures were carried by a combination of the extremists on both wings, who were anxious to stop the dominance of the moderates committed to working with a limited monarchy. The effect was to cut off from the conduct of government the main body of men who had begun to acquire some experience of it.

CHAPTER 4
The French Revolution: War, Terror and Dictatorship, 1792–95

From the spring of 1792, the course of the Revolution was shaped by a new development: war. Many members of the Legislative Assembly were idealists like those of the National Assembly who had earlier passed a motion renouncing all wars of conquest. However, the threatening attitude of the émigré nobles on the eastern borders under the spurrings of the Count of Artois, one of Louis' brothers, combined with the danger of Louis' suddenly receiving help from Austria or Prussia, created in France a panic of the kind which breeds war. At the same time a political group in the new Assembly later called the Girondins (for several of them came from the Gironde district in south-west France) began to want war for reasons of their own.

Prominent Jacobins as the Girondins mostly were at this time, they were by no means the most extreme group in the Jacobin Club; for though they were determined to preserve the gains of the Revolution and even to advance to a Republic, they were opposed to the ultra-democratic and terrorist views of the minority in the Club further to the left. Under the leadership of Brissot and Vergniaud in the Assembly, they became strong enough to force Louis in March 1792 to appoint some of their outside associates as ministers. One of the foremost of these was a former inspector of commerce, Roland, whose talented wife provided a centre for the group in her *salon*.

By this time the Girondins had conceived the idea that war would unite the country behind its true leaders – the Girondins – and at the same time show up Louis' sympathies with the enemy. This would provide the excuse for getting rid of him. The Girondins, however, were not alone in wanting war. The monarchists among Louis' ministers also wanted it, for a very different reason: the military forces of the Crown, if victorious, could be used to crush the Revolution, or if defeated could not prevent France's enemies doing so. In April 1792 the royal Council accordingly decided on war against Austria, and the Assembly agreed with only seven contrary votes. A few weeks later, in July, the war became extended to Austria's allies, Prussia and Sardinia, when she formally requested their help. The Assembly's attitude by now was one of 'war against kings, peace with all peoples'. This was a challenge against the rulers of the world, and one which they were not slow to accept.

For France, the immediate consequences of declaring war against Austria were

Approach of war

The Girondins

France declares war on Austria, April 1792.

War with Prussia and Sardinia, July 1792

PEACE TO THE PEOPLES, WAR TO THE TYRANTS!
From a French engraving of 1792.

Louis dismisses
Girondins: mob
action in
Assembly and
Tuileries, June 1792

disastrous. The entirely unprepared French armies tried to invade the Austrian Netherlands, and retreated almost without fighting. The King then took the opportunity to veto two of the Assembly's decrees, and to dismiss some of his Girondin ministers including Roland. The result was another mob explosion, which may or may not have been stirred up by the Girondins. A crowd, supposedly meeting to celebrate the anniversay of the Tennis Court Oath, found its way into the Assembly where they sang the revolutionary song *Ça Ira* and one of them brandished a calf's heart (labelled 'aristocrat's heart') on the end of a pike. From there the mob invaded the Tuileries and forced Louis to fraternise with them, drink their health, and wear the red cap of liberty. He stood out, however, against their more serious demands.

Shortly afterwards Lafayette, who was now commanding one of the French armies and who feared that the Revolution would be carried beyond the settlement of 1791, made a last effort to save the monarchy. He offered to lead the National Guard against the Jacobins and other extremist clubs, but he came up against the invincible folly of Marie Antoinette. Distrusting Lafayette as a former leader of the Revolution, she declared that she would 'sooner perish than be saved by M. Lafayette' and actually had the Jacobins warned of Lafayette's intentions. She seems to have hoped that by sowing discord among the Revolutionaries she would make the task of her foreign helpers easier.

As the suspicion grew that Louis had betrayed to the enemy the armies' plans for the recent campaign, the movement to depose him developed apace. Orators on the left repeatedly pointed out the dangers of a stab in the back, and at the Cordelier Club the lawyer Danton, a patriot and democrat of extreme violence despite some good-natured qualities, began to urge and prepare the next great move in the Revolution. Rightly, the Girondin group began to fear that the revolutionary leadership was slipping from their own into other hands – the hands of those who relied on the support of the voteless poor. Republicans though they were, the Girondins accordingly offered to save the throne if Louis would recall Roland and others to the ministry. Louis did not accept the bargain, but responded sufficiently to make the Girondins uncertain of their better course of action – whether to save the monarchy or destroy it.

Movement to depose Louis

The impending blow from the Left fell in August 1792. By this time France was aflame with anger at a Manifesto issued by the Austro-Prussian commander, the Duke of Brunswick. This Manifesto was inspired by the French and Austrian courts, and Brunswick himself thought it unwise. It threatened drastic punishment to Paris if the citizens dared to make any further move against the royal family, and proclaimed that all resistance to Brunswick would be treated as rebellion. From this point on, the deposition of Louis was loudly demanded in Paris by the Clubs and by contingents of National Guard called in from the provinces. One such contingent, from Marseille, had come marching in singing the stirring new patriotic song of the French Army of the Rhine, recently composed at Strasburg by Captain Rouget de l'Isle. The *Marseillaise*, as it was soon called, swept through France to become the prime song of the Revolution and later the French national anthem.

Brunswick's Manifesto, July 1792

It was probably Danton, President of the Cordeliers and a member of the Commune who now took the initiative. At a given signal, the bell of the Cordeliers, the forces controlled by the Clubs in the various sections of Paris converged on the Hôtel de Ville. There they seized power, replacing the moderate rulers of the Commune by men of the extreme Left. These included Hébert, a violent Cordelier whose followers became known as the 'Enraged'. Then came an attack on the Tuileries, led by the Cordeliers' forces and the men from Marseille. Firing began, and though Louis' Swiss Guard resisted valiantly, they were ordered to retire at the wrong moment and their lives were spent in vain. Meanwhile, as the attack threatened, Louis and his family were persuaded to seek refuge in the Assembly – which, however, now proved powerless before the forces of the new leaders of the Commune. Like it or not, the Assembly had to suspend Louis from his royal functions and confine him and his family in the Temple prison. Lafayette, who left his troops

Danton's coup d'état.

Attack on the Tuileries, 10 August 1792

Suspension and imprisonment of Louis

DANTON

Robespierre demands
a Convention to frame
a republican
constitution.

and came to the Assembly to protest, was promptly declared a traitor and had to
flee abroad. At the same time the provincial lawyer Robespierre, an ardent
disciple of Rousseau and a Jacobin of the Left, led a movement to dissolve the
Assembly and elect a Convention on a completely democratic basis. Its task would
be to draft a new and more democratic constitution in which the King would have
no place. This was agreed. Meanwhile Danton became Minister of Justice, and his
revolution was on its way to success and a republic. It had, however, set a fatal
precedent. In the attack on the Tuileries some hundreds had perished, and subse-
quently about 800 royalist sympathisers and Swiss Guards had been massacred.
Thenceforward the story was largely of one group of revolutionaries replacing
another, and disposing of them by the process of wholesale butchery.

The suspension of the King was the first step in the reorganisation of the
defences. France was actually in a dangerous state. In the Vendée district revolts
against the government had broken out, prompted by Catholic horror of the measures against the Church. Now, on 19th August, 1792, the Prussians (whose

grievances included the confiscation of the lands of German nobles in Alsace) crossed the frontier, and quickly captured Longwy. On 2nd September they followed this by taking Verdun. Panic and anger gripped the country, and led to further extreme measures against royalists. In Paris on the night of 2nd September Marat (a doctor and leading Cordelier who ran a violently democratic paper *L'Ami du Peuple*) was amongst those who organised a massacre of the priests and royalists who were being held in prison. The proclaimed intention was to empty the prisons before their inmates could help the invaders. Impromptu tribunals visited each prison, and turned out those they found guilty – about half of those examined – to be butchered by killers waiting in the courtyards. All told, about 1,400, two-thirds of whom were ordinary criminals, perished in the course of five days. At least one aristocrat was sliced into shreds, and the Princesse de Lamballe was appallingly mutilated: one man was later accused of roasting and eating her heart. As if these deeds in Paris were not enough, Marat and others at the Commune sent a circular to the provinces urging other cities 'to adopt these methods, so essential to the safety of the nation'. All this foreshadowed, in a horrible way, the later Reign of Terror.

Suddenly, however, the course of the war altered. On 20th September, the day before the new democratically-elected Convention first met, the French repulsed the Prussians at Valmy. It was a mere cannonade; and the Prussians retirement was due rather more to their suspicions of Austrian and Russian intentions and to Danton's bribery than to French reorganisation. But it made all the difference to the spirit of the French. The invasion was checked – the Revolution might be saved. 'Here and now', said the great German poet Goethe, who witnessed the action, 'begins a new era in the history of the world.' The next day the Convention deposed Louis and declared France a republic. Within a few weeks the French proceeded to advance to the Rhine and the Austrian dominions in Italy. In November 1792 the Convention intoxicatedly voted that France would give her help to all peoples desiring to recover their liberty, and so hurled a further challenge at the world.

The trial of the King before the Convention soon followed, on charges of treason to the nation. He had no chance of acquittal although technically by the 1791 constitution his ministers should have been responsible for all his actions. But as Robespierre said, 'You are not judges – you are statesmen', and the King was unanimously declared guilty. When it came to the question of the punishment, the Girondins and Danton, who really wished to save him, hesitated to lay themselves open to a charge of royalism, and Robespierre's policy of execution narrowly triumphed. On 21st January 1793 Louis XVI met his death courageously by the new 'humane' method of execution – the guillotine.[1]

The execution of the King resulted for France in further terror, dictatorship, and war with most of Europe. Within a few days the Revolutionary government declared war on Britain and Holland, and within another month on Spain as well.

Prussians take Verdun, 2 Sept 1792

Marat and the September Massacres

Valmy, 20 September 1792

Louis deposed: France a republic, 22 September 1792

Execution of Louis, January 1793

War declared on Britain, Holland and Spain, February–March 1793

[1] The name came from a member of the National Assembly, Dr Guillotin, who in the interests of humanity had proposed that those convicted of capital crimes should be beheaded instantly by a machine (such as was then in use in some parts of Italy) instead of suffering the usual long drawn-out torments. A suitable machine was perfected – not by Guillotin – and was first used in France in April 1792.

All these powers had objected to the doctrines of the Revolution and the execution of the King, and all were keenly conscious of the danger to their security arising from the French advances, particularly the occupation of the Austrian Netherlands and the opening of the lower Scheldt in violation of past treaties.

France's difficulties

Very quickly, the French armies again began to suffer reverses. In the Austrian Netherlands the French commander, Dumouriez, was defeated and soon afterwards deserted to the enemy. Meanwhile in the Vendée and Brittany a second and greater rebellion arose, prompted this time not only by religious feelings but also by opposition to conscription. All this discredited the Girondins, who had clamoured most loudly for the war and who had worked closely with Dumouriez. It also led to dictatorial measures, such as the setting up of a Revolutionary Tribunal to deal with offences against the State, and a Committee of Public Safety. The

War dictatorship

function of the latter, which was elected from the Convention for a month at a time, was to supervise the rather weak Executive Council of ministers. To control this temporary but powerful Committee of Public Safety soon became the main object of the various political factions. A similar committee formed soon afterwards, the Committee of General Security, had special responsibilities for police and internal security, and acted as the main 'feeder' of the Revolutionary Tribunal.

Girondins _v._ extreme Jacobins

The stage was now set for a struggle between the discredited Girondins and their opponents farther to the Left, the more 'democratic' Jacobins now in control of the Paris Jacobin Club. Seeking victory, the Girondins had the Jacobin president at this time, Marat, who was also a member of the Convention, hauled before the Revolutionary Tribunal. Acquitted, he and his colleagues of the Mountain (the most extreme section of the Convention, so called from their raised seats) soon helped to turn the tables on the Girondins by organising a public demand for the arrest of the Girondin leaders. To do this they worked hand in glove with the still more revolutionary Commune of Paris, whose newly installed leaders favoured measures which were not merely democratic but socialistic, such as control of prices in the interests of the poor.

Arrest of the Girondins, June 1793

With the support of the Paris _sans-culottes_[1] the Jacobins were able to have the Girondin leaders arrested in June 1793. A few months later they were guillotined in a batch – the perpetual fate of liberals who start revolutions. Roland, who had escaped, wandered hunted and miserable till he heard of his wife's execution, and then committed suicide. His wife at least left behind her a true and memorable phrase. Gazing at the Statue of Liberty erected near the guillotine awaiting her, she exclaimed 'Ah, Liberty, what crimes are committed in thy name!'

Meanwhile a further rebellion had broken out in the Girondins' support, only to be quickly defeated. Its most lasting effect was that it spurred one Norman girl, Charlotte Corday, into a memorable act. Burning with hatred of the brutal and irreligious policy of the new leaders, she sought an interview with Marat. Ad-

Murder of Marat, July 1793

mitted to him as he sat in the enclosed steam-bath which gave him relief from a painful skin disease, she killed him with one thrust of a knife. This was a dose of his own stringent medicine. He had once said: '270,000 heads to cut off, and mankind will be happy,' 270,000 was the estimated number of the First and Second Estates.

---

[1] The _sans-culottes_ were the men without culottes, or knee-breeches. They were the class of petty tradesmen, lower artisans, labourers and below, who wore the humbler trousers.

Shortly before this the Convention had approved a new constitution. Extremely democratic, this guaranteed the right to vote to all adult males and provided for plebiscites on important questions. But it was kept in abeyance while the war crisis continued – and was never introduced. Government remained chiefly in the hands of the Committee of Public Safety, whose decisions the Convention (or those who still attended it, for hundreds of the members now began to stay away) rubber-stamped for fear of the consequences of acting otherwise. Within three years the Convention sanctioned 11,250 decrees, without giving so much as one of them a second reading.

New constitution

All over the country the Committee of Public Safety was now using the local Jacobin societies to enforce its policy, which included conscription. This had been voted earlier, over a wide age-range, but never rigorously applied. Now it was applied without exception to men aged eighteen to twenty-five, and it produced armies far bigger than was customary. Carnot, a Committee member who was a former officer, was the leading figure in the task of raising, arming and training these conscript armies. He accomplished it brilliantly, so well in fact, that he later escaped execution because he was regarded as (in Napoleon's phrase) 'the Organiser of Victory'. To enforce conscription and suppress opposition of all kinds the Committee used not merely local agents but also their own members sent down to the provinces as 'representatives on mission'. They met resistance with extreme ruthlessness, and blood flowed freely not only in Paris but in many of the great provincial towns.

The *levée en masse*, August 1793

Carnot

What France now had, then, was Committee dictatorship based on the support of one part of the Convention, the Mountain. During July 1793 there was a significant change in the more important of the two Committees, that of Public Safety. Danton, not extreme enough to please the Mountain, lost his place, and Robespierre and his associates moved in. Honest in money matters (he was nicknamed 'the Incorruptible'), no lover of women, and believing in his democratic, Rousseauite creed far more sincerely than many of the other revolutionary leaders, Robespierre was also vain and fanatical, and determined to enforce his own ideas at all costs. Believing that 'terror' was necessary to inspire 'virtue' (i.e. correct behaviour according to Robespierre's own principles) he was one of those primarily responsible for what came to be called the 'Reign of Terror'.

Decline of Danton; rise of Robespierre, July 1793

Others helped Robespierre in unleashing this, or even surpassed him. They acted either from similar fanaticism, or from sheer criminality, or from a realisation that the choice was now between being a guillotiner or a guillotined. In Paris Fouquier-Tinville, the ruthless Public Prosecutor to the Revolutionary Tribunal, claimed over 2,500 victims in sixteen months – from Marie Antoinette and the Girondins down to harmless old women like Madame du Barry, whose days of glory as the mistress of Louis XV were long since over. Among the more depraved parts of the Paris population a dreadful bloodlust grew, developing into a kind of worship of 'Madame Guillotine'. Huge crowds attended the 'Red Mass' (as indeed they attended public executions anywhere) and it may be that the government also ordered executions to provide entertainment for the people and distract their minds from the war. Individual executions in Paris, however, paled into insignificance compared with the vengeance taken by the Committee's representatives in the provinces when there was armed revolt. At Nantes, for instance, over 4,000 were butchered in four months, some by being sent out in a

Reign of Terror, 1793–94

ROBESPIERRE

Above left: EN ROUTE FOR THE GUILLOTINE
A sketch made by Jacques Louis David, foremost artist of the day and an ardent Jacobin, as the former Queen was borne to execution in 1793. David had been painter to Louis XVI and enjoyed much royal favour. This did not stop him becoming a leading member of the Convention and voting for Louis' death.

boat which was then deliberately sunk; and at Lyons 2,000 perished in mass executions conducted by volleys of gunfire.

France was now virtually a police state, in which few could trust their neighbours and all dreaded 'the knock on the door after dark'. But though the royalists were utterly powerless, the revolutionists themselves were far from united. Many resented the virtual dictatorship of the two Committees, and there was a growing move by the extremists of the Paris Commune, led by Hébert, to push the revolution in a socialist direction, in the interests of the poor. This agitation forced Robespierre and the Convention to pass a 'Law of the Maximum' controlling the price of bread and other necessities. As atheists, the Hébert group also set out to destroy Christian worship: the Commune ordered the closing of all the Paris churches, and enthroned a 'Goddess of Reason' in the cathedral of Notre Dame. Disapproving of these measures, and fearful lest the revolution slip from his

Hébert and the
Commune

'Law of the Maximum'

control, Robespierre and his associates then struck. Hébert and the other leaders of the Commune went the way of the Girondins, and in their place Robespierre secured the appointment of men subservient to himself.

By now, however, the French armies, conscript and ragged but full of revolutionary fervour, had recovered from their setbacks and were again triumphant. In this situation, and alarmed also at the continued threat to personal liberty, Danton, Desmoulins and others began to feel the need for peace abroad and reconciliation at home. The Terror, they argued, had worked its purpose and should be ended. Sickening of the bloodshed and happy in the love of a young girl he had just married, Danton led a campaign to halt the whole ghastly business. The move was fatal; denouncing him as 'too indulgent', Robespierre immediately accused him of counter-revolutionary sentiments, and Danton and Desmoulins met the fate they had helped to mete out to so many others. Danton behaved with his invariable courage. As he passed Robespierre's house on the way to the guillotine he shouted: 'Infamous Robespierre, you will soon follow me!' And on the scaffold itself he made one of the most famous remarks in history: 'Show my head to the people – it is worth the trouble!'

Having struck down the Hébertists on his left and the Dantonists on his right, there was little to restrain Robespierre. He established the worship of the Supreme Being (his own particular form of religion) and stepped up the Terror. By one ruthless law, known as the Law of 22nd Prairial,[1] suspects were deprived of the help of counsel and could be condemned to the one possible punishment, death, on the reputation of a 'bad moral character' alone – which might be made to mean anything. After this in fifty days nearly 1,500 heads fell. But opposition grew. Too many leaders, far less honest men than Robespierre, began to fear that their turn would come next. They ganged up together, and their momentary alliance cost Robespierre his hold on the Committee of Public Safety and his control of the Jacobin Clubs. Shouted down in the Convention, he was lodged with his closest followers in prison – only to be released by his creatures in the Commune. But his opponents in the Convention persisted, and he was recaptured in the Paris Hôtel de Ville on 9th Thermidor (27th July) as he was about to sign an illegal appeal to the troops. The next day he and twenty-one of his associates were led to the scaffold in their turn, and the day afterwards the knife fell on seventy-one of his supporters in the Commune.

Strangely enough, though those who overthrew Robespierre were far worse than he, the execution of the Robespierrists led to the end of the Terror. The country now was so obviously tired of fear and bloodshed that the new rulers, after ensuring their own safety by executing the chief remaining terrorists, eventually destroyed the war dictatorship organisation which had made the Terror possible. They weakened the powers of the Revolutionary Tribunal, the

Marginal notes:

End of the Hébertists, March 1794.

The end of Danton, April 1794

Law of 22 Prairial, (10 June 1794)

End of Robespierre, July 1794

---

[1] Prairial was one of the months of the new Revolutionary calendar adopted in 1793. The practice of dating years from the birth of Christ was abandoned, and the new era began as from 22nd September 1792 with Year 1 of the Republic. The year was divided into twelve thirty-day months, named with reference to the climate and seasons: e.g. Nivose (the snowy month), Pluviose (the rainy month), Germinal (the month of buds), Thermidor (the heat month), and Prairial (the meadow month). Each month was divided into three decades, or groups of ten days. Sundays and saints days of course disappeared. The tenth day, décadi, was a holiday, as were the five odd days at the end of the year. These were known as *sansculottides*.

36

Committees of Public Safety and General Security, abolished the Paris Commune, closed the Jacobin Clubs, and repealed the Law of 22nd Prairial. Finally the Convention voted yet another new constitution, in which the electorate would be restricted to taxpayers (a reaction against extreme democracy), and power split between a two-housed Assembly and a Directory of five men. Aided by the long drawn-out war and by public feeling against Britain's attempts to promote a further rising in La Vendée and a landing in Brittany, the men who had ousted Robespierre kept their hold on affairs and one of their leaders, Barras, later secured appointment to the Directory. When there was a royalist rising in Paris shortly before the new constitution came into force, they ordered out the troops, and a 'whiff of grapeshot' dispersed the mob. The officer in command was a sallow-skinned Corsican named Napoleon Bonaparte, who from being the Directory's saviour and servant was soon to prove its master.

How are we to explain this almost incredible French Revolution, this astounding mixture of idealism and villainy, courage and cowardice, reform and tyranny? Chiefly by bearing in mind this fact – that France, a country undergoing a radical reshaping of her organs of government, at the critical moment was plunged into war, both national and civil. War, with the fear it generates, often produces reckless violence against opponents at home, and so it was in the French Revolution. Further, the democratic creed of the French Revolutionaries, based on idealism rather than practicability at the time, encouraged the belief that the mob is always right, and robbed leader after leader of the will or courage to halt the mob when it was obviously wrong. By the system of open debates in Assembly, Convention, Clubs and local committees, those who urged moderation were always liable to be shouted down and accused of the unforgivable offence of counter-revolutionary sentiments. Worst of all, perhaps, was the permission given in July 1792 to the local assemblies of the forty-eight Paris sections (the electoral districts) to consider themselves in permanent session. This meant that the fanatics could always outstay the wearied moderates and reverse any decisions they disliked. At critical moments, too, the undue importance of the Municipal Government of Paris, or Commune, which was early captured by the extreme Left, had a disastrous effect on the more moderate Convention.

Thus partly because of the war, internal and external, partly because of the genuine difficulty of keeping a hold on a country freed from the shackles of centuries, partly because of the unrealistic theories of the revolutionaries and the practice of open debating, partly because of the independence of the Commune and the sections, the conduct of affairs rapidly drifted into the hands of extremists, and the Revolution developed from a movement for peaceful reform into a welter of terrorism and bloodshed. Yet it must never be forgotten that when the frenzy of violence died, the permanent benefits of reform remained. These did not include democracy, for France had shown herself as yet incapable of it. They did, however, include equality before the law, administrative reform, fairer taxation, liberated industry and commerce, and the foundation of schools, colleges, museums, libraries and the metric system. Together with all this went the abolition of feudalism, the distribution of feudal land among the peasantry, and the transference of the major share in the State from nobles and clergy to the bourgeoisie. It was the greatest achievement of Bonaparte not to destroy the Revolution but, while maintaining law and order, to preserve most of these essentials.

End of the Terror and the war dictatorship.

The new constitution: the Directory

Bonaparte

Origins of the Revolution's violence

Permanent benefits of the Revolution

CHAPTER 5
The Revolutionary Wars and the Rise of Napoleon Bonaparte

1. From the First Coalition to the Treaty of Amiens, 1793–1802

We must now follow the career of the fascinating and repellent genius who in almost equal measure restored and ruined France. We have seen how, for a number of reasons including the threat of her doctrines and the occupation of the Austrian Netherlands, the war which revolutionary France had declared against Austria in 1792 had by 1793 developed into a war against a European coalition. The price of France's initial failure in this was the Terror and dictatorship.

First Coalition, 1793

This dictatorship, directed mainly by the Committee of Public Safety, succeeded in redeeming the military situation. By 1795 the work of Carnot and others on the Committee (Carnot not only planned campaigns and organised armies but also turned up in civilian dress to lead the advance at Fleurus in 1794 which recaptured the Austrian Netherlands) and the enthusiasm of the ragged French troops had driven Prussia and Spain from the war. Holland, too, had not only failed on land and lost a fleet captured by a cavalry charge across the ice, but had also been compelled to make a peace which put her forces at the disposal of France. The Prince of Orange fled, the republican party collaborated with the French, and Holland found herself reshaped along French lines into the Batavian Republic. Of the First Coalition, only Austria, Sardinia and the main originator and pay-master, Britain, still remained active by the autumn of 1795.

Fleurus

Formation of Batavian Republic

Britain's record in the war thus far had been uninspiring in Europe, though she had picked up some territory overseas. Her efforts included the capture of Toulon with the Spanish in 1793 (and its loss four months later), an unsuccessful expedition to aid revolt in Brittany, defeat under the Duke of York in the Netherlands, and an incomplete 'Lord Howe' victory (as Nelson termed it) outside Brest on 'the Glorious First of June', 1794, when Howe's fleet, which had been blockading Brest, captured six warships, but allowed a big grain convoy from America to get through to the French port.

The strategy of France's new government, the Directory installed in November 1795, was to knock out Austria before concentrating on Britain. It was a good moment to deal with Austria, not only because she had lost most of her allies, but also because she was busy absorbing a further slice of Poland, the last stretches of which had been finally partitioned between Austria, Prussia and Russia in October 1795. In the ensuing campaigns the French conscript still managed to maintain – it was one of the secrets of his success – an astonishing degree of faith in 'liberty' and 'equality'; but the actual government of France, the Directory, soon moved very far from the crusading spirit of 1792. Instead, it approached the war in the Louis XIV tradition of foreign conquest and glory, to which it added the idea of

extending France to her 'natural frontiers' – the Rhine, the Alps, the Pyrenees, and the oceans. Already in October 1795 the Austrian Netherlands had been declared incorporated in France, and other additions were now planned. The Directory indeed still offered the new liberty to the peoples of Europe, and was soon able to set up more satellite republics like that formed in Holland; but usually the new liberty was to turn out no more acceptable than the old tyranny.

The French planned to attack Austria from more than one direction. Not only were two French armies to attack directly along the Rhine-Danube route, but in addition a third army was to enter Italy, capture the Austrian possessions there, and then join the attack on Austria itself via the Tyrol. The soldier appointed by the Directory, on the motion of Carnot, to command the Italian expedition was

the Napoleon Bonaparte who had already proved his worth in ousting the British from Toulon in 1793 and the royalists from the streets of Paris in 1795. A penniless, friendless, one-meal-a-day young artillery officer in 1789, he had welcomed the Revolution as a keen disciple of Rousseau, and had maintained sufficiently close relations with Robespierre to be thrown into prison when he fell. But he had learnt to despise the mob and to loathe mob violence in the scenes he witnessed in Paris, and gradually his sense of order triumphed over his revolutionary principles. Still partly in disgrace, he had been on the spot in the difficult situation of 1795, and his prompt order to fetch cannons and fire on the mob had saved the new Directory. His rewards were the command of the Italian Expedition and the hand of a mistress of the Director Barras, Josephine Beauharnais, with whom he was passionately in love and who had useful aristocratic connections.

On 11th March 1796, after a two-day honeymoon, Bonaparte departed for Italy. Within a month he had pulled his lax, ill-equipped, and disorganised troops together, and was ready for action. His words to them on the opening of the campaign are famous: 'You are badly fed and nearly naked – I am going to lead you to the most fertile plains in the world. You will find there great cities and rich provinces. You will find there honour, glory, and wealth.' A few days after he entered Italy he had succeeded in his first object of separating the Austrian and Sardinian armies, and the King of Sardinia was demanding peace from a general whose troops had practically 'no artillery, no cavalry, and no boots'. The rest of the campaign continued on the same lines. By brilliant strategy and marching he contrived to manoeuvre numerically superior opponents into positions where they could engage only a small proportion of their forces against his entire strength. He had, too, a powerful moral weapon – the appeal of the doctrine of 'liberty' to peoples under autocratic or foreign rule. Within little more than a month after

setting foot on Italian soil he had forced the bridge at Lodi and entered Milan, capital of Lombardy and the Austrian headquarters, amid the rejoicing of its Italian population. Here, as in other conquered areas of Italy later, the French set up a dependent republic. A check came when for some months the enemy held out

in Mantua, but finally by the battle of Rivoli, in early 1797, this resistance was crushed. The Austrians became demoralised, and the victorious Bonaparte chased them out of Italy to within seventy-five miles of Vienna. There he stopped only because the Austrians signed a truce, converted some months later into the severe treaty of Campo-Formio.

By this treaty Austria was compelled to recognise not only France's conquest of the Austrian Netherlands and her newly-won Rhine frontier, but also the loss of Lombardy, and its incorporation into a new state, the Cisalpine Republic, which, although nominally independent, was entirely under French control. In return France threw Austria a shameful bribe – Venice, which had no quarrel with France and which had preserved her existence as an independent republic for 1,100 years. The Italians, who had helped the French, were thus soon to find that 'liberty' was not everywhere applied, and that even where it was, it was expensive. From Venice and the Cisalpine Republic and the Papal States (which were equally at his mercy, and parts of which were incorporated in the Cisalpine Republic) Bonaparte poured back tribute over the Alps in the form of cash and masterpieces of art – the Papacy alone, for instance, had to pay 300,000,000 francs compensation for the murder of a French envoy by the Roman people. Thus within eighteen months Austria had been beaten out of the Coalition, North Italy

Treaty of
Campo-Formio, 1797

REPUBLICAN ELECTRICITY
This French cartoon of about 1800 is entitled 'la chute en masse' (mass downfall) – a play on the common contemporary expression 'levée en masse' (mass raising – i.e. recruitment – for the French republican armies). It shows the Austrian Emperor, the Pope, and the King of Spain being knocked down by the forces of liberty, equality and fraternity, generated from an electrical machine, labelled 'Declaration of the Rights of Man'. Elementary experiments with the newly discovered force of electricity were a fashion of the time.

completely reorganised, France enriched and glorified, and the name of Napoleon Bonaparte sent ringing throughout Europe.

Britain's critical year, 1797

There remained one stubborn opponent, Britain, who would never feel secure while a major sea-power occupied the coast of the Low Countries. Accordingly 1797 saw a determined French effort to crush her. It was, indeed, a critical year for Britain with no allies, an imminent revolt in Ireland, mutinies in the fleet, corn shortage, a financial crisis, and control in India threatened by the French-inspired Tippoo Sahib. But the schemes of France went astray, in spite of the fact that Holland and Spain had now to act as her allies and move their fleets at her dictation. At the end of 1796 an attempted French invasion of Ireland at Bantry Bay had been scattered by storms, and the French efforts of 1798 to carry aid to the revolt of Wolfe Tone and his United Irishmen were little more successful. The graver danger to Britain during these years in fact came from France's compulsory allies rather than her own disorganised navies, until Jervis and Nelson (his second-in-command, whose initiative won the day) defeated the Spanish off Cape St Vincent and Duncan disposed of the Dutch at Camperdown. Britain for the moment was safe.

The Egyptian Campaign, 1798–99

It was left to the conqueror of Italy to devise a more brilliant, if fundamentally impracticable, scheme of attacking the obstinate island. Knowing that Britain was a world power to whom commerce was the life-blood, Bonaparte planned to capture Egypt (which was part of the Ottoman or Turkish Empire), ruin British trade in the Mediterranean, and possibly even advance overland and seize India. The fascination which the East had exercised over his mind from boyhood urged him on, as well as that vaulting ambition which could say: 'My glory is threadbare. This little Europe is too small a field. Great celebrity can be won only in the East.' The Directory readily approved the proposal – Bonaparte was becoming so powerful that it might be wise to keep him away from France. So with an army of 38,000, a large group of scientists and antiquarians and 400 boats, and with the whole expedition financed by plunder from two new French vassal-republics (the Helvetic and the Roman), Bonaparte sailed from Toulon for Egypt. Eluding Nelson, he took Malta from the Knights of St John *en route*, cleverly continued to give Nelson the slip, and arrived off Alexandria in July 1798. Before the month was out he had overwhelmed the famous Turkish cavalry force, the Mamelukes,

Battle of the Pyramids

at the Battle of the Pyramids ('Forty centuries look down on you,' he said to his troops before the battle), and Egypt lay at his feet. Within a few days, however, Nelson came on the French fleet at anchor in Aboukir Bay and utterly destroyed it,

Battle of the Nile

so cutting off French communications with Europe. Without sufficient reinforcements Bonaparte could not advance to India, and he was thus driven into adopting an alternative plan, almost equally ambitious, of invading Syria, pushing through Asia Minor, capturing Constantinople, and smashing the Ottoman Empire. Syria proved an easy victim (he again posed as the 'deliverer' from Turkish rulers),

Acre

till he was held up at Acre by Admiral Sir Sidney Smith, who swept up the French transports and landed a British naval force to help defend the city. Frustrated, Bonaparte had finally to retire to crush a Turkish attempt at recapturing Egypt.

At this stage, in August 1799, master of Egypt but a prisoner there because of the loss of his fleet, Bonaparte learnt some astonishing news from English newspapers thoughtfully sent him by the eccentric Sir Sidney Smith. In Europe the French were on the run. A second great Coalition had been formed, this time between Britain, Turkey, Austria, Russia, Portugal and Naples. Austria was alarmed at the fresh French aggression in Italy, which had driven the Pope from Rome, set up another republic in Naples, and captured Piedmont, while the new ally, Russia, joined because her half-mad Tsar Paul was sentimentally attached to the Order of St John and resented Bonaparte's move towards the East. This, the Tsar considered, should be reserved for Russian and Turkish influence. From Italy, Bonaparte learnt, the French troops were being expelled by the fierce Cossack general Suvorov, while the other French armies were hanging on with difficulty to their conquests on the Rhine, in the Netherlands, and in Switzerland. There were, too, rumours of royalist plots and treachery among French generals. In France a wave of unpopularity was almost submerging the Directory. The moment was ripe. Bonaparte and a few followers stole away from Egypt in two small ships, leaving his deserted expedition to its favourite sports of measuring ruins, trying to find a substitute for hops, and fishing in the Nile with bent bayonets for dead Mamelukes, and leaving it also to the later prospect of a certain surrender to the enemy. By luck and skill, he again eluded the British fleet, landed in southern France and received a great welcome as the conqueror of Egypt and the man who could recapture Italy. Within a few weeks he had carried out a *coup d'état* by an intrigue with some of the Directors, and had dismissed the Assembly. For once his nerve failed him, for he nearly fainted when the Assembly at first refused to accept his statements; he was saved by his brother Lucien, the President, who was in the plot and who ordered in the waiting troops in the nick of time. Bonaparte now established a new government of three Consuls, of whom he was the first – and the only one who counted. The other two were former Directors. A show of democratic government was preserved, but no one was taken in by appearances. The new dictatorship was approved by an overwhelming plebiscite – a new political weapon of Bonaparte's.

Secure in his new power, Bonaparte marched to restore the situation in Europe. In fact the tide had already begun to turn in France's favour, but Bonaparte monopolised the credit. By 1800 his military genius and a good slice of luck at the battle of Marengo made the recapture of Italy possible, while in Germany Moreau defeated the Austrians several times, concluding with a victory in the snow at Hohenlinden. Russia had already quarrelled with Austria and Britain and retired from the conflict. Austria had therefore little option but to make peace. By the Treaty of Lunéville of 1801 she again recognised the French dependent republics and other arrangements in Italy, Switzerland and Holland, as well as France's conquests along the left bank of the Rhine.

France could now concentrate again on Britain, for whom a very difficult situation developed in the form of the 'Armed Neutrality of the North' – a league of the Baltic powers (Prussia, Sweden, Denmark, and Russia) opposed to the extensive 'right of search' claimed by the British admiralty over neutral powers. This claim had caused wars with Holland in the past, was to cause a war with the United States from 1812 to 1814,[1] and was to make great trouble between the U.S.A. and Britain in 1915. Russia, too, was prompted by Tsar Paul's concern for the Knights of St John, to whom the British had not restored Malta, despite having taken it from the French. The British government dealt with this situation partly by

Second Coalition, 1799

Napoleon overthrows the Directory October–November 1799: the *coup d'état* of Brumaire

The Consulate, 1800

Treaty of Lunéville, 1801

The Armed Neutrality

[1] See pp. 56–7.

Copenhagen, 1801

relaxing some of the harsher claims, (that iron, timber, and corn could be seized in any ship trading with the enemy, for example), and partly by smashing the Danish fleet at Copenhagen. (The Danes were given twenty-four hours to withdraw from the league, and refused; during the subsequent British attack Nelson did his famous telescope trick to ignore the instructions of Sir Hyde Parker).

Assassination of
Tsar Paul

Further, the assassination of Tsar Paul by a court party in Russia tired of his insane suspicions helped the British cause, for his successor, Tsar Alexander I, was opposed to France.

The year 1801 thus finished with Britain triumphant in the Mediterranean and the Baltic. Farther afield, on the suggestion of the exiled Prince of Orange, she had occupied the Dutch possessions of Ceylon and the Cape of Good Hope; and she had also captured Trinidad from the Spanish. France was equally supreme on the European continent. On both sides there were accordingly overtures for peace, and in March 1802 the two enemies signed the Treaty of Amiens. Its most important terms were that Britain was to restore the Cape to the Dutch and Malta to the Knights of St John, while retaining Ceylon and Trinidad; and in return France was to evacuate Rome and southern Italy and restore Egypt to Turkey. Bonaparte, approved First Consul for life by an overwhelming plebiscite, could now, it seemed, devote his genius to the arts of peace.

Treaty of Amiens, 1802

2. Napoleon Bonaparte's Achievements in France as First Consul and Emperor, 1800–14

As a general, Bonaparte's genius was, finally, unproductive, because he took on too much. As a statesman, however, he gave France institutions which in different forms have endured to this day. Most of this creative work dates from his years as First Consul (1800–04) which included a period free from war when he could concentrate on his country's internal problems.

His first care was to consolidate his own power. To begin with, he had been appointed First Consul for ten years, but in 1802 he improved on this by becoming First Consul for life. In 1804 he then took the logical step of turning the central government into an imperial dictatorship, with himself as the Emperor Napoleon. He kept representative institutions only in a powerless form, but secured the approval of France by plebiscite.

The Empire, 1804

Napoleon's central government perished with him. However, his earlier reorganisation of local government (an area which the revolutionaries of 1789 had plunged into near-chaos) became the basis of the modern French system. As First Consul he retained the new division of France into *Départements*, but created a new sub-division, the *Arrondissement*, to replace the District (which had been abolished by the Convention). More important, under Bonaparte's scheme the leading official in each division and sub-division was appointed, directly or indirectly, by the central government. Local councils continued to be elected, but their powers became largely advisory; the real business was done by officials who represented, and owed their positions to, the central government, They were the Prefect in the *Département*, the sub-Prefect in the *Arrondissement*, and the Mayor in the Commune. Bonaparte, in fact, as First Consul nominated the Prefects and sub-Prefects, and the Prefects chose the Mayors. Thus control over the provinces, lost in 1789–91 and increasingly re-asserted by every government

Reorganisation of
local government, 1800

since then, by 1800 was permanently recovered. From then on Frenchmen had little effective share in governing their own localities; but they got well-chosen officials, good order, and the possibility of a strong and unified national policy.

In the realm of education Bonaparte's government during the Consulate made some important advances. It neglected elementary education, leaving this largely to the Church, but encouraged secondary education by founding secondary schools (to be run by the Communes) and *lycées*, or semi-military secondary schools (to be run by the government). In these, science and mathematics were second only to military training (at Eton at this time the main subjects studied were still Greek and Latin). Later, under the Empire, a university, too, was founded: the University of France, consisting of seventeen Academies (or branches) in different districts. The Grand Master of this university, chosen directly by the Emperor, was expected to control virtually the whole educational system of France. None of these new institutions catered for girls. 'I do not think we need trouble ourselves with any plan of instruction for young females,' said Napoleon, '. . . Public education is not suitable for them, because they are never called upon to act in public. Manners are all in all to them, and marriage is all they look to.'

As a clever man who had himself risen solely by his abilities, Bonaparte was determined that the great state positions should be open to all men of talent, however humble their origins. He sought such men for his Council of State, a purely advisory but important body whose expert knowledge helped him greatly in the various tasks of government. Accordingly, while he allowed the *émigrés* to return, he no longer permitted them to consider themselves the true nobility of France; instead he created a kind of nobility of talent by founding the Legion of Honour. Membership of the Legion came to be a cherished distinction, awarded for services in such matters as politics, civil service, local government, and the arts; but in its founder's time the appointments were nine-tenths military. 'Men,' he said, 'are led by toys.' When he became Emperor he developed this theme, but in many ways contradicted the idea of the Legion of Honour by creating a new hereditary nobility to grace his Imperial Court. All told he created some 3,000 new hereditary nobles, including four princes, thirty dukes and nearly four hundred counts, quite apart from the members of his own family to whom he allotted kingdoms.

In religious affairs, too, Bonaparte, for all his irreligious nature, left his mark on France. During the Revolution the extremists had severed the Church in France from its head, the Pope, and by so doing had brought about religious conflict and chaos. Although such revolutionary deities as the Goddess of Reason and the Supreme Being had quickly passed out of fashion, the Church in France in 1800 was still disunited and cut off from Rome. Nevertheless, the overwhelming majority of French peasants were Catholic at heart, even if the intellectuals were not. Anxious to secure his régime by pleasing the peasants and at the same time ending the religious strife in the west of France, Bonaparte as First Consul came to an agreement with the Pope. By the Concordat of 1801 Catholicism was recognised as the religion of France's rulers and of the majority of Frenchmen, although other religions were not forbidden.

Bonaparte, however, was able to drive a hard bargain with Rome, for the Pope feared a French occupation of the Papal States. The French State was to choose the bishops (whom the Pope would instal), pay the clergy, and generally control the Church, which would be under only the nominal leadership of the Pope. Above all, the Church lands confiscated at the Revolution were not to be returned. Thus the peasants were won over to Bonaparte not only because he restored their religion but because he saw that they kept their recent gains. The Concordat did not please everyone – one distinguished general was overheard to remark at the *Te Deum* which celebrated the reconciliation: 'The only thing lacking at this ceremony is the million dead men who died to get rid of this nonsense.' Bonaparte, however, knew he was on firm ground in appealing to the old religious instincts. He saw in religion what he called 'the cement of the social order' – something useful in binding men together and keeping them satisfied, something that young ladies especially should study to make them meek and obedient wives. In other words, religion was for Bonaparte only an instrument. The true depth of his Catholicism may be judged from the way he later annexed the Papal States and had the Pope carried off to France.[1] Nevertheless, the Concordat helped to restore social stability to a France which badly needed it at the time.

Industry and Commerce

Both as First Consul and Emperor, Napoleon was actively interested in French industry and commerce. Commercial exchanges and chambers of commerce were created, and advisory boards set up for many manufactures, arts, and crafts. High protective tariffs sheltered French industries from foreign competition; technical schools, prizes, loans, and exhibitions encouraged new processes; and France, deprived of certain staple articles by the Continental System,[2] managed to develop effective substitutes such as chicory for coffee and beet for cane-sugar. New cotton machines were invented and factory acts passed. Further, by main-

Bank of France, 1801

taining a stable currency based on gold, and by his creation of the Bank of France while First Consul, Napoleon won the support of all the business interests.

In fact, by an elaborate series of decrees Napoleon's government regulated almost the whole of the national life – art, the theatre, the press, commerce, industry, and religion. This regulation was not all gain. High tariffs meant great hardship for many consumers in the form of increased prices, government censorship greatly limited freedom of publication, and regulation of industry hindered as well as helped industrial development.

Public works

Whatever the merits of his general financial and commercial policy, there is no doubt that Napoleon's great schemes of public works as Emperor permanently beautified and enriched France. Canals, bridges, and roads were constructed, marshes drained, sea-ports enlarged and fortified. Museums were founded, and the Louvre completed and filled with the priceless treasures stolen from Italy. Palaces like Fontainebleau were restored. The planning of a great group of arterial roads radiating from the Arc de Triomphe and the clearing of the Tuileries Gardens gave Paris the beginning of its modern beauty. It is little wonder that Napoleon was immensely popular with the French until about 1808 – until, in other words, his plans grew too vast, he began to taste defeat, and he cost France too much in men and money.

The *Code Napoléon*, 1804

Of all Bonaparte's non-warlike achievements, his greatest was perhaps the Civil Code or the *Code Napoléon*, a summary of the laws of France on such topics as rights and duties, marriage, divorce, parentage, inheritance and property, and a

[1] See p. 50.
[2] See p. 49.

statement of the general legal principles concerning them. After the old tangle of Frankish, Roman, Royal, Provincial, and Baronial laws which had been complicated rather than unravelled by the revolutionary legislation, the *Code* was crystal clear. It was, of course, not the actual work of Bonaparte: the decision to compile a *Code* had been taken before he came into power, but as First Consul he presided over about half the meetings of the committee which reviewed the lawyers' drafts, and had a decisive influence on its development. Often he was able to secure greater clarity, or to place his weight behind clauses which increased the power of the State, the husband or the father – Napoleon's great pillars of authority.

This civil code was not a very progressive document. It allowed few legal rights to women and permitted a father to have his child temporarily imprisoned. However, it confirmed the legal equality of male citizens, helped to bring social stability, and enabled Frenchmen – and others – to understand the main principles underlying the laws. In the words of one historian 'it was at once the summary and the correction of the French Revolution'. Other codes on commerce and criminal law followed, but the civil code was recognised as outstanding and was soon widely adopted by different states in Europe and in South America. Through the *Code* therefore Napoleon helped to give one of the main bulwarks of domestic peace – a great legal system – not only to France, but to the world.

CHAPTER 6
The Struggle Against Napoleon

1. From the Renewal of War to the Height of Napoleon's Power, 1803–10

The Peace of Amiens was always unlikely to give more than a short breathing space. It did not mention a question of the greatest importance to Britain – the French annexation of the Austrian Netherlands; and it left both sides still deeply suspicious and without the real will to peace. France refused to give any greater freedom to British trade; British caricaturists refused to be kinder to Bonaparte. France, too, was clearly planning to extend her influence in the Near East, India, and the West Indies – but equally clearly Britain would brook no important colonial rival.

In this highly-charged atmosphere the break came over Malta. Britain decided to violate the treaty by holding on to Malta till Bonaparte stopped scheming to revive his power in Egypt; Bonaparte decided to violate the treaty by holding on to southern Italy till Britain withdrew her forces from Malta. By 1803 the two rivals were at war again, France being helped by Spain after the British seizure of some Spanish treasure ships destined as subsidy for France.

The struggle which followed was a more personal one than the earlier bout of war against France. By 1804, when Bonaparte rid himself of his fellow Consuls and became the Emperor Napoleon, the flame of the French Revolution was plainly dying down. Thenceforth Europe had to deal with the ambition of one man rather than the burning zeal of a nation.

With the intention of mounting a direct attack on Britain, Napoleon first marshalled an enormous force in camp at Boulogne. 'The Channel', he said, 'is a ditch which it needs but a little courage to cross.' So an army of 100,000 men was held ready for the venture, and some 1,500 flat-bottomed ferry-boats constructed. But the scheme depended entirely on the absence of the British fleet, for Napoleon's first idea of slipping across in the calm of a dark or foggy night was obviously absurd. (Even after Boulogne harbour had been enlarged, five or six tides would be required to embark so great a body of men). Accordingly he directed his fleets to escape the British blockade (which was normally maintained as near the French naval ports as conditions permitted), join up with the Spanish, lure the British away from the Channel by a feint attack on the West Indies, and race back across the Atlantic before the British grasped the plan. Having thus secured an over-whelming predominance in the Channel, the Franco-Spanish fleets could safely cover the sailing of the invasion.

Villeneuve, the French admiral at Toulon, was successful in the first part of the scheme. He escaped according to plan, linked up with some Spanish ships off Cadiz, and proceeded to the West Indies. This drew Nelson there, in the belief that Villeneuve would be attacking British West Indian possessions. While the British admiral searched, Villeneuve duly gave him the slip, and set off back to Europe. But within three days Nelson became wise to the manoeuvre, sent off a fast ship to race Villeneuve and warn the Admiralty, and began to follow with his fleet. The British Admiralty, in fact, learnt of Villeneuve's return twelve days before Napoleon did, and he got it once more from the English newspapers! When Villeneuve approached Spanish waters he therefore found a British force from the Channel under Admiral Calder ready to intercept him. Moreover, though a few French ships had managed to slip out of Rochefort, the main naval force in the French Atlantic ports, that at Brest, had not escaped blockade at all. Seeing his scheme tottering, Villeneuve obeyed his alternative orders and put in at the Spanish port of Ferrol, and from there soon sailed to Cadiz. By this time, he was deeply pessimistic at the state of his fleet – 'bad masts, bad sails, bad officers, and bad seamen – obsolete naval tactics: we only know one manoeuvre, to form line, and that is just what the enemy wants us to do.'

In a rage, Napoleon now broke camp at Boulogne and prepared to lead his army against Austria, as a third Coalition, in which Britain and Russia were joined by Austria, had been formed earlier in the year. It was aimed against Napoleon's ever-increasing ambition, which showed itself during 1805 when he annexed large areas of northern Italy and declared himself King of Italy. Napoleon was not one to leave the initiative to the enemy. Speedily the men from the Boulogne camp were marching to central Europe as only the French armies could march – Napoleon 'wore his long boots', as they put it.

Meanwhile from his refuge at Cadiz, which Collingwood dared to begin blockad-ing with only three vessels, Villeneuve was persuaded to emerge by the taunts and orders of Napoleon, who commanded him to convey forces to Naples. Disregarding a last-minute order superseding him, the French admiral sailed, and on 21st October 1805 the thirty-three French and Spanish ships confronted the twenty-seven of Nelson and Collingwood off Cape Trafalgar. When the day finished Nelson's favourite mode of attack (breaking the enemy line and concentrating a superior force on one section of it at a time) had won its last and greatest triumph. The French navy was crippled, and the luckless Villeneuve committed suicide. For the rest of the war Britain was safe from invasion, and British sea-power, supreme from the beginning of hostilities, was from then on more or less un-challenged in European waters.

Unfortunately for the Allies the great success of Trafalgar was offset by two disasters which followed Napoleon's move to central Europe. Almost simul-taneously with the British victory at sea, a hopelessly outmanoeuvred Austrian army surrendered to Napoleon at Ulm, on the Danube in Bavaria; and before the end of the year, in his first great battle as supreme commander of all the French armies, Napoleon inflicted a crushing defeat on the Austrians and Russians at Austerlitz, in the Austrian province of Moravia. The news of this second and

Nelson follows Villeneuve

Villeneuve at Cadiz

Third Coalition, 1805

Trafalgar, 1805

Ulm and Austerlitz, 1805

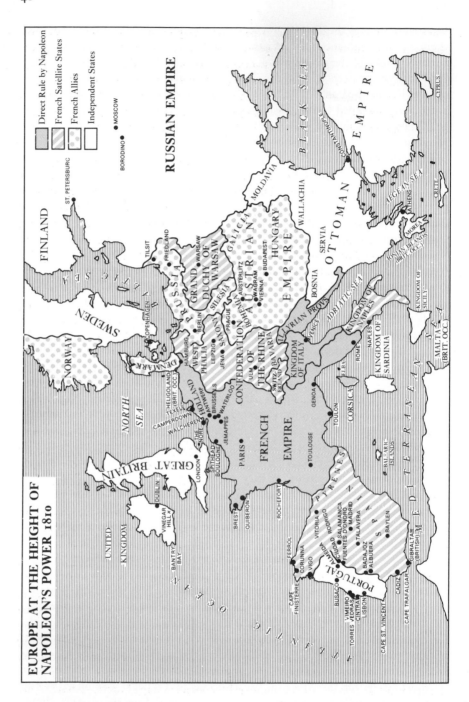

EUROPE AT THE HEIGHT OF
NAPOLEON'S POWER 1810

Direct Rule by Napoleon
French Satellite States
French Allies
Independent States

unexpected disaster came as a death-blow to Britain's Prime Minister, Pitt, old
and worn-out at forty-seven from the strain of government during more than ten
years' warfare.

Peace of Pressburg,
1805

To secure peace, Austria now agreed to hand over to Napoleon the Tyrol and
all her possessions in Italy including Venice, and to reduce her influence over the

south German states. With Austria powerless, Napoleon a few months later was able to set up a union of west German states known as the Confederation of the Rhine, the princes of which were sworn to carry out his orders in foreign policy. They soon declared their resignation from the old Holy Roman Empire, which Napoleon then declared he could no longer recognise. Francis of Austria thereupon resigned as its head, to become Emperor of Austria instead; and the Holy Roman Empire, which had endured in name at least for a thousand years, came to an end.

Confederation of the Rhine; end of the Holy Roman Empire, 1806

The turn of Prussia came next. Prussia had not joined the Coalition at its outset, for Napoleon had bribed her by allowing her to occupy the ancestral territory of Britain's George III – Hanover. He then thought better of this, and proposed to hand back Hanover to George III as part of a bargain with Britain. This and other actions stung Prussia to the point of belatedly declaring war, in which she put pressure on Saxony to join her. Only five days later, the battlefield of Jena in Thuringia witnessed the most crushing defeat ever inflicted on Prussian arms. The Prussian military machine fell to pieces, and Napoleon entered Berlin.

Jena, 1806

From Berlin Napoleon next moved east to deal with Russia, which still remained active against him. In doing this he could count on the help of the Poles, to whom, as to many other peoples at first, he appeared as 'the liberator'. He encountered the main Russian armies at Friedland, in east Prussia, and beat them and the Prussians so severely that Alexander decided to reverse his whole policy and make peace. The Treaty of Tilsit, first broached by the two Emperors on a raft on the River Niemen, proved to be almost the height of Napoleon's power. By its terms Alexander recognised Napoleon's arrangements on the Continent, including the Confederation of the Rhine and the setting up of a new Grand Duchy of Warsaw. In return Alexander received the promise of a free hand in Eastern Europe and a share in the Turkish Empire when it was to be annexed. More important still, he agreed, if Britain should refuse to give up her colonial conquests or her right of search, to join Napoleon's 'Continental System'. At the same time, Prussia made similar promises.

Treaty of Tilsit, 1807

The Continental System was the basis of Napoleon's strategy from this point. After Trafalgar Napoleon had come to realize that Britain could not be conquered by sea, and he therefore sought to use against her not a military or naval but an economic weapon – in other words, to strike a deathblow to her trade and wealth. It was a policy which the earlier Revolutionary governments had initiated, but which he was to systematise. For this purpose he issued from Berlin in 1806, after the Battle of Jena, and later from Milan a series of orders known as the Berlin and Milan Decrees, the effect of which was to forbid France or any of her allies or subject territory to accept British goods, which were to be confiscated whenever found. British ships were to be excluded from all ports, and by thus cutting off Britain's means of export, while still allowing her to import certain French goods (i.e. allowing Britain to buy but not to sell), Napoleon hoped to rob Britain of her gold reserve, start a financial crisis, and bring his enemy to bankruptcy.

The Continental System

Berlin and Milan Decrees, 1806

It followed that, if the scheme were to be successful, it would have to be applied practically all over Europe – hence his effort to make it really a 'Continental' System. And if the whole of Europe had to be controlled in order to beat Britain, Napoleon was certainly beginning to bite off rather more than he might be able to chew. Yet his capacity for chewing seemed unlimited. By 1807 he had crowned himself King of Italy in the old Austrian dominions in the north; made his brother Joseph King of Naples in the south; made another brother, Louis, King of Holland, and a third, Jerome, King of Westphalia (formed from the western lands of Prussia); while from eastern Prussian territory he had formed the Grand Duchy of Warsaw. Master of the Continent and secure in the new Russian alliance, he hoped that the exclusion of British goods would soon settle his last outstanding problem.

Orders in Council, 1807

Britain's retaliation was swift and effective. By a series of Orders in Council of 1807 and later, all countries which accepted Napoelon's orders were declared to be in a state of blockade, and any port excluding British vessels was to be deprived of the opportunity of welcoming those of other nations. Britain thus aimed at starving the Continent of alternative sources of supply, causing rising prices and hardship in each country, and therefore discontent against Napoelon, who had started the whole business. The absence of any French navy worth mentioning made the British blockade practicable; and when the British Government heard that Napoleon was planning to seize the Danish navy, it took prompt if lawless

Capture of Danish fleet, 1807

action, ordered the Danes to hand over their fleet to British keeping till the end of the war, and on their refusal bombarded Copenhagen till the vessels were duly surrendered. The last considerable danger being thus removed, Britain could carry out her Orders in Council effectively, and the grim trade war began to stifle the commerce of Europe.

The Peninsular War

The first country to revolt against the system was Portugal, which had long carried on a very profitable trade with Britain. Napoleon used the occasion typically, collecting five French armies on Spanish soil for the advance on Portugal, then, when this was conquered, bullying the Spanish royal family into resigning their throne to his brother Joseph.[1] But the move was fatal. Doctrines of liberty made no impression on the extremely backward and intensely Catholic Spaniards. Encouraged by their priests, they firmly resolved not to accept the rule of the man who, by 1809, had caused the Pope to be kidnapped and the Papal States to be incorporated in France. Moreover, the hostility of the Peninsula to Napoleon supplied Britain with a place for the operation of her army – a highly important development. With the Spanish victory at Baylen and the British and Portuguese victory at Vimiero in 1808 fortune began to desert the French in the Peninsula. For the moment Napoleon restored matters by coming from central Europe to take charge himself; but under Sir John Moore the remaining British army in Portugal – another had withdrawn, by a mutual arrangement with the French known as the Convention of Cintra – staged a desperate hit-and-run attack into Spain. It ended in a hurried embarkation at Corunna, but prevented the Emperor from overrunning Portugal.

Torres Vedras

As soon as Napoleon was gone from the Peninsula the tide turned again. The British under Wellesley (the future Duke of Wellington) landed again in Portugal and advanced successfully into Spain, where he defeated King Joseph at Talavera. For this he was made Viscount Wellington. Driven back by French reinforcements, Wellington retired to the Lisbon area. Around here, at Torres Vedras, after devastating the country in front to rob it of supplies and cover, he constructed an elaborate series of defensive earthworks so strong that even Marshal Ney, 'the bravest of the brave', refused to attack them. From these defences Wellington could emerge and support the peasantry in their ceaseless guerrilla

---

[1] Joseph's place as King of Naples was taken by one of Napoleon's marshals, Murat.

THE THIRD OF MAY 1808 AT MADRID
From a painting by Goya in the Prado, Madrid. There has been an unsuccessful rising against Joseph Bonaparte, and the French are shooting captured rebels. On the one side, Goya seems to say, is merciless organised power; on the other side, humanity, courage, the love of freedom, defiance.

warfare against the French – a warfare so intense and so savagely cruel on both sides that prisoners who were merely shot or blinded thought themselves lucky. One captured French general was thrown into a vat of scalding water. Like previous invaders the French had the eternal difficulty of fighting in mountainous country where communications were almost non-existent, where 'a small army is beaten and a large army starves'. Nowhere else had they operated in a barren country and amid a fanatically hostile population. French commanders in different parts of Spain learnt of each other's movements only from Napoleon in Austria, who often depended on the English newspapers for his information; a force of two hundred cavalrymen was necessary to get a message from one village to another, as a smaller number would be murdered by peasants. Slowly Wellington grew stronger and prepared to advance. The first cracks were appearing in Napoleon's great edifice.

Walcheren expedition

Elsewhere, the system as yet remained intact. In 1809 Britain sent an expedition to Walcheren, off the mouth of the Scheldt, to free Holland, but it did not even succeed in fighting, let alone winning, a battle. Lingering under inefficient commanders it fell a victim to the swamps and fevers of the island, and perished miserably. Austria, too, tempted to try conclusions once more by French failures in Spain, found Napoleon still far too strong at the battle of Wagram, lost even more territory, and had to promise to enforce the Continental System. Moreover, she was made to ally with Napoleon and supply him with a new wife, the Princess Marie Louise – for Josephine had not provided the Emperor with an heir and was now conveniently divorced.

Wagram

Austrian Alliance

So by 1810, with opposition again crushed in Europe, with Sweden compelled to adhere to the Continental System and Holland now completely incorporated in the French Empire following Louis Bonaparte's unwillingness to apply the System rigorously, Napoleon might hope that his mastery of Europe was secure and that his last remaining problems – Britain and the Peninsula – would soon be cleared up.

THE EFFECT OF THE CONTINENTAL SYSTEM ON BRITAIN (THROUGH FRENCH EYES)
Before. After.

2. The Decline and Fall of Napoleon, 1810–15

Napoleon's hopes of 1810 were not to be realised. The Continental System rapidly made him more and more unpopular as trade stagnated, as tea, coffee, sugar and tobacco became unobtainable or enormously expensive, as ships were laid up and firms closed down. He even found himself compelled to issue licences for the large-scale importation of certain British goods into France such as boots for his armies. The conscription and taxes he applied to his dependent allies or conquests made matters worse, and completely failed to compensate for all the improvements in other directions that his government had made. In 1811 came the revolt which was to prove the beginning of the end. The Tsar, tired of doing without British and overseas goods, annoyed at the annexation of a relative's territory (Oldenberg), slighted by Napoleon's marriage with an Austrian rather than a Russian princess, and dissatisfied at Napoleon's failure to help him in his Eastern ambitions, broke away from the Continental System. The result was one of the most appalling military disasters in history – the Moscow campaign.

Unpopularity of Continental System

In 1812, with an overwhelming army of 610,000 men, forced from almost every country in Europe, Napoleon crossed the river Niemen into Russia to teach Alexander his lesson. Before such a force the Russians could only retreat; and as they retreated they devastated the country, denuding it of supplies and shelter. The vast invading army could not be fed; death and desertion carried off thousands, so that long before the cold set in two-thirds had disappeared. Napoleon struggled on to Moscow, hoping that its capture would end not only the war but all the difficulties of supply. Outside the capital the greatest battle of the campaign was fought – Borodino – which the French won at the cost of 30,000 horses and 50,000 men, with the dead left seven or eight deep on the field of conflict. Moscow now lay open to the invaders – only for them to find their longed-for haven turned into a raging inferno when the Russians set fire to the city rather than let it provide shelter for their opponents. After five weeks in the ruined city, Napoleon realised there was nothing to do but turn back – and, since Russian armies blocked other routes, to retreat over the desolate line of the advance. The dreadful sight – and sounds – of Borodino had to be encountered again, but one man at least was not sickened: 'the most beautiful battlefield I have ever seen in my life', remarked Napoleon. By November the cold had come to complete the catastrophe. As they struggled on, with Ney in the rear heroically fighting a battle a day against the ever-harassing Russian forces, the Emperor realised that his presence was essential in Paris if he was to rebuild the shattered military strength of his Empire. As before in Egypt, he left his forces to escape as best they could and hastened ahead back to Europe. By December there were 60 degrees of frost. Finally, of the 610,000 men who started on the great campaign, a tattered, starving, disorganised, delirious, and shell-shocked remnant of 20,000 recrossed the Niemen. Not more than a thousand were of any further military use. The largest army in history had been completely wiped out.

The Moscow Campaign, 1812

Borodino

The retreat from Moscow

The tide of disaster did not stop at that point. Encouraged by the shattering blow to the French in Russia, Prussia and later Austria came to grips with the old enemy, thus forming with Britain and Russia the Fourth Coalition. Prussia, since Jena, had witnessed a remarkable revival of national spirit and efficiency. Although allowed by Napoleon an army of only 42,000 men, the Prussians had adopted a

Fourth Coalition, 1813, and the Revival of Prussia

THE RUSSIAN TEACHING BONEY TO DANCE: 'IF YOU TRESPASS ON OUR GROUNDS, YOU MUST DANCE TO OUR TUNES'
Cartoon by George Cruikshank on the Moscow campaign of 1812.

Scharnhorst, Stein, and Hardenberg

system of short service, and so had a reserve about 120,000 strong within three years. The Prussian War Minister, Scharnhorst, had also revised methods of arms training and tactics, had achieved universal liability to serve and the abolition of degrading punishments such as flogging, and had completely reorganized the Prussian military forces. Moreover, Prussia had been fortunate in two statesmen, Stein and Hardenberg, who in five years transformed an almost medieval into a modern state. Stein had secured the emancipation of the serfs, thereby allowing them liberty to leave their ancestral soil and work for wages elsewhere; had broken down restrictions by which certain land was only for nobles, certain trades only for burgesses; had abolished the monopolies of the old gilds; had given a measure of municipal self-government by allowing the craftsmen and landowners in each town to elect a council; and had set up a new Ministry of State which had been lacking before, competent to deal with all the various provinces in the Kingdom of Prussia. Hardenberg's most famous land law had given the peasants two-thirds of their former land as freehold, the other one-third going to their lords in place of services owed. New patriotic literature had appeared, education was being reformed, universities had been founded at Berlin and Breslau. Prussia at last felt itself not only united in wanting to overthrow Napoleon but competent to do it. So began 'The War of Liberation'.

The War of Liberation, 1813

By a miracle of organisation Napoleon within three months of the Russian campaign had a new army of a quarter of a million in the field. But he had enormous odds to face, including yet another powerful opponent, Sweden, whose new ruler, Bernadotte, though one of Napoleon's marshals, declared he was 'not going to be one of the Emperor's customs officials'. Bernadotte, having refused to apply the Continental System, was tempted to join the Allies by the promise of receiving Norway. Against the Prussian forces Napoleon won three battles, including the big victory of Dresden, but he was becoming less superhumanly active and he missed an opportunity of following up the retreat. Finally numbers triumphed after the Prussians, Austrians, Russians, and Swedes had managed to link up their armies, and at the battle of Leipzig, 1813 (sometimes known as the 'Battle of the Nations'), the French forces were overwhelmed. Rapidly they retreated across Germany with the Allies in pursuit. Rejecting a very generous peace offer which would have given France her 'natural frontiers' and so left her with the Rhineland and Belgium, Napoleon laid himself open to the inevitable – an invasion of France.

Leipzig, 1813

Meanwhile in the Peninsula Wellington during 1811 had succeeded in liberating Portugal and beginning to fight his way into Spain. In June 1813, after many fierce battles *en route* he and his allies defeated Joseph Bonaparte at Vittoria and went on to capture Madrid. Thence they began to push the French back towards the Pyrenees. By the end of 1813 the British, Spanish and Portuguese forces were invading France from the south while their continental allies were about to do so from the east.

Peninsular War
Vittoria, 1813

On the sacred soil of France itself, Napoleon put up a brilliant fight against over-whelming odds. With armies containing youngsters ignorant even of the way to load a rifle, he won four victories before Blücher, the Prussian commander, wisely decided to give up chasing such a military genius and marched straight on to Paris. With the capital at the mercy of the Allies (who by the Treaty of Chaumont had now organised their alliance systematically and agreed on some of their peace demands) the French marshals compelled Napoleon first to accept terms and then to abdicate. By the treaty of Fontainebleau, which he ratified after an unsuccessful attempt at suicide, he gave up the throne but was allowed the title of Emperor, an income of about £200,000, and the Mediterranean island of Elba as his kingdom.

Invasion of France

Abdication of Napoleon: Treaty of Fontainebleau, April 1814

A replacement for Napoleon was already waiting in the wings. Just before his abdication the French Senate, guided by Talleyrand, a former bishop and foreign minister to the Republic and Napoleon, set up a provisional government and arranged for the restoration of the Bourbon line. This was in accordance with the wishes of the Allies. The new king was the elder surviving brother of the executed Louis XVI. He took the title of Louis XVIII, and to make his accession more acceptable to the French, promised to rule by the terms of a Charter which guaranteed a parliament and a constitution. He had some difficulty in leaving his exile in England promptly, on account of a bad attack of gout.

Restoration of Bourbon monarchy: Louis XVIII

The Allies now concluded a peace treaty with this restored monarchy. It was extraordinarily generous, since they did not wish either to antagonise France permanently or to make the restored régime unpopular. By what was later called the First Peace of Paris (to distinguish it from the Second Peace of Paris in the following year) the Allies stripped France of her great conquests, such as Belgium, Holland and the territories in Germany and Italy (from all of which the French armies had already been driven) and returned her to her boundaries of 1st November 1792. This still left her half a million more inhabitants than she had had before the Revolution. With even greater forbearance, the Allies demanded no indemnity from France, imposed no army of occupation, and even allowed the French to retain most of the great works of art which Napoleon had pillaged

First Peace of Paris, May 1814

BY PERSEVERANCE, VALOUR, PEACE UNION, AND MAGNANIMITY.

EUROPE REPOSES FREE

COMMERCE & THE ARTS REVIVE

GAS ILLUMINATIONS FOR THE PEACE OF PARIS, 1814

Boulton & Watt's factory at Soho, Birmingham, illuminated to celebrate the peace. Gas-lighting began in coal mine offices near Whitehaven in 1765 and was used by William Murdoch for lighting factories in the English Midlands from about 1792. It was later used for lighting selected streets and bridges, but did not become general in households until the second half of the nineteenth century. Even then it was largely confined to towns, and gave a poor light until the invention of the incandescent gas mantle by Von Welsbach around 1890.

from the European capitals. Apart from this, France had to agree to certain proposed features of the post-war settlement, such as the enlargement of Holland, the formation of a new confederation of the German states, the guaranteed independence of Switzerland, and Austrian gains in Italy. There was also a colonial settlement with Britain, the French recognising the British retention of Malta, Mauritius and two of the French West Indian islands. Nearly all other questions were to be referred to a great European congress, which was to meet at Vienna. The French would be represented at this – but had to promise to accept Allied decisions about the redistribution of territory.

War between Britain and U.S.A., 1812–14

The satisfactory progress of the war in Europe enabled Britain to pay more attention to a vexatious conflict on the other side of the Atlantic. At about the same time as Napoleon invaded Russia, the recently formed United States of America had declared war on Britain. The Americans were prompted partly by desire to annex Canada, partly by resentment against British actions at sea – notably the prevention of American commerce with French-controlled ports, and the seizure of British-born American subjects from American ships. Britain in fact was on the point of exempting American vessels from her regulations, and three or four days after the declaration of war actually did so, but the war still went on. It was fought mainly along the Canadian border, on and around the Great Lakes, and off the American eastern seaboard. In general, the American invasion of Canada was successfully resisted; but at sea British ships suffered some nasty shocks from the very efficient American vessels, until, with the closing of the war in Europe, the British strength became irresistible. One memorable incident, which created lasting ill-feeling, occurred when a British landing party burned the public buildings of Washington in retaliation for a similar American action in Canada. Loss of commerce finally made the war unpopular on both sides, and in December 1814 a peace was signed at Ghent on inconclusive terms. This was too late to stop a British expedition in the following month attacking New Orleans – unsuccessfully.[1]

Treaty of Ghent, December 1814

The Congress of Vienna opened in November 1814. Both beforehand and from then on, the Allies strove to thrash out the many problems on which they disagreed. Though the Congress included representatives of nearly all the states of Europe, the major bargaining and decision-making was reserved to the four greatest Allies, Britain, Austria, Russia and Prussia. Their disputes over the future of Poland and Saxony soon reached such a pitch that the chief French delegate, Talleyrand, was able to capitalise on the division and bring France into the select group of major decision-makers. He did this by inducing Britain and Austria to join France in an alliance, to operate should Russia or Prussia attempt to enforce their ideas by war (as Prussia was threatening). When news of this leaked out, Russia and Prussia moderated their proposals, and the Congress got back on a more even keel.

Congress of Vienna, November 1814– June 1815

This dangerous episode was scarcely over when a still more alarming piece of news burst upon the Congress – the news that Napoleon had decamped from Elba. This galvanised the four main Allies into instant action. Within about an hour, they agreed to declare Napoleon an outlaw and renew hostilities against him, a decision in which they were soon joined by many smaller powers. More striking still, they rapidly reached agreement on all the outstanding issues of the European settlement. The Final Act of the Congress, a document of 121 articles summarising the agreed decisions, was signed on 9th June 1815, nine days before the last great clash with Napoleon at Waterloo.

Napoleon escapes from Elba, February 1815

Of all the episodes in Napoleon's career none is more remarkable than 'The Hundred Days' of his rule between the exile of Elba and the exile of St Helena. He landed at Antibes with only a few hundred soldiers, in a country which less than a year before had been heartily glad to see the back of him. Louis XVIII instantly sent forces to capture him, Marshal Ney vowing that he ought to be 'brought back in a cage'. But the magnetism of Napoleon's personality, the memory of campaigns shared in common, resentment at the loss of the Empire, the shabby treatment of the army by the restored Bourbon government, the fear of the peasants that the government was about to confiscate the lands they had acquired at the beginning of the Revolution, all led to a very different result. The tactics of Napoleon helped too, for he promised peace and a parliament; he also showed his considerable talent for falsehood when he informed the first troops sent to capture him that he had been summoned to Paris by the Allies. So the soldiers, including Ney, simply fell in behind him and helped him to continue his march to Paris. Before long Louis XVIII was in flight, while the French newspapers underwent a rapid change of tone – 'the scoundrel Bonaparte' becoming first 'Napoleon,' then finally 'our great and beloved Emperor'. Three weeks were enough for him to establish himself again as master of France. Confronted with the hostility of the Allies, he decided to take the offensive. On 12th June he marched into Belgium to strike at the British and Dutch under Wellington and the Prussians under Blücher

The Hundred Days, March–June 1815

---

[1] The Americans had acquired Louisiana by purchase from France in 1803.

before they could be joined by the Austrians and the Russians, whose armies were in distant parts of Europe.

Waterloo, 1815

The campaign of Waterloo consisted of three main battles. As Napoleon had only half the forces of his opponents he sought to engage them separately. On 16th June he defeated the Prussians at Ligny, but fatally neglected to follow up the victory. The same day he challenged Wellington at Quatre Bras, imagining the Prussians to be in flight. On 18th June at Waterloo Wellington knew that the Prussians had retired in good order and would probably succeed in joining him during the day. He therefore stood his ground, while Napoleon, confident that his opponent was 'a bad general' commanding 'bad troops', flung his men recklessly against Wellington's. But the attacks of the French columns, for all their dash, could not penetrate the thin British lines whose rifle fire was so deadly, and when Blücher appeared in the late afternoon Napoleon's fate was sealed. In Paris the parliament demanded his abdication. Resisting the temptation to start a civil war for his own throne, he gave in, and surrendered to the British as the 'most generous of his enemies'. The compliment, however, cut no ice. Anxious to have no further trouble, the British government banished him to the inaccessible island of St Helena, in the South Atlantic.

Second Peace of Paris, November 1815

Nearly five months haggling followed between the Allies and France before a new peace treaty was signed. This time the Allies were not so generous: they determined that France should make some amends for the renewed support she had given to Napoleon. By the Second Peace of Paris, they made her revert to her boundaries of 1790, thus taking from her part of Savoy (which she had occupied early in the Revolution) and some frontier areas in the north-east. In addition they stipulated that France should pay an indemnity, and suffer an army of occupation; they had already insisted on the return of the remaining looted works of art. At the same time the four great powers of Britain, Austria, Russia and Prussia renewed their Quadruple Alliance in case of further trouble with France, and promised to meet from time to time for consultation in congresses.

Death of Napoleon, 1821

Six years after his defeat at Waterloo Napoleon died in his remote place of exile. He had spent much of his time discussing and arranging the history of his career to present it to the best advantage. Europe would never again be troubled by his brilliant talents, his restless energy, his inflexible will, and his lack of moral sense. With an eye, as ever, to the best effect on public opinion, he directed in his will that his ashes should rest 'by the banks of the Seine, in the midst of the French people, whom I have loved so much'. And this was the man, who, in 1814, had remarked that he 'cared little for the lives of a million men'!

Reasons for Napoleon's success and failure: military talents

In considering the extraordinary success and the equally outstanding failure of Napoleon, it must be remembered that he was a general of unparalleled brilliance. Wellington said that 'his presence in the field was worth a difference of 40,000 men'. But as the years went on a decline showed itself, not in his talents, but rather in his energy, still tremendous enough, but not quite so superhuman as before. At Ligny, for example, the failure to pursue the Prussians made a vital difference.

increasing scope of the war

Even more important is the fact that as the scale of the war grew, as hundreds of thousands instead of tens of thousands became involved, so it inevitably followed that his marshals must direct a greater proportion of the army. And though the marshals were mostly young, talented and brave, they had not Napoleon's genius, and they quarrelled among themselves – in Spain, for example, they refused to help each other's armies, and in Russia one even tried to murder another. When ex-Marshal Bernadotte, King of Sweden, deserted Napoleon in 1813 the simple advice he gave to his new allies was: 'When you face the marshals, attack; when you face Napoleon, retreat.'

But while military reasons were, of course, vital in causing both Napoleon's rise and his downfall, other factors were equally important. Among these was the fact that in his early days Napoleon was practically carrying the French Revolution to repressed peoples eager to welcome it. To Italians ruled by Austrians or despotic princes, to Poles ruled by Russians or Austrians or Prussians, to Germans looking beyond the hundreds of petty princedoms in Germany, to all dissatisfied with the absolute or backward rule of their monarch, Napoleon appeared as a kind of saviour. Even in Britain Napoleon always relied on being supported by a popular uprising should he land. In other words, his rise was inspired by the two enormously powerful forces whose history makes up so much of the history of the nineteenth century – the forces of liberalism and patriotism.

Strangely enough – or perhaps not so strangely – these same two forces contributed powerfully to his downfall. While he fought against governments which lacked a liberal or popular backing he was consistently successful; but when the middle or lower classes fell in strongly behind their governments he began to

Liberal and patriotic feeling – at first with Napoleon, later against him

A STUDY IN DEGENERATION
Left: Napoleon as a young artillery officer in 1792, from a painting by Philippoteaux.
Right: Napoleon in exile at St Helena, from a sketch by de Vinck.

fail. German liberals, for example, turned against him wholeheartedly after 1806, when French domination had proved to give them little freedom. The Italians, the Swiss, the Dutch were all overtaxed. In Russia and Spain the French revolutionary doctrines made no impression at all on very backward peoples, and here he was faced with disaster right from the beginning. Further, after his introduction of the Continental System, the middle and lower classes in every country felt the effect of his rule in high prices, strict customs rules and declining trade. Everywhere the tide of patriotic sentiment, whether national or local, turned against Napoleon, and he was defeated largely by the hostility of those whose good will had enabled him earlier to triumph.

excessive ambition

Finally, it is obvious that Napoleon, in his increasing pride and self-confidence and in his determination to beat Britain, simply took on too much. To beat Britain he proclaimed the Continental System: to maintain that system he had to control the whole of Europe. It was a task beyond the power of any one man or any one nation, even when the man was Napoleon and the nation the French. Even if he had crushed all Europe utterly, he would have gone on to the Turkish Empire, to India, to the Americas. A restless demon of energy drove him on, a demon he him-himself was aware of when he loved to picture himself as the Man of Destiny, driven on by Fate. His schemes were all too big; he simply could not last. If the end had not come at Waterloo, it would surely have come at another battle a little later.

What, then, is the significance of the career of Napoleon Bonaparte? To France he gave durable institutions and the social benefits of the Revolution. To Europe, he gave a taste of modern government and such a stir that vast new forces began to be aroused, including those of liberalism and, in Germany and Italy, the beginnings of nationalism. To the world, he gave an appalling example of the damage that can result from colossal talents corrupted by an overwhelming desire for power.

CHAPTER 7
The 'Congress System'

1. The Congress of Vienna and the Post-War Settlement, 1814–15

When the Allies and the other European powers met at Vienna in the autumn of 1814 they faced two main tasks. The first was to make or approve detailed arrangements for sharing the spoils of victory, bearing in mind that the great powers had already made a number of preliminary agreements. This had to be done without setting the victors at each other's throats. The second task was, in so doing, to create a stable Europe unlikely to suffer further great upheavals.

Though representatives of all the European states were invited, and the conference was convened in the name of seven Allies and France, it was understood that the major decision-making would be reserved to the 'Big Four' among the Allies – Austria, Britain, Prussia and Russia. The chief delegates of these powers – the Austrian Foreign Minister Metternich, the British Foreign Secretary Castlereagh, the Prussian Chancellor Hardenberg, and the Russian Foreign Minister Nesselrode (who was overshadowed by his master, Tsar Alexander I) – met regularly in Metternich's house to discuss the whole range of Congress business, but the other powers were confined to more restricted matters and their own particular problems. Before the Congress was very old, however, the chief French delegate, Talleyrand, cleverly played on the comparative neglect of the minor Allies and the growing disputes between the major ones to insert himself into the heart of the discussions. Metternich and company had to acknowledge that they could not get very far without the cooperation of France, and the 'Big Four' became the 'Big Five'.

This was a remarkable diplomatic feat on the part of the representative of the defeated power which had caused all the trouble. Talleyrand, however, was always very skilful in claiming that the blame for past events lay with the Revolution and Napoleon, not with the legitimate ruling house of France, which had now been restored in the person of Louis XVIII. 'Legitimacy', the restoration of the pre-Revolution rulers and their territories, in fact became Talleyrand's theme-song, and it served the interests of France well. It was also acceptable as a broad principle to the other great powers, who used it in their re-settlement of Europe, except when it suited them to do otherwise.

Since the 'Big Five' hogged the major business, most of the other representatives had plenty of time on their hands. For this reason the Congress proved to be one of

Social aspects of the Congress

the most sparkling social events in European history, with brilliantly uniformed emperors, kings, princes, ministers and ambassadors attending to the lighter pursuits of dancing and love-making between the more serious business of discussion, intrigue and spying. The bills for entertainment were enormous and cost the Austrian Emperor, the main host, a fortune. Only one function was arranged for which the delegates were invited to pay – a picnic organised, not surprisingly, by Sir Sidney Smith, who was there as a representative of the former royal family of Sweden. It turned out to be a fiasco.

As we have seen, the arrangements concerning France had been settled by the first Peace of Paris in May 1814, before the Congress opened. They were later revised by the second Peace of Paris in November 1815, after the end of the Congress and the episode of Napoleon's Hundred Days.[1] The treatment of France, however, was a fairly simple problem compared with some of those which confronted the Congress itself. Of these more difficult questions, the worst concerned

Problem of Poland and Saxony

the future of Poland and Saxony, a matter so hotly disputed that Talleyrand was able to form an alliance with two of the Big Four against the other two, and so assert the importance of France.[2]

The pressure in this matter came primarily from the Tsar. Alexander I, whose unstable mind (possibly inherited from his eccentric father Paul) was at this time in a highly religious and fairly liberal phase, wanted to gratify the Poles by restoring the ancient Kingdom of Poland. He planned to give it a parliament and a constitution, but to assume the kingship himself. Austria and Britain were opposed to this, because it would have allowed the Russians to exercise a disguised power much farther west than ever before. Also, the Austrians and the Prussians would have to disgorge the Polish territory they had acquired in the three Partitions, and Austria was unwilling to do so. Prussia, however, was agreeable, despite the fact that her section of Poland was very important and included the city of Warsaw. She was agreeable because, in compensation, Alexander had promised to support her claim to the whole of Saxony, a kingdom which had been one of the last to desert Napoleon, and which, being small and powerless, could be regarded as expendable.

After the dispute between the powers over this matter had reached crisis-point, and France had lined up with Austria and Britain, there was a compromise. A

Kingdom of Poland

Polish kingdom was to be set up, with Alexander as King, but it was not to include all the old Polish territories, some of which would remain with Austria and Prussia. For the important part of Poland which she surrendered, Prussia was indeed to have compensation in Saxony – but she was only to have half, instead of all, of that Kingdom. By way of additional compensation she received Swedish

Prussia's gains

Pomerania (the last Swedish territory on the main continent) and a number of the small Rhineland states. This extension of Prussia in the Rhineland area was also intended to create a barrier against further French aggression. It did this, and in so doing made Prussia a main guardian of German interests and a natural future enemy of France.

The principle of creating a strong barrier against France also underlay some other decisions made or ratified by the Congress. One of these was the merging of the

[1] See p. 58.
[2] See p. 61.

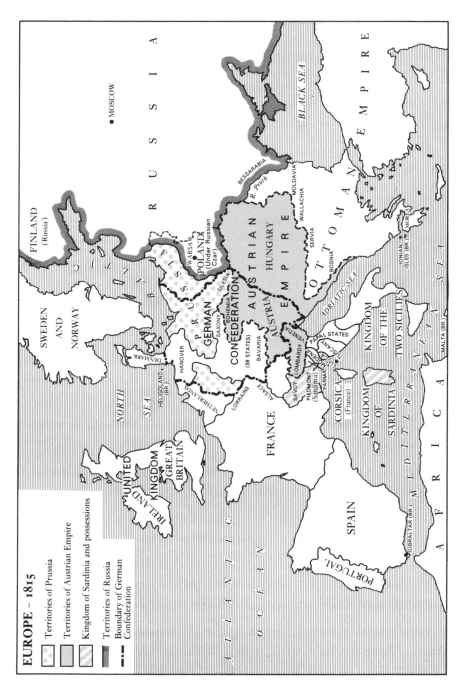

EUROPE – 1815

Territories of Prussia

Territories of Austrian Empire

Kingdom of Sardinia and possessions

Territories of Russia

Boundary of German Confederation

former Austrian Netherlands (Belgium) with the United Provinces (Holland) to form a new Kingdom of the Netherlands, under the House of Orange. This also served to compensate Holland for the loss of colonies to Britain.

Another check to France was the build-up of Austrian power in northern Italy, an arrangement which also compensated Austria for surrendering her part of the Netherlands. Not only did Austria recover Lombardy and supply Hapsburg

Kingdom of the Netherlands

Austrian gains in Italy

rulers for the three central duchies of Modena, Parma and Tuscany, but she also retained Venetia, including the city of Venice, and much of the Dalmatian coast. The Italian barrier against France was also strengthened by allotting Genoa to the Kingdom of Sardinia. Both Genoa and Venice had been great republics in the days before the armies of the French revolution broke into Italy, and had the Congress been solely concerned with 'legitimacy' they should have been restored as republics. But the Congress was also concerned with compensation, and with forming a strong ring round France. So Genoa and Venice had to swallow the loss of their former independence. 'Republics,' as Alexander put it crisply, 'are no longer fashionable'. Elsewhere in the Italian peninsula, however, 'legitimacy' could be applied: the Pope recovered all his former territory, and farther south the Spanish Bourbon monarchy was restored in Naples and Sicily. Murat, King of Naples, who had helped the Allies in 1814, had rejoined Napoleon during the Hundred Days, and so could be shot without compunction.

Russia's gains

So Prussia, Austria, Sardinia and Holland had their rewards and compensations, and rotting thrones were propped up again in southern Italy and Spain. What was Russia's reward, apart from the resurrection of a Poland under Russian kingship? The main answer lay in recognition of two gains recently made by Russia in the course of fighting powers other than France – her acquisition of Finland from Sweden and Bessarabia from Turkey. But Sweden had deserted Napoleon and been of great service to the Allies from 1812 onwards. If she had to surrender Finland to Russia and Pomerania to Prussia, how should she be compensated? The answer had already been spelled out when she joined the Allies – she should have Norway, which would also help to make a strong single power in the North. And who lost

Norway to Sweden

Norway? Denmark, punished, like Saxony, for remaining too late in Napoleon's camp – though in this case she was given minor compensation elsewhere. Actually, at some time or other all the main powers except Britain had collaborated with Napoleon, and which of them got punished for doing so became, as Talleyrand put it, 'a question of date'. But it was not only that. It was also a question of being a small power unable to resist the larger ones.

British gains

Britain's rewards for her very strenuous efforts had already been settled by previous agreements. Her main gains, apart from islands in the West Indies, included recognition of her possession of Ceylon, the Cape of Good Hope (for which she made a money payment to the Dutch), Mauritius, Guiana, Malta, the Ionian Islands and Heligoland. Armed with such additions to her empire, Britain was able to develop still further her commercial and maritime supremacy.

The German Confederation

The new organisation in Germany to replace the old Holy Roman Empire and its successor, Napoleon's Confederation of the Rhine, occupied much discussion before agreement was reached. In the end, the thirty-eight remaining states of Germany, including the major ones like Prussia, Bavaria and Hanover (now enlarged into a kingdom), agreed to form a German Confederation under the presidency of Austria. It was to have a Diet, or Parliament, with representatives of each state, but with very limited authority. Almost all powers remained with the individual states, who looked to the Confederation not to run everyday matters but to harmonise foreign policy and prevent the member-states concluding alliances hostile to each other.

So the map of Europe was redrawn, and the weak points became easy enough to see as time went on. In particular, the Congress ignored one of the new factors which had helped to bring about the downfall of Napoleon – the rise of national feeling: nations and peoples were bandied about as though they were goods, to supply 'compensation' here or constitute a 'barrier state' there. Norwegians, Belgians, Boers, Finns, Italians, Serbs, Poles were placed under foreign governments they soon intensely disliked. Very little was done to satisfy the desire of the Poles and of many Germans, awakened by Napoleon's work, for large and powerful states to represent their nationality. Nothing at all in this direction was done for the Italians. Since the growth of nationalism proved to be one of the main currents of the nineteenth century, wars inevitably occurred to upset the Treaty. One by one as time wore on its provisions were cancelled, and nearly always by force.

Weaknesses of the settlement

This, however, is to judge the settlement from the vantage-point of the future. The powers at Vienna did not see anything very wicked in foreign rule, for it had been common throughout history. They did not, it is true, perceive the strength of the rising force of nationalism: but the aggressive nationalism that they had recently seen, that of France, seemed to them a threat to European civilisation and a danger that must be contained. So they restored the old régimes, and sought to strengthen by territorial additions the powers most likely to keep France in check. At the same time by their hard bargaining among themselves they tried to prevent any one of their own number becoming too dominant. They sought, in other words, to avoid future trouble by preserving some sort of balance of power.

In their desire to prevent further trouble, the powers also agreed to a new departure in European politics. By the terms of their Quadruple Alliance as renewed in the second treaty of Paris in November 1815, Russia, Austria, Prussia and Britain agreed not only to ally if necessary in defence of the post-war settlement, but to meet in future congresses to discuss problems as occasion arose. This arrangement contained the germs of a League of Nations or United Nations idea, except that it was confined to the four great powers and so had a dictatorial slant from the beginning. The conception was particularly Castlereagh's, though he was later to disapprove of the way the other powers tried to use the Alliance.

The Quadruple Alliance (renewed 1815). Agreement to meet in congresses.

Sometimes confused with this practical attempt to lessen the conflicts of the great powers is another agreement concluded in the months after Waterloo and known as the Holy Alliance. This was not a military compact, but a league of heads of states who promised to rule on Christian principles, acting as fathers to their peoples and brothers to each other. It was the creation of the religious and well-meaning Alexander, and had no effect worth mentioning. Castlereagh disapproved of it, terming it a 'piece of sublime mysticism and nonsense'. Metternich called it 'a loud-sounding nothing' and said that 'the Tsar's mind was quite clearly affected'. But though no one except Alexander took it seriously, every sovereign in Europe signed it, with the exception of the Sultan (who, not being a Christian, had not been invited), George III (who was insane) and the Pope! It was one of those amiable gestures of good will which people sign because they sympathise with its objects and because they know there is no particular provision for carrying them out if to do so would prove inconvenient. The confusion with the Quadruple Alliance arose because Liberals in Europe, finding the adjective 'holy' in connection with the arch-conservative Metternich too rich to forget, insisted on referring to the Russia–Austria–Prussia grouping as the 'Holy' Alliance.

The Holy Alliance, 1815

Both the Quadruple Alliance and the Holy Alliance, then, were intended to help preserve the peace and an atmosphere of brotherhood. They were, in fact, a quite

Defects of the Quadruple Alliance

original attempt to improve the lot of mankind. Unfortunately, however, the problem of peace is a thorny one. In the absence of international government or enforced arbitration, peace implies keeping territories and their ownership arranged as they are, except in the rare cases where both parties to a dispute can agree on a peaceful alteration. But what if one side feels genuine injustice and the other refuses to remedy the grievance? The Italians in Lombardy might have appealed peacefully for a century to the Austrians to clear out, without anything coming of it. In such cases it is possible that keeping the peace may perpetuate what one side passionately feels to be a wrong. Even nowadays, when there are international organizations ready to settle disputes – as there were not then – peoples often feel so strongly that they prefer to fight rather than accept the verdict of arbitration.

This was the problem with the 1814–15 settlements. There soon proved to be many peoples who longed either to throw off their foreign rulers or else to claim a constitution and a parliament. But everywhere the Quadruple Alliance was anxious to keep the peace. Thus it is not difficult to see what the Alliance, so good in intention, developed into. Directed by men who had spent their whole lives in fighting the French Revolution and its heir, Napoleon, it was inevitable that the Alliance should regard extreme nationalism and democracy of the French kind as wicked delusions which had plunged Europe into untold bloodshed. So the Alliance became, in effect, a kind of trade union of Kings in Possession to stop the possibility of Peoples in Possession. As this aspect of it came more to the fore it incurred the hatred of Liberals all over Europe, and British support of it grew more and more lukewarm. The guiding spirit became, not Castlereagh, with his practical common sense, nor Alexander, with his religious enthusiasm, but the supreme anti-liberal, Metternich. Metternich well knew that to give free rein to either democracy or nationalism would smash the ramshackle Austrian Empire in pieces, for in it lived Germans, Poles, Czechs, Croats, Slovaks, Ruthenes, Magyars, Serbs, and Italians, all more or less restrained by Vienna. And it was Metternich who had declared that democracy could only 'change daylight into darkest night', and who had attacked the ideas of the French Revolution as 'the disease which must be cured, the volcano which must be extinguished, the gangrene which must be burned out with the hot iron, the hydra with jaws open to swallow up the social order'.

2. The Later Congresses and the Breakdown of the Alliance, 1818–30

In 1815 the reactionary side of the Quadruple Alliance was not yet uppermost, and the Allies approached their problems in a reasonably constructive way. The first which they had to tackle in the post-war period was the position of France. France had proved punctual in the discharge of her obligations, but was naturally resenting the army of occupation. In 1818 a Congress of the four powers met at Aix-la-Chapelle and there it was unanimously agreed to withdraw the army of occupation and to invite France to co-operate in future congresses. The Alliance thus admitted France very quickly to what became called the 'Concert of Europe' and so prevented her previous enmity becoming long-lasting. At the same time, however, the Allies took precautions. They secretly renewed their Quadruple Alliance, to

Congress of Aix-la-Chapelle, 1818

France enters the 'Concert'

operate against France if need be – and confidentially informed the leading French representative that they had done so!

In other respects, too, the Congress was a great success. Agreement was reached on the protection of Jews in Europe, on Swedish debts to Denmark, on the treatment of Bonaparte on St Helena, on the old matter of the British claim to a Channel salute. Significantly, however, the powers could not agree on a joint expedition to punish the notorious Barbary pirates, because of fear of Russian vessels in the Mediterranean. Above all, on one highly important matter there was considerable disagreement before Russia and Prussia gave way. These two powers wanted the Quadruple Alliance to guarantee not only all the frontiers established at Vienna, but all the *governments* – in other words, it would be the Alliance's duty to intervene whenever there was a successful revolution in any country in Europe. Prussia even wanted an international army under Wellington to be kept at Brussels for this purpose. Castlereagh, however, managed to secure an agreement limiting promised intervention to the case of France, if she should again undergo a revolution which obviously threatened the peace of Europe. His argument was masterly – 'nothing would be more immoral . . . than the idea that . . . force was collectively to be prostituted to the support of established power without any consideration of the extent to which it was abused'. Till there was perfect justice everywhere, he maintained, it would be wrong to guarantee all existing governments.

In opposing the Russian and Prussian plan Castlereagh was firmly supported by his colleagues in the British Cabinet, including Lord Liverpool (the Prime Minister) and the former Foreign Secretary and brilliant orator George Canning, who was now re-establishing himself as a great political figure. Many years earlier Canning had criticised Castlereagh for incompetence in organising the Walcheren expeditions, and the two had fought a duel in which Canning was wounded. Now they were reconciled, and Canning heartily shared Castlereagh's desire to avoid foreign commitments which could involve Britain in intervention beyond her own spheres of interest. Castlereagh and Canning oppose general guarantee of governments.

The British view of a limited Alliance triumphed – for the moment. The Congress of Aix-la-Chapelle broke up, after the powers had agreed to meet again whenever necessary. The meeting had been the first conference of the European powers ever to be held except to make a peace treaty at the end of a war. Not surprisingly, then, the idea of holding congresses from time to time appeared to Castlereagh as Castlereagh's hopes of the Congress 'system'

> a new discovery in the European government, at once extinguishing the cobwebs with which diplomacy obscures the horizon, bringing the whole bearing of the system into its true light, and giving to the counsels of the Great Powers the efficiency and almost the simplicity of a single State.

This verdict, however, proved over-optimistic. In fact, the very term 'Congress *System*' which historians have traditionally applied to the experiment, suggests that Europe was more closely regulated by congresses at this time than was actually the case. There was a genuine effort to produce a unified policy among the great powers, but their interests were too diverse for this effort to have much success.

Unfortunately, any hopes that Europe had suddenly discovered the way to govern itself peaceably were soon dashed. By 1820 there was a rising tide of protest against established governments and the spirit and arrangements of Vienna. In Spain in that year a revolution against the restored Bourbons forced King Ferdinand Unrest in Europe, 1819–20 to grant a constitution that was very liberal for the time – it had been originally drawn up in 1812 during the revolt against Joseph Bonaparte. A similar revolution followed in Portugal; while on the other side of the Atlantic the Spanish colonies, which had thrown off the rule of Spain during the war, still refused to acknowledge the rights of their mother country over them. In Italy there was restlessness everywhere, fomented by the Carbonari, a secret society aiming at liberalism and the expulsion of foreign rulers. 1820 saw a major revolution on Italian soil – the Spanish Bourbon king of Naples being compelled to adopt a constitution similar to the Spanish one of 1812. The following year the King of Sardinia also had to grant liberal reforms, after agitation in Piedmont.

Other countries were also affected. In Germany, where some of the state rulers granted constitutions from 1816 onwards, university students agitated for German union and a national constitution; A high point came in 1819 when a student assassinated a leading opponent of these ideas, Kotzebue, an anti-liberal writer and a secret Russian spy. In England between 1816 and 1820 there were riots at Spa Fields, brutal acts of repression like the Peterloo Massacre, and even a plot to murder the whole Cabinet. In France, in 1820, the popular young Duke of Berri, who was in line to inherit the throne, was murdered as he left the Paris Opera House. Events like these shook the Tsar out of his earlier liberal tendencies. Backed by France, he demanded the calling of a new Congress where measures might be concerted against such violence.

Congress of Troppau, 1820–

In 1820 the Congress duly met at Troppau, in Austrian Silesia, to consider these and similar problems. Already by this time the German Confederation, on the suggestion of Metternich, had taken powers, notably by the Carlsbad Decrees, to suppress revolutions in its component states.[1] Castlereagh knew before the start of the Congress that the objects of Metternich and the Tsar were to use the Alliance to put down the revolutions in Naples and Spain, and perhaps even to restore to the latter her revolted American colonies. But though Castlereagh, like Metternich, detested revolutionary movements, he was not prepared to see Britain associated with the other two powers in wholesale revolution-breaking. His reasons were threefold: partly that there had existed genuine grievances in Naples and Spain; partly that opponents in Parliament would be difficult about the matter; but principally that internal affairs of other countries were no business of Britain's where they did not directly interfere with her interests. Britain thus refused to join in the declaration of the other three powers at Troppau concerning their right to intervene to suppress revolutions. Indeed, Castlereagh even declined to take part

–and of Laibach, 1821

Austrian intervention in Italy

in the Congress, sending instead of a participant only an 'observer', as did France. The Congress, coupled with its continuation at Laibach in 1821, in fact had two direct results. One was Austrian intervention in Naples and Piedmont, with Congress approval, to restore the kings concerned to their full powers and suppress the recently granted constitutions. The other was the beginning of a split within the Quadruple Alliance.

Greek Revolt begins, 1821

By 1821 the situation had been still further complicated by a revolt of the Greeks against their Turkish rulers. The Greeks gambled on receiving help from their fellow Orthodox Christians, the Russians, who were notoriously eager to break up the Ottoman Empire and extend their influence south to the Mediterranean.

[1] See p. 107.

Britain and Austria, on the other hand, were equally anxious to uphold Turkey as a bulwark against Russian expansion. The Tsar himself was faced with a difficult problem: should he help fellow Christians and extend Russian influence, or should he show his usual disapproval of revolutions? For the moment Castlereagh and Metternich were able, by playing on Alexander's fondness for the Alliance, to hold Russia off Turkey. The Greek revolt broke out while the Congress of Laibach was meeting. To consider it more fully, together with the questions of Spain and her colonies, a new Congress was called to meet at Verona in 1822.

Before this Congress could meet, Castlereagh, worn out by incessant labours and saddened by his unpopularity among the British liberals and working classes, had suffered a mental breakdown. With typical efficiency, though left unguarded for only two or three minutes, he succeeded in cutting his throat. His position as British Foreign Secretary was filled by Canning, who by now was positively anxious to break up the European Alliance. Castlereagh himself, by refusing to associate Britain in the suppression of revolutions in Spain, the Spanish colonies, Naples, and Piedmont, was already drifting apart from Russia, Prussia, and Austria. Canning went further. Unlike Castlereagh, he was not one of the original framers of the Alliance; he had no parent's fondness for it, and was eager to assist, rather than prevent, its demise – the more so because his sympathies were more liberal than Castlereagh's.

Canning

At the Congress of Verona in 1822, then, the British representative, Wellington, was instructed to take a firm stand against Allied intervention in Spain. France, however, was ready to intervene on her own responsibility, and she later secured promises of support from Russia, Prussia and Austria. Within a year French troops restored King Ferdinand to complete power. Free to take revenge, he set up the Inquisition once more and imprisoned and executed so many of the rebels that France and her supporters grew ashamed of the monarch they had helped.

Congress of Verona, 1822

French intervention in Spain, 1823

Now that absolute monarchy was restored in Spain, came the crux of the matter. Would the king, backed by France, go on to reclaim his rebellious Latin-American colonies? On this point Canning's views and policy soon proved decisive. South and Central America offered valuable outlets for British trade, which had gained a hold while Spain was powerless during the Napoleonic Wars; Spain now refused to promise open trading conditions for Britain with her colonies if she should recapture them; therefore, quite simply, Spain must not be allowed to recover her lost possessions. Moreover the problem was soon not confined to the colonies of Spain. In September 1822 Brazil proclaimed its independence of Portugal.

The Latin-American States

Canning's firm line

The warning to the Alliance not to interfere in Latin America came from two directions: Britain and the United States. For the first, Canning warned Polignac, the French ambassador in London, that Britain would fight France if she attempted to intervene in America. By this time the United States, fearful of Russian operations in America and the claims she might develop through her ownership of Alaska, and seeing the drift of Canning's policy, had already granted official recognition to four of the new and struggling Latin-American Republics: Columbia, Chile, Buenos Aires and Mexico. Now, at the close of 1823, the United States President, Monroe, in a message to the U.S. Congress, warned Europe that America was not open to further European colonisation and that any interference by European powers on the American Continent would be regarded 'as the manifestation of an unfriendly disposition to the United States'.

U.S.A. and the Monroe Doctrine, 1823

Seeing his cue taken up, Canning promptly welcomed the 'Monroe Doctrine' and before very long, when the last Spanish troops in America were defeated, recognised three of the same four Latin-American republics. Faced with the prospect of fighting both Britain and the United States if the Alliance persisted in interference, Austria, Russia, Prussia and France drew back and let revolution triumph in Latin America. Thus the principle of interference was defeated, and mainly by Britain, who in so doing had split up the Alliance. The Congress 'System' was now on its last legs. Its death-blow was soon to come over the question of Greek independence.

The Greek revolt had by this time reached a critical stage.[1] In 1824 the Sultan called upon his powerful vassal, Mehemet Ali of Egypt, for help; and Mehemet Ali's son, Ibrahim Pasha, was soon suppressing the rebels with a brutality which threatened to leave the Sultan with no Greek subjects at all. In 1825, too, Tsar Alexander died, and was succeeded by his brother Nicholas I, a man of more stable and determined character, who was resolved to help his fellow Orthodox Christians in Greece. Seeing that Nicholas in any case meant to help the Greeks, Canning decided it would be wise to associate Britain with the action, to give her a voice in the subsequent peace settlement and to stop Russia monopolising the benefits of intervention. He therefore acted with Russia, to control her, and in 1827 by the Treaty of London, Britain, Russia, and France agreed to secure independence in all but name for Greece. Against this policy Prussia and Austria protested strongly, being anxious both to discourage rebellion and to reserve the Balkan peninsula for their own influence. The intervention ended by the British, French and Russian fleets destroying the Turkish and Egyptian navy almost accidentally at Navarino Bay, and thereby making certain of independence for the Greeks.[2] But it had another effect, too. Since the powers of Europe were so hopelessly divided over the matter, it could no longer be pretended that there was any effective Quadruple or Quintuple Alliance. The 'Congress System' was dead.

So, on the questions of intervention in Italy, Spain, the Spanish colonies and Greece, Britain had gradually drawn away from her Continental allies. Canning, indeed, almost revelled in the work of destroying the first experiment in international co-operation, saying after the Congress of Verona: 'Things are getting back to a wholesome state again. Every nation for itself, and God for us all.'

The Congress System thus broke down in the first place because vital issues arose, such as the matter of the Spanish colonies, on which Britain could not possibly agree with the other powers. In the second place it never captured the sympathy of European public opinion, even in the way that the League of Nations was to do. This was partly because it did not represent the small powers, and partly because the views and characters of men like Metternich and Alexander after 1820 made the Alliance appear something like a league of despots for the suppression of liberty, constantly urging intervention to put down popular movements. Thirdly, as so often after the end of a war, Britain began to object to the policy of Continental obligations which the war had rendered necessary. There came the inevitable desire to have a free hand, to be without alliances and commitments which would certainly involve the country in war again if another European

The Greek revolt

Treaty of London, 1827

Navarino Bay, 1827

The powers divided

European intervention dropped

End of the 'Congress System'. Reasons for its failure

[1] See p. 157.
[2] See pp. 157–58.

'UNTOWARD EVENT' IN NAVARINO BAY, 1827
Considering that the British, French and Russian vessels were trying to impose an armistice by peaceful means, and that they began firing on the Turkish and Egyptian fleets only in retaliation, the destruction of the latter was remarkably complete.

conflict developed. This, indeed, was one of the chief factors which prompted Canning to destroy the 'Congress System'.

In helping to break up the Alliance, Canning actually claimed to be 'resisting the spirit of foreign domination'. It is in this light, as a factor in the fight for freedom, that Canning's and Britain's opposition to the Alliance has often been presented. British historians have frequently depicted Canning as a sort of George the Giant Killer battling against the wicked Russian and Austrian ogres, when what he was really doing was returning to Britain's standard post-war policy, in those days, of isolation. We can easily exaggerate Britain's liberalism if we lose sight of the fact that Castlereagh, for example, was the leading spirit in the Tory Government which approved the Peterloo massacre and ruthlessly

British motives

opposed all working-class political movements at home. (Canning's 'resistance to foreign domination' did not go so deep, either, as to make him question the existence of the British Empire, much of which was founded on it.) Britain thus destroyed the 'Congress System' a little out of love of constitutional liberty, but much more from the desire to avoid unnecessary Continental obligations and because the Alliance threatened British interests in important and pocket-touching matters, such as trade with the former Spanish colonies.

CHAPTER 8
France under the Bourbon and Orleans Monarchies

1. The Restored Bourbons, 1815–30

The final defeat of Napoleon at Waterloo in 1815 meant for France the second Louis XVIII, 1814–24 return of the Bourbon line in the person of Louis XVIII. Already previously restored by the Allies in 1814, he had left Paris, when the news of Napoleon's landing from Elba was announced, with a speed remarkable in view of his advancing age and figure. Now in 1815 he was back again, to exhibit in his fat, gouty, and unromantic frame the Divine Right of Kings. This, however, did *not* mean that the whole gains of the Revolutionary and Napoleon periods were lost and that France simply went back to the position before 1789. Louis, a sensible old gentleman, retained most of Napoleon's great institutions, such as the Code, the University, the Legion of Honour, and the system of local government. Also he had, as mentioned before, promised to rule constitutionally by the terms of a Charter.

This Charter, a suggestion of the Allies in 1814 to make Louis' return less Constitutional Charter unpopular, was of great importance. Its main effects were to provide France with a parliament and to prevent any return to absolute government. All Frenchmen were to be subject to the same system of law, all were to be free from the possibility of arbitrary imprisonment by *lettres de cachet*, and all were to be equally eligible for important civil and military positions. Furthermore, liberty was guaranteed in the form of a free press (though the government could suppress abuses of this) and of complete religious toleration (though Catholicism was recognised as France's official religion). The middle classes' fears were quietened by a provision that those who had bought confiscated property during the Revolution were entitled to keep it. All these were valuable concessions to liberalism; but to most Frenchmen who had known the extreme theories and practices of 1791 the new parliament seemed very undemocratic. The upper Chamber of Peers was nominated entirely by the king, and though the lower Chamber of Deputies was appointed by indirect election voters had to be over thirty years of age and pay at least 300 francs in direct taxes. Deputies had to be over forty and to pay direct Narrow franchise taxes of at least 1,000 francs. Of a population of 29 million, less than 100,000 people had the right to vote. Here was a sure source of future trouble.

Louis XVIII in 1815 was in some ways in a very similar position to Charles II of England in 1660 – willing to let bygones be bygones and chiefly anxious 'not to go on his travels again'. But like Charles II, too, he found himself surrounded by groups of returned nobles who were fiercely keen to recover their positions and revenge themselves on their late enemies. Of these nobles the relentless leader was Charles, Count of Artois, the King's younger brother. So, just as the English Royalists of 1660 savagely persecuted the Cromwellians against all the wishes of Charles, so the French Royalists of 1815 (returned in full strength by the upper middle classes to the Chamber of Deputies) savagely persecuted the Bonapartists

against all the advice of Louis. A 'White Terror' took place in 1815–16, both before the elections and afterwards, in the course of which some 7,000 supporters of Napoleon were imprisoned, massacred or executed. Marshal Ney, 'bravest of the brave', who had set off to capture Napoleon and fallen in behind him, was shot after a trial before the peers. These excesses in turn produced the opposite reaction, and by 1817, when the upper middle classes had lost their panic-stricken fear of Bonapartism, the more moderate outlook of Louis began to take effect.

Till 1820 Parliament and Louis then proceeded along fairly conciliatory lines. All at once, however, the extreme Royalists (or Ultras, as they were called) were presented with a magnificent opportunity in the murder by a Bonapartist of the Duke of Berri, a son of the Count of Artois. Berri was next in line to the throne after Artois as Louis XVIII had no surviving children. The assassin who stabbed him as he was leaving the Paris Opera House imagined that the deed could result in the end of the Bourbon dynasty. The Ultras were of course not slow to see the value of the crime to their cause: they used the murder to persuade King and Parliament that liberalism and Bonapartism must be stamped out. So by 1822, when a severe law was passed limiting the freedom of the press and trial by jury, the short moderate phase of Bourbon rule was ending. Louis XVIII, too, succumbing to diabetic gangrene, was almost literally breaking up – his valet was horrified one day to discover pieces of the King's toes inside the royal stockings he had just pulled off. Louis was thus without the physical reserves to resist Artois and the Ultras. In Spain, for instance, as we have seen, the French under Ultra inspiration intervened to restore the absolute rule of the unsavoury Ferdinand. All the same, by the time Louis' reign closed in 1824 a great deal had been done for France by

his government: a heavy war indemnity paid off, the country rid of the foreign occupying troops, the army reorganised under Marshal St Cyr, and France readmitted to the ranks, councils, and alliance of the Great Powers. Moreover, although the Parliament was undemocratic and beset by troubles, it was educating the nation, through the speeches of its many talented members, in most of the great issues of the time.

The reign of Artois, who ascended the throne as Charles X, was almost bound to come to grief before long. If Louis XVIII was the Charles II of French history, Charles X was the James II. He longed to restore the French monarchy to all its ancient power, and despised constitutional kingship. 'I had rather chop wood than reign after the fashion of the King of England', he said. Further, he had as passionate a conviction as Robespierre that his enemies were not only mistaken but sinful. The first acts of his reign were typical. For his coronation he revived all the ancient medieval ceremony: while he lay prostrate on cushions, he was pierced in seven parts of his body, through seven apertures in his clothes, with a golden needle dipped in holy oil said to have been miraculously preserved from the fifth century. He then visited hospitals to heal the diseased by his holy touch. Before long an act was passed making profanation of the holy sacrament in church punishable by death; and every encouragement was given to the religious revival which had set in against the excesses of the Revolutionary period. The religious orders were quickly allowed to return, the Jesuits re-emerged as an important force, and nunneries flourished abundantly. To those who still harboured revolutionary sentiments, further affront was given by an act, not unwise in itself, which granted 1,000 million francs compensation to those who had been dispossessed of their property by the Revolution.

These things were not done without opposition which in turn only served, however, to harden Charles's opinions. In face of the growing protests of the liberals and Bonapartists he resolved not to compromise, for compromise in his opinion had brought down Louis XVI. He therefore dismissed the last of his moderate Royalist counsellors and appointed as his chief minister the Prince de Polignac, a former prisoner of Napoleon and an Ultra of the Ultras.

Events now moved fast towards their conclusion. Polignac's aims were simple – 'to reorganise society, to give back to the clergy their weight in state affairs, to create a powerful aristocracy and to surround it with privileges' – a programme which would have largely cancelled out the Revolution. To carry it out, he had, so he claimed, the assistance of visions from the Virgin Mary. Opposition to him quickly boiled up even in Parliament, which reproached Charles with choosing a minister who did not represent them. Charles's answer was the one which might have been expected of him – to dissolve Parliament. The new elections, however, showed an ever greater majority against Polignac. Charles, therefore, to deal with this situation, issued in July 1830 a series of drastic proclamations, known as the Ordinances of St Cloud. By the terms of these ordinances even stricter laws were passed to control the press, the newly elected Parliament was declared dissolved before it met, and three-quarters of the electors were deprived of their right to vote. The whole effect would have been to destroy the Charter. 'At last you are ruling', said Charles's daughter-in-law, with more enthusiasm than accuracy.

The opposition was instantaneous despite the fact that almost at this moment the government scored a great success abroad by the capture of Algiers. Foremost among the protesters against the Ordinances were the very printers who were supposed to set up the Ordinances and the journalists whose livelihood was threatened by the enslavement of the press. Their leader in the preliminary agitation was a writer, Adolphe Thiers, whose name is to recur many times in the history of the next forty years. It was not he, however, whose action was decisive. While the liberal deputies and the upper middle classes were still wondering what to do, the working classes had taken action. The revolutionary tradition was strong in Paris, and it did not take long for a mob, under Republican leaders, to seize the Hôtel de Ville, Notre-Dame, some important guard-houses and arsenals, and crown their captures with the fluttering 'tricolore'. The troops, who anyway had no great enthusiasm for the Bourbons, were unable to make headway against the barricades of the populace, constructed by cutting down the trees of the boulevards and tearing up the paving-stones. The disheartened soldiers had no food, owing to the fact that the rebels had captured the military bakeries. Yet even at this stage of the revolt Charles and Polignac did not realise the gravity of the situation. The latter, comforted by a fresh vision from the Virgin Mary, declared that a couple of hours, four men, and a corporal would settle the whole business. But the next day

His religious and royalist policy

Polignac chief minister, 1829–30

Ordinances of St Cloud, 1830

The 1830 Revolution

Thiers

the mob proceeded to rout the troops who were guarding the Tuileries. Seeing the evident success of the popular insurrection the middle-class deputies realised that they had better take advantage of it, and Thiers returned from the day he had been tactfully spending in the country.

Charles now in haste offered to dismiss Polignac and restore the full terms of the Charter, but the time was past for such concessions. Events were fast moving towards the establishment of a republic when Thiers, on 30th July, had the walls of Paris posted with placards in favour of Louis Philippe, Duke of Orleans, head of a younger branch of the Bourbon line. He was a prince who might be calculated to appeal to the middle and lower classes, since he was the son of the Duke of Orleans ('Philippe Egalité'), who had voted for his cousin Louis XVI's death, and had fought on the revolutionary side at Jemappes. But he was not well known, and when, a day later, he appeared at the Hôtel de Ville to receive the 'call of the people', his reception was distinctly lukewarm until he embraced the veteran republican Lafayette and received from his hands the sacred tricolore. The main fact, however, was that at the critical moment Thiers had produced a candidate when all was confusion, and so the claims of Charles X, and the grandson in whose favour he soon abdicated, and the Republic for which the revolutionaries had been fighting, were pushed into the background. Charles X and his family were soon on ship for England, and Louis Philippe of Orleans, the 'Citizen-King', was King of the French – on condition he ruled as a constitutional monarch.

The Orleans monarchy: Louis Philippe, King of the French

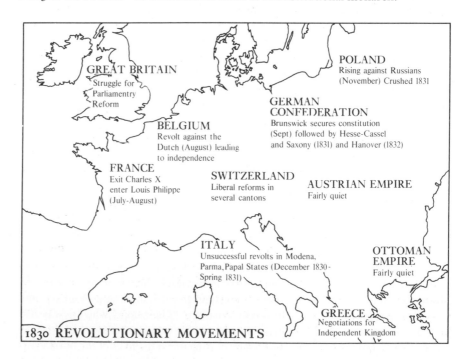

1830 REVOLUTIONARY MOVEMENTS

2. The Orleans Monarchy, 1830–48

Unpopularity of Louis Philippe

The reign of Louis Philippe proved to be eighteen years of disappointment. Clever, sensible, kindly, and well-intentioned, he yet came to grief in an even more undignified way than his predecessor. Apparently with much to attract the people to him – his revolutionary parentage and past, his years of poverty, during which he had earned his living by giving lessons in drawing and mathematics, his simple and unaffected ways – he nevertheless failed to capture the true loyalty of any major group apart from the wealthier middle classes. The old Royalists despised his democratic habits of lighting his own study fire, shaving himself, living principally on soup, and strolling round the shops with no greater protection than an eternal umbrella. They thought nothing of his proudest accomplishment – that he had learnt in exile, from a waiter with whom he shared lodgings, how to cut ham in beautifully thin slices. The working classes equally disliked his government for the simple reason that, though it was their blood which had established it, it did almost nothing to improve their lot. The consequence was that throughout his reign there were plots and attempts to assassinate him, which Louis Philippe for his part met with cheerful and unfailing courage. He had some amazing escapes: once an infernal machine consisting of an arrangement of twenty-four muskets to be fired simultaneously mowed down the front of his bodyguard in a procession, one of the bullets grazing his chin. Another time a bullet lodged in his hair, but he was quite unperturbed. 'It is only in hunting me that there is no close season', he remarked.

The problems which faced his government were immense. In the first place he had to secure recognition of his accession from the European powers, which, frightened of French revolutions, might have been tempted to intervene to restore Charles X. Nicholas I of Russia, indeed, nearly did, only he was soon too busy suppressing a Polish rebellion against himself. But by an inflexible policy of peace, much as this was distasteful to certain elements in France, Louis Philippe calmed down the fears of the powers; and (first of all, winning over the new Whig Foreign Secretary in Britain, Palmerston) he soon secured general recognition. To do this, however, he had to sacrifice certain opportunities of action which would have appealed strongly to a large section of the French.

His peaceful policy

The first such occasion was the Belgian revolt of 1830. The Belgians, forcibly joined with the Dutch by the decision of the victorious allies in 1814–15, had resented the union ever since. Their chief grievances arose from the use of Dutch as for some purposes the only official language, the religious difference between Catholic Belgium and Protestant Holland, and the fact that the Dutch practically monopolised all official positions. At one time, for example, six cabinet ministers out of seven were Dutch, as were thirty out of the thirty-nine ambassadors and all the nine generals. The Belgians, it is true, were allowed half the total number of MPs, but as there were three and a half million Belgians to two million Dutch, even this struck them as unrepresentative and unfair. Further, as some of the Belgian MPs were government officials who depended for their livelihood on not offending the Dutch King, these men constantly voted with the Dutch against their own compatriots. This, by giving the Dutch a majority, led to many laws being passed against the Belgian interest. Bread, for example, the main article of Belgian diet, was heavily taxed, while potatoes, the principal Dutch fare, escaped. Laws in general, too, tended to favour the Dutch commercial and sea-faring interests rather than the Belgian industrial ones, and inclined to the Dutch preference for free trade rather than the Belgian desire for protection. Belgian newspapers, too, were severely censored.

Belgian Revolt, 1830

The consequence of all this was a steadily growing state of unrest leading to mass petitions against Dutch injustice. Then came the July revolution in Paris and one or two high-handed actions by the Dutch King. Extremists plotted a revolution in Brussels, and the action began when students and others poured out from a performance of an opera dealing sympathetically with a rising in Naples against the Spanish and rioted in imitation. The Dutch army was successfully resisted, other towns followed the example of Brussels, and soon a National Congress had declared Belgium to be independent of Holland. A separate constitutional monarchy was voted, with the usual institutions of two houses of parliament, liberty of speech and worship, and so on. By the standards of the time, this constitution was exceptionally liberal.

Meanwhile, what was the attitude of France and the other powers? Would they accept such a cancellation of one important part of the 1814–15 settlement? There was no doubt of France's answer, for the difficulty of Louis Philippe so far had been to restrain the enthusiastic French from rushing to the help of the Belgians. Fortunately the other powers too, in conference at London, agreed to accept Belgian independence, and offered to guarantee the neutrality of the new state, but only on condition that Belgium shouldered over half the debt of the Netherlands, did not include Luxemburg in its boundaries, and chose a king of whom the Powers approved. The Belgians, annoyed at these terms, promptly invited Louis Philippe's son to be the new king – knowing that this would be highly disagreeable to everyone except France.

The Belgian Crown – Louis' dilemma

Louis Philippe was now faced with a delicate choice. If he accepted on behalf of his son he would risk involving France in another European war, while if he did not he would offend his own people. He was firm and sensible enough to refuse and to agree to the British nomination, Prince Leopold of Saxe-Coburg, the future Queen Victoria's uncle. The Belgians then accepted Leopold, and there was no European war about the matter – but there was a general feeling in France that Louis Philippe had been outmanoeuvred by Palmerston, and his prestige suffered accordingly. In fact, however, he was able to recover a little of his reputation when, in 1831, the Dutch king, William, who had refused to accept the Powers' decision, invaded Belgium. The Dutch started sweeping all before them in a brilliant ten-day campaign, and Louis Philippe was hastily authorised by the Powers to intervene to protect Belgium. This he did successfully, and so was able to claim that France after all had aided Belgian independence. Nevertheless he was obviously only going as far as Britain allowed him, and this cautious and pacific policy struck Frenchmen brought up on the Napoleonic traditions as distinctly inglorious. Eventually the whole matter of Belgian independence was concluded in 1839, when the Dutch king, after some years of sulking about the matter, cleverly accepted the Powers' original terms. He thus got back Luxemburg, which the Belgians had been holding meanwhile. The Powers then signed a treaty in London guaranteeing the independence and neutrality of Belgium – the celebrated treaty which Germany was to violate in 1914.

Treaty of London, 1839

Other instances of Louis Philippe's peaceful foreign policy abound. In spite of the urgent demands of many Frenchmen (which they frequently proclaimed by rioting), he did nothing to help the Poles in their revolt against the Russians or the Italians in their agitation against the Austrians. Twice Thiers, as principal minister, resigned because the King would not let him risk a more adventurous policy: once in 1836 when Thiers wanted to support the liberal side in a Spanish civil war, and once in 1840 when France's ally, Mehemet Ali, was ordered by Britain, Austria, and Prussia to restore Syria to Turkey.[1] The second occasion showed so clearly that the bolder Palmerston could humiliate France whenever he chose, by relying on Louis Philippe's anxiety to preserve the peace, that the result was widespread dissatisfaction in France with the King's foreign policy.

When Guizot, a Conservative whose views on politics agreed very well with the King's, replaced Thiers in 1840 the same foreign policy continued. The French annexed Tahiti, until Britain protested, when the annexation was cancelled. In fact, up till 1846 the universal charge against the monarch was subservience to Britain, with whom he and Guizot developed a close understanding or *entente*. In that year, however, Guizot and Louis Philippe carried out their only bold and successful piece of foreign policy apart from the conquest of Algeria (which, in any case, had been started under Charles X).

Ministry of Guizot, 1840–48

Entente with Britain

Both the Queen of Spain, Isabella, and the heir to the throne, the Infanta, her sister, were unmarried. There was naturally competition among the Powers to supply husbands. Palmerston favoured the claims of a German prince, Louis Philippe a French one. Both agreed to withdraw their claim, on condition the other did. Then suddenly Palmerston revived the claim of his candidate. At this, Guizot and Louis Philippe went secretly to work and within a short time astounded Britain by arranging a double marriage – of Isabella to an old nobleman who was rumoured to be impotent, and of the Infanta (who would thus inherit the throne) to a son of Louis Philippe. For once someone had stolen a march on Palmerston. But while France rang with applause over the matter and the King's popularity revived a little, Britain smarted and withdrew her friendship. Two years later she

The Spanish marriages, 1846

End of Anglo-French entente

[1] See p. 159.

THE LEGISLATIVE BELLY, 1834
A very unflattering view, by the great caricaturist Honoré Daumier, of a ministerial bench in the French Chamber. Among Louis Philippe's ministers depicted here are Guizot (extreme left) and Thiers (next but one to Guizot).

watched the Orleans dynasty dethroned without lifting a finger to save it. Thus the King's only bold piece of foreign policy had the unfortunate effect of alienating his country's best friend in Europe.

Home policy

Damaging as the foreign policy of Guizot and the King was to the King's reputation, their home policy was even more so. Both were highly intelligent men, and Guizot's reputation as an orator, a scholar, and a historian-philosopher stood second to none. Yet both completely failed to realise the need for state-action on behalf of France's poorer classes, or for any great measures of political or social progress. At a time when France, in turn undergoing her Industrial Revolution, was beginning to learn the horrors of factory life, slum-dwellings, and propertyless workers, Guizot could get no farther than the fashionable doctrine of *laissez-faire*. In his view the main concern of the government in such matters should be to keep outside them. Apart from a law providing elementary education and a factory act limiting the employment of children, the eighteen years of Louis Philippe's reign saw no real effort to improve the living conditions of the bulk of the people. That some improvement was needed may be seen from the single fact that nine-tenths of town-dwellers examined for the army during the reign were rejected as physically unfit. All this time, however, the wealthier middle classes, the bankers and industrialists, were prospering greatly – railways were built, while the production of French wine increased two-fold, coal four-fold, and machinery ten-fold. Thus the situation was doubly galling for the working classes who were not only poor, but poor in a period of prosperity. And the only contribution the government seemed to make to the matter was to break up strikes by bloodshed, suppress trade unions and political clubs, and deny the ever-increasing demand for an extension of the right to vote.

Parliamentary reform demanded

It was the refusal of this demand which finally brought about the fall of the monarchy. The parliamentary system had never really functioned smoothly under Louis Philippe. The exact extent of the King's power was rather vague, and there grew up a feeling that he was exercising more influence than he should. Further, there had not as yet been time for the formation of two highly organised parties to assure one side or the other of a stable majority, and so even an upright man like Guizot maintained himself in power by a system of bribery. Government posts, pensions, business contracts (especially in connection with the new railways) were distributed among members of parliament. Guizot was thus supported throughout the years 1840 to 1848 by a parliamentary majority, though he was bitterly opposed by most of the country. While the right to vote, too, was restricted to such a small class – only 200,000 out of 35 million – such a state of affairs could continue indefinitely. So 'parliamentary reform' became the rallying-cry of all who were opposed to the conservatism of the King and his minister. Some, like Thiers, probably wanted to extend the franchise slightly to capture power for themselves. Others, like the Republicans, aimed at the vote for all men in order to carry out a complete reform of the social system. In any case a great campaign for parliamentary reform was begun, and against the slightest concession to this Louis Philippe and Guizot resolutely set their faces. Guizot's answer, in fact, to those who demanded the vote was 'get rich'. Then they would qualify for it automatically.

Socialism

By 1846 or 1847, moreover, the dissatisfied in France were able to look to certain positive programmes of reform. One of these increasingly attractive alternatives to the stagnation of Louis Philippe was the new doctrine of socialism, propounded since 1828 by a series of brilliant French writers. Socialism claimed that by abolishing private ownership of great industries, banks, transport systems and the like, and by putting them under the control of the state, all citizens could become more or less equal partners in the wealth of the country, and the grotesque inequalities of capitalism would be avoided. One of the foremost socialists, Louis Blanc, in his book *L'Organisation du Travail*, tried to show how the state could begin to take over the control of industry by running national works and work-shops for the benefit of the unemployed. He argued too that the whole unemployment problem would be solved when the state, which would not be concerned merely with profit, acted as the general employer. His phrase 'the right to work' became a demand of the poorer classes, who naturally saw in socialism not only a means of avoiding the dreaded spells of unemployment, but a method of winning for themselves a much fairer and greater share in the wealth of the country. Socialism in various forms thus began to divert the loyalty of the urban working classes away from the Orleans dynasty. Socialism itself underwent a rapid development from 1828, when it was full of idyllic schemes, such as the proposal that men should work in fields to the sound of grand pianos, till by 1848 it had become an almost scientific doctrine. Not only were there Blanc's proposals and hundreds of suggestions for really practical undertakings (such as the cutting of a Suez Canal), but in addition the Germans Marx and Engels were maturing the elaborate creed known now as communism, or revolutionary socialism.

The second alternative to which the working classes could turn was Bonapartism. It may seem difficult to understand the attraction of this, since Napoleon had led the French to disaster. The military triumphs of the Empire, however, were a great source of pride to Frenchmen, and the principles of Bonapartism had been entirely reconstructed since 1815. In exile at St Helena, Napoleon had cleverly 'edited' the history of his career to show that the constant warfare was more or less accidental and caused by other nations, and that his dictatorship was intended to be temporary. He would, he declared, have given France peace, prosperity, and liberal institutions had Europe permitted him to fulfil his life-work. These elements in Napoleon's defence of himself were seized on and magnified by the heir to the Bonaparte claim, Louis Napoleon Bonaparte, a nephew of the great Emperor. In a series of pamphlets he proclaimed his care for both the army and for peace, and his desire for free institutions. He outlined many schemes of public works and of agricultural and commercial reform, all designed to abolish unemployment and bring prosperity. Though he twice failed ridiculously in attempts to seize power, the cult of Bonapartism gradually developed. Unimportant at the beginning of Louis Philippe's reign, it became gradually more and more of a menace as industrial distress grew and the government still did nothing. As shaped by Louis Napoleon, it appealed to the neglected working classes, to the slighted army, to all those who disliked Louis Philippe's cautious foreign policy, and even to liberals who swallowed the promises of free institutions.

To rob the growing agitation of something of its sting, Thiers and Louis Philippe completed the Arc de Triomphe in celebration of the victories of the Empire, opened a 'Museum of Conquests' at Versailles, and had the Emperor's remains brought from St Helena to be interred in Paris. The manoeuvre was unsuccessful; they hoped to satisfy the Napoleonic clamour by a little cheap pageantry, but in

Louis Blanc

Bonapartism

Louis Napoleon

fact they only caused men all the more to contrast the colourful days of the Empire with the drab existence of the present reign. The contrast was heightened by the work of a number of skilled French historians, such as Lamartine and Blanc, who in their treatment of the revolutionary period depicted the leaders of that generation as gigantic figures who completely dwarfed Louis Philippe and Guizot.

General dissatisfaction with Guizot

By 1847, when an economic crisis was adding to other troubles, the government thus had few enthusiastic supporters. It had done almost nothing for the workers; it was corrupt; it had knuckled under to Britain. Its very real services in keeping the peace for eighteen years, and thereby allowing industry and commerce to develop, were not generally appreciated. Either socialism or Bonapartism promised more. Further, France, as Lamartine put it, was simply 'bored' with the existing régime. It was all too colourless and stagnant. The fat old King, often drawn by caricaturists in the shape of a William pear, became a figure of ridicule. His middle-class taste, shown in the new apartments at Versailles, seemed utterly unattractive when compared, in the same building, with the splendour of Louis XIV or the brilliant vulgarity of Napoleon. Above all, the ministry of Guizot, 'the austere wirepuller', in eight years of power had virtually barred all progress. As Lamartine, the republican poet and historian, said: 'If that were all the genius required of a statesman charged with the direction of affairs, there would be no need for statesmen – a milestone would do just as well.' To many it became clear that the first step to progress was to shift the 'milestone' ministry, as Guizot's government was rapidly nicknamed.

To accomplish a real change in the direction of the government, however, it was necessary to extend the franchise, for the existing class of wealthy electors was quite satisfied with Guizot. The agitation for parliamentary reform grew apace; there was not so much a desire to uproot the monarchy, as to make the government more democratic and more aware of industrial and social problems. The full result of the 1848 revolution, like that of 1830, though everything had been leading up to it, was something of an accident.

Reform Banquets

The opposition started a big series of Reform Banquets. At these, opposition orators would speak on the need for giving more people the vote. Gradually they advanced from a request for modified electoral reform to omission of the King's name from the toast-list and a demand for a republic with a vote for everybody. In February 1848 a great Reform Banquet was announced, with a Reform Procession. Scenting danger, the government banned the banquet; a number of complicated moves followed, and the organisers finally decided to call off the procession. Half the banqueters did not know whether the whole affair was really on or off, but by this time the Paris masses had got it into their heads that *something* exciting would happen anyway, and so turned up for the procession in force. Then the government made the fatal mistake of calling out the National Guard to disperse the crowd – fatal because the Guard showed their sympathy with the crowd and so encouraged it. A more ruthless man than Louis Philippe would have ordered out the regular troops to fire on the Guard, and perhaps quelled the whole matter by a brutal display of force. Louis Philippe, old and peaceful, refused to face the prospect of blood, and consented to dismiss Guizot. The next day an accidental clash between a small section of the crowd and some troops led to the barricades going up all over Paris again, and the working classes preparing to resist the troops by force. In the fighting which ensued the troops put no heart into the work, and

PUT OUT!

Louis Philippe's candle is snuffed out by the 1848 Revolutionaries. Cartoon by John Leech, March, 1848.

when the King reviewed them, instead of 'Vive le Roi!' he got shouts of 'Vive la réforme!' Discouraged at the collapse of all his work, murmuring 'This is worse than Charles X', the old King lost heart for the first time and abdicated in favour of his grandson, the Count of Paris. But as it turned out, the Orleans monarchy, mourned by very few, was at an end. A provisional government was formed in Parliament, and France became a republic for the second time in her history. The Tuileries meanwhile had been looted by the mob, some of whom were drowned in the floods of wine released from the royal cellars.

The Revolution of 1848 – exit Louis Philippe

CHAPTER 9
The Second French Republic and the Second French Empire

1. The Second Republic, 1848–52

Demand for a
republic

When Louis Philippe abdicated, he had no intention of ending the monarchy. The more determined of the revolutionaries, however, were eager for a republic – and got one. Yet they were not at all a united body. Some of them were intellectuals of the middle or upper classes who were members of the Assembly, like the poet and historian Lamartine; well-read in history, they desired a republic largely for sentimental reasons (such as admiration for the old Roman Republic or for the first French Republic). But others were men of the working classes, or else middle-class champions of the working class, like the historian Louis Blanc, who wanted a republic as the best means of achieving socialist measures and a higher standard of living for the poor. These republicans of diverse views were able to seize control by acting together, but they did not of course represent the whole of the nation. Equally important, if not more so, were the people who for the moment were only in the background – the peasantry and small landowners of France. Having made considerable gains in 1789, these were soon to show themselves deeply suspicious of further revolutions and republics made in Paris. Conservative by instinct, they were anxious above all for a régime which would guarantee law, order and the security of their property.

Provisional govern-
ment formed,
February 1848

On the abdication of Louis Philippe in February 1848, Lamartine was one of those who took the lead. When a mob burst into the Chamber of Deputies to demand the end of the Orleans dynasty and the setting up of a republic, he persuaded them to agree to the formation of a provisional government consisting largely of republican deputies. To this list of names the working class groups who had meanwhile seized control of the Paris municipal government compelled him to add some of their own nominees, including the socialist Louis Blanc. At the same time, a republic was declared. The provisional government as thus formed then arranged for elections to be held in April to return a new assembly which would settle the details of the republican constitution. For these elections, the vote was granted to all adult males, whether they could read or not – and France's electorate suddenly leapt from 250,000 to 9 million.

Elections for
constituent assembly

The result of the election was that most of the seats went to moderate republicans, a fair-sized minority to declared royalists, and only a very few to the socialist extremists. Whatever the feelings in Paris, France itself seemed to be a fairly conservative country. The Paris working classes, however, could not be ignored. Since February they had been armed, and they were determined not to let their efforts merely serve the interests of the middle classes, as had happened in 1830. They were driven, too, by real need, for the 1840s were hard times with much unemployment. Twice in March extremist groups rioted, without success; and in May a throng of extremists invaded and momentarily took over the Assembly, from which they were expelled only by the arrival of the National Guard.

Working-class agitation

Frustrated in the attempts of their more violent leaders to seize direct control, the Paris working classes had to pin their hopes on Blanc, some of whose ideas the provisional government had promised to put into effect. Blanc had long advocated Social Workshops or co-operatives where the workers would pool their efforts for their common good. These, he thought, could be the first step towards socialising all the vital elements in the nation's economic life. At the same time they would help to absorb some of the many unemployed. Blanc was a member, however, of a government which was by no means socialist and which therefore tried to limit the application of his ideas. The result was that, though National Workshops to absorb the unemployed were set up in response to popular clamour, they were nothing like the workshops of Blanc's dreams. They were not co-operatives; and the work offered was almost entirely of the labouring order – replanting trees, paving roads, building railway stations – at a rate of two francs a day.

'National Workshops'

Nevertheless in the harsh conditions of 1848 the unemployed, and even many of the employed, flocked to these national works. The results were unfortunate. In the first place the government, unimaginative in supplying work and frightened of offending wealthy manufacturers by setting up in competition with them, began to order the same tasks to be done over again to employ all the applicants. As this got more absurd, greater and greater numbers were placed on 'inactivity' pay of one franc a day. Taxation began to mount to pay for all this, and a financial crisis occurred. The interests of the tax-paying middle classes and the propertyless working classes were now seen to be sharply opposed, and the new Assembly, consisting almost entirely of the former, demanded an end to the Workshops. To close them without breaking too many promises the government offered the workers (and idlers) who attended them the choice of joining the army (if young) or clearing land in the provinces. This offer was summed up by one French historian as 'a choice between being shot by the Arabs in Algeria or dying of fever in the swamps of Sologne'.

Workshops closed

Faced with this action on the part of the government, in June 1848 the armed workers of Paris rose in a fresh revolution. Up went the barricades; over went buses and locomotives to strengthen them. The Paris working classes fought bravely in this struggle against the government, but they were opposed by the army, the National Guard, the upper and middle classes, and the whole of the provinces. Heavy artillery was used to smash the resisting streets, and the blood of over 10,000 Frenchmen flowed before the revolt was crushed. After the struggle was over, thousands more were deported. It was a dreadful experience, and it gravely weakened the Second Republic. Henceforth the working classes would never feel confidence in its good intentions, and the middle classes would never feel confidence in its stability.

The 'June days' of 1848

A few months later, in October, the new republican constitution was completed.

The Presidency of the Republic

Power was to be split between a President and an Assembly, both elected by universal suffrage. The question of who was to be President had still to be settled. The three main candidates were General Cavaignac (the Minister for War who had just put down the Paris revolutionaries), Lamartine, and Charles Louis Napoleon Bonaparte, nephew of the great Emperor.

Early history of Louis Napoleon

The son of the Emperor's brother Louis, who from 1806 to 1810 was King of Holland, Louis Napoleon Bonaparte had lived adventurously. A romantic, believing firmly in his destiny as his uncle's heir, he had been involved in a bewildering variety of scrapes, revolutions and love affairs. In 1831 he had joined the Italian secret society, the Carbonari, in their revolt against Papal rule in Rome, and had eventually escaped from the Austrians disguised as a footman. Exiled from France, he wrote books on military subjects to make himself popular with the French army and on social subjects to show his care for the French people. In 1836, with a few followers, he had tried to 'invade' France, raise the garrison of Strasbourg, and claim the throne from Louis Philippe – but had shrunk from using violence, had failed even to make a good speech to the soldiers, and had let the whole affair degenerate into a scuffle. This was followed by his arrest and deportation to the United States. Undeterred by this miserable failure he continued to press his claim; and in exile in Switzerland and England he wrote a book, *Des Idées Napoléoniennes*, in which ideas of peace, socialism and Bonapartism were intermingled. In 1840, thinking the time ripe for a further attempt, he landed at Boulogne with about fifty men and a captive vulture (to represent the Imperial eagle). Again the 'invasion' developed into an undignified scuffle. Louis Napoleon tried to escape by swimming out to a boat, but it capsized; he was wounded and captured – and in a few hours was once more the laughing-stock of France. At his trial, however, he cut a more impressive figure, maintaining stoutly that the plebiscite which had confirmed his uncle in power had never been revoked by the French people, and that therefore a Bonaparte should still be ruling. The lenient government of Louis Philippe, anxious not to make a martyr of him, ordered him to be confined for life in the fortress of Ham, and his 'eagle' in the Zoological Gardens. He was taken to Ham on the very day that the ashes of his famous uncle, brought back from St Helena, were interred in the Invalides.

Attempts to seize power at Strasbourg (1836) and Boulogne (1840)

Captivity at Ham, 1840–46

At Ham, under very free conditions which allowed him to study and to keep a mistress, Louis Napoleon had then devoted further attention to social problems. He soon produced schemes for the development of the French beet-sugar industry, for improving army recruitment, for a Panama Canal, and for doing away with poverty by making the state take over and develop all unoccupied land. His book *L'Extinction du Pauperisme* appeared in 1844. The result was that he grew popular with the French working classes and became regarded as a man of vision. In 1846, having decided that the time was ripe for his escape, he damaged his rooms so badly that they needed repairs, and in the course of these disguised himself as a workman and walked out of the fortress with a plank over his shoulder.

Return to France, 1848

Safe in London again, Louis Napoleon showed his love of humanity by his attentions to the ballet girls. When the revolution of February 1848 overthrew Louis Philippe, he quickly returned to France and offered his services – only to be asked to leave. Back in London once more, he helped the forces of law and order by enrolling as a special constable during the Chartist riots. Then the law against the Bonapartes was repealed in France (for the benefit of Louis Napoleon's cousins, not himself) and he returned to Paris. Securing election to the Assembly, he made such a poor impression that his opponents did not rate him seriously in his ambition to become President. Thiers, in fact, even began to encourage his candidature on the ground that 'he was a noodle whom anyone could twist round his finger'. But they miscalculated badly. The name 'Napoleon' offered to the middle classes a guarantee of law and order, while the books which Louis himself had written promised a host of useful social reforms acceptable to the working classes. In all his propaganda, Louis Napoleon kept the military dictatorship of Napoleon I in the background, and stressed only the great Emperor's reforms and liberal 'intentions'. So it came about that, on a national vote in December 1848, Louis Napoleon was elected President of the French Republic with 5,400,000 votes, while Cavaignac received 1,400,000 and poor Lamartine only 17,000.

Louis Napoleon President, December 1848

The term of office of the Prince President (as he was called) was four years. He immediately set out to combine enjoyment with popularity. He especially courted the army, the Church, big business and the broad mass of the people. When a new Assembly of a fairly Catholic and conservative character was elected in 1849, he co-operated with it in some matters (for example in the Loi Falloux which allowed the religious orders and other private groups to set up schools) but he opposed it in others. One measure in particular, which the Assembly had passed with his approval, he later strove to undo. In 1850, alarmed at the fact that the vote had been given to so many who were as yet unable to read or write, the Assembly disqualified 3 million casual labourers from voting by a law which stated that they must have resided continuously for three years in the same district. Louis Napoleon later decided to champion the cause of these men, and this, combined with his plans outlined in 1850 for railways, roads, harbours, canals, model farming, drainage and sanitation, increased his popularity with the poorer classes.

Louis Napoleon's period of office was due to expire in 1852 and there was a law against re-election. His attempt to have this repealed having failed, he began planning an extension of his power by other means. He was spurred partly by ambition, partly by the fact that he was deeply in debt and could not afford to lose his presidential income. At the same time some of the leaders of the Assembly began plotting to get rid of him as Prince President, for he was already beginning to act very like a dictator. Thiers, for example, openly boasted 'before a month is up, we will have Louis Bonaparte under lock and key'.

It was the Prince President who struck first. At 10 p.m. on the night of 2nd December 1851 (the anniversary of Austerlitz), following usual evening reception, a brilliantly engineered *coup d'état* began. Seventy-eight separate police officers during the night arrested seventy-eight separate leaders of the opposition, both police and prisoners being quite ignorant of the fact that they were part of a large-scale operation. Troops were posted in strategic positions and printers were forced to print proclamations announcing the change in the presidential position. Paris woke up to find Louis Napoleon supreme over his opponents.

The *coup d'état*, December 1851

Louis Napoleon's announced intention was to rule as President for a further ten years and to draw up a fresh constitution after holding a plebiscite to confirm him in his power. In protest there was a little barricade-work in Paris on 3rd and 4th December, but order was restored with the loss of about 500 lives. In the provinces there were outbreaks which led to about 27,000 people being arrested,

YOUNG FRANCE'S NEW TOY.

France neglects Louis Philippe, Lamartine (with lyre), and General Cavaignac for Louis Napoleon. Cartoon in Punch, *3rd January 1849.*

of whom 10,000 were deported. However, the subsequent plebiscite, during which the President's officials used every form of pressure they could, came up to his highest hopes, 7,400,000 voting for him and only 600,000 against. The moral was drawn by the President: 'France has realised that I broke the law only to do what was right. The votes of over 7 million have just granted me absolution.' The use of the word 'absolution' suggests that the *coup d'état* weighed on Louis Napoleon's conscience, as does the fact that he released all the prisoners by 1859. If it did not weigh on his conscience it should have done, for the new constitution turned out to be virtually a dictatorship, whereas he had solemnly sworn before God to be faithful to the French Republic as established in 1848. But a politician's promises, as he himself observed, 'are even more brittle than lovers' oaths'.

2. The Second Empire, 1852–70

It was not long before the logical sequel occurred – the restoration of the Empire. A year of useful reforms (housing schemes, abolition of Sunday labour, provision of baths, wash-houses, asylums) combined with pageantry and triumphal tours to impress some and wandering round slums on foot to impress others, and various public bodies began to urge the Prince President to become Emperor. The invitation did not fall on unwilling ears: this, after all, was what he had been scheming for nearly all his adult life. On 2nd December 1852, the first anniversary of his *coup d'état*, the Second French Republic ended and the Second Empire began, the ex-President assuming the title of Napoleon III.[1] A further plebiscite confirmed the step by 7,800,000 to 250,000, while 2 million did not vote. *The Empire*

In the imperial constitution Parliament was allowed very little power, the Emperor reserving to himself the conduct of foreign affairs, the selection of all ministers, and the command of the armed forces. In addition, political meetings were forbidden, except in the presence of a government agent, federations of political associations were banned, newspapers could not be published without government authorisation, and all steps were taken to see that opposition was too weak to overthrow the Emperor. This dictatorship Napoleon III, with his mixture of ideals and ambitions, proposed to modify later when France had settled down. For the moment, however, he was careful to point out that an isolated plebiscite was a different matter from perpetual democracy, and aptly expressed the difference by saying that he 'did not mind being baptised with the water of universal suffrage', but that he 'refused to live with his feet in it'.

The reforming zeal of the new Emperor was soon evident. For some years it was said that he never visited a town without making better arrangements for its future. In Paris, in collaboration with the Prefect of the Seine, Baron Haussmann, he initiated one of the biggest slum-clearance schemes on record. Thousands of narrow, insanitary, unlit streets with verminous dwellings were destroyed, to be replaced by magnificent wide boulevards, complete with trees and lamps, a piece of reform which had the secondary object of making the erection of barricades more difficult. In addition water-pipes, gas-mains and rain-water sewers were laid under the Paris streets and similar modernisation was accomplished in several other cities, notably Lyon. In the improvement of the country's communications the Emperor showed an equal zeal; railway, telegraph, and steamship services all expanding thanks in part to his interest. In 1848 there were only 3,000 kilometres of railway track but by 1870 there were 17,000. During the same period the volume of foreign trade was multiplied about three times, and the production of coal, iron and steel increased enormously. All this was greatly aided by the new banking *Reforms*

[1] Bonapartists reckoned there had been a Napoleon II – the infant son of Napoleon I and Marie Louise. In 1814 Napoleon I abdicated in favour of his three-year-old son (then known as the King of Rome), and he was the titular Emperor for a few days before the Bourbons were restored in the person of Louis XVIII. Napoleon II died in 1832.

90

and credit institutions, such as the *Crédit Mobilier* and the *Crédit Foncier*, founded with the encouragement of the Emperor.

All told the Second Empire ushered in for France a period of considerable prosperity, though one marked by much financial speculation. There were no

TERRIFIC ASCENT OF THE HERO OF
A HUNDRED FÊTES.

Louis Napoleon climbs higher, aspiring to become Emperor, while the Parisian working man regards him with suspicion. Boulogne and Strasbourg refer to his own two ridiculous attempts to capture the throne in Louis Philippe's reign. The setting is the Place de Vendôme in Paris, where Louis Napoleon took up residence – the column is the Vendôme column raised in 1805–10 to celebrate the victories of Napoleon I. Cartoon in Punch *by John Leech, 4th September 1852.*

signs at first of the adventurous foreign policy which was to bring ruin on the Second Empire as it had done on the First, and there was every sign of Napoleon III's care for the masses. So acute an observer as Queen Victoria's Prince Consort soon remarked of the Emperor, 'Louis Napoleon wishes for peace, enjoyment, and cheap corn'. Apart from the 'enjoyment', this is not unlike the Emperor's own statement of his aim – 'to reconcile order with progress'.

The court life of the Emperor rapidly became notable for its brilliance. Rebuffed in an attempt to secure a royal bride (the other sovereigns of Europe for the most part regarded him as an upstart) he concentrated instead on looks. In 1853, at the age of forty-five, he married a beautiful Spanish noblewoman twenty years younger. The Empress Eugénie, as she became, was unfortunately less well equipped mentally than she was physically. This would not have mattered had she not tried to influence the Emperor's policies, usually in an anti-liberal and pro-clerical direction. This, however, was to occur later. For the moment all was enjoyment at Court, with spiritualistic diversions (tables talking and accordions playing by themselves), grand receptions, appearances at the Opéra, visits from interesting people such as Pasteur, Verdi, Gautier, the interminable love-affairs of the Emperor, and the rather more innocent pastimes of the Empress such as blind man's buff. In was Napoleon III, in fact, with his love of amusement and his rebuilding schemes, who gave Paris that atmosphere of elegance and enjoyment which for long made it the Mecca of Britons escaping to holiday abroad.

The Court

There was something in the Napoleonic character, however, which would not be content with either reform or enjoyment. Though by no means a hardened militarist, Napoleon III was unable to resist the traditions of his uncle and the pressures which came from various quarters, including the army, the church and the Empress. His ambition and sometimes his ideals prompted him to undertake military campaigns, but he lacked the ruthless character of the first Napoleon, and after a successful beginning his foreign policy led him to disaster.

Foreign ventures

The first foreign venture was comparatively a success. Already nurturing a personal grievance against the Tsar Nicholas for refusing to address him as 'brother' in the manner customary between sovereigns, and anxious to assert French claims wherever possible, he had quarrelled with Russia. The original question at issue, which was much less important than the power-struggle behind it, was the guardianship of the Christian Holy Places of Palestine. Napoleon claimed that this had been accorded to Charlemagne and his French successors on behalf of the Catholics. In recent centuries, however, the care of these places had come more and more under clergy of the Orthodox Church, who were naturally supported by the great Orthodox power, Russia. When Russia not only refused to surrender existing Orthodox rights but also demanded from Turkey the protectorship of all the Sultan's Christian subjects – which would have given Russia the right to interfere widely in the Turkish Empire – Napoleon III, supported by Britain, prompted Turkey to refuse. The subsequent invasion by Russia of the Turkish provinces of Moldavia and Wallachia and the sinking of the Turkish fleet at Sinope then caused Britain and France to ally with Turkey for the purpose of reducing Russian influence. When Austria also threatened to join this coalition, the Tsar withdrew his troops from the two provinces (which were then occupied by Austria on behalf of the Turks) and the war danger seemed to recede.

1. The Crimean War, 1854–56

Despite this relaxation of tension, Britain, France and Turkey then decided to invade the Crimean peninsula. The intention was, by destroying Russian forts and naval stores, to drive Russian warships off the Black Sea and so reduce their ability to threaten the Balkans and Anglo-French interests in the Mediterranean. The key to the Black Sea was the naval base and fortress of Sebastopol, and for a year British and French generals vied with each other in their mistakes while besieging it. Eventually, when some 65,000 French and British soldiers had lost their lives after suffering the untold miseries of campaigning in a Crimean winter, Sebastopol was taken, and Russia began to think of making peace. Even so, it took another threat from Austria, who had joined the alliance but had not so far done any fighting, before Russia finally came to terms.

During the conflict the French Emperor had some worrying moments and in 1855, after the early failures, he reached the point of wanting to take charge in the Crimea himself. From this he was dissuaded only by the entreaties of Queen Victoria, whose truly feminine heart had been mildly fluttered by his personal charms. But the end of the war compensated for everything. The Treaty of Paris of 1856, with Russia forced to accept the neutralisation of the Black Sea and to abandon her exclusive claims to protect the Sultan's Orthodox Christians, gave Napoleon III a taste of the sweets of victory.[1]

Treaty of Paris, 1856

The next foreign venture at first seemed equally successful, though before the end it involved Napoleon III in a bewildering series of difficulties and contradictions. The enthusiasm of the Emperor as a young man for the cause of Italian unity has already been noted. He had, however, to be more careful now that he was in control of the destiny of France. Part of his problem was how to aid the Italians in their struggle for unity without making an Italy which would be too powerful a neighbour and without offending the very important clerical circles in France, who would not wish to see the Pope's rule over the Papal States abolished. He had also to avoid getting into trouble with too many other nations; yet unless he actually did something to help the Italians he would offend liberal circles in France. He was thus almost bound to offend one of the two main sections of opinion in France, and probably he would have done better to go all out on one side or the other. Instead he tried to please both, and failed to satisfy either.

**2. Intervention
in Italy**

On becoming President in 1848 Louis Napoleon had found the French republic committed to help Pope Pius IX against the Italian revolutionaries Mazzini and Garibaldi, who were trying to establish a Roman Republic. For a time he continued this policy and even sent French troops to restore Pius to power in Rome – to please the clericals. He combined this, however, with assurances that he would press the Pope to carry out a liberal policy – to please the anti-clericals. Italian problems for a while then took a secondary place in the Emperor's mind – though Count Cavour, Prime Minister of the kingdom of Sardinia, which became increasingly the centre of Italian hopes of unification, staked a strong claim on the Emperor's gratitude and future services by sending a contingent of troops to help the French in the Crimean War.

At the peace conference in 1856 in Paris, where he thus gained a place, Cavour raised the question of Italian unity. The Emperor, however, did nothing further till a violent incident jogged his memory. In January 1858 a number of fervent

The Orsini attempt

---

[1] The Crimean War is treated in more detail in pp. 160–65.

Italian patriots attempted to assassinate the Emperor as he was driving to the Opéra. They were led by Felice Orsini, a distinguished republican revolutionary who had come to the conclusion that Napoleon III was the greatest obstacle to Italian unity. The explosion of the bombs killed eight people and wounded 150, but to the great relief of the French the Emperor and the Empress were unhurt. From prison Orsini wrote to Napoleon urging him to help the cause of a united Italy, and at the trial he conducted himself heroically. The Emperor, strangely affected – and possibly a little scared – by this incident, determined to do something more to carry out his youthful vows and ideals. He would even have reprieved Orsini, had not his advisers reminded him that the attempt had resulted in a massacre of innocent bystanders.

A few months later Napoleon met Cavour at the spa of Plombières as though by accident – his Foreign Minister even telegraphed to tell him that Cavour was there! – and came to an understanding with the Sardinian Prime Minister. The terms of the understanding, part of which was made formal later, were that Napoleon would support Sardinia in a war to drive the Austrians from northern Italy. Lombardy and Venetia, freed from Austrian rule, could then be joined with Sardinia, which, with the addition also of Modena and Parma and part of the

Plombières Meeting, 1858

'L'Empire, c'est la Paix,' said Napoleon III frequently – but Europe could never quite believe it.

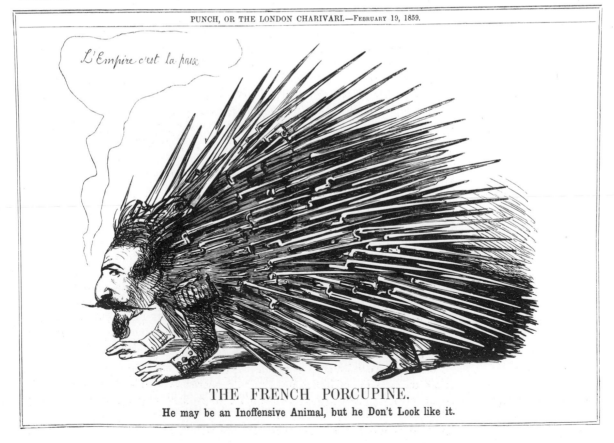

PUNCH, OR THE LONDON CHARIVARI.—FEBRUARY 19, 1859.

L'Empire c'est la paix

THE FRENCH PORCUPINE.
He may be an Inoffensive Animal, but he Don't Look like it.

papal territory, could thus expand into a strong northern Italian kingdom. In the centre of the peninsula, there would be another, and smaller, Italian kingdom, based on Tuscany, and below this a reduced papal territory. In the south the kingdom of Naples and Sicily would remain unchanged. The three kingdoms and the papal territory would achieve Italian unity by forming a loosely organised federation like the German Confederation, under the presidency of the Pope. In return for her services in driving out the Austrians, France would receive Savoy and Nice, which though under Sardinian rule were predominantly French in language and sentiment. With this bargain sealed, it remained only to provoke, not too obviously, an Austrian declaration of war on Sardinia.

The war begins, 1859

Shortly afterwards the Austrian ambassador was amazed to hear Napoleon III say to him, 'I regret that our relations with your government are not as good as they have been'; and it was not long before Sardinia was mobilising her troops in preparation for the war. These preparations alarmed several European states, including Britain, who demanded that they should stop. Shaken, Napoleon put pressure on Sardinia to disarm; but before she could do so Austria rashly marched into Piedmont to enforce disarmament, in defiance of a French warning not to do so. The war had begun, and Cavour's scheme had succeeded just when it seemed about to fail. With the French army under the Emperor's personal command two

Magenta and Solferino. Lombardy freed

big victories over the Austrians were then won at Magenta and Solferino. Most of Lombardy was freed, to be united with Sardinia. It remained now to complete the task by sweeping the Austrians from Venetia.

Peace of Villafranca, 1859

Suddenly came the astounding news that the Emperor had concluded an armistice with the Austrians, leaving an infuriated Cavour and Sardinia in the lurch. Many motives have been suggested for this sudden reversal of policy, among them the fact that the Emperor, sickened with the horrors of war at first hand, had lost all zest for the enterprise. Perhaps a more important reason was one he

Napoleon withdraws

himself put forward – that his victories had been by a narrow margin, and that attacking Venetia meant capturing the four formidable Austrian fortresses known as the Quadrilateral. Further, there was a lurking fear of Prussian intentions in his mind, and an increasing belief that Cavour and the pressure of events might carry Sardinian expansion farther than the French intended. At any rate he retired from north Italy with only half of his aim accomplished. Shortly afterwards,

Modena, Parma, Tuscany united with Sardinia

however, by diplomatic means he helped prevent Austria from re-imposing pro-Austrian rulers on the central Italian duchies of Modena, Parma and Tuscany – rulers who had been expelled by the local populations during the excitement of the war in the north. This enabled these three duchies to vote for union with Sardinia. For these services Napoleon claimed from Sardinia his reward of Savoy

Savoy and Nice for France

and Nice, a transfer confirmed, as usual, by a plebiscite.

The whole adventure of 1859 thus shows up Napoleon III's Italian policy in all its contradictions. We see him helping Italian unity in the north (while his troops still kept the Pope in power in Rome), then backing out at a critical moment, then helping again. We see him offending half France by beginning at all and the other half by stopping when he did. All the same, by 1859 Italy had provided a second field of victory for French arms, the French army was regarded as the best in Europe, and the Emperor was at the height of his power. Successful minor enterprises in Syria and China contributed to the general effect.

The following year, however, marked the turning of the tide. In 1859 the Emperor, mindful of his declared policy of allowing greater liberty as time went on, allowed all political exiles to return, and so laid his Empire open to attack from within. In 1860, too, he allowed Parliament more freedom to criticise and amend proposals brought before it, which led to the same result. Above all, in 1860 he provoked widespread discontent among the manufacturing classes by concluding a commercial treaty with Britain (whose negotiator was the famous free-trader Richard Cobden). By this agreement the French duties on British textiles, iron, steel, and hardware goods were lowered considerably in return for British reductions on French wines, silks, and fancy-goods. Similar agreements with most of the other western European countries followed. This exposed many French

An amnesty

The Cobden-
Chevalier Treaty, 1860

The Amnesty to his old opponents (1859) was Napoleon III's first small step towards the 'Liberal Empire'. Cartoon by John Tenniel.

THE FIRST LESSON.
Not so Bad for a Beginner!

manufacturers to the full blast of foreign competition, and the Emperor's popularity suffered accordingly.

3. The Mexican Adventure, 1861–67

A further foreign adventure, dragging on over several years, damaged the Emperor's prestige in a serious fashion. In 1861, the Mexican Republic, which had been formed by a break-away from Spanish rule forty years earlier, came under the reformer Juarez, a leader of peasant origin. Having just fought a ruinous civil war, he was obliged to default on the Republic's debts, and he refused for the time being to pay interest on bonds held by foreign creditors. France, Britain, and Spain thereupon agreed to send a joint expedition to enforce payment. When the object of the expedition had been attained, Britain and Spain withdrew their forces, but Napoleon III, urged on by Eugénie and the clerical party, kept his troops there and embarked on a far more ambitious project. His plan, specially designed to enhance French prestige and please those clericals offended by his Italian policy, was to overthrow the anti-clerical Mexican Republic of Juarez and substitute a Catholic Empire. The Archduke Maximilian, brother of the Austrian Emperor, was persuaded, by the promise of French support, to become the imperial claimant.

The fighting that followed was long and expensive, but by 1864 French arms had duly installed Maximilian on his throne. Unfortunately for Napoleon III, however, another power now came on the scene in full force – the United States. Engaged from 1861 in its own desperate Civil War, the United States had thus far been powerless; but when the war ended in 1865, she warned France that she would tolerate no violation of the Monro Doctrine.[1] France, in other words, must keep out of Mexico – or be prepared to fight the United States. Napoleon, already tired of a costly war, and worried about the position in Europe, welcomed the excuse, and in 1867 withdrew his last forces. The result of the whole episode was again that both parties in France were aggrieved – the liberals because Napoleon had engaged in the venture and the clericals because he had ended it too soon. Maximilian's desperate wife, unable to extract a promise of further help from Napoleon, went mad at the thought of the impending fate of her husband; and finally when the news came in 1867 that Maximilian had been captured by his enemies and shot, Napoleon, who had led him into the whole adventure and then deserted him, suffered a serious loss of reputation.

The 'Liberal Empire', 1869–70

By now Napoleon III was having difficulty in restraining political opposition in France. His Italian and Mexican policies had pleased hardly anyone, his economic reforms had not gone far enough to prevent outbreaks of strikes and the growth of Socialism and Communism, and there was an increasing demand for greater political liberty. Again following his proclaimed intention of 'liberalising' the Empire as time went on, he now gave greater freedom to the press, slackened the control over political meetings, and granted a limited right of forming trade unions. The right to strike had been granted a few years earlier, in 1864. To 'crown the edifice' Parliament was now given a further measure of power, and in 1870 a ministry was appointed which at last really did reflect the views of the majority in the Assembly. By 1870 Napoleon, urged not only by his theories but by a most painful illness – a stone in the urinary tract – which was sapping his strength, had thus turned himself from a dictator into a constitutional monarch. The constitutional changes were approved in another plebiscite – 7,500,000 voting for and

Advance of Prussia

[1] See p. 69.

1,500,000 against. Less than a year later the reign of Napoleon III came to an end.

The death-blow to the Empire, torn as it now was by fiercely expressed disagreements in France, came from a state which Napoleon had not sufficiently considered in the early years of his rule – Prussia. The nightmare of the growing power of Prussia under Bismarck had, however, begun to haunt him from 1865 on. The change had come with the Austro-Prussian war of 1866 – the 'Seven Weeks' War'. The year before, France and Britain had failed to support Denmark against Prussia and Austria when the two latter states, acting in the name of the German Confederation, had wrested the disputed duchies of Schleswig and Holstein from the Danes.[1] Shortly afterwards, however, the two victors quarrelled over the final disposition of the duchies, and war threatened between Austria and Prussia. In preparation for it, Bismarck, guiding the fortunes of Prussia, secured a promise of military aid from the new kingdom of Italy: in return Prussia undertook to help the Italians free Venetia from the Austrians. This agreement was to run for only three months, but Bismarck had no difficulty in provoking war during this short period. When the struggle broke out most of the main German states supported Austria, and Europe naturally expected the conflict to be a long one. Napoleon in fact had visions of a strong France at the end of the war dictating policy to the two exhausted opponents. He accordingly decided to remain neutral, more especially as Bismarck had hinted at territorial compensation in the Rhineland if he did so, while Austria had definitely promised France, as the price of French neutrality, to hand over Venetia to Italy.

These calculations were upset, however, by the rapidity of the Prussians' success. One great battle in Bohemia near the villages of Königgrätz and Sadowa (the Germans call the fight by the first name, the French by the second) in 1866 virtually sufficed to defeat Austria. It was little consolation to her that she beat the Italians at Custozza and at the naval battle of Lissa: she had to hand over Venetia to them all the same. Shocked by these developments, and by Prussia's annexation of some of the north German states who had sided with Austria, Napoleon rather hysterically began to demand 'compensation' for France in German territory west of the Rhine. He also made secret proposals to secure Prussia's assent if France should acquire Luxembourg and Belgium. Bismarck however was much too clever for him; while giving nothing away, he used Napoleon's anglings for two vital ends. The first was to persuade the south and west German States, through fear of France, to ally with Prussia. The second was achieved by revealing details of these secret negotiations at two critical moments – one just at the outbreak of the Franco-Prussian war. The result, by showing Napoleon eager to grasp surrounding territory, was to throw European sympathy into the Prussian rather than the French scale, and to rob Napoleon of any possibility of British support in 1870.

The fatal moment for the Empire had now come. With first Denmark then Austria beaten, the south German States won over to Prussia through fear of France, Italy indebted to Prussia for the acquisition of Venetia, and Britain offended with France from knowledge of her ambitions in Luxembourg and Belgium, Napoleon was isolated. At home his prestige was low; physically, he was a dying man. Bismarck knew that the moment was ripe to strike. And, most foolish

The Seven Weeks' War, 1866: Prussia defeats Austria

4. The Franco-Prussian War, 1870–71

[1] For this problem see pp. 143–46.

and fatal of all, France, now desperately anxious to come to grips with Prussia, went out of her way to play Bismarck's game.

The actual conflict arose over the candidature for the vacant Spanish throne, for which a prince of the Hohenzollern family was, on the insistence of Bismarck, a reluctant candidate. Bismarck's idea was to sandwich France between two Hohenzollern powers, for the head of the family ruled in Prussia. When news of this candidature became public, France, fearing Prussian expansion and determined not to be again outmanoeuvred, not unnaturally demanded its withdrawal. The Prussian king, William, as the head of the house, would by the normal dynastic rules of the time decide the issue. He had never personally favoured the candidature, and he agreed to urge his young relative to withdraw. Shortly afterwards the prince's withdrawal was announced, by his father, and France's object was achieved. Unhappily, however, some of the French ministers, and to a lesser extent Napoleon himself, were not content with this. Distrustful of Prussia, and anxious for an even more resounding diplomatic triumph to restore the Emperor's waning prestige, they clamoured for a renunciation more official and permanent. The French foreign minister (the Duke of Gramont) accordingly concocted with Napoleon, urged on by Eugénie, a further demand: that in no circumstances would the Prussian king allow the candidature to be revived. They then instructed the French ambassador in Prussia to secure this undertaking.

The French ambassador did his best. He broached the demand to King William on the riverside promenade at the German spa of Ems, where the King was staying, and asked for an interview on the subject. The King, who had thankfully regarded the matter as closed and was now offended at the implied slight on his good faith, declined to receive the ambassador for this purpose, and instructed one of his ministers to inform Bismarck of the incident. The telegram from Ems which did this also gave Bismarck permission to communicate the details to the Press. Bismarck, who had come to the conclusion that the moment was ripe for war with France and who was depressed by the withdrawal of the candidature, saw his chance. He issued the telegram to the press, but condensed it to leave out the politer aspects and conveyed the impression of a studied Prussian snob to France. A howl of wrath at once arose in the Paris Press, and a momentary war-fever swept over the French government, which only a month before had reduced the army by 10,000 men, (with premier Ollivier informing the Assembly that 'at no epoch was the peace of Europe more assured'). It appears that Napoleon did not entirely share in this general French confidence or in the fatuous blindness of the Minister for War, who boasted that there was 'not so much as the button of a gaiter missing'. But the sick man was borne along by the imperious will of Eugénie, who revelled in the prospect of the conflict and proclaimed proudly, 'This is *my* war'.

The fighting

Disillusionment was to come speedily. Almost at once the French, whose mobilisation was very slow compared with their enemy's, found Alsace and Lorraine invaded by forces vastly better trained and equipped, particularly in artillery. Some heavy fighting soon sufficed to shut up the main French army under Marshal Bazaine in the fortress-town of Metz, where, besieged, it could help no other part of France. The Emperor, dispirited and in agony, proposed to fall back on Paris from Châlons-sur-Marne with the chief remaining force. Such an action would have prolonged the struggle and given France a chance of drafting millions more into the conflict. But Eugénie and her advisers could not brook the temporary

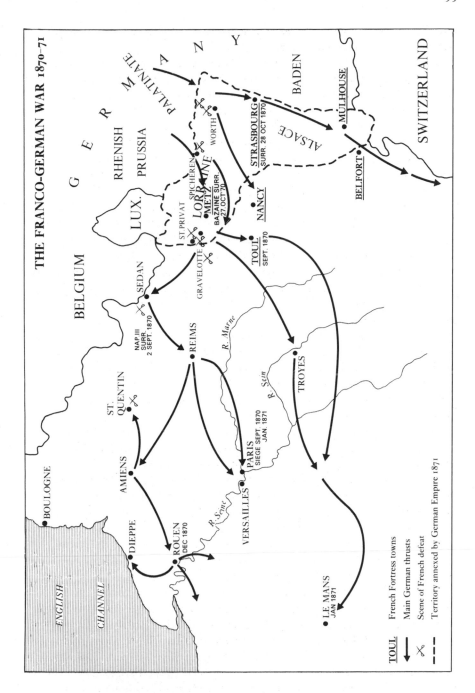

THE FRANCO-GERMAN WAR 1870-71

BELGIUM

LUX.

GERMANY

RHENISH PRUSSIA

PALATINATE

BADEN

SWITZERLAND

MÜLHOUSE

STRASBOURG
SURR. 28 OCT 1870

ALSACE

BELFORT

WÖRTH

SPICHEREN

LORRAINE

METZ
BAZAINE SURR.
27 OCT 70

NANCY

ST. PRIVAT

GRAVELOTTE

TOUL
SEPT. 1870

SEDAN
NAP III
SURR.
2 SEPT. 1870

REIMS

R. Marne

TROYES

R. Seine

ST.
QUENTIN

BOULOGNE

AMIENS

DIEPPE

ROUEN
DEC 1870

R. Seine

VERSAILLES

PARIS
SIEGE SEPT. 1870
JAN. 1871

R. Seine

ENGLISH CHANNEL

LE MANS
JAN 1871

Territory annexed by German Empire 1871

TOUL   French Fortress towns

↓   Main German thrusts

✕   Scene of French defeat

¦ ¦ ¦   Territory annexed by German Empire 1871

humiliation and forebade such a step, assuring the Emperor that his throne was
lost if he retreated.

Against all his own inclinations the harassed Emperor then moved with
Marshal MacMahon to the relief of Metz. He was caught, as was almost inevitable,
in an unfavourable position, and suffered the crushing defeat of his army at Sedan.   Sedan
On 3rd September came to Paris the dramatic despatch: 'The army of Châlons has

End of the Empire,
September 1870:
the Republic restored

surrendered; I myself am a prisoner. Napoleon.' Within a day a mob had invaded the Assembly with cries of 'Down with the Empire', and Léon Gambetta, a fiery young politician already distinguished for his daring opposition to Napoleon, had demanded the restoration of the Republic of 1848. The Assembly agreed; a Government of National Defence was formed (under the military governor of Paris) to include the parliamentary opposition, and Gambetta took the key post of Minister of the Interior. There was no contest, not a finger lifted to save the Empire. Napoleon himself accompanied William as a prisoner into Germany, soon to be released and to die later in England – whither Eugénie, escaping from Paris

PUNCH, OR THE LONDON CHARIVARI.—October 15 1870.

VERSAILLES, OCT. 5, 1870.

"The Royal Head-Quarters were transferred here to-day."—*Telegram.*

Ghost of Louis the Fourteenth (*to Ghost of* Napoleon the First). "IS THIS THE END OF '*ALL THE GLORIES?*'"

Cartoon by John Tenniel.

with the help of her American dentist, had already fled. The Empire, it has been said, 'crumbled like a castle of cards under the flick of a child's finger'.

So the reign of Napoleon III, which opened in revolution, ended in revolution. It had been a thing of contrasts. It had combined dictatorship with democracy; professions of peace and the first Paris international exhibitions with territorial ambitions; support of nationalism in north Italy with opposition to it in Rome and Mexico. Beneath its 'gas-lit pomp' lay squalor, industrial and moral. And the whole contradictory nature of the Empire had been perfectly mirrored in the character of Napoleon himself, at once idealistic and self-seeking, reforming and reactionary, profound and superficial. Less complex in character, Eugénie had done almost as much as her husband to bring about the downfall. Her influence on the Roman question, on Mexico, on the Franco-Prussian war had been decisive. She, at any rate, learnt her lesson, for in the long years of her exile she never again interfered in politics. A vigorous old lady, even after the terrible blow of the loss of her son the Prince Imperial (killed fighting for the British against the Zulus), she maintained her activity to the last, learning to ride a bicycle, buying one of the first motor-cars, and even wanting to fly at the age of ninety. But 'the Empress Eugénie', she said, 'died in 1870'.

The Empire had collapsed, but meanwhile the restored Republic fought on. For four months Paris, besieged like Metz, endured heroically while Gambetta, who escaped in a balloon, organised armies and resistance in the countryside. But before long Bazaine gave in at Metz, with the garrison on the point of starvation, and nearly 200,000 French soldiers laid down their arms. The Prussians thus released from conducting the siege were added to the forces before Paris or used in holding back Gambetta's attempts to relieve the capital. Up to the last the Parisians resisted, till everything had been eaten, including the elephant in the Zoo and the rats of the streets and sewers, and the fuel was exhausted. Then there was no alternative but to surrender. Ten days before the armistice was signed Bismarck set the seal on his work when, in a ceremony at Versailles, King William of Prussia was proclaimed German Emperor – the head of a united Germany'.[1]

Between the armistice and the final peace at Frankfurt nearly four months elapsed. During the latter part of this period the German forces outside Paris had the pleasure of seeing Frenchmen fight each other in the bloody episode of the Paris Commune.[2] The terms of the treaty of Frankfurt were regarded at the time as extraordinarily severe. France was to pay an unprecedented war indemnity of 5000 million francs in three years, to suffer an army of occupation, and to lose Alsace and most of Lorraine, including Metz. These territorial losses, by leaving deep and lasting resentment among the French, helped to produce the European conflict of 1914, in the usual way in which one war begets another.

Siege of Paris, September 1870– January 1871

Surrender of Bazaine at Metz, October 1870

Armistice, January 1871

Treaty of Frankfurt, May 1871

[1] See p. 154.
[2] See pp. 215–17.

CHAPTER 10
The Metternich Period in the Austrian Empire and the German Confederation

1. From the Congress of Vienna to the Outbreak of Revolution, 1815–48

Metternich –

From the end of the Napoleonic wars to the revolutionary movements of 1848 the history of Germany and Austria was influenced to a remarkable degree by one man – Prince Metternich. Few statesmen have had to face so difficult a series of problems, and few have received so much blame for their attempted solutions. In some respects he was and still is a greatly misjudged man. In any case, for more than a generation he occupied a unique position, not only as foreign minister of the Austrian Empire, but also as the embodiment of the older Europe of the monarchies which was fighting a desperate battle with the newer Europe of the revolutionary ideals.

To understand Metternich's pre-eminence we must remember that it was he more than anyone else who, within four years of his appointment as foreign minister in 1809, successfully manoeuvred Austria away from her temporary alliance with Napoleon and brought her in with the Allies. It was his skill in 1814 which inspired the manifesto of the Allies, invading France, to the effect that their quarrel was with Napoleon, not the French people. 'I know Metternich: only he could have thought of that!' exclaimed Napoleon. It was he, too, whose spirit was so active at the Congress of Vienna and whose diplomacy was so successful in bringing the famous Final Act, or summary of the arrangements, rapidly to completion when Napoleon escaped from Elba – a Final Act of 121 articles, which took twenty-six secretaries all day to write out a single copy! Above all, it was he who, with Castlereagh, was the inspirer of the Congress movement – the movement to establish a 'Concert' of Europe, or, in the words of a contemporary, 'to put all heads under the same thinking cap'.

his ideas and outlook

The ideas of this man, born the son of a count and later created a prince, and educated from the first for an outstanding position in the Imperial Court, had become fixed. He had spent all his public life thus far in striving to protect Austria from Napoleon, who claimed to represent certain ideas associated with the French Revolution. As a young man, he had witnessed the excesses of a French revolutionary mob in Strasbourg; and later he had seen the intense nationalism of France bring untold misery to Europe. He was an enthusiastic traveller, a student and patron of art and science, the boundaries of which are far from being national. He was the foreign minister, from 1821 dignified with the title of Chancellor, of an Empire which included thirteen races and many religions. It was his habit, he said, to write 'to Paris in French, to London in English, to St Petersburg in Russian, and to Berlin in German'. In a word, his outlook was that of a cosmopolitan aristocrat of the eighteenth century. It was an outlook which in its culture, its love of peace, and its opposition to anything which smacked of the vulgarity of 'the rabble', such as disorderly agitation or nationalist hysteria, had much to commend it. Unfortunately it was also an outlook which ignored the need for development.

It was because Metternich represented so completely and so ably the views of his task European aristocracy generally that he occupied such an outstanding position in the generation after Waterloo. Apart from his prime duty of safeguarding Austrian interests, he saw his task as twofold: to preserve the European peace and to maintain for monarchy and aristocracy their privileged position against the assaults of the growing forces of the age, liberalism and nationalism. In all these objects he met with a fair degree of success. Although the 'Congress System' collapsed by 1829, no major European war occurred from 1815 till the Crimean War of 1854, and no liberal or national outbreak really shook the Austrian Empire till 1848. Even then the revolutionary movements were suppressed within a year or so, and it was not till 1859 that, in the loss of Lombardy, the dismemberment of the Empire began. At the same time it is apparent from the vantage-point of the twentieth century that in the struggle against what was for the most part extremely inefficient monarchy, the liberal and national forces were almost bound to win. It has required the technical resources and ruthless efficiency of modern dictatorship, of the left or right, to suppress the liberal movement. Metternich himself was sometimes acutely conscious of the fact that his task was almost hopeless. 'I have to give my life to propping up a mouldering edifice', he once remarked in a moment of pessimism. The Emperor Francis, referring to the claims of the different nationalities within his Empire, put the matter even more strongly: 'My realm is like a worm-eaten house – if one part is removed, one cannot tell how much will fall'. Let us see how Metternich strove to act, in his own words, as 'a rock of order' in Austria and Germany.

The Allies of 1813, in the War of Liberation, had taken advantage of the patriotic stirrings in Germany aroused by the Continental System and the oppressive demands of Napoleon. As Napoleon had appealed to the forces of local or national patriotism in the early days of his victories, so the Allies had later been able to use the same weapon against him with considerable effect. Napoleon himself, with his usual acuteness, prophesied that the Allies would pay for their encouragement of nationalism when it turned against their own empires. However, the arrangements of the peace settlement of 1814–15, in regard to Germany and the Austrian Empire not less than elsewhere, show how little importance the Allies as yet attached to nationalist principles. What they were mainly concerned with in the Vienna and other treaties was how to restore the old rulers, reward themselves, and restrain the aggressive nationalism of France. In so doing, of course, their great hope was to achieve a stable, and not a changing, Europe.

The Austrian Empire, as recognised by the treaties of 1815, included as its main The Austrian Empire sections Austria proper (which by origin and population was German), Bohemia and Moravia (inhabited chiefly by Czechs, Slovaks, and Germans), Hungary

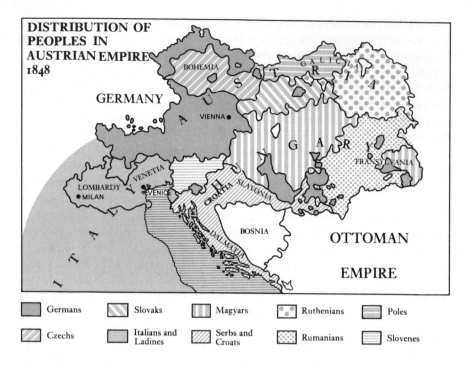

DISTRIBUTION OF
PEOPLES IN
AUSTRIAN EMPIRE
1848

Germans	Slovaks	Magyars	Ruthenians	Poles
Czechs	Italians and Ladines	Serbs and Croats	Rumanians	Slovenes

(Magyar, with many minorities, notably Serb and Croat), Galicia (mainly Ruthenians and Poles, acquired during the partitions of Poland), Transylvania (Roumans, of Latin origin), Illyria and Dalmatia (Serbs and Croats), and Lombardy and Venetia (Italians). It thus contained, besides oddities like the Magyars, representatives of the so-called great 'racial' divisions of Europe – the Teuton (the Germans), the Slav (the Czechs, Croats, Poles and Serbs), and the Latin (the Roumans and Italians). As yet, with the exception of some of the Italians and possibly some of the Germans of Austria itself, the new wine of nationalism and democracy had not yet reached the heads, or even the lips, of most of these peoples, and so the central government in Vienna was not in immediate danger of being challenged.

This was all the more so since the government at Vienna permitted a wide variety of local difference, employed local officials rather than bureaucrats from Vienna, and generally allowed a very considerable degree of liberty, provided that no political agitation of any kind took place. Hungary enjoyed a separate parliament, or Diet, in which its intensely feudal nobility frequently asserted their privileges against Vienna. It was, further, no part of the policy of Metternich to attempt to 'Germanize' or 'Austrianize' the whole of the Empire – he was not keen enough on nationalism to enforce his own particular brand of it, while he correspondingly denied the right of the other brands to break away from his 'international' Empire. The government of Vienna, however, while well-meaning and not unduly tyrannical, was for the most part inefficient. It was badly in need of reorganisation, and Metternich made several efforts to induce his imperial master to accept schemes of reform. Purely internal matters, however, were the subject on which he possessed least influence, for his role above all was that of foreign minister: 'I have sometimes ruled Europe', he once remarked, 'but I have never governed Austria'.

Germany

In the matter of race, Germany presented a very different picture from the

Austrian Empire, as it was inhabited solidly by Germans. Politically, however, it had even less unity. Before the Napoleonic wars some eight or nine larger states (including Prussia, Bavaria and Saxony) and over three hundred smaller ones had existed, all forming part of the Holy Roman Empire and acknowledging the authority in name, though very little in fact, of the Emperor – to which position the Hapsburg ruler of Austria had for centuries been elected.[1] Napoleon's campaigns in Germany, however, had broken down many of the old divisions and finished off the shadowy Holy Roman Empire. Napoleon had also created some new and more powerful units, such as his Confederation of the Rhine. Within these a great deal of administrative reform had been carried out, and large sections of Germany had been released from medieval restrictions for the first time. The peacemakers of Vienna naturally allowed no place to such Napoleonic creations – they had collapsed, anyway, with the breakdown of Napoleon's power – and consequently a fresh settlement was necessary in 1814–15.

The Congress of Vienna made no attempt to revive the defunct Holy Roman Empire. The Hapsburg Emperor himself readily consented to the abandonment of the title whose history had begun with Charlemagne in 800 AD, because Austria had set herself the task of consolidating a really strong Austrian Empire centred round the great natural economic link of the Danube. At the same time she was not prepared to see the growth of a powerful northern rival, to take over her role as leader of Germany, and this fact, taken together with the claims of the various royal houses of Germany, made it certain that there would be no strong German state created. The hundreds of states had, now, by the force of circumstances, been boiled down to a mere thirty-nine, but the Confederation into which these were formed was deliberately kept as weak as possible. Its Diet consisted purely of ambassadors of the various states, not representatives elected by the peoples. Its members undertook not to declare war on one another and to provide protection if attacked, but no law was binding on any member-state unless that particular state approved of the law in question. This alone, with the fact that unanimity was necessary for any change in the constitution, made the Confederation almost powerless. The monarchs of Austria (on account of her German lands) Britain (on account of Hanover), Denmark (on account of Holstein), and Holland (on account of Luxembourg) were all represented in the Diet, and none of these had any interest in the development of a strong Germany.

The weakness of the Confederation disappointed those Germans who had hoped for a greater measure of national union, but it was not surprising. There was in fact no agreement on any particular form of closer union and the powerful forces of local patriotism were all against any effective central government. However, though the Confederation was left weak, its members were enjoined by the Vienna Act to grant constitutions to their subjects. Germany might thus perhaps look forward to a period of increasing liberalism, though not to one of increasing German unity.

This hope proved false. Only four or five rulers carried out their promise to grant a constitution, and none of these constitutions went very far in the direction of popular rights. The natural consequence was an outbreak of liberal agitation, particularly among the numerous university students and their professors. Often this found a centre in the newly formed student patriotic organisations (*Burschen-*

The German Confederation

Liberal protests

---

[1] For Germany before 1789, see p. 4.

DEMONSTRATION AT THE WARTBURG FESTIVAL, 1817
French corsets – worn by Prussian officers – were among the 'unpatriotic' articles burnt by German students during the Festival, which turned out to be a demonstration in favour of a more united and liberal Germany.

1. Wartburg Festival, 1817

schaften) which had sprung up in sixteen of the German universities. In 1817 in Saxony there occurred the 'Wartburg Festival', a meeting of the *Burschenschaften* to celebrate the fourth anniversary of the battle of Leipzig and the tercentenary of Martin Luther's protest against papal indulgences. The intention was also to form a closer union among German university students. The students marked the occasion by burning a number of selected 'guys', some books and periodicals the views of which they resented, and a few emblems of Prussian militarism, which was disliked both for itself and for having adopted French fashions. These emblems included a corporal's cane, a pig-tail as worn by the infantry, and a pair of corsets as sported by the cavalry. It was only a student demonstration, but its spirit was unmistakable, and Metternich took good notice of it, the more so since he suspected the Tsar Alexander, who from 1815 had been under the influence of liberalism, of fomenting similar trouble throughout Europe.

Two years later a much more sensational student act occurred, the murder of Kotzebue. He was an unpopular author of reactionary views and a spy in Russian pay who was regarded as poisoning the mind of Alexander against liberalism. Round about the same time, another student attempted to assassinate a leading minister in one of the German states. At once Metternich seized his opportunity. He won over Alexander so completely from the last of his liberalism that in 1820 the Tsar said to him:

> 'To-day I deplore all that I said and did between 1815 and 1818. I regret the time lost: we must study to retrieve it. You have correctly judged the condition of things. Tell me what you want and what you want of me, and I will do it.'

It was a remarkable admission, but then, as Metternich said, 'Alexander's mind never could pursue one line of thought for long'. More important still, he used the occassion to secure the endorsement by the Diet of the Confederation of a series of laws designed to crush all political agitation. These, originally drawn up in Carlsbad at a conference of nine of the leading states called by Metternich, were known as the Carlsbad Decrees. By them a strict censorship was everywhere set up, 'investigators' of recent activities were appointed, student societies were suppressed, political meetings were forbidden; professors were dismissed, liberal leaders sentenced to years of imprisonment. The result was for Metternich a triumph; liberalism in Germany and Austria was crippled for nearly a generation to come. The German race, hampered in its efforts at political expression, had to find full scope for its genius in such strictly non-political subjects as science and music.

The stranglehold which Metternich thus helped to secure was remarkably complete. Though the fall of the Bourbons in France in 1830 produced repercussions all over Europe (including revolutions in Belgium, Poland and Rome), the Austrian Empire and Germany remained free from any really serious disturbance. In Germany, indeed, there was agitation and the inhabitants of four states succeeded in wringing constitutions from their rulers, but that was all. By 1833 it was clear that the rulers everywhere were once more on top. In fact, from the Carlsbad Decrees till the revolutionary stirrings of 1847–49 there was no political event of significance for the future of German liberalism or nationalism.

There was, however, a movement of a mainly economic character which was destined to have very great results. In 1816 Prussia had abolished a vexatious remnant of medievalism when she repealed all her internal customs duties and made the transit of goods from one district of Prussia to another quite customs-free. Two years later she instituted a common tariff for her whole kingdom, as against the goods of other states. It was very low or non-existent on raw materials, and only about ten per cent on most manufactures. She also invited neighbouring states to join this large customs-area, and those small states which were completely surrounded by Prussian territory quickly saw the advantages of doing so. From about 1828 this invitation was made a little more pressing by putting very heavy tariffs on the goods of external neighbours who did not accept it. This Prussian customs union quickly showed remarkable signs of success – so much so that it was resented by other German states, which formed opposition groups, including a south-western union of Bavaria and Würtemberg and a 'middle' union covering

2. Murder of Kotzebue, 1819

'Conversion' of Alexander

Carlsbad Decrees, 1819

The Zollverein

Hanover, Hesse Cassel and other states. The opposition groups, however, found themselves gradually forced by economic pressure to come to terms with the Prussian one, so that by 1829 the association centring round Bavaria had signed a treaty and the middle association was beginning to break up, with its members coming in one by one. In 1833 the southern union finally joined the enlarged Prussian one, and with the addition the same year of Saxony and the Thuringian states the scene was set to proclaim, as from 1st January 1834, the existence of the German Customs and Commercial Union, usually known as the Zollverein. In the ensuing years, helped by the building of the first German railways, this union prospered and attracted other German states, so that by 1844 the Zollverein covered nearly all Germany. Hanover and Hamburg were perhaps the most important exceptions.

Though Germany in the 1840s still lacked any effective political union, it was thus on the way to economic union, and the importance of this fact must not be overlooked. Moreover, through the Zollverein Prussia rather than Austria was taking the lead in Germany. The economic advancement by this time, especially in Prussia, was not confined to getting rid of customs barriers. New roads had been built, a modern postal system initiated, railways constructed, steampower introduced, while side by side with this, great developments in education, such as the founding of polytechnics, schools, gymnasia, were apparent. After a period during

Development of Prussia

which Prussia had seemed to lose all desire to follow the tradition of her great reformers of the 1806 period, Stein, Hardenberg, and Scharnhorst, she began to revert to her policy of equipping herself as a really modern state. In this the main guiding force was her devoted and efficient civil service.

A change of monarchs

The changes on the thrones of Austria and Prussia during these years were matters of importance. In 1835 the Emperor Francis, steady, conservative, far from brilliant but trusting implicitly in Metternich, died. He was succeeded by

1. Ferdinand in Austria

Ferdinand, described by Palmerston in his usual round terms as 'the next thing to an idiot'. Thenceforward Metternich's advice was not always followed, and from about 1840 on he had to intrigue to keep his position at court. The presence of an opposite party to the Chancellor's at court encouraged liberalism in Austria to hope once more.

2. Frederick William IV in Prussia

In Prussia, too, the greatly respected old man, Frederick William III, like Metternich and Francis a survival from Napoleonic days, also died, and was succeeded in 1840 by Frederick William IV. The character of the new King, who was known to be religious, humane, and anxious to avoid all forms of persecution, caused a great revival of the partly neglected moves for constitutionalism and a greater degree of national union. The composition in 1840, for example, of the famous patriotic song 'Die Wacht am Rhein' ('The Watch on the Rhine') showed which way sentiment was moving. The appointment of well-known patriots and

Revival of liberalism

even liberals as the principal Prussian ministers, together with a relaxation of the censorship, seemed to confirm Prussians in the opinion that their King was indeed of progressive outlook. Unfortunately, however, it is difficult for a king (or a pope) to be liberally or democratically inclined when the increased demands resulting from his encouragement begin to outrun what he himself desires. Frederick, who was in truth no liberal at all but a religious autocrat with humane sympathies, rapidly found himself in this position. He soon ended the experiment of a milder censorship. He did, however, do something towards the establishment of the constitution which Frederick William III had promised Prussia as far back as 1815; he permitted a Parliament or Diet to meet for all Prussia in 1847. It consisted of the deputies from the local and rather powerless Diets of the separate Prussian provinces. As it was not directly elected, however, and as Frederick William refused to allow regular meetings or anything more than mere debating rights, it was of little use to enthusiastic liberals. In fact, the idea of a written constitution which would truly limit his power deeply shocked him, for he had a strong conception of the Divine Right of his position. 'Never will I consent', he said, 'that a written paper should intrude like a second Providence between our Lord God in Heaven and this country, to govern us through its paragraphs.'

The demand for more representative forms of government in both Austria and Germany, however, was soon to enter a new phase. In Germany the failure of the potato crop of 1846, the doubled price of wheat in 1847, the thousands dying of hunger-typhus, had all reacted powerfully on the various state governments. **Economic distress** These factors were partly responsible for Frederick William's decision to call a Prussian parliament. All over Europe, economic distress was giving an extra spur to political agitation. The first big instance of actual rebellion came in 1846 – unsuccessfully – from discontented Poles in the last piece of semi-independent Polish territory, the 'Free City' of Cracow, in Galicia. For help against the rebels the city authorities turned to the Austrians – who soon took advantage of the situation to incorporate the territory into the Austrian Empire. Then in 1847 the more demo- **Risings** cratic cantons of Switzerland took action against the Sonderbund (a 'separate league' of the seven Catholic and more conservative cantons formed in 1845 under Austrian patronage), and broke it up. In January 1848 there were risings in Sicily, followed the next month by outbreaks on the mainland of Italy. Finally, on 24th February 1848 the Orleans monarchy of Louis Philippe fell in France. Like fireworks touched off one from the other, liberal revolutions then erupted throughout Europe – and not least in Austria and Germany.

2. The Revolutionary Movements in the Austrian Empire, 1848–51

The revolutions of 1848 were remarkable for their dramatic suddenness. The news of the fall of the Orleans monarchy reached Vienna on 1st March; by 13th March Metternich, the statesman of forty years' experience, was fleeing from the capital with a forged passport 'like a criminal' and rulers were making frantic concessions all over Germany to save their tottering thrones. The revolutions in Germany were profoundly affected by the revolutions in Austria, and for the sake of clarity it may be well to follow first the revolutionary movements in the Austrian Empire.

The part of the Austrian Empire which enjoyed the greatest opportunity for the **Hungary** expression of national feeling was Hungary. Here a separate Diet had long existed, in which the proud Magyar nobility frequently strove to assert independent claims against Austria. At the same time Hungary itself, like most of the Austrian Empire, was in an intensely backward state, with the nobility still preserving medieval feudal privileges over the peasantry and enjoying complete exemption from taxation. Already in Hungary, led by the fiery young lawyer-journalist Louis Kossuth, a movement to introduce liberal reforms had arisen. Kossuth's first **Kossuth** demand was that the debates of the Diet should be held in Magyar, not Latin. He

KOSSUTH IN 1848

Lajos (Louis) Kossuth, lawyer, journalist, orator, and great Hungarian patriot, became the main figure in the Hungarian revolt of 1848–49 against Austria. After its suppression he lived in exile, demanding a separate Hungarian republic and refusing to accept the Austrian concessions of 1867 which established the Dual Monarchy of Austria-Hungary.

also insisted, contrary to government regulations, on circulating reports of the debates held in the Diet and in the local assemblies. In his efforts to outwit the police and the law he was reduced to having his pamphlets lithographed instead of printed, and then finally to having them copied out by hand. Not surprisingly imprisonment followed, but on his release after three years he continued the campaign with heroic determination. By 1844 he had helped to force the Austrians into recognising that Magyar should be the language not only of the Hungarian Diet, but of law, government business, and public education throughout Hungary. In 1847 Kossuth, despite his lack of landed property, was elected as member for

Budapest to the new Diet. Though the Magyar nobility disapproved of most of his ideas, nearly all could accept his championing of Hungary as against Austria.

Immediately after hearing the news of the 1848 revolution in France, sensing that the hour of radical change had struck, Kossuth on March 3rd came out with a flaming speech in the Hungarian Diet. 'From the charnel-house of the Viennese system', he said, 'a pestilential breath steals over us which paralyses our nerves and deadens our national spirit.' He demanded not only that Hungary should be equal to Austria in all respects, enjoying a separate Hungarian ministry, but that serfdom and the nobles' privileges should be abolished and a constitutional system established, with liberty of the Press, of meeting, and of association. Support of Kossuth's policy was not lacking from the ordinary citizens of Budapest, who succeeded in making their own nobles accept a 'People's Charter'. In March and April 1848 a series of laws (the 'March and April Laws') were carried through the Hungarian Diet at Pressburg (Bratislava), establishing the main reforms demanded by Kossuth, and setting up a new Parliament at Budapest. This was to be elected on the basis of a property qualification and Magyar speech, and it was to cover all the lands to which Hungary traditionally laid claim, including those like Transylvania and Croatia where the Roumans and the Croats respectively greatly outnumbered the Magyars. It now remained for the victorious Magyar nationalists to wring approval of these arrangements from the Austrian government.

Meanwhile in Vienna, too, events had moved in a revolutionary direction. Taking their cue from France and from Hungary, a number of students and professors held a great demonstration on 12th March. The mob cheerfully extended this the following day into fighting and an invasion of the palace, and secured important promises from a paralysed and inefficient government. The outcry naturally included yells of 'Down with Metternich!', and the government had no better policy than to sacrifice the aged Chancellor to the storm. When it called troops into Vienna they only fraternised with 'the rabble' (to use Metternich's expression). On 15th March the government promised a constitution and the formation of a National Guard, and then on 17th March had to accept the Hungarian demand for a separate ministry responsible to the Hungarian Diet alone. During the following month the Imperial Government worked out the details of the promised constitution (which proved to be a very restricted one), and conceded all the main demands put forward from Budapest. *Vienna* *Fall of Metternich*

These events were rapidly paralleled in other sections of the Empire. Before March was out local revolts had driven the Austrians out of Milan and Venice (where a republic was set up under Daniele Manin), and the King of Sardinia had declared war with the intention of expelling them from the entire Italian peninsula. At Agram in Croatia the Croats demanded the restoration of their ancient rights, while at Prague, capital of Bohemia, the Czechs framed constitutional demands similar to those of the Hungarians. To all these the shaken Imperial government agreed. Only in Italy, where war was deciding the issue, and in Galicia, where the energetic Austrian governor, Count Stadion, kept the Poles in check, did it attempt any real resistance. *Revolutions in Italy and Bohemia*

The salvation of the Austrian monarchy, however, soon came in spite of itself. In May it touched its lowest depths, when, after a feeble effort to oppose further demands by Viennese radicals, the Emperor and his family suddenly left Vienna for Innsbruck, on the frontier. At the beginning of June, too, a great Congress of *A constitution granted* *The Slav Congress*

METTERNICH IN FLIGHT FROM VIENNA, 1848
A caricature of 1848. Metternich's resignation and flight from Vienna in March 1848 opened the flood-gates to revolution in the Austrian Empire. The revolutions were suppressed and in 1851 Metternich returned – but never again held office.

the different branches of the Slav race opened in Prague to discuss possible ways of organising their racial kinship, a movement which spelled danger to an Empire of which the ruler was not by race Slavonic. But just when things seemed at their worst for the Empire, the tide began to turn. From Italy came news of the first success of the Austrian commander, Radetsky. In Prague itself the Austrian Governor, Prince Windischgrätz, found himself confronted by crowds of Czech radicals, largely students, agitating for Bohemian independence. He resisted the demand of the mob for armaments, and after a struggle in which his palace was attacked and his wife shot dead at a window, he withdrew with his troops from the

Recovery in Italy

Recovery in Bohemia

city, bombarded it all night, and by morning had completely subdued the rebels. The separatist Czechs of Bohemia had failed and one part of the Empire at least was saved.

The solution of the rest of the difficulty for the Imperial government was to come from the very fact which had caused most of the trouble – the existence of such a welter of different nationalities within the Empire. The point to bear in mind is that not only was the Empire so composed, but that each province within the Empire was practically a smaller edition of the Empire in its varying races. The Croats and Roumans under Hungarian government now found, for example, that the rule of the dominant Magyars in Hungary was rather less to their taste than that of their previous and more distant masters, the Austrians. When they claimed from the Hungarians the same liberty as the Hungarians claimed from the Austrians, they were denied it. Before long the Croats, under their beloved leader Count Jellaçic, who hated the Magyars and was a loyal servant of the Emperor, were in conflict with Hungary. They trusted Jellaçic's optimistic view that loyalty to the House of Austria would earn them more concessions than revolt. It was the obvious if unsavoury policy of the Imperial government to accentuate these national jealousies, and then watch its various enemies rend each other in pieces. Fresh hope gleamed for the monarchy, the more so since Radetsky had, in July, won a great victory over the Sardinian forces at Custozza and was soon to re-enter Milan.

The Croats quarrel with the Hungarians

Jellaçic

THE THREE PROPS OF THE AUSTRO–CROAT CIVILISATION
A French satirical cartoon following the suppression of the 1848 risings in the Austrian Empire. Left to right the three generals are Count Jellaçic, the Croat who helped to crush the Hungarians; Count Radetsky, the veteran who won the struggle in Italy; and Prince Windischgrätz, who suppressed rebels in Prague, Vienna and Hungary.

Spurred by this success and stung to action by Kossuth's extreme financial measures, which were budgeting for Hungary as a separate state, the Austrian government now definitely urged Jellaçic and his Croats to attack the new authorities in Hungary. He did so in September, and for a while was held in check and part of his army had to surrender. But a use was soon found for his troops. When another and more violent democratic outbreak occurred in Vienna itself, the government called on Jellaçic to advance there, and at the same time summoned help from Windischgrätz in Prague. So in October Windischgrätz arrived to bombard Vienna into submission as he had done Prague, while Jellaçic defeated a force of Hungarians sent by Kossuth to the rescue of the Viennese democrats. The Imperial government was thus now in control not only of the Czechs, the Croats, and the Italians, but of the Austrians themselves. With the abdication of Ferdinand in December 1848 because of his mental condition, a new Emperor, Francis Joseph, a youth of eighteen, succeeded unencumbered by any promises about constitutions. The fast-reviving monarchy could now deal with Hungary.

The Hungarians, of whom Kossuth was now virtually the dictator, soon found themselves paying the price of their intolerance to their minorities. All round Hungary the non-Magyar peoples were hostile, and in January 1849 it proved a fairly simple matter for Windischgrätz and Jellaçic to advance and capture Budapest. Kossuth and the government, however, who fled, organised resistance to the Austrians from the provinces. Much to the surprise of Europe, this proved very successful, the Hungarians defeating the racial risings on their frontiers and compelling the Austrians to withdraw from Budapest. Kossuth had by now cut the last ties asunder, and declared Hungary, in March 1849, an independent republic, of which he was 'Governor-President'. The decisive moment had arrived. The Austrian government appealed to a source from which they knew they could, in the last resort, derive help – Russia.

The Tsar Nicholas I, who hated revolutions and republics, was only too willing to aid the young Francis Joseph. Palmerston protested against the intervention, but in vain. By July an advance by the Russians from the east, by the ruthless Austrian general Haynau from the west, and by Jellaçic from the south made the result a foregone conclusion. The frantic Hungarian government's belated concessions to its minorities were useless. Kossuth and the Hungarian generals quarrelled senselessly, and finally Kossuth abdicated and fled into Turkey, burying the Iron Crown of St Stephen on the way. The last Hungarian army then laid down arms and surrendered to the Russians. The Russians handed control over to Haynau, who found the task of ordering the scores of executions and hundreds of imprisonments so congenial that at last even Vienna grew ashamed and recalled him. Both Kossuth and Haynau, incidentally, later paid visits to England. Kossuth won a tremendous welcome from the people and a reception by Palmerston in spite of the opposition of the entire Cabinet. Haynau, who had received the nickname of 'Hyena,' was chased by liberal-minded draymen when he visited a London brewery.

It remained for Austria to take advantage of her escape. In Italy, with the decisive defeat of the Sardinian army at Novara in March 1849 and the suppression of the Venetian Republic in August, the anti-Austrian movement had collapsed. The Imperial government resumed control in Lombardy and Venetia, and was apparently established there more firmly than ever. Elsewhere Roumans, Croats,

Jellaçic and Windisch-grätz save the government

Francis Joseph

Hungary declares its independence

Russia intervenes

Collapse of Hungary

Reaction triumphant

"HE WENT AWAY WITH A FLEA IN HIS EAR."—*Old Saying.*

SKETCH OF A MOST REMARKABLE FLEA WHICH WAS FOUND
IN GENERAL HAYNAU'S EAR.

A humorous presentation of one of the draymen who 'rough-housed' Haynau on his famous visit to Barclay's Brewery. The 'flea's' remark refers to a threat of disciplinary action against the draymen. It is obvious where Punch's *(and Britain's) sympathies lay. Cartoon by John Leech, 28th September 1850.*

Czechs, Hungarians, Poles, all underwent for their varying activities a tightening-up of control. By the end of 1851 the government felt sufficiently secure in Vienna to abolish the constitution for the Empire which it had granted (but not implemented) in March 1849, and reaction was everywhere triumphant. But though no portion of the Empire finally received greater national independence or constitutional freedom as a result of the events of 1848 to 1851, the feudal privileges of the nobility and the serfdom of the peasantry had disappeared never to return.

Just as the first French Revolution, in spite of the later dictatorship of Napoleon, conferred lasting benefits on the French peasantry, so did the revolutionary movements of 1848 achieve similar results for the peasantry of the Austrian Empire, in spite of the later re-establishment of full Hapsburg control.

3. The Revolutionary Movements in Germany, 1848–51

The revolutionary struggles of these years in Germany followed another pattern, since German liberal feeling was not complicated by racial differences. Whereas the subject nations of the Empire wished to weaken the central government to gain greater local liberties, most German liberals wished to set up a stronger central government to give expression to their national pride.

Liberal demands

Frederick William IV's accession to the throne of Prussia was, as we have seen, the signal for a revival of German liberalism, and he had so far kept the promise of Frederick William III that in 1847 he had called a Diet, or parliament, for his whole kingdom. It consisted of representatives from the various provincial Diets which had already existed, but which met only intermittently. With the bad harvests, starvation, and typhoid epidemics of 1846 and 1847, the liberal demands had become more urgent and the new all-Prussia parliament soon put forward requests for freedom of expression, trial by jury, an income tax, and a single National

A National Parliament

German Parliament elected by the people for the whole of Germany. They were prepared to let the old powerless Confederation Diet exist side by side with this. Frederick William, however, had quite other ideas – he had refused a written constitution for Prussia, and he had, instead of supporting the idea of a popularly elected Parliament for all Germany, wished simply to enlarge the powers of the Confederation Diet. He was particularly concerned with the problem of Austria, for as her lands were largely non-German this might lead to her exclusion from an all-German Parliament. 'Germany without Austria', he said, 'would be worse than a face without a nose.' It is not kings of this stamp who get the big things done in

Attitude of Frederick William IV

history, and Frederick William was throughout extremely nervous of allowing Prussia to take the lead. In consequence he soon fell out with his newly called Prussian parliament and dissolved it.

The fall of Louis Philippe in February 1848 – 'going out by the same door as he came in', as the Tsar Nicholas bluntly put it – aroused the same ferment in Germany as it did in the Austrian Empire. Popular movements at once occurred in many of the states, and everywhere the rulers after singularly little resistance granted their subjects constitutions or at least appointed liberal ministers. As one historian puts it – 'the fruit fell from the trembling tree at the first shock'. But for most liberals a local state constitution was not enough: some wider form of German union must be attained. Already by 5th March fifty leading liberals, chiefly from south Germany, met and debated plans for summoning a preliminary parliament (*Vorparlament*) to discuss and establish a constitution for all Germany. Most of the state governments knew better than to oppose such a scheme at such a moment, and even the old Diet contrived not to get too much in the way. So on

The *Vorparlament*

31st March the *Vorparlament*, consisting of 600 present and past members of the various state parliaments, actually met at Frankfurt. That could not have happened, however, unless not only the minor governments but Austria and Prussia had been

RIOT IN BERLIN, 1848
From a contemporary engraving.

seriously weakened by revolution. Austria, we have seen, was out of action by 15th March, when Metternich fled. Prussia's turn, as we shall now see, came on 18th and 19th March.

Following the news of the fall of Metternich in Vienna an outcrop of public meetings, addresses for reform, and the like occurred in Berlin until soldiers were eventually called on to fire to clear the streets. Frederick William, however, a great lover of peace, sincerely hated actions like this, and on 18th March he agreed to the idea of a constitution and parliament for the whole of Germany. He also abolished the censorship in Prussia. But in the afternoon another, almost accidental, clash between crowd and troops took place, and in two or three hours Berlin was up in barricades and revolution. The poor King went nearly frantic wondering whether

Rising in Berlin

to order the troops to attack the barricades. Finally, on the morning of the 19th, after a tortured night, he decided to withdraw his soldiers and even to go one step further by granting the rioters' demand for arms. Later in the day a new liberal ministry was appointed and the King and Queen had to appear on the balcony of the palace to salute the corpses of citizens killed fighting against the royal troops.

'Prussia merged in Germany'

On the 21st he issued a proclamation in which he used the famous phrase that 'henceforth Prussia is merged in Germany', and was compelled to spend the day riding round promising nearly everything demanded. He afterwards referred to it as the most terrible day in his life.

When the German *Vorparlament* met at Frankfurt on 31st March it thus felt confident in the fact that the monarchs of both Austria and Prussia were too weak to oppose the national movement. The *Vorparlament* (a hundred and forty-six members of which came from Prussia, but only two from Austria) was consequently able to order elections to be held for a real parliament, or National Assembly, and to dissolve itself. By May this National Assembly had met, also at Frankfurt.

National Assembly at Frankfurt

It was an extraordinarily talented body, containing several of the best-known names in German literature and scholarship at the time. Many of its members, like those of the parliaments of the first French Revolution, were lawyers; many were state officials; landowners and manufacturers on the one hand, and working-class citizens on the other, however, were sadly lacking. It was essentially representative of the professional middle classes, the leaders of liberal opinion at the time.

A number of extremely difficult tasks confronted the Assembly, the first one being the drawing up of a constitution which would be at once liberal and acceptable to the various state governments. It was not too hard to compile a list of citizens' rights, such as equality in law, freedom from arbitrary arrest, freedom of speech, of the press, and of public meeting – the French 'Declaration of the Rights of Man' served as a classic example of this sort of thing. It was, again, quite easy to announce that all German states should have a constitution and a really representative government. All this was actually pronounced as law in December 1848. What was not so simple, was to get it all carried out by Austria, Prussia, and the other governments, even if they were temporarily weak. Yet a far more serious problem arose when the position of Austria was considered. Before this happened the

The difficulties about Austria –

Assembly had already lost prestige when it reluctantly approved Frederick William's withdrawal of support from the German party in Schleswig-Holstein, who were fighting against the incorporation of these two duchies into the Danish monarchy.[1] A day of bloodshed and riots in Frankfurt had followed, nationalist

– and Schleswig-Holstein

extremists in the mob demonstrating in favour of continuing the war and if necessary fighting the King of Prussia too.[2] Consequently by the time the Assembly came to tackle the vexed question of who or what was to be the central authority in the new Germany and what exactly Austria's position was to be, much of the early confidence had disappeared.

The difficulty about Austria was the fact that most of the Austrian Empire was non-German. The Assembly was thus faced with three possible solutions: to admit

[1] See pp. 143–47.

[2] Many of the liberals in the National Assembly were highly nationalist. They would have had no compunction about taking over all the territory they claimed as German, even though some of it had large non-German populations (e.g. Danes and Poles).

all the Austrian Empire into the new Germany, to admit only the German part of it, or to admit none of it. All of them had fatal drawbacks. It would be nonsensical to admit Austria's thirteen different races into a state specially formed to express German nationalism; but to exclude them would be to offend Austria. The third possibility, of omitting Austria entirely, was viewed with horror by Frederick William and by many other Germans. Thus the solution eventually favoured was the second, that of inviting Austria to be a part of the new state in virtue of Austria proper, but to exclude her Empire. This could not be acceptable to Austria, as it would mean that she would be split into two different states. The Austrian government therefore refused such an invitation, and maintained that the whole Assembly should be abolished and the old Confederation restored, possibly with larger powers. As yet, however, Austria could not take any more active steps in opposition, for with the Empire crumbling on account of the various nationalist movements she was powerless.

The opposition of Austria to the ideas of Frankfurt compelled the Assembly to look to the next greatest state, Prussia, for leadership. It was not by any great majority that the Crown of the new 'German Empire' was offered to Frederick William, for by this time there were few illusions as to his views and character. He had, too, by now recovered his position in Prussia somewhat by granting a constitution which still preserved a great deal of monarchial power. Nevertheless if it could not be Austria it must be Prussia, and so the invitation was duly tendered to Frederick William (March 1849).

The Assembly offers Frederick William the German Crown

Frederick William, now feeling more confident, had little hesitation in refusing the 'crown of shame' offered by a revolutionary assembly, or rather, declaring that he would not accept it until it was offered by the various kings and princes of Germany. This at the time, as he well knew, was an impossibility. Further, he knew that Austria was entirely opposed to the whole movement and equally to Prussian leadership of it, and that acceptance of the crown might mean war. The Tsar Nicholas too was almost equally likely to pour troops into Germany to stop a nationalist liberal movement. There was, moreover, his historic duty as King of Prussia – would it not be better from that point of view to follow the ideas of a young politician named Bismarck, and aim at absorbing other German states into Prussia rather than sinking Prussia into Germany? So Frederick William kept to the path of conservatism and prudence, admitting frankly that 'Frederick the Great would have been the man for such an occasion – as for himself, he was not a great ruler'. He followed this up by refusing the consent of Prussia to the whole laboriously compiled national constitution, and by withdrawing the Prussian delegates from Frankfurt. Prussian troops, too, were used to put down subsequent insurrections in Germany. Austria had already withdrawn her delegates, the other monarchs soon followed suit, and by the end of 1849 the last vestiges of the Assembly and its constitution had disappeared. Thus ended in failure a great design to combine German nationalism and liberalism, nobly planned but extremely difficult to execute. It was one of the great tragedies of nineteenth-century history that Germany should eventually achieve union not through the liberal idealism of Frankfurt but through the Machiavellian realism of Bismarck.

Prussia withdraws from Frankfurt

The story had one tail-piece. In 1849 Frederick William agreed to the creation of some more acceptable and less democratic alternative in the form of a union of any willing states under Prussian leadership. This started promisingly, receiving

An alternative Prussian union

IRELAND
Minor revolt
against Britain

ENGLAND
Chartism
flares up

BELGIUM
Riots

FRANCE
Exit Louis Philippe
(Feb) The Second
Republic

GERMAN CONFEDERATION
Many revolts for constitutions and National
Parliament (February-March onwards)

SWITZERLAND
Defeat of Sonderbund.
New Federal
Constitution

RUSSIA
Nicholas I helps Turkey to
crush revolts (July). In 1849,
helps Austria against
Hungarians

AUSTRIAN EMPIRE
Revolts by Viennese, Hungarians
and Czechs (March- April and onwards)

ITALY
Revolts in Sicily, Naples, Tuscany,
Papal States (Jan.-Feb.) and Parma.
Lombardy and Venice, later helped
by Sardinia-Piedmont, revolt against
Austrians (March)

OTTOMAN EMPIRE
Revolts in Moldavia and
Wallachia

EVENTS OF 1848

the adhesion of several petty states and a few of the larger ones, besides the approval of a large group of the late delegates to Frankfurt. A constitution was even drawn up, elections held, and a parliament called. At the critical moment, however, owing to the opposition of Austria and the largest states, Frederick William abandoned this his latest offspring, which accordingly perished. For a moment he thought of resisting when the old Confederation was not only resurrected by Austria but also encouraged to support one notorious German tyrant in his quarrel with his subjects. But at the last minute, after Prussian troops were mobilised, he again gave way, and at Olmütz agreed to the Austrian demands. Nothing was left but to accept the revival and the activities of the Confederation in its 1815 form.

The Olmütz
Submission, 1851

So Austria, secure again in her own house, triumphed all along the line, not only over revolution but also over Prussia. Of all the turmoil of 1848–49 in central Europe the only notable gain for liberalism, apart from the freedom won by peasants from their lords in the Austrian Empire, was the watered-down constitution which survived in Prussia. Monarchy was 'on top' again, the various 'rabbles' subdued, nationalist claims frustrated. In 1851, as though to complete the restoration of the old Europe, shaken but still supreme, there returned to Vienna, to live for some years yet as a revered 'Elder Statesman' – Metternich.

Monarchy on top again

CHAPTER 11
The Unification of Italy

1. From the 1815 Settlement to the 1848 Revolutions

We are often apt to forget that Italy, like Germany, is a fairly recently created state. England was already a single national state in the Middle Ages, but both Italy and Germany were made up of many different states until little over a century ago. In the case of Italy some of these states were even under foreign rule. We now have to follow the process by which, during the nineteenth century, the *country* Italy (or 'geographical expression', as Metternich put it) became the *state* Italy.

The first big changes, though most of them were only temporary, came during the Revolutionary and Napoleonic wars. Napoleon's Italian campaigns and subsequent arrangements wiped out many of the old divisions,[1] but his re-organisation lasted only until his downfall. He himself at first aroused the enthusiasm of many Italians by his promises of reform and freedom, and almost everywhere his government introduced modern ideas and improvements in administration. He abolished relics of feudalism, broke down church monopolies, established the enlightened French legal codes, built roads and bridges. He also greatly simplified the political arrangements of Italy. Although the islands of Sardinia and Sicily, protected by the British navy, remained outside his grasp, he reduced the mainland to only three divisions. These consisted of: first, an area under direct French rule as part of the French Empire (including, after 1809, the Papal States); secondly, a so-called Kingdom of Italy in the north and east; and thirdly, the Kingdom of Naples (under Jerome Bonaparte and later Murat). Ultimately, however, as in all territories he conquered, Napoleon aroused the hostility of the inhabitants by repressive police measures and taxation. He also imposed conscription and robbed Italy of many of its most precious works of art. Nevertheless, as the heir to the French Revolution he inspired many of the more educated Italians with a strong desire for political progress.

Work of Napoleon I

The post-war arrangements ran counter to any wishes of this kind. As we have seen, the men who framed the settlement at Vienna and elsewhere were out of sympathy with the growing forces of liberalism and nationalism. They were much more concerned with stability, and so usually favoured a return to the old order.

Divisions of Italy in 1815

[1] For Italy before the French Revolution, see pp. 3–4.

When Italy was reorganised on the fall of Napoleon many of the old political divisions accordingly reappeared – and the power of Austria was doubled by her acquisition of Venetia. In all more than a dozen states were now recognised in Italy. With some unimportant exceptions, these fell into five main groups. From south to north, they were:

1. *Naples and Sicily*, or the 'Kingdom of the Two Sicilies,' poverty stricken, infested with brigands, and ruled with cruelty and inefficiency by Ferdinand I, a member of the Spanish branch of the Bourbon family. Originally Naples and Sicily had been separate kingdoms under the same ruler, but Ferdinand brought them together into a single state.

2. *The Papal States*, or the States of the Church, ruled by the Pope and therefore by now invariably by an Italian, but among the worst-governed regions of the country. The clergy had a stranglehold over freedom of expression, and the Inquisition and torture might be used against those whose politics were liberal or whose ideas were considered too modern. It was even dangerous to state that the earth revolved around the sun, since the medieval Church had thought otherwise. Only about two per cent of the rural population could read. As the century wore on, the development of communications was to be hindered for many years by the Pope's refusal to allow the railway and the telegraph within his domains.

3. *Modena*, *Parma and Tuscany*, in central Italy, were the three main independent duchies. All of them were better governed than the states of the south, and their rulers were more concerned with the cultural welfare of their subjects than were the Pope or Ferdinand. This applied especially to the Duchess of Parma, Napoleon's second wife, the easy-going Marie Louise. But all three rulers were tainted with one unforgiveable sin in the eyes of nationalistically-minded Italians – they were under the domination of Austria. The rulers of Parma and Tuscany were Hapsburgs; the ruler of Modena was married to one.

4. *Lombardy and Venetia*, linked together in a new kingdom under an Austrian viceroy, formed part of the Austrian Empire. Lombardy, with its capital Milan, was the most fertile province in Italy, and Venetia, with Venice as its chief port, was probably the richest trading centre. The Austrians governed much better than did the Pope or Ferdinand. Nearly every town had an elementary school and most had secondary schools. But the most efficient department of government was unfortunately the police, whose supervision was extremely strict. Austrian spying was very highly organised. One lady remarked in Vienna at the time of the Congress: 'My daughter cannot sneeze but Prince Metternich will know of it'. Every modern history book was sent to Vienna for censorship, and no freedom of discussion on political matters, either in public or in the press, was allowed. Thousands of political prisoners soon filled the gaols. Such a system naturally cost a great deal to maintain, and Lombardy and Venetia, though containing only an eighth of the population and an eighteenth of the territory of the Austrian Empire, had to provide a quarter of the taxes. In these circumstances the other merits of Austrian rule earned Austria no gratitude.

5. Finally, there was the *Kingdom of Sardinia*, which included Piedmont, Genoa, and Savoy, all recovered from the French. (We will call this state Sardinia for the sake of brevity, but its centre of government was Turin, in Piedmont.) None of its territories was prosperous – Sardinia was a barren island and Savoy a mountainous region inhabited largely by French. Piedmont itself was more important,

THE UNIFICATION OF ITALY 1859-70

but the only territory of much wealth was Genoa – and that resented the loss of its ancient republican status when it was merged in the Kingdom in 1815. The King then restored, Victor Emmanuel I of the house of Savoy, was a reactionary who even had parks torn up and gas-lighting abolished because they had been introduced by the French. Nevertheless to many Italians he had the supreme merit, in an age of growing national feeling, of being an Italian.

Extent of Austrian influence

To understand the situation in 1815 it is necessary to bear in mind the fact that Austrian influence was not confined to Lombardy, Venetia and the Duchies. There was an agreement between Ferdinand and Austria that no alteration should be made in the government of Naples without Austria's consent; and equally the Pope relied on the long arm of Austria to support his despotic government in the Papal States. Austria, determined to maintain existing conditions as a barrier against revolution, was thus regarded by politically-minded Italians everywhere with detestation. To those who hoped for progress, it seemed that improvement could come, unless the Papacy should suddenly reform its whole administration, only from the one really Italian state, the kingdom of Sardinia. In the course of time eyes gradually focused on this kingdom as a possible nucleus of Italian unity. That, however, occurred later; the first step was to win, not union, but local freedom from foreign or despotic rule. Meanwhile in 1815 it was true that 'Italy could no more be called a nation than a stack of timber could be called a ship'.

Carbonari and their revolt in Naples, 1820

It was not long after the Congress of Vienna that the first explosion occurred. Italy was honeycombed by secret societies aiming at political reform or the ending of foreign rule. There were many of them, but the most important were the Carbonari (literally 'charcoal-burners'), a society, or rather societies, in which much of the ritual was taken from the popular occupation of charcoal-burning, but in which liberals of the upper classes were more numerous than the poor. The great Carbonarist watchword was 'freedom'. In 1820, following a momentarily successful revolution in Spain, some leading Carbonari in Naples rebelled against Ferdinand, and being either unopposed or assisted by the royal troops, managed with absurd ease to force that monarch to issue a constitution. This was based on the Spanish one of 1812, a fairly advanced document involving the limitation of the king's power in favour of parliament, together with the abolition of many noble and clerical rights and privileges. The King swore a great oath to observe it faithfully: 'Omnipotent God – if I lie, do thou at this moment annihilate me'. Then he obtained permission from his ministers to go to the conference of Laibach 'to obtain the sanction of the powers for our newly acquired liberties'. At Laibach he

Suppression by Austria

promptly disowned the whole movement and besought Austria to send troops to restore him to his former powers. This, as we have seen, Metternich soon did.[1] The first big revolutionary effort in post-1815 Italy had failed.

Carbonari revolt in Piedmont, 1820

Meanwhile a similar outbreak had occurred in Piedmont. Its object was to wring a constitution from the elderly Victor Emmanuel I. Again taking the lead, Carbonari tried to link the movement with a revolt against the Austrians in Lombardy. After Victor Emmanuel had abdicated and Prince Charles Albert, acting as regent, had granted a constitution, the new King (the late King's brother) revoked this measure. The result was a civil war in which the forces of absolutism, aided

Collapse at Novara, 1821

by the Austrians, beat the liberals at the battle of Novara (1821). So no constitution was gained in the Kingdom of Sardinia, and in Lombardy the Austrian hold was firmer than ever.

1830-Revolt in Papal States

The year 1830, with revolutions in France and Belgium, evoked similar tremors in Italy. Again under the influence of the Carbonari, Modena, Parma and the Papal States came out in rebellion. As usual the distressed rulers' appeals to Austria fell on ready ears, and the Pope had the satisfaction of seeing the Austrian

[1] See p. 68.

whitecoats suppress his rebellious subjects. A new complication then arose, for the French, jealous of Austrian interference in the Papal States, also sent troops there to support the Pope. By this time it was clear that the local, uncoordinated Carbonarist conspiracies would make no headway against the forces of absolutism. Something greater, some more national movement was needed before anything could be done.

It was the work of Giuseppe Mazzini to supply this need. In the story of Italian unification there are three great names which stand out, all of them subjects of the King of Sardinia – Mazzini, Cavour, and Garibaldi. Of these Garibaldi was the

Mazzini

MAZZINI

Giuseppe Mazzini, liberal and republican in his political views, was the greatest prophet and propagandist of Italian unity. A member of the Carbonari and the founder of Young Italy, he was sentenced to death and spent much of his life in exile hatching plots against the rulers in his native land. A man of the highest ideals and character, he wore black – as in this portrait – in mourning for his disunited, and in many regions oppressed, country.

soldier, Cavour the statesman, and Mazzini the prophet and full-time revolutionary. From his childhood onwards Mazzini never ceased to think of the woes of his country – in fact, he always wore black as a sign of mourning for it! As soon as his student days were ended he joined the Carbonari, abandoning his hopes of becoming a great writer for the even more thorny paths of political agitation. Indeed, he came to the conclusion that no great art *could* be produced by Italians until Italy was free. Arrested and imprisoned for conspiracy after 1830 by the Sardinian government, he was soon driven from the Kingdom. The accession of the more liberal Charles Albert to the throne of Sardinia in 1831 then brought a great appeal from Mazzini, in exile in Marseille, to the King to assume the leadership of the movement for freedom.

> All Italy waits for one word – one only – to make herself yours . . . place yourself at the head of the nation and write on your banner, 'Union, Liberty, Independence' – proclaim the liberty of thought – liberate Italy from the barbarians – on this condition we bind ourselves round you, we proffer you our lives, we will lead to your banner the little States of Italy – we will preach the word that creates armies. Unite us, Sire, and we shall conquer.

'Young Italy'

Charles Albert, however, was not ready for such a programme (any more than was Italy as a whole) and Mazzini had to fall back on organising the society of 'Young Italy', This association was an effort to improve on the work of the Carbonari by appealing to a wider number of people, including the poorer classes, and by supplying a great ideal which would have the force of a religion. Its watchword was 'Unity and Independence'. As a fervent preacher of the necessity of education, self-sacrifice, and rebellion, Mazzini was so successful, and the 'Young Italy' Society took such a hold, that he was eventually exiled from France too.

From Switzerland, his next home, in 1833 Mazzini helped to organise a mutiny in the Sardinian army. This only brought down terrible punishment on the liberals from the frightened Charles Albert. In the following year Mazzini planned an invasion of Savoy, an invasion which collapsed before a shot was fired. Exiled from Switzerland, he then found refuge in England, whence he continued to direct the affairs of his Society. By this time he was a convinced republican, having long since ceased to hope anything from the King of Sardinia. His missionary work greatly fostered the desire for unity and freedom among Italians, but his strict republicanism was later to prove an obstacle when a King of Sardinia appeared who was willing to lead the national movement.

A 'liberal' Pope, 1846 – Pius IX

The next moment of importance in the making of Italy occurred in the year 1846, when a new Pope, Pius IX, was elected. The personality of Pius IX proved to be a matter of extreme importance. He was kind-hearted, hated the tortures he had witnessed in the Papal States, was prepared for limited concessions in a well-meaning and rather muddle-headed way, but was temperamentally unstable (with a tendency to epilepsy) and not at all the whole-hearted liberal he was at first taken for. But the fact that there was now a Pope who was not an out-and-out reactionary, and above all that this Pope, as the first act of his régime, released all the hundreds of political prisoners in the Papal States, was bound to make Italians expect more of him than he could give. Popular enthusiasm for the Pope rose to a great height, and intelligent reformers not only in the Papal States but also elsewhere, such as the Abbé Gioberti in Piedmont, began to hope for a great union of Italy, not under Sardinia, but under the Papacy. Metternich, like the rest of Europe, was astounded. 'We were prepared for everything except a liberal Pope', he said; 'now that we have got one there is no answering for anything.'

2. The Movements of 1848–49 and the Preparations in Piedmont

The year 1848, so momentous in France and central Europe, inevitably involved Italy in its ferment. It was from Italy, in fact, that the first explosion came, for in January 1848 the practically unarmed population of Palermo, in Sicily, rose and within a fortnight expelled Ferdinand II's garrison and defeated a relieving force. Within another fortnight, the rebels had control of almost the entire island. Once more the old 1812 constitution was proclaimed; and the King had rapidly to extend similar concessions to the other half of his realm, Naples. The agitation then spread like wildfire through the rest of Italy. In March 1848 Charles Albert of Sardinia, anxious to have the liberals with him in the war against Austria he had at last decided on, published a constitution for his realm; in the same month Pius IX reluctantly followed suit. On 17th March came the news of Metternich's flight from Vienna, and 18th March at once saw a desperate rising in Milan, where in 'the five days' of street fighting the Milanese expelled Radetsky's 20,000 troops. There was nothing for the veteran Austrian general to do but retire to the Quadrilateral, the district bounded by two rivers, the mountains, and four fortresses. On the 22nd Venice rose, expelled its Austrian garrison, and under Daniele Manin proclaimed itself an independent republic.

The moment was obviously favourable for Charles Albert to declare war on Austria. His objective was not to create a united Italy, but to expel the foreigners from northern Italy and enlarge his own kingdom. For a few precious days he hesitated, then marched an army from Piedmont into Lombardy to assist the inhabitants in their revolt against the Austrians. From the new government of Naples came a force to help him; but in April Pius IX, after reluctantly allowing a small papal force to march north, denounced the war and refused from then on to aid in any way the national cause. It was quite natural, as Pope, that he should hesitate to fight a major Catholic Power, Austria; but the decision proved a bitter disappointment to those who had hoped so much of the Pope, and it cost him the leadership of the reform movement. It was a leadership he was more than willing to surrender.

Despite the recall of the Neapolitan troops by King Ferdinand, a few minor successes greeted the opening of Charles Albert's campaign in the north. But after Radetsky had received reinforcements the chances of the Italians, fatally handicapped by divisions between Piedmontese, Lombards, and Venetians (to say nothing of those between monarchists and republicans), were slight. At last desperately attacking one wing of the Quadrilateral, Charles Albert was defeated in July at Custozza, and had to retire. By August Radetsky was back in Milan. In March 1849, following a renewed outbreak in Vienna, Charles Albert was again encouraged to march his forces into Lombardy, but once more he was beaten, this time on the battlefield of Novara, already before fatal to Italian liberal hopes. Having in vain sought death on the field, the unfortunate monarch abdicated

Revolt in Sicily, 1848

Constitutions in Sardinia and Papal States

Austrians expelled from Milan and Venice

Charles Albert attacks Austria

Pius IX disappoints

Charles Albert defeated at Custozza and Novara, 1849

Abdication of Charles Albert

in favour of his son Victor Emmanuel II and retired to Portugal, where he died heartbroken within a few months.

Meanwhile exciting events had been taking place in the southern states. In Naples King Ferdinand had succeeded in taking advantage of the chaos brought about by popular riots and inexperienced liberal ministers, and had recovered his authority. By May 1849, following intense and most cruel bombardment of Sicilian towns, which earned for Ferdinand the nickname of 'King Bomba,' Sicily too gave way. Stouter resistance, however, occurred in the Papal States. Here, in February 1849, after the murder of the reforming Papal prime minister, Rossi, the refusal of the Pope to grant a democratic constitution and his consequent

Roman Republic, 1848–49

flight to seek Ferdinand's protection, a republic had been declared. It soon came under the influence of Mazzini, who hurried there to advance the movement, and who initiated a series of great reforms in the Papal States. The Pope, however, had appealed to the powers of Europe, and had found in Louis Napoleon, President of the French Republic, a source of aid. It was not, of course, that Louis Napoleon, a man of the modern world, wished simply to restore the temporal power of the Pope – it was only that he was anxious to placate opinion at home, which at

French suppression

that time appeared to him predominantly pro-clerical. In any event the French

Louis Napoleon's holds the 'bottle' of Rome. He would like to get rid of it, but can't. From Punch, *September 1849.*

force eventually overcame the heroic resistance of the revolutionists in Rome, and by July 1849 the Roman Republic was at an end and the Pope restored. So Venice alone was left as a centre of resistance to absolutism, and by August 1849, faced with starvation, cholera, and ceaseless bombardment, Manin had at last to give in. The triumph of despotism was complete – Sicily, Naples, Rome, Lombardy, Venice, and the central Italian duchies, had all rebelled and all failed. For the cause of Italian unity the years 1848 and 1849 seemed to be entirely negative.

End of Manin's rebellion in Venice, 1849

Yet if nothing positive was achieved during the revolutionary movements of 1848–49 in Italy, at least two steps forward were taken. In the first place a bold, patriotic king genuinely concerned with national unity had succeeded to the throne of Sardinia – Victor Emmanuel II. He was a fiery little man, revoltingly ugly, with coarse tastes and passions, but his devotion to the national cause was never in doubt – a great advance over any previous king of his line. Secondly the defence of Rome against the French had not only provided an epic of resistance and proved that Italians could be heroic in the service of their ideal, but it had brought to the fore another of the real makers of Italy – Giuseppe Garibaldi.

Victor Emmanuel II of Sardinia

This remarkable man, born at Nice in Savoy, had run away from his parents at the age of fifteen and taken up a career on the sea. Won over to the society of 'Young Italy', he entered the Sardinian navy with the object of inducing it to mutiny in 1833 in favour of Mazzini's plot. The first time he saw his name in print was when, having escaped to France, he read that he had been condemned to death. He then disappeared to South America for twelve years. There he fought for Uruguay against the Brazilian Empire and Argentina, survived extreme tortures when taken prisoner, and learned in the wild South American conditions the arts of intrepid horsemanship and guerrilla warfare. He also acquired a wife, Anita, who shared his dangerous life in the saddle and on the battlefield. He had seen her from his ship through a telescope, gone straight to her house, said 'You must be mine', and stolen her from under the nose of a baffled rival! As well as a wife he acquired in South America a political or military uniform – the famous red shirt. Originally these were probably the shirts worn by Argentine slaughter-house workers, to make the blood-stains from the cattle less noticeable, but they were soon to become in Europe the garb and emblem of one of the most remarkable guerrilla forces ever created, Garibaldi's volunteers.

Garibaldi

Experiences in South America

Returning to Italy in 1848, Garibaldi threw himself into the struggles of that year with all his enthusiasm, fighting at first for the Piedmontese and Lombards against the Austrians and next for the Romans against the French. He achieved a notable victory against the attacking French troops in April 1849, but eventually had to retire before overwhelming forces, who perjured themselves by breaking an armistice before the agreed period elapsed. Hunted across Italy by the armies of France, the Pope, Austria and Naples, he succeeded in bringing a remnant of his faithful followers to the Adriatic coast, where he embarked for Venice, to assist her in her struggle. At this point, however, his wife Anita, who had insisted on joining him in all the dangers of Rome, was taken mortally ill, and he had to land prematurely to watch her die in his arms. With one companion, followed at every track and turn, he won his way across again to the other side of Italy, and finally re-embarked opposite Elba. Italy's guerrilla chief was safe for another campaign – as long as he stayed outside Italy.

Garibaldi and the Roman Republic

Though 1848 had passed in vain, at least one part of the peninsula had taken a

Reorganisation of the
Sardinian Kingdom

step towards liberty. The constitution granted to Sardinia by Charles Albert still held good, and the young King, Victor Emmanuel II, whatever his defects in taste, morals, and personal appearance, was ardently patriotic. The most interesting and significant development of the next few years was the process by which Victor Emmanuel's kingdom was transformed into a modern state. Not only was the 1848 constitution adhered to, but the problem caused by the excessive power of the Church was boldly confronted. In 1850 a series of laws was passed by which the Church was deprived of its special courts, its right of sanctuary for criminals, its right to inherit property without the consent of the government, and its monopoly of performing the ceremony of marriage. The result was not only modernisation and a quarrel with Rome which lasted till Mussolini's time, but the emergence into the limelight of a great supporter of these proposals, Count Camillo Cavour.

Cavour

Cavour, perhaps greatest of the makers of Italy, was, unlike Mazzini and Garibaldi, born an aristocrat. Trained for the army, he rapidly tired of military routine, and after coming into conflict with the authorities for supporting the French revolution of 1830 he resigned his commission. For some years he then devoted himself to agriculture on his estates in Piedmont and gained knowledge which he was later to use for his country's benefit. He became, too, a great student of British affairs, hailing with approval Catholic Emancipation and the passing of the great Reform Act of 1832. On his travels he spent many an evening in the Strangers' Gallery of the House of Commons, following the debates and making himself familiar with every detail of parliamentary practice and government. Economic subjects, like the Poor Law, Free Trade, Railways, he studied above all.

Il Risorgimento

By 1847 Cavour had helped to found a newspaper in Piedmont, *Il Risorgimento* ('Resurrection' – the name often applied to the whole movement for Italian unification). Its main object was to advocate constitutional government and the independence of all Italy from foreign rule; and Cavour's articles in this paper helped to spur Charles Albert into taking up arms against Austria. Not surprisingly, therefore, Cavour was one of the members of Sardinia's first parliament, called at Turin in Piedmont after the granting of the constitution in 1848. By 1850, following his success in pushing through the ecclesiastical laws, he was created Minister of Agriculture, Industry and Commerce; the following year he became

Prime Minister of
Sardinia, 1852

responsible for finance as well; and by the close of 1852 he was Prime Minister. In these positions he began a work of the greatest importance: the building up of the prosperity of Victor Emmanuel's realm, and particularly of Genoa and Piedmont. He removed duties, concluded trade treaties, built railways, started a service of Atlantic mail steamers, passed important laws about companies, co-operative societies and banks, and reorganised the army. Under his skilful guidance the Kingdom of Sardinia, by transforming itself into a modern state, acquired the essential equipment for the coming conflict.

3. The Unification of Italy, 1859–70

The strength of the modern state Cavour was creating was soon to be tested. Always martially-minded, Victor Emmanuel II was eager, when the Crimean War broke out, for Sardinia to join France and Britain against Russia. Not only

Sardinia and the
Crimean War, 1855–56

would this help to prevent any possible Russian supremacy in the Mediterranean, it would also stake a claim on the gratitude of Britain and France and bring Sardinia into the limelight at the peace conference. It used to be thought that this policy originated with Cavour, who was always a schemer of the deepest kind; but in fact Cavour merely seems to have played along, somewhat doubtfully but very skilfully, with the bellicose King. At all events, the outcome was successful. The Sardinian troops distinguished themselves in at least one engagement in the Crimea, and at the close of the conference of Paris in 1856 Cavour was able to draw attention to the woes of Italy and point to Austria as their main cause. Further, in answer to Napoleon III's unexpectedly direct question, 'What can I do for Italy?' Cavour not only told him but showed him how to do it. During the next two years the Franco-Sardinian friendship slowly matured. Then came the news of the terrible attempt on the Emperor's life by Orsini.[1] Italy held her breath and Cavour thought his life-work was ruined; but the strange consequence was only to bring home even more strongly to Napoleon the desirability of helping the Italian cause. So in 1858 he and Cavour concluded the pact of Plombières and the subsequent treaty by which France was to help drive the Austrians from Lombardy and Venetia, receiving as her reward from Sardinia the provinces of Savoy and Nice.

Alliance with Napoleon III, 1858

The next step was to get Austria to declare war, and to do it in such a way that Sardinia and France were not obviously in the wrong. This was achieved very skilfully by piling up arms in Piedmont, adjoining Lombardy, and arranging

War with Austria, 1859

The two 'bad men', Napoleon III and the Austrian Emperor, duel to settle the fate of the Babes (Italy and Victor Emmanuel II of Sardinia). Cartoon by Tenniel.

[1] See pp. 92–3.

appeals from the Milanese and others, till Austria, suddenly losing patience, sent an ultimatum demanding that Sardinia should disarm. She naturally refused, and Austria declared war, so appearing the aggressor. It was all against the advice of the aged Metternich, who pleaded in vain to the Austrian Emperor: 'For God's sake no ultimatum!' But Cavour was joyful – 'The die is cast' he said, 'we have made some history: now let us have some dinner.' France duly stepped in to stop the invasion of Piedmont, and by June 1859 Victor Emmanuel and Napoleon III had won the two great battles of Magenta and Solferino, thereby liberating most of Lombardy.

Magenta and Solferino

It was at this stage, as we have seen, that Napoleon, disgusted with the bloodshed, daunted by the strength of the Quadrilateral, suspicious of Cavour's designs in central Italy, and frightened by the clerical outcry at home and the menacing attitude of Prussia on the Rhine, suddenly made an armistice with the Austrian Emperor at Villafranca.[1] Cavour's rage was terrible: he resigned his post and contemplated suicide as he thought how his country was being cheated of complete success. In his desperation he even urged Victor Emmanuel to continue the war without France's help, a piece of advice which the King very sensibly rejected. Victor Emmanuel wisely concentrated on the fact that Lombardy had been freed, even if Venetia still remained in Austria's hands. He could also soon take comfort from developments in central Italy.

Napoleon III withdraws: resignation of Cavour

In 1859, when the Austrians were in the midst of their difficulties, the three main duchies of central Italy (Modena, Parma and Tuscany) had exiled their dukes, and one of the Papal States, Romagna, had successfully revolted. In each of these territories power had been taken over by men favourable to Sardinia and working closely with Cavour. These leaders managed, despite Villafranca and Cavour's resignation, to maintain their hold and persist in their policy of union with Sardinia; and by the end of 1859 Napoleon III became reconciled to this. His agreement became certain when Cavour returned to power early in 1860 and struck a bargain that if these central Italian territories were allowed to unite with Sardinia, France could have her reward (Savoy and Nice) originally arranged, but forgone when she withdrew with the job half done. Napoleon, true to the principle of the plebiscite by which he himself had risen to power, agreed to allow the union only if the people of the territories concerned so wished. The people of the three duchies did wish, and since France supported them, Austria could do nothing. Almost simultaneously Savoy and Nice, also conveniently approving the decision by plebiscite, were transferred to France. Thus the result of Napoleon's intervention finally proved to be the addition not only of Lombardy but of much of central Italy to the Sardinian Kingdom. Despite the unrelenting opposition of the republican Mazzini, who plotted desperately against Cavour, union with Sardinia was clearly the only practical way of achieving total Italian unity, now fast coming into view as a real possibility.

Revolutions in central Italy

Cavour returns to power, 1860

Lombardy, the duchies and Romagna (renamed Emilia) to Sardinia; Savoy and Nice to France, 1860

The excitements of 1859 and early 1860 were scarcely over when another decisive move occurred, this time in the south. Since the failure of the movements of 1848–49 the Kingdom of Naples had had much hostile publicity. The British liberal statesman Gladstone, who had visited some of the Neapolitan prisons during a holiday, had startled the world with the publication of his findings. Over 20,000

Naples under 'Bomba'

[1] See p. 93.

political prisoners were, he said, kept by King 'Bomba' in dungeons where the atmosphere was worse than that of a London fog. Men of the highest character and education were chained to ferocious criminals by fetters which were never on any occasion removed, night or day. Perjured evidence and unfair judges were the regular thing at trials. It was, thundered Gladstone, 'the negation of God erected into a system of government'. In vain France and Britain had protested at these conditions, and finally recalled their ambassadors. 'Bomba' remained notorious for cunning and cruelty; and even his more playful moments were marked by a fondness for crude practical jokes, such as withdrawing a chair from behind a guest about to sit on it. In 1859 he died while still king, but not before he had left to his unfortunate successor a legacy of hatred which was bound to break out in rebellion before long.

The rebellion duly came in 1860, in the southernmost half of the Neapolitan kingdom, Sicily. It was the opportunity for which Garibaldi, whose thoughts had long dwelt on the southern tyranny, had been waiting. Following his escape from Rome in 1849, when he eluded 'four armies and ten generals', he had wandered round Europe and the New World, and earned his living as a candle-maker, a sea-captain, and finally, in a little island, Caprera, off Sardinia, as a farmer. In the war of Sardinia and France against Austria in 1859 Cavour had employed him as a guerrilla captain, and he had carried on a very successful campaign in the Alps. But he, like Mazzini, was infuriated by Cavour's cession of his native Nice to France – 'They have made me', he said, 'a foreigner in the land of my birth.' Napoleon was to him 'a vulpine knave' and Cavour 'a low intriguer'. He was even planning a raid on the ballot boxes to stop the Nice plebiscite when fortunately the expedition to help the Sicilian revolt caught his imagination.

The enterprise, originally suggested by Mazzini, turned out to be one of the most thrillingly successful exploits of the century. A thousand picked volunteers gathered at Genoa, ready to sail at a moment's notice. Cavour and Victor Emmanuel played a tricky game, encouraging Garibaldi in secret but publicly hindering and disavowing him. This was partly because they were genuinely doubtful about the merits of the enterprise, partly because they had to avoid official Sardinian complicity, which might have meant war with Austria. So they stopped Garibaldi getting recruits from the army in Piedmont; they stopped him getting the modern rifles a patriotic fund had paid for. But in the long run, frightened though they were that he would, if successful, go on to attack the Papal States, which might bring about a fatal clash with France, they let him sail. Firearms, old converted flintlocks, though Cavour may not have known their condition, eventually arrived, registered as 'books'. Above all, in spite of official orders issued, nothing was done to prevent the volunteers embarking, though futile telegrams were later despatched by Cavour to order Garibaldi's arrest 'if he put into a Sardinian port'. Cavour knew, like the rest of the world, that Garibaldi was going to Sicily; but there was no harm in building up evidence which would help to keep Sardinia in the clear if the expedition failed.

The landing in Sicily at Marsala was amazingly fortunate. The governmental batteries and troops could easily have prevented it, but the two little steamers arrived together with a powerful detachment of the British navy. There was actually no connection between them – the British ships had turned up to enforce respect for British property at Marsala – but the garrison thought there was, and

Garibaldi and the Thousand, 1860

Conquest of Sicily

GARIBALDI'S LANDING AT MARSALA, 1860
Giuseppe Garibaldi and his thousand Redshirts landed at Marsala, in Sicily, almost unopposed. This started a chain of events which led within less than a year to a united (though incomplete) Kingdom of Italy. In this contemporary lithograph, Garibaldi is seen bearing the flag of Victor Emmanuel II – the tricolour of revolutionary Italy on which is superimposed the white cross of the House of Savoy.

frightened at the prospect of taking on the might of Britain, refrained from firing at the Thousand, who coolly disembarked. Even the red shirts at first were taken for British uniforms, and when at length the government commander realised his mistake it was too late: the invading force had landed with the loss of one man wounded in the shoulder and one dog wounded in the leg. From that romantic beginning, the Thousand, brilliantly led by their chief and supported by the sympathy and finally the physical force of the inhabitants, soon conquered Sicily. Perhaps the peak point was when Garibaldi's men, with only 370 muskets left between them, watched 20,000 defeated Neapolitan troops march away. It had all been accomplished inside a bare two months.

Conquest of Naples   The elated Garibaldi, after toying with the idea of invading the Papal States by sea, next proposed to cross the Straits of Messina, land in southern Italy, and continue the good work on the mainland of the Neapolitan kingdom. This was very satisfactory to Cavour as long as Garibaldi still managed to forget his old republicanism and remained faithful to the new watchword he had agreed to adopt: 'Italy and Victor Emmanuel'. But would he? And would he go on to take the dreaded step of attacking Rome? Cavour was highly nervous, but again he decided to risk it. The ability of Garibaldi to cross the Straits depended in the last resort on the dominant naval power in the Mediterranean – Britain. If Britain ranged her battleships there, he could not get across. Napoleon III, frightened of an attack on Rome and now also disturbed at the rapid growth of Sardinia, proposed to Britain that a joint Anglo-French force should close the Straits to Garibaldi. The leaders of the British cabinet, however, were three very good friends of Italian unity – Palmerston, Russell and Gladstone. They appealed to Cavour to know what were his wishes. Cavour, again using the tactics of deceit, openly requested Britain to join with France in stopping Garibaldi – and privately sent a special envoy to beseech Russell to do no such thing. So Britain let it be known that she was strongly against any Anglo-French intervention; and with the way cleared, Garibaldi was on the mainland by September 1860. Victor Emmanuel, incidentally, had as part of the same double game sent him a public message forbidding him to cross and a private one suggesting he should disobey! As Cavour not inaptly remarked, 'If we had done for ourselves the things which we are doing for Italy, we should be great rascals.' **Britain gives indirect help**

Once on the mainland Garibaldi's progress resembled a triumphal march. His welcome on all sides was such that the King fled his capital to a more easily defensible position, and Garibaldi was able to enter Naples without opposition. Then came the critical moment – would he remain faithful to Victor Emmanuel or, if he now swept into the Papal States, might he not alienate France by attacking Rome? Might he not even cling to his temporary dictatorship in the south until he could ensure the establishment of a republic? The republican Mazzini had now arrived in Naples; and Mazzinian republicans had helped to organise the original expedition to Sicily. Cavour, after desperate thought, took the biggest decision of his life. Risking the chance of Austria's declaring war on Sardinia, he advised Victor Emmanuel to send his army from Tuscany and Lombardy to invade the Papal States, so forestalling Garibaldi. **Sardinia invades Papal States**

Cavour's object was twofold. Undoubtedly he wanted to stop the fame of Garibaldi overshadowing Victor Emmanuel too completely. More important, however, was the consideration that while capturing most of the Papal States, the Sardinian forces could do what Garibaldi would never do – stop short of Rome itself and so avoid falling out with France. The move was brilliantly successful. Victor Emmanuel's troops easily defeated the small Papal army at Castelfidardo, and quickly overran the Papal States. Garibaldi, with Victor Emmanuel's army now crossing into the Kingdom of Naples, had to recognise the inevitable. In October, having reluctantly arranged for a plebiscite (which resulted, as elsewhere in the south, in enormous majorities for annexation to Sardinia), Garibaldi met Victor Emmanuel north of Naples and greeted him as 'King of Italy'. It remained then for Garibaldi to surrender his temporary dictatorship, to introduce Victor Emmaneul to the city of Naples, to hear with pain the monarch's inevitable decision to disband his volunteers, and to sail off to retirement in Caprera. He **Castelfidardo**

Naples, Sicily, and Papal States (except Rome) annexed to Sardinia, 1860

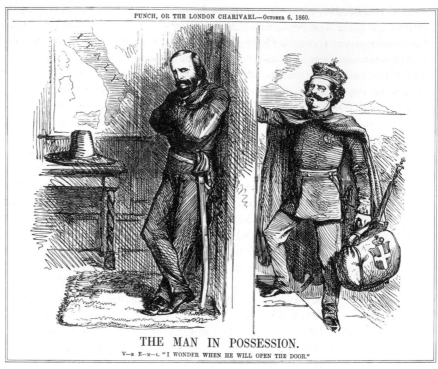

THE MAN IN POSSESSION.

V—r E—m—l. "I WONDER WHEN HE WILL OPEN THE DOOR."

Will Garibaldi surrender Sicily and Naples to Victor Emmanuel? Cartoon by Tenniel.

refused all honours, including a dukedom. He took with him only a few hundred francs of borrowed money and a bag of seed-corn.

The unification of the greater part of Italy was now an established fact. Following the addition of Lombardy in 1859, and the duchies and Romagna (Emilia) in 1860, Naples, Sicily and all the Papal States except Rome had now thrown in their lot with Sardinia. In 1861 a new parliament for all the realm met at Turin and the constitutional kingdom of Italy was proclaimed. Yet there remained, in addition to a few less important districts, two vital parts of Italy still outside the fold – two gaping wounds still unhealed. They were Venetia and Rome itself – the one held by the Austrians, the other by French troops on behalf of the Pope.

Kingdom of Italy, March 1861

Death of Cavour, 1861

Only three months after the establishment of the new Kingdom Cavour died at the age of fifty. He was worn out by over-work, and upset by a violent scene with Garibaldi in the new parliament. His untimely death robbed the new Italy of the man who might have prevented the chaos of the next few years. In 1862 Garibaldi, impatient as ever, with some volunteers from Sicily made a dash for Rome. He had to be held up by Victor Emmanuel's troops, and while trying to prevent civil war was shot in the foot. It was a terrible humiliation. Another was to follow in 1866,

Italy and Prussia fight Austria, 1866

when Prussia persuaded Italy to ally with her in a war against Austria.[1] The Italians were badly beaten by the Austrians on land at Custozza and on sea at Lissa. Only Garibaldi in the Alps was successful. The war, however, was won by the over-

[1] See p. 146.

whelming Prussian victory over the Austrians at Königgrätz (Sadowa) and in spite of the Italian failure Bismarck allowed Italy her promised reward of Venetia. Even the way she received this, however, was humiliating: Austria did not surrender it direct to the Italians, but handed it over to Napoleon III to pass on. This was in accordance with an agreement made before the war, Napoleon having stipulated that Austria should surrender Venetia as the price of his neutrality.

Venetia incorporated in Italy, 1866

Only Rome, the natural capital in nearly all Italian eyes, now remained outside the new kingdom. In 1866 Napoleon III had withdrawn the French garrison; and once Venetia was safely acquired this tempted Garibaldi into raising volunteers for another attack. Quickly the French returned and with their new 'Chassepot' rifles soon ended, at Mentana, Garibaldi's initial run of successes. Finally, however, in 1870 when the Franco-Prussian war broke out, Napoleon III in his need for troops had again to withdraw the French garrison from Rome and this time for good. The Pope's last stronghold could now fall to the Italians without the danger of a war with France. In protest Pius IX retired as a voluntary prisoner to his palace of the Vatican, from which no Pope ever emerged until 1929, when the dictator Mussolini ended the long quarrel between the new Italian state and the Papacy.[1]

The last goal – Rome

Rome the Italian capital, 1870

By 1870 Italy, apart from some disputed areas beyond the north-eastern frontiers, was united and free. The story had been a stirring one, yet disillusion was already beginning. Perhaps the country was made too quickly. Without the guiding hand of Cavour it soon proved to have little skill in managing parliamentary affairs or even in suppressing beggary and brigandage. In the south and in the former Papal States the application of the Sardinian Kingdom's anti-ecclesiastical laws, such as the dissolution of the monasteries, caused great distress. The dominant northerners tended, in fact, to take over the south and run it in their own interests. Bitterness and ill-feeling, even rebellion, began to spoil the atmosphere in the new state. Disgusted with the events of 1867–70, Garibaldi, on the fall of Napoleon III, dashed off to France to fight for freedom and the new French republic against the Prussian military machine. (It was a tradition his descendants maintained, for six of his grandsons raised a volunteer Italian regiment to help France in another hour of need in 1914.)

Mazzini, in exile, was heartbroken about the course events had taken. The free republic of self-sacrificing patriots he had dreamed of was far from a fact. Garibaldi, who could have achieved it, had in Mazzini's opinion been fooled all the time by Cavour and Victor Emmanuel. The great guerrilla chief, said Mazzini, had 'a heart of gold and the brains of an ox' – a similar impression to that made on the English poet Tennyson, who spoke of Garibaldi's possessing 'the divine stupidity of a hero'. At any rate, to Mazzini, brilliant as Cavour's tactics had often been, the whole process of unification had been carried out by the wrong means, with foreign help, and by double-dealings and shifty diplomacy bound to end in demoralisation. 'Unity', he said already by 1860, 'you may consider as settled, and so far, so good. The rest is all wrong.' Or again: 'I shall have no more joy in Italy.... The country, with its contempt for all ideals, has killed the soul within me.' This was an over-harsh saying; for between 1859 and 1870 unquestionably a great

---

[1] By the terms of the agreement of 1929, the Pope was recognised as possessing sovereign rights over the 'Vatican City' – a territory a mile and a half square.

ITALY IN ROME.

PAPA PIUS (*to* KING OF ITALY). "I MUST NEEDS SURRENDER THE *SWORD*, MY SON; BUT *I KEEP THE KEYS!!*"

The inclusion of Rome in the Italian kingdom and the disappearance of the Papal States ended the Pope's temporal power but left his spiritual authority untouched. Cartoon by Tenniel, 1st October 1870.

ideal, that of a free and united Italy, was achieved, and with astonishing speed. It was achieved in spite of such formidable obstacles as the hostility of Austria and the Pope, the wavering friendship of France, the quarrels between republicans, monarchists and federalists, and the conflicting pull of centuries-old local loyalties. Nevertheless the unification of Italy, like that of Germany, seems to illustrate one of the eternal tragedies of politics – that great ends can often be achieved only by means which rob the ends of much of their worth.

CHAPTER 12

Bismarck and the Unification of Germany

1. The Rise of Bismarck, 1851–63

As recounted earlier,[1] the great ideal of a united and liberal Germany for which the Frankfurt Parliament strove had come to nothing within two years. Frederick William IV of Prussia had refused to accept the leadership of the national movement, and without Prussian leadership it was lost. By 1851 the supremacy of Austria in Germany was again established, the old powerless Confederation of 1815 was revived, and everything seemed to be as before the revolutions. Yet within twenty years Germans of all the historic German states except Austria were united in the new German Empire, proclaimed at Versailles in 1871. Such a transformation, such an achievement was the work of one man above all others – Otto von Bismarck.

Bismarck, one of the most brilliant diplomatists of all time, dwarfed every other politician in Germany, called even Lord Palmerston's bluff, and outwitted Napoleon III so completely as to make him rather a pathetic figure. By origin he was a Prussian 'Junker,' or landed gentleman, whose family had enjoyed the rank of nobility and shared in local government from the fourteenth century. He inherited an estate of which he was passionately fond, a magnificent set of brains, a tremendous physique, indomitable will-power, and the political principles of the Junker class. These were monarchical and highly autocratic, intensely conservative, and distrustful of new ideas, especially those of a liberal tendency. It was nevertheless this aristocrat, who despised both the ideals and the political capacity of the majority, who succeeded where the liberals of 1848 had failed.

Bismarck

After a conventional university education, with much duelling and beer-drinking, he entered the Prussian civil service and served his year in the army. His civil service career, however, was too monotonous to absorb his restless energies, which found an additional outlet in gambling and general dissipation. In 1839 he retired from the service to devote himself to his estates, studying the science of agriculture as hard as another maker of destiny, Cavour. He rapidly gained a demonic reputation locally for his vices, his physical energy, his enormous consumption of drink and cigars, and for playful pranks such as awakening guests by firing pistol shots through their windows. But he was, too, devouring books

Early life

[1] See pp. 116–20.

of all kinds, making himself the master of many fields of knowledge. With his belief in religion at length restored and a happy marriage to tame his wildness, by 1848 Bismarck was stable enough to be on the threshold of great achievements.

Bismarck in 1848

The liberal revolution of that year found in Bismarck one of its bitterest opponents. As an aristocrat he disliked any approach to democracy; as a Prussian he hated the thought of Prussia being merged in Germany. In the Prussian Parliament of 1847, to which he was elected, he opposed with all his force the liberal schemes, speaking against them with a stinging and reckless eloquence. He even voted, alone with one other member, against an address of thanks to the King when the monarch at length granted a constitution. His attitude was so extreme that Frederick William feared to promote him to office, regarding him as 'only to be employed when the bayonet reigns'. In truth Bismarck believed that nothing could be done without force: he therefore strove to preserve the greatest force available in Germany, the extremely militarist state of Prussia. Though he was not called to office in the critical days of 1848, his advice made its impression on Frederick William. In 1851, when the Prussian monarchy, at the expense of humiliation by Austria and desertion of the national movement, had regained its power in Prussia, Bismarck was appointed Prussian representative at the revived Confederation Diet.

Bismarck as Prussian representative in the Diet

While he was representing Prussia in the Diet from 1851 to 1858, Bismarck's views underwent considerable development. Up to 1851 his ideas had been purely conservative; now he became aware of the fact that there were real problems in the weakness of a divided Germany. He began to favour uniting Germany, but not at the price of surrendering the tradition and the power of Prussia. His solution of the German problem became not the liberal one of a free union under a Prussian king stripped of his autocratic powers, but a virtually dictated union under a Prussian king with his power intact. 'The God of battles,' he had already said, 'will throw the dice that decide.' With typical realism, he also recognised that the practical objective of the immediate future was the unification of *north* Germany, rather than of the whole area covered by the German Confederation. In the same way Cavour, in extending the territory of Sardinia-Piedmont, aimed originally at uniting only the north of Italy.

Against this growth of Prussian power, he saw clearly in his duties as representative, Austria would fight with all the weapons at her disposal. She would exploit the ascendancy which she had gained over Frederick William to remain the dominant power in Germany. As it was easier to dominate a number of small states than a single great one, and as Austria would not willingly separate herself from her non-German lands, she would block any schemes for German unification which involved the creation of a strong central government. Bismarck accordingly saw in Austria his first enemy. His attitude was soon shown in the famous stories of the cigar and the shirtsleeves. At the Diet only the Austrian delegate as a special mark of honour ever presumed to smoke – Bismarck as soon as he arrived lit a cigar. And once, when an Austrian representative received him informally in his shirtsleeves, Bismarck promptly threw off his own jacket with the remark: 'I agree. It's a very hot day.' Before long he had defeated an attempt by Austria to break up the Zollverein. Such a man would never rest till Austria was deposed from her place of supremacy in Germany.

Yet before Austria could be tackled, there were other enemies nearer home to

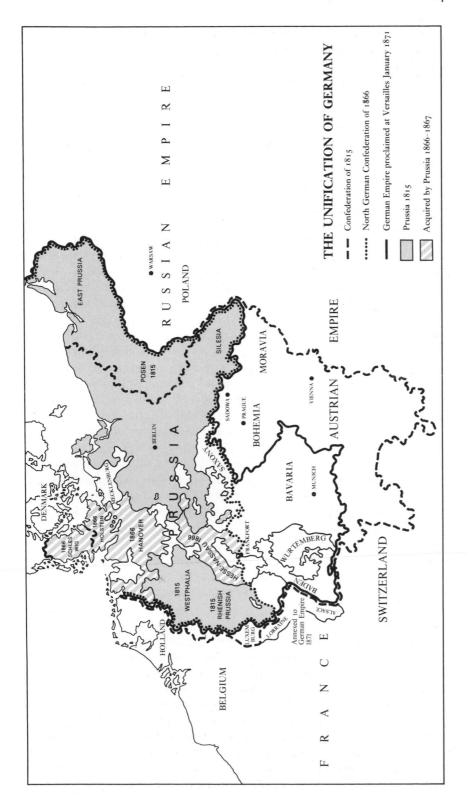

THE UNIFICATION OF GERMANY

– – – Confederation of 1815

· · · · · North German Confederation of 1866

——— German Empire proclaimed at Versailles January 1871

Prussia 1815

Acquired by Prussia 1866–1867

defeat – the liberals of Prussia. By 1858 the reign of the unfortunate Frederick William IV had ended in madness, and his younger brother William occupied his throne as Regent. King William I by 1861, he was by training and temperament a soldier. He had appointed two keen military minds, both violently anti-liberal, to the key positions of the Prussian army. Roon became Minister of War and Moltke Chief of the General Staff. It did not take Roon long to decide, in collaboration with Moltke and the King, that the Prussian army must be greatly increased. Together they planned to raise its strength, including reserves, from just under half a million to just over three-quarters of a million men. This, with its creation of new regiments, would naturally involve considerable expenditure. Here was the crux of the matter – would the liberal majority in the Prussian parliament agree to these military items in the budget?

William I

Roon and Moltke

Army reforms

Liberal opposition

It soon became apparent that they would not. The reason for their attitude was not so much that they disapproved of a large Prussian army, as that they strongly disliked two of the proposals: that the professional army should have fuller control over the militia, or reserve citizen army, and that conscripts to the professional army should serve the full legal three years, instead of the customary two. The liberals also hoped, by insisting on their views, to assert the control of parliament over the King and ministers. Obviously a matter which concerned everybody in two ways, military training and finance, was a suitable issue over which to take up the struggle. The conflict, in fact, began to run on similar lines to that between Charles I of England and his opponents – who, at base, was the real ruler, king or parliament? Meanwhile the King went ahead and created the new regiments, with money from existing taxes which by a loophole in the constitution he could continue to collect. A parliament overwhelmingly against him threw out the budget prepared by his ministry. The situation was becoming perilously near civil war or the surrender and abdication of William.

Bismarck 'Minister-President' of Prussia, 1862

It was at this stage that the King turned to the strong man whose appointment meant no compromise. In 1862 Bismarck, who since 1859 had been out of the way as Prussian ambassador first at St Petersburg and then at Paris, was summoned to Berlin by a telegram from Roon. It read: 'Pericula in mora. Dépêchez-vous.' ('Danger in delay. Hurry.') This was the sign for which Bismarck had been waiting. Hastening to the capital he persuaded the King to tear up the document of abdication and carry on the struggle to a finish. On the same day as the budget was again rejected by parliament, Bismarck was appointed Minister-President. The destiny of Prussia was at last in his hands, and with it the destiny not only of Germany but of much of Europe.

Bismarck's conception of force

The appointment created the greatest surprise throughout Europe, where statesmen betted how long the new minister would last, and the greatest consternation throughout Prussia, where it was regarded as a deliberate affront to the liberals. Not one of these was appointed to the new ministry, though there had been several in the old. Hardly anyone realised either the outstanding ability of Bismarck or the growing strength of the state he was to govern, with its army, its devoted civil service, its advanced educational system, and its expanding commerce. Bismarck himself seemed to go out of his way to slap the liberals soundly in the face by such remarks as the famous: 'Germany has its eyes not on Prussia's Liberalism but on its might. The great questions of the day will not be decided by speeches and resolutions of majorities, but by blood and iron.' The phrase 'blood and iron' ever afterwards stuck to Bismarck; and however much we may dislike the fact, the events of the next few years proved that Bismarck's prophecy was completely accurate. He had, in fact, penetrated to the heart of European politics, that affairs were arranged not by right but by might, and he was determined to accept the logic of this by making Prussia mightier than any possible enemy. It was the old policy of Frederick the Great. Bismarck argued that in the long run people always thought those who were successful were also right. In any case the word 'right' held no real meaning for him in international politics, though it had some in private life. So Bismarck believed, not like Cavour that wrong must sometimes be committed in the interests of the state, but that nothing committed in the interests of the state could be wrong – and particularly if that state was Prussia. In expanding Prussia he was always able to convince himself that he was carrying out the will of God. Bismarck was later to suffer many sleepless nights from indigestion, but none from a guilty conscience.

The first step towards the creation of the great Prussia and Germany he dreamed of was to crush the liberal opposition to the army reforms. This was done by advising the King to carry on in spite of the rejection of the budget and to collect existing taxes all the same. The press was gagged, liberals were driven from official positions, and Bismarck's unpopularity reached such heights that he could later say of it: 'Men spat on the place where I trod in the streets.' But Bismarck had rightly judged that the leading German liberals would shirk an appeal to force and he calculated that everything would be forgiven him when he had achieved something great for Prussia. He deliberately aimed, in other words, at successes in foreign policy in order to win the battle at home. Yet his foreign adventures were always strictly and closely connected with his main aim, Prussian leadership in Germany, and never, like Napoleon III's, on occasion designed largely to placate opinion at home.

Anti-liberal measures

Foreign policy

2. Bismarck's Wars, 1863–71

There were three main steps by which Bismarck achieved his desired end. Each was marked by a war – in turn against Denmark, against Austria, and against France. There has been much debate about how far Bismarck conceived this whole programme in advance, and how far his success came rather from seizing opportunities as they arose. He himself was in no doubt about the matter: he later boasted how he had steered his predetermined course. There is no reason to doubt that the broad outline was in his mind from the mid-1860s – certainly that Austria and France would have to be dealt with if Germany were to be unified under Prussian domination – but the actual steps which led to the wars owed a great deal also to chance, to the seized opportunities of the moment, and to the mistakes of opponents. Bismarck, though constant in his aim, was always very flexible in his tactics. One mistake he himself never made. It is proof of the brilliance of his statesmanship that in spite of the obviously growing power of Prussia, he succeeded in preventing his enemy from allying with any major power. His first aim in any war, the isolation of the enemy, was always achieved. Let us follow the process by which the unification of Germany was accomplished along Bismarck's lines.

In 1863 a question which had long troubled German nationalists became once more acute. The King of Denmark had for centuries ruled over two duchies,

The Schleswig-
Holstein question

Schleswig and Holstein, not as the Danish king but as their Duke. The more northerly duchy, Schleswig, was inhabited by people of Danish origin in the north, but in the south the majority were German-speaking. The other duchy, Holstein, was largely German in character, was a member of the German Confederation, and resented the Danish connection. As the nationalist movement developed in the nineteenth century, keenly national Danes wanted to absorb the two duchies – or at least Schleswig – completely into the Danish kingdom. On the other hand, keenly national Germans wanted to avert this, so that the duchies could later be brought into a united Germany. Already there had been fighting over the matter in 1848 and a dispute over the succession to the duchies – a German claimant, the Duke of Augustenburg, having challenged the rights of the heir to the Danish throne (whose succession to that would come through the female line, a practice not accepted in the duchies). In 1852, after Augustenburg had resigned his claim in return for a monetary payment, a conference of the great powers at London had settled the succession in favour of the King of Denmark. On the bigger question, however, it had simply decided that the duchies should be kept as they were, an indivisible part of the lands of the king of Denmark, but not subject to the laws of the Danish Kingdom.

Treaty of London, 1852

Unfortunately this did not satisfy either the Germans or the Danes. By 1863 the intricacies of the situation were such that Palmerston maintained that only three persons in Europe were completely acquainted with the truth – the Prince Consort, who was dead; a German professor, who was in a lunatic asylum; and he himself, who had forgotten all about it. In 1863 the Danes came out with a new constitution which linked Schleswig in common arrangements with Denmark, but treated Holstein separately. At once violent protests arose from the duchies, which clung to their traditional status, and from all Germany. The Danes were undoubtedly breaking the London treaty of 1852, and the eyes of Germans turned to Prussia to see if she were going to act as leader of Germany in the matter. Would she represent German feeling and the Confederation Diet's demands, and help to instal the Prince of Augustenburg (son of the rejected candidate of 1848) as ruler of the duchies?

Danes try to link
Schleswig with
Denmark, 1863

This was Bismarck's first great opportunity. In Holstein, Augustenburg was now claiming to be duke, and the Confederation Diet voted to send in troops to support him. Bismarck wanted neither to break the Treaty of London, nor to tie himself too firmly to Augustenburg – so it was Saxon and Hanoverian troops, not Prussians, who marched into Holstein on behalf of the Confederation. How could Bismarck now manoeuvre the situation so that Prussia would take over the lead on behalf of Germany, but finish up in possession of the duchies? A glance at a map shows that Schleswig and Holstein (with its port of Kiel) were of immense strategical importance to Prussia, particularly since Schleswig could be used as a base for naval operations against her. No one as yet, however, saw through Bismarck's policy of annexation, for the simple reason that Prussia had no more 'right' to the duchies than had China or Japan. Europe had not yet realised that the real attitude of Prussia was represented by Roon, who remarked that the question of the duchies was not one of right or law, but of force, and that Prussia had it.

Prussia and Austria
fight Denmark, 1864

Bismarck's handling of the question was consummately skilful. He first secured the friendship of Russia by supporting the Tsar in every possible way short of war during the Polish rebellion of 1863. Then he concluded an alliance with Austria, the terms of which were that the two powers would intervene unless Denmark

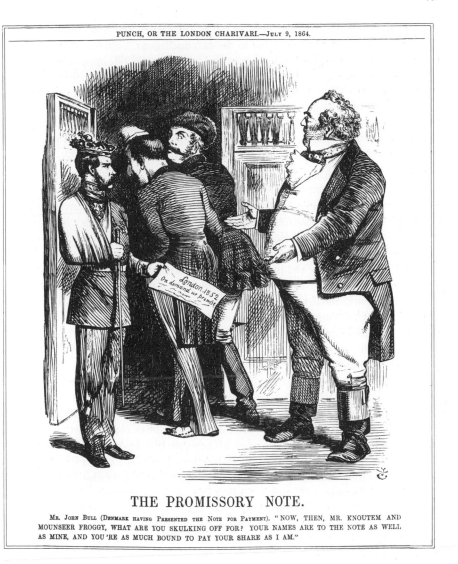

PUNCH, OR THE LONDON CHARIVARI.—JULY 9, 1864.

THE PROMISSORY NOTE.

Mr. John Bull (Denmark having Presented the Note for Payment). "NOW, THEN, MR. KNOUTEM AND MOUNSEER FROGGY, WHAT ARE YOU SKULKING OFF FOR? YOUR NAMES ARE TO THE NOTE AS WELL AS MINE, AND YOU'RE AS MUCH BOUND TO PAY YOUR SHARE AS I AM."

Britain complains that no one joins her in supporting Denmark against Prussia over the Schleswig-Holstein question. A little before, Britain had refused to co-operate with France on the matter, and now France had her revenge. Cartoon by Tenniel.

withdrew the new constitution, and that the future of the duchies should be settled by joint agreement between Austria and Prussia. This made the Confederation powerless in the matter. Having thus ensured that the balance of local force would be on his own side, Bismarck then demanded that Denmark should submit the whole matter to a European congress. Encouraged by Britain, Denmark refused, and the Austrian and Prussian armies promptly invaded Schleswig. Bismarck had seen that France and Britain were not on good enough terms to co-operate in stopping the invasion, had encouraged Napoleon to abstain by hints of future compensation for France in the Rhineland, and had called Palmerston's bluff that 'if Denmark had to fight, she would not fight alone'. Britain, hastily backing down,

. . . and administer the duchies

was humiliated before all Europe, and after the Danes had been soundly beaten they duly surrendered their rights in the two duchies to Austria and Prussia.

The affair at this stage, however, was far from ended. Public opinion in Germany and the duchies expected that Augustenburg would now be installed as duke in both territories. Bismarck, however, proposed that he should be installed on conditions which would have left him completely under the power of Prussia. Eventually, after they had quarrelled violently over their joint administration, it was agreed by the two powers, though not by the unfortunate Augustenburg (who now faded out of history) that for the time being Austria should administer Holstein and Prussia Schleswig. The 'Convention of Gastein' (1865) as this agreement is called, simply, in Bismarck's phrase 'papered over the cracks'. He knew that he could now at any time pick a quarrel with Austria over the government of Holstein, and he was confident that the Prussian army could smash the Austrians as it had smashed the Danes. Thus he could finish up with the whole of north Germany under Prussian control and Austria forever driven from her dominant position in Germany. It was subtle and immoral statesmanship, and for it to appeal to certain essential persons with more delicate consciences than himself, such as King William, Austria must first be put 'in the wrong'. At these finer aspects of the diplomatic game Bismarck was a past-master.

In preparation for the war against Austria he had now decided on, Bismarck took two important steps. Again he secured the neutrality of Napoleon III by talk of future compensation. Prussia, his representative hinted, would not take offence if ever Napoleon should think of acquiring Belgium, and there was always the possibility of ceding to France German territory along the left bank of the Rhine. Napoleon for his part welcomed the prospect of an Austro-Prussian conflict for another reason: he imagined that it would exhaust both combatants, and that he could step in at a later stage to reap big advantages. It was actually with Napoleon's blessing that Bismarck, as his next step, concluded an alliance with the new Kingdom of Italy to attack Austria in the rear if war should come within three months. Italy's reward was to be Venetia. All that then remained was to make certain that war came within the stipulated time. Failing to provoke Austria by sending Prussian forces into Holstein to expel the Confederation troops, Bismarck proposed a reform of the Confederation by which Austria would be entirely omitted from German affairs. In an effort to win the German liberals and nationalists to his side against Austria he even urged that the new German parliament to replace the Confederation Diet should be elected by universal suffrage. Austria naturally objected to these proposals, and moved that the members of the Confederation should jointly attack the insolent Prussia. Nine of the German states agreed, including all the larger ones, while six took the Prussian side. Prussia thereupon left the Confederation and declared it dissolved. The war had come – and Bismarck had managed to convince William and the Prussians that it was purely defensive!

The course of the 'Seven Weeks' War', as it is called, astonished Europe. Against the hostile states in the north and centre, including Hanover, the Prussian army had little more to do than to walk in and take possession, while against Austria and Saxony everything was settled in one overwhelming victory at Königgrätz in Bohemia.[1] Even the fact that the Austrians were entirely successful against the

---

[1] The French call the battle Sadowa, the name of a neighbouring village.

Convention of Gastein, 1865

Bismarck plans war with Austria

He secures:
1. France's neutrality

2. Italy's alliance

The Seven Weeks' War, 1866

Königgrätz (Sadowa)

KÖNIGSSTRASSE

PEACE—AND NO PIECES!

Bismarck. "PARDON, MON AMI; BUT WE REALLY CAN'T ALLOW YOU TO PICK UP ANYTHING HERE."
Nap (the *Chiffonnier*). "PRAY, DON'T MENTION IT, M'SIEU! IT'S NOT OF THE SLIGHTEST CONSEQUENCE."

Napoleon III's expectations from the Austro-Prussian War are disappointed. Cartoon by Tenniel.

Italians could not alter the result in the main seat of the war. Prussian training and tactics, the breech-loading needle-gun and the well-planned movement of troops by railway, had done their work. Everything was over before Napoleon could reap any advantage from it: when he frantically tried to claim Rhineland territory as compensation, Bismarck encouraged France to put her demands in writing and then turned them down flat. 'It is France that is beaten at Sadowa', said Thiers.

The wisdom of Bismarck's statesmanship is nowhere seen more fully than in the conditions he imposed after the decisive Prussian victory. The first point was the rapidity with which he ended hostilities, to rob France of any chance to intervene. The King and the army were anxious to march in triumph to Vienna and punish Austria by annexing Austrian Silesia or some other territory. Bismarck instead

Treaty of Prague, 1866

HONESTY AND POLICY.

BRITANNIA. "WELL! I'VE DONE MY BEST. IF THEY WILL SMASH EACH OTHER, THEY MUST."
NAP. (aside). "AND SOME ONE MAY PICK UP THE PIECES!"

Napoleon III hopes for 'pickings' from the Austro-Prussian War. Cartoon by Tenniel, 16th June 1866.

demanded a halt. His object was not to make of Austria a permanent enemy, but simply to expel her from German leadership so that the field there was clear for Prussia. He insisted that not a yard of Austrian territory should be annexed by Prussia, and that the only loss suffered by Austria should be Venetia, which had been promised to Italy. Reluctantly King William agreed, and this arrangement formed part of the final treaty of Prague. Outside Austria, however, Prussia

Prussia's gains annexed Holstein, Hanover, Nassau, Hesse-Cassel and the free city of Frankfurt. She also retained Schleswig. These gains gave her an extra four and a half million inhabitants, a very compact territory running across north Germany, and an important outlet to the North Sea.

The main blow to Austria, however, was that by the treaty of Prague she also had to recognise the abolition of the old Confederation and the setting-up of a new body in its place – the North German Confederation – from which she was excluded. The object of this was to ensure the supremacy of Prussia. Most of the defeated German states were compelled to enter the new organisation, including the Kingdom of Saxony. The main south German territories, however, notably Bavaria, Baden, and Würtemberg, had to be left outside owing to strong local feeling and the attitude of Napoleon III (who was prepared to stand aside only if the new Prussian-dominated Confederation extended only as far south as the river Main).

The King of Prussia was the President, Bismarck the Chancellor of the new organisation. Home affairs were left almost entirely to the individual states, but matters of foreign policy were placed in Prussian hands by the stipulation that Prussia controlled the armies of all the members. A concession to democracy was made by allowing all men a vote for the Parliament or Reichstag – though, as the Chancellor was responsible to the King and not to the Reichstag, this concession was more apparent than real. The feelings of individual states, too, were solaced

The North German Confederation, 1867

William I President, Bismarck Chancellor

THE EUROPEAN EQUILIBRIUM
A cartoon by Daumier published in the French paper Le Charivari *in December 1866. With Prussia having just fought and defeated Austria, and with Napoleon III full of adventurous schemes, the equilibrium of Europe rested on the riskiest of foundations – the bayonets of the Powers.*

by setting up of a Federal Council, or Bundesrat, consisting of their representatives, in which it was possible for all combined to outvote Prussia. This meant that the unannexed north German states, while definitely acknowledging the supremacy of Prussia, did not lose all the liberty of action and prestige they would have surrendered by definite annexation, and thus their relations with Prussia were not unfriendly in spite of defeat in the war. Further, Bismarck as a condition of peace had insisted that the south German states should sign military alliances with Prussia – and had made them willing to do so by revealing to them Napoleon's plans for expansion at their expense. He induced them also to link up with the Northern Confederation in a new customs parliament, elected by universal suffrage, which replaced the old Zollverein. Thus by the arrangements following the war Bismarck achieved the remarkable feat of expelling Austria from her old leadership and uniting most of Germany under Prussia without making permanent enemies of any of his victims. This leniency was absolutely essential to Bismarck's policy. He knew only too well that the day of reckoning had to come with Napoleon III, and when it did it was important to have Austria and south Germany as friends rather than foes. Like a good chess-player, Bismarck thought several moves ahead.

Military alliance with the south German states

Austrian reorganisation

The Seven Weeks' War, greatly as it benefited victorious Prussia, was not without advantage for defeated Austria. Driven out of Germany and Italy, she at last recognised her real mission as an Empire centred on the Danube. Realising that if reorganisation was to be successful something must be done to satisfy racial feeling within the Empire, Austria decided on a large measure of compromise with her biggest non-German territory, Hungary. This agreement of 1867, known as the 'Ausgleich' ('Compromise'), divided the Austrian Empire into two halves – Austria, which included Bohemia and the northern provinces, and Hungary, which covered also the south Slav states and Transylvania. Each section recognised Francis Joseph as Emperor, but preserved its independent parliament for most matters. Three subjects, however – foreign affairs, defence, and the finance for these – were to come under a joint body representative of the two divisions, and meeting alternately in Vienna and Budapest. Thus the Austrian Empire was reorganised as a dual monarchy, or Austria-Hungary, under which name it continued to be known until it broke up into its various racial fragments at the end of the First World War.

The Ausgleich creates 'Austria-Hungary', 1867

For Bismarck there remained one more stage in the unification of Germany under Prussia. Austria had been displaced from her supremacy and the North German Confederation formed. In Prussia itself the old opposition of the liberals, dazzled by his success, had died down, and he had been forgiven everything. The more nationalistically-minded among the liberals even broke off from the radicals to form a separate National Liberal party and became Bismarck's main supporters. Yet the main south German states, Bavaria, Würtemberg, and Baden, although now bound by military and economic alliance, still remained outside. Bavaria especially clung to her independence and her local peculiarities. Bismarck, however, held all the trump cards. He knew that France was unlikely to allow Prussia to gain control over south Germany peacefully. He also knew that if war between Prussia and France broke out these south German states, uncomfortably situated between the two combatants, could not remain neutral. As Germans and as military allies of Prussia they must oppose France. Once let them fight side by side with Prussia against the historic enemy, once let Prussia take control in the emergency of war, and Bismarck knew that the Prussian hold would not be lightly shaken off again. Accordingly he deliberately willed and prepared for war with France to complete the unification of Germany along the lines he desired, a unification which would spring, not from free bargaining (as a much later unification might have done) but from Prussian power.

Bismarck plans war against France to unite Germany

This fact, however, must not blind us to the equal truth that France, on her side, gave Prussia every provocation Bismarck desired. Ever since Sadowa, terribly alarmed at the growth of a new power on her eastern boundary, France had determined to stem the tide of German unity. Ill-feeling grew when Napoleon III,

Errors of France

PUNCH, OR THE LONDON CHARIVARI.—May 4, 1867.

LUXEMBURG
FOR SALE BY
PRIVATE CONTRACT
HIGHLY ELIGIBLE
PROPERTY
TEN MINUTES WALK
FROM THE
GERMAN FRONTIER
RIGHT OF SHOOTING
&c   &c   &c

"TO BE SOLD."

EMPEROR NAPOLEON. "I—A—HAVE MADE AN OFFER TO MY FRIEND HERE, AND——"
THE MAN IN POSSESSION. "NO, HAVE YOU, THOUGH?—I RATHER THINK I WAS THE PARTY TO APPLY TO."
EMPEROR NAPOLEON. "OH, INDEED! AH! THEN IN THAT CASE I'LL—— BUT IT'S OF NO CONSEQUENCE."

Prussia stops Napoleon III buying Luxembourg from the King of Holland. Cartoon by Tenniel.

desperately hoping to secure his throne by successes in foreign policy, tried to buy the Grand Duchy of Luxemburg from the King of the Netherlands. This move, which Bismarck himself had promised to accept to keep his options open with Napoleon, and to which the Dutch King agreed, was thwarted by an outcry in Germany. Luxemburg had been a member of the old German Confederation, and Prussian troops were still garrisoning the fortress town of Luxemburg itself. Bismarck promptly fell in with the mood in Germany, and warned Napoleon off. A conference of the powers then decided on the neutralisation of Luxemburg as a separate state: the Prussian garrison was withdrawn, but the King of Holland continued to be the Grand Duke – a bitter blow to the French Emperor. Baulked of lands on the Rhine in 1866 and of Luxemburg in 1867, humiliated in Mexico and in a contradictory position in Italy, Napoleon could not now risk another rebuff. If he suffered one, the many enemies of his régime at home would seize the chance to dethrone him. So Roon and Moltke prepared the Prussian armies and Bismarck laid his diplomatic plans, secure in the knowledge that at the right moment France could be manoeuvred into threatening war. The south German states would then fight gladly side by side with Prussia to protect Germany from danger – and Bismarck would know how to use the opportunity. Like Cromwell, he believed that it was a good thing to strike while the iron was hot, but a better thing to make the iron hot by striking.

Hohenzollern candidature in Spain

The opportunity came in 1870. The throne of Spain being vacant, a Hohenzollern relative of William's was encouraged by Bismarck to stand as a candidate. Bismarck knew perfectly well that France, already frightened at the growth of Prussia to the east, would not accept a German on the throne of Spain to the south. William and the prince concerned knew this too, and not wishing to cause a European outcry were unwilling to advance the Hohenzollern candidature. Bismarck, however, overrode them both and almost compelled the prince to go forward. The announcement of the news caused the reaction in France that Bismarck had expected – intense indignation and a demand that the candidature should be withdrawn. Acting now on his real inclinations, William advised the candidate to retire – such advice from the head of the royal house was equivalent to a command – and France had won a striking success. Unfortunately France had had experience of Bismarck's double-dealing, and was suspicious that the prince's son might become the candidate instead. She was, too, anxious for an even more resounding diplomatic triumph than she had just achieved. Consequently the French decided also to seek an apology, and an undertaking from William that the Hohenzollern candidature would never in any circumstances be renewed. This demand William brushed aside as a reflection on his good faith and an attempt to pick a quarrel. How Bismarck, who had thought his chance was slipping from his hands, seized the opportunity by editing the King's decision from Ems to read more provocatively has already been told in the account of the Second Empire.[1] In face of the fury of France Bismarck persuaded William to order the mobilisation of the Prussian army. In face of the mobilisation of the Prussian army, France declared war.

Franco-Prussian War, 1870–71

The Franco-Prussian war, as we have seen, astonished Europe by the ease with which the much vaunted French military prowess crumpled before the ruthless

[1] See p. 98.

MAIL–CARRYING BALLOON LEAVING BESIEGED PARIS, 1871
An engraving from a contemporary journal. Ballooning dated from 1783, when the brothers Montgolfier used hot air to lift a balloon, and the French scientist Charles made passenger flights possible by the use of hydrogen. During the siege of Paris in the Franco-Prussian War mail was sent out from the capital by night in balloons, and later Gambetta escaped by the same means to organise resistance in the provinces.

Sedan, 1870

Bismarck's
diplomatic brilliance

German Empire
created, 1871

efficiency of the Prussian troops. Strasbourg, Sedan, Metz – France was at Prussia's feet. But the organisation of the Prussian armies, the work of Roon, Moltke, and the King, would have been in vain had not Bismarck first secured the requisite political conditions. The secret of it was that France had been isolated from all possible help. Italy was no more than half a friend while France occupied Rome, and had recently fought as an ally of Prussia. Russia was bribed not to interfere by the suggestion that she should repudiate the clauses of the 1856 treaty restricting her right to warships on the Black Sea. Britain was alienated by Bismarck's publication at the critical moment of the French proposal of 1866 to annex Belgium. Austria and the south German states had been partly reconciled by the lenient treatment after the Seven Weeks' War, and the south German states were bound in military alliance to Prussia. France had no friend in Europe, and left alone in a state of internal dissension to face the Prussian armies she was powerless. It was Bismarck's master-stroke.

Already before the war was over and the treaty of Frankfurt signed, by which Prussia was to strip France of Alsace, most of Lorraine, and an indemnity, Bismarck's main object was achieved. In the flush of enthusiasm for the common cause the south German states were ready, after due negotiation, to unite with the North German Confederation into a German Empire. Special concessions were given to Bavaria in the way of independence, and a special secret payment to the Bavarian King Ludwig II, and Ludwig then undertook to invite William in the name of the princes to accept the imperial crown of the new Germany. It was only by such an invitation that the Prussian King would deign to assume his new position. So on 18th January, 1871, in the Hall of Mirrors at Versailles, the German Empire was solemnly proclaimed, with William as the first German Emperor, or Kaiser. The setting was appropriate. Versailles stood more than anything else for the historic, aggressive glory of France. Now, in Versailles, while Paris lay starving ten miles away, a triumphant Germany rose by and through the humiliation of the most brilliant civilisation in Europe. But Empires, even when they are the work of a Bismarck, are not seldom built on shifting sands. Overbearing Germany and heart-broken France could not know that before fifty years were out the Hall of Mirrors would reflect another scene of equal importance – with the roles of victor and vanquished reversed.

CHAPTER 13
The Eastern Question, 1815–78

1. The War of Greek Independence and the Syrian Question, 1820–41

From the fourteenth to the seventeenth century the Ottoman Turks, a Central Asiatic race, built up by unremitting conquest a Mediterranean Empire. After Armenia and Asia Minor had fallen to these ruthless invaders from the East, the Balkan peninsula came next. The capture of Constantinople in 1453 and the break-up of the Eastern Roman Empire, which had endured a thousand years, sealed the fate of Serbians, Bulgarians, Albanians, Rumanians, and other tribes and kingdoms in south-eastern Europe. Even Hungary was conquered, and the victorious host advanced twice to the walls of Vienna itself (1529 and 1683). Meanwhile, the North African coast – Egypt, Tripoli, Tunis, Algeria – had also been compelled to submit together with islands like the Ionian Isles, Cyprus and Crete. Even large stretches of south Russia, including the Crimea, came under Turkish sway.

Ottoman conquests

At length, however, the tide of conquest spent itself and began to recede. Through the might of Austria the Turks were compelled to relinquish Hungary, through that of Russia the Crimea. At the end of the eighteenth century the Ottoman Empire, though still enormous, was a power in decline. The efforts of the various subject nationalities in the Balkans to secure independence, together with the ambitions and policies of states such as Austria, Russia, and Britain in relation to the decaying empire, constituted the nineteenth-century Eastern Question. Very roughly, this question might be expressed as: who was going to take over from the Turks, and when, where, and to what extent?

Ottoman Empire in decline

The Eastern Question

In the general approach to the question it is possible to discern certain main trends. The traditional British attitude was the preservation of the power of the Sultan as a bulwark against a possible Russian advance to the Mediterranean. This was roughly the policy of Pitt, Wellington, Palmerston and Disraeli – though not of Gladstone. Turkish misgovernment did not greatly concern most British statesmen compared with the advantages of keeping a great military power like Russia from capturing Constantinople, one of the most strategically important cities in the world. They hoped, quite in vain as it proved, to secure better conditions for the subject races by 'representations' to Turkey. Russia, on the other hand, felt more strongly for the Balkan peoples, who were mostly, like herself,

Britain supports Turkey

Orthodox in religion and Slavonic in race. She also coveted Constantinople, headquarters of the Orthodox faith and sentinel over the passage between the Black Sea and the Mediterranean. Her aim thus became to break up or weaken the Ottoman Empire and free the subject races, at least to a limited degree, while securing concessions and privileges for herself in the bargain. These broad lines of policy were sometimes departed from, but in general they held true for most of the nineteenth century.

The War of Greek Independence, 1821–1827

The first phase of this long-enduring problem in the nineteenth century arose in connection with the War of Greek Independence (1821–1827). The Greeks, like all the subject nations of the Turks, enjoyed certain privileges which made their lot more tolerable than might have been expected. They were allowed complete educational and religious freedom, the head of their Church, or Patriarch, having a recognised governmental position. They were exempt from military service – an exemption which was theoretically a great dishonour and in practice a considerable advantage, as they thus monopolised commerce and became wealthy. Such concessions, however, did not alter the fact that they were an enslaved race, subject to the arbitrary will of local governors. Much depended on the character of the governor, for the whole Turkish system had become lax in its central control. As long as the governor got in the required taxes (provided almost entirely by the subject peoples) and sent along a few detruncated heads as a sign of his efficiency, he administered his province practically as he pleased. This meant that Turkish rule varied greatly in severity from one district to another; mostly, however, it was light, but inefficient and corrupt, and punctuated by periods of savage re-pression whenever there were signs of revolt.

The early years of the nineteenth century saw a great development in the Greek national spirit. The modern Greeks, through a mixture of races, were a far cry from their classical forebears. Yet with the birth of a new literary language in the early nineteenth century, midway between peasant speech and classical Greek, Greeks of various kinds, previously separated by differing dialects, experienced a greater national consciousness. The liberal ideals of the French revolution, and the growing prosperity of Greek merchants, also helped in this development. The educated classes recalled 'the glory that was Greece' and felt a responsibility to revive the heroism and culture of the days of antiquity. A society, at first secret, known as the 'Philike Hetairia', or friendly society, was founded to foster these ideals among the Greeks. The first step was obviously to expel the Turks from the sacred soil of Greece, and the society became the spearhead of revolution.

Hypsilanti's plan, 1820–21

To this end, in 1821, Alexander Hypsilanti, a distinguished Greek officer in the Tsar's army who had recently become president of the society, raised a revolt. Its scene was not Greece itself, but farther north in the two Danubian principalities of Moldavia and Wallachia (now part of Rumania). The main population of these provinces, which were under Turkish sovereignty, was not Greek, but many of the upper classes were, and Hypsilanti was the son of a former hospodar, or prince, of Moldavia who had himself raised Greek revolts and served with the Tsar. In March 1821 Hypsilanti and a small force including brother Greek officers entered Moldavia from Russia and proclaimed the two provinces independent of Turkey. His intention was, after liberating the two territories, to proceed to Greece itself and perhaps even to revive a Greek Empire. He claimed to have the support of 'a great power', which was naturally understood to be Russia. But he carried out his task in a very dilatory way, gave offence by acting too much as a monarch, and lost his good name when he failed to stop his Greek supporters indulging in barbarous massacres. Not surprisingly, Tsar Alexander I soon disowned him. By June 1821 he had been hopelessly defeated, for the local population apart from the Greeks gave him very little support, and he fled to Austria, where he was imprisoned.

While Hypsilanti was engaged in Moldavia another and more serious revolt against the Turks broke out in Greece itself, in the peninsula known as the Morea, (in classical times the Peloponnesus). Called on to revolt by one of the bishops, the local Greeks, chiefly illiterate herdsmen, seafarers and brigands, fell on all available Mohammedans and massacred them. In all, something like 50,000 were butchered, and within a few weeks there was not a Mohammedan left in the Morea outside the fortified towns. Naturally the Turks retaliated in kind. They hanged the Greek Patriarch and two other bishops in Constantinople and slung their corpses into the Bosphorus in the traditional fashion, and generally matched atrocity with atrocity. In the Greek islands off Asia Minor their reprisals were particularly terrible against Scio (Chios), one of the most flourishing communities. Such deeds attracted the attention of all Europe; and the Russians, infuriated at the outrage on the bishops, demanded intervention against the Turks. Men of liberal sympathies everywhere began to give their support, in spite of Greek barbarities and the terrible feuds between their various local leaders, to a small nation struggling to be free – a notable case was Lord Byron, who established himself in Greece and wore himself out in the Greek cause, which he hallowed by his death in 1826 at Missolonghi. It says much, too, for the classical education of the British upper classes that they now reacted strongly in favour of, and not against, Greece. As yet, however, though private individuals volunteered, no government actively intervened, for Metternich persuaded Alexander that he must not assist 'revolution'.

The turning-point came when the Sultan, unable to make progress in the Morea because the Greeks of the surrounding isles had the mastery at sea, called on his powerful vassal Mehemet Ali of Egypt for help. Mehemet Ali was an Albanian who had fought for the Turks against Napoleon in Egypt, and had established such a position there, and in the adjoining lands, that he was recognised as Pasha by the Sultan. With the help of French officers he had built up a strong army on the European model. He also developed a powerful fleet, and it was by means of this that an Egyptian army under the command of his son Ibrahim was landed in the Morea. The previous barbarities now appeared insignificant before the conduct of Ibrahim, who set his troops to wipe out ruthlessly the entire Greek population. Russian demands for intervention now grew irresistible, strengthened by the death of Alexander and the accession of Nicholas I, who was determined to protect his fellow Christians. At this point, seeing that Russia was bound to intervene before long and anxious that she should not acquire too much influence, Canning decided to join in with the object of supervising Russia. The main powers then met and Britain, France and Russia concluded the Treaty of London, by which they agreed that Greece should be self-governing, though under Turkish overlordship. They also agreed to enforce a truce while details of the new arrangement were being settled. Austria and Prussia would not accept this policy and refused to sign.

Seeing the powers divided, the Turks not surprisingly declined to accept the treaty proposals. Britain, France and Russia then sent naval forces, with Admiral Codrington as senior officer, to cut off Ibrahim from his supplies in Egypt.

Revolt in the Morea

Turks retaliate

Turks call in Mehemet Ali, 1826

Russian intervention

Treaty of London, 1827

Codrington's instructions were to enforce an armistice, preferably by peaceful means. In the course of staging a 'demonstration', however, at Navarino Bay, before the assembled Egyptian and Turkish fleets, the allied squadrons encountered some Turkish fire ships which refused to move out of the way. An exchange of shots led to a general battle, at the end of which the Egyptian and Turkish navies were at the bottom of the sea. Although Wellington, who became Prime Minister early in 1828 – Canning having died soon after the Treaty of London – disapproved of armed intervention against the Turks and regretted the battle of Navarino as an 'untoward event', its effect remained. Ibrahim had to evacuate the Morea, and the war there was won for Greece. By the beginning of 1828 a provisional Greek government was in some sort of control there under the presidency of Count Capodistrias, a Greek who had been one of Tsar Alexander's leading ministers.[1]

It required a further development to complete the liberation of Greece. Still refusing to accept an armistice, the Sultan called for a holy war against the Christian powers, and especially Russia. Disregarding Wellington, who was anxious to preserve the strength of the Ottoman Empire, Russia reacted strongly, invaded Moldavia and Wallachia, and drove her troops southwards in a hard-fought advance. With Constantinople finally at Russia's mercy the Turks had to agree to the Treaty of Adrianople (1829), by which Greek self-government, though still under Turkish overlordship, was recognised. In addition Moldavia and Wallachia were to enjoy a similar degree of independence and Russia acquired some Turkish territory in Asia. But Britain and Austria had begun to fear that a semi-independent Greece would give Russia further excuses for intervention; so they determined on complete independence or nothing. To sustain Turkey, they insisted on confining the new independent Greek state (which was to have its own 'sovereign prince') within very narrow boundaries, and for the sake of peace Russia agreed. This agreement was signed in London early in 1830. Happily for the Greeks, however, the defeat of the Tories later that year and the appointment of Palmerston as Foreign Secretary brought about a more generous British attitude and in the end more extended boundaries were permitted. In 1832 Britain, France and Russia signed a treaty by which the Greek boundary was fixed farther north, and Greece was to become an independent monarchy under the youthful prince Otto of Bavaria – who began his reign early the next year. The first great episode in the nineteenth-century Eastern Question was over, and the first great hole had been made in the rotting fabric of the Ottoman Empire.

The next phase began almost immediately with the question of Syria. Mehemet Ali, bribed by the Sultan with Crete at the beginning of the war of Greek Independence, was dissatisfied. Syria, Damascus, and the Morea had been promised to him for his help – and now the Greeks had the Morea, while the Sultan, already alarmed at the power of his vassal, refused to hand over the other territories in view of the Turkish failure to win the war. Knowing that the Sultan was re-organising the Turkish army and that it might soon be directed against himself, Mehemet Ali decided to forestall the danger and claim his due at the same time. Accordingly in 1831 Ibrahim Pasha was once more despatched with an Egyptian army, and within a very short time had overrun Syria. Two or three Turkish

---

[1] Capodistrias, who had a difficult time with the various Greek factions, was assassinated in 1831.

forces were overwhelmed, and within a year Ibrahim was in a position to threaten Constantinople itself.

In his extremity the Sultan turned for aid to an unexpected quarter. Since the Treaty of Adrianople Nicholas of Russia had come to the conclusion that Russian influence might perhaps be better served by maintaining a weak Turkish Empire than by setting up strong national Balkan states – especially if he thus avoided falling out with Britain. Accordingly he offered to help the Sultan against Ibrahim – and the Sultan's danger was such that he had no option but to accept. 'A drowning man', a Turkish minister remarked, 'will clutch at a serpent'. Russian intervention, deeply distrusted not only by Turkey but by Britain, saved the situation for the Sultan. All the same, he had to abandon Syria, Damascus, and Palestine to Ibrahim, while the new friendship with Russia was expressed in the Treaty of Unkiar-Skelessi (1833). This document contained officially only a treaty of alliance between Russia and Turkey, but secretly another clause promised that Turkey would close the Dardanelles to the warships of all nations *au besoin* (at need), or in other words at Russia's demand – a provision which might have enabled Russia to carry out an aggressive Mediterranean policy and then, if need be, retire securely into the Black Sea.[1] The secret clause was betrayed to Britain by a Turk who objected to his master's subservience to Russia, and the consequent outcry was immense. Russia, it seemed, had stolen a march on Britain, even though, following the outcry, Nicholas let it be known that he had no intention of exercising his treaty rights.

Britain's opportunity for a revision of this treaty soon arrived. In 1839 the Turks, whose Sultan had devoted his life to vengeance on Mehemet Ali and the recovery of his lost provinces from Ibrahim, invaded Syria. But their armies again failed, and disaster became complete when the Turkish navy, sent to attack Mehemet Ali's fleet, surrendered to the Egyptians on the ground that the ministers at Constantinople were in the pay of the Russians! At this stage the Powers of Europe intervened once more, Britain and Russia for once taking up a similar attitude. The solution finally agreed on by Britain, Russia, Austria, and Prussia was that Mehemet Ali should enjoy the title of Pasha of Egypt on an hereditary basis and retain the southern half of Syria, while surrendering his other conquests. This proposal, however, met with great opposition both from Mehemet Ali and from France, who cherished strong sympathy for this introducer of Western organisation. France, too, hoped to gain influence in Egypt – always attractive to her since Napoleon's expedition – through support of Mehemet. When the latter, backed by France, refused to agree to the loss of half Syria, the Powers withdrew even that concession and determined to restrict his power to Egypt. A force sent to Syria soon cleared out Ibrahim, who had become detested by the local peasantry, while the appearance of the British fleet off Alexandria induced Mehemet Ali to submit. For a moment it seemed that France would declare war on Britain, but the counsels of Louis Philippe prevailed against the firebrand activity of his new chief minister Thiers – who was forced to resign – and France climbed down. The Sultan, of course, now wanted to take Egypt too from Mehemet Ali, and had to be restrained from this course by the Powers.

The Sultan appeals to Russia

Treaty of Unkiar-Skelessi, 1833

Turkey invades Syria

The powers intervene

France supports Mehemet Ali and Ibrahim

Syria restored to Sultan

France climbs down

[1] Actually it seems that Nicholas was much more concerned to dominate Turkey and to stop any attack on Russia up the Straits than to send Russian vessels into the Mediterranean.

The Straits
Convention, 1841

To close the incident, after Syria had been completely restored to the Sultan and Mehemet confirmed in his position of Pasha of Egypt, a new treaty was entered into by the powers, including France. This, known as the Straits Convention, guaranteed that in time of peace Turkey would close not only the Dardanelles but also the Bosphorus to the warships of all nations. This was regarded as a re-statement of the old position before 1833. It was thus a great triumph for Palmerston and Britain, since Russia could not, as she had threatened to do by Unkiar-Skelessi, regulate the Straits purely at her own individual will. By applying the prohibition to the Bosphorus as well as the Dardanelles it also banned Russia, as well as the other naval powers, from threatening Constantinople by sea. At all events the latest trick in the game was Palmerston's, who had maintained the power of the Sultan against his rebellious vassal and thereby brought back Turkey to reliance on Britain and the powers in general rather than on Russia alone. The ambitions of France, too, had been checked. No wonder 'Pam' was a popular foreign minister – in Britain.

2. The Crimean War, 1854–56

The Crimean War

Causes:
1. distrust of Russia's attitude to Turkey

The third and thus far the most acute phase of the Eastern Question led to the first war between the great Powers since the days of Napoleon I. Something has already been said of the Crimean War,[1] but it is worth recalling the main causes. The chief general cause was undoubtedly distrust of Russian intentions concerning the Ottoman Empire. There was justifiable fear among the Powers that Nicholas's recent policy of friendship with Turkey and preservation of the Empire was only a cloak for some dark design. Both in 1844 and in 1853 the Tsar broached schemes of partition with Britain – in the former year he had suggested that Russia should take Constantinople, while Britain 'compensated' herself with Egypt and Crete. The proposal was not entertained, partly because Britain feared to be trapped in some way, partly because there seemed no legitimate excuse for the whole business, and partly because Britain did not agree that Turkey was as weak as Nicholas implied. Indeed, the Tsar's favourite phrase in connection with the Sultan was a reference to him as 'the sick man of Europe'. As early as 1833 he had used it in negotiating with Metternich – 'Prince Metternich, what do you think of the Turk – is he not a sick man?' To which that astute diplomatist had countered – 'Is it to the doctor or to the heir that your majesty addresses the question?' At any rate Britain decided it was wiser not to strike a bargain of the sort suggested. (The interest of the two Powers in these territories nevertheless continued. In 1882 British troops occupied Egypt; and in 1915 Britain, at war with Turkey, at last promised Russia Constantinople.)

2. the right to protect the 'Holy Places'

It was the general and indeed justifiable distrust of Russia which made what appeared to be an unimportant quarrel develop into a great war. In and around Jerusalem and in Bethlehem there were 'Holy Places' connected with the life of Christ which were traditional centres of pilgrimage for Christians. The protection of these Holy Places had been granted by an ancient treaty to France, who had long since ceased to trouble herself much about them. Moreover pilgrims of the Greek Orthodox faith had come to outnumber Catholic pilgrims by about a

[1] See pp. 91–2.

hundred to one. Accordingly Russia, a nearer neighbour, had repaired the shrines, and generally filled the vacancy caused by French lack of interest. This led to frequent and bitter disputes between the local Catholic and Orthodox monks. In 1850, however, Louis Napoleon, soon to be Napoleon III, in order to please the clerical party in France revived the old French claim – which the Sultan accepted, though not to the exclusion of the Russians. Russia protested strenuously against any concessions to the French, and the Sultan was in the unfortunate position of being bound to offend one of the two powers. This particular dispute was almost patched up, however, when in 1853 the Tsar, as though to make things as awkward for Turkey as possible, added fresh claims and demanded in effect that Russia should exercise a general right of protection over all the Orthodox Christians in the Ottoman Empire.

3. Russian claim to protect all Christians in Ottoman Empire

TURKEY IN DANGER.

Britain's constant view of Russian ambitions in the Balkans. Cartoon in Punch, *9th April 1853.*

This additional demand on the part of Russia led on to the war. The danger was that Russia might use such a privilege to interfere in every part of the Ottoman Empire purely for her own benefit. Turkey, though alarmed and resentful, might possibly have given way to so powerful a foe, but the Sultan was unofficially encouraged to reject the Russian demands by the British ambassador at Constantinople, Lord Stratford de Redcliffe. The ambassador's action was upheld by the British Cabinet, and France took much the same line as Britain. Diplomatic complications followed and then a more positive move on the part of the Tsar – the occupation by Russian troops of the two semi-independent principalities of Moldavia and Wallachia, which though under Turkish suzerainty had no Turkish garrison. The Tsar announced that he would hold these territories until the Turks met the Russian claims. Further diplomatic negotiations then failed when Turkey, sensing the support of the two western powers, at length delivered an ultimatum calling on Russia to evacuate the two territories. When she did not, the Turkish armies marched north and later in October 1853 a state of war set in between the Russians and the Turks.

As yet, however, diplomatic efforts to arrange the dispute were still being pursued, and the war remained tentative. To be prepared for any eventuality, Britain and France (whose ruler Napoleon III also had a personal quarrel with Nicholas about incomplete recognition of his title)[1] had ordered their warships up the Dardanelles during September. This broke the Straits Convention of 1841, for the situation at that time was still short of declared war. By mid-November the British and French fleets were concentrated off Constantinople. Nicholas, thinking the two powers would soon sail with the main Turkish fleet up the Bosphorus to the Black Sea and threaten Russia there, decided to act quickly. He ordered the Russian fleet to attack a light Turkish squadron on the Black Sea. This action, at Sinope, in which the new Russian shell-guns rapidly set the Turkish vessels ablaze, was for some reason regarded in Britain and France as an unjustifiable massacre, and war-feeling at once ran high. It has to be remembered, by way of explanation, that the working and middle classes of both Britain and France were delighted at the prospect of striking a blow against the most despotic monarch in Europe, who in addition to allowing his own people no liberty, had also deprived the Poles and Hungarians of theirs. Swept on by public enthusiasm, Britain and France sent their ships up the Bosphorus into the Black Sea. They then demanded that Russia should withdraw her troops from Moldavia and Wallachia and recall her ships from the Black Sea to their base at Sebastopol. When she refused, war followed.

The first object of the war was rapidly attained in August 1854 when the Russians withdrew from Moldavia and Wallachia. They did so, however, only because Austria and Prussia were now demanding the evacuation of these two principalities – which Austria, by agreement with the Turks, then occupied for the duration of the war. This, however, brought little prestige to Britain and France, who scarcely felt that they had yet enjoyed a war at all. Accordingly the Allied governments decided to destroy the great naval base, Sebastopol, and to this end in September 1854 they landed an expeditionary force in the Crimean Peninsula. Elsewhere they also conducted naval operations in the Baltic, while the Turks and the Russians clashed in the Caucasus.

Russia occupies Moldavia and Wallachia, July 1853.

War with Turkey begins, October 1853

Turkish flotilla destroyed at Sinope, Nov. 1853

Popular sentiment against Russia

Crimean War begins, March 1854

[1] See p. 91.

CAPTURED GUN EMPLACEMENT AT SEBASTOPOL
The main Allied objective in the Crimean War was the capture and dismantlement of Sebastopol, the great Russian naval base on the Black Sea. Nearly a year – of great hardship for the besieging troops – passed before this was achieved. The photo shows part of one of the redoubts after the final assault in September, 1855.

The Crimean campaign will live for all time as a fantastic exhibition of military inefficiency and political futility at their worst. One historian has termed it 'a contest entered into without necessity, conducted without foresight, and deserving to be reckoned from its archaic arrangements and tragic mismanagements rather among medieval than modern campaigns'. The object of the Allies was scarcely worth wasting a man on – even if Sebastopol were destroyed and Russian warships driven from the Black Sea, that state of affairs could not be made permanent. As

Futility of the war

soon as the British and French force was removed, for the Sultan would not want the continued presence of such embarrassingly powerful allies, Russia was bound to build up a Black Sea fleet once more. It was about as sensible as for Russia to hope to prevent Britain or France building a fleet on the Atlantic.

As though the object of the war were not senseless enough, its conduct reached the very height of absurdity. After the successful landing in the Crimea and the subsequent allied victory on the River Alma, the obvious move should have been an attack on Sebastopol itself, which was not well fortified. To a land attack on the south it could offer little resistance, though from the sea, especially since the Allies had allowed the Russians time to block the harbour by sinking ships, it was almost untakeable. Accordingly the allied army was marched round to the south of the town, the generals being so confident of rapid victory that orders were given for knapsacks, clothes, tents, and the like to be left behind – with a Crimean winter approaching. When the commanders seriously examined the place, they decided that a preliminary bombardment was necessary. Since the guns had now to be fetched and since it had not occurred to the British War Office to make arrangements for the construction of the necessary five-mile railway from the base, the artillery took three weeks to arrive. During this period the only really able commander in the district, a Russian engineer-officer of German descent named Todleben, designed and constructed an elaborate series of earthwork defences round the town. These linked together certain existing stone towers or redoubts, such as the Malakoff and the Redan. In fact, by the time the Allies had finished their bombardment Sebastopol was much stronger than when they first arrived outside it. Not only that, but the Russians had by now brought up a further army of 100,000 men, which gave them in all about 140,000 against 60,000 of the Allies. A more disastrous military decision than that of Marshal St Arnaud and Lord Raglan to postpone the original assault it would be difficult to find.

The battle of Inkerman, which followed in November, gave the Allies a taste of victory, while Balaclava a week or so beforehand had shown in the famous charge of the Light Brigade that not even the appalling blunders of their own commanders could shake the courage of the British troops. In the words of one French general, it was magnificent but it was not war. The engagements did not produce any important results, and the Allies had to settle down to winter in the Crimea. The men had no cold-weather equipment; snow blocked the roads and made it impossible to bring up ammunition, food or forage. Horses died of starvation, making the transport problem still worse. With inadequate nourishment and disgraceful sanitation the army suffered dreadfully from cholera. Owing to the complete lack of any but local dressing-stations, serious casualties had to be shipped right across the Black Sea to the nearest big hospital at Scutari, a journey which in war conditions often took three weeks. And there, too, chaos reigned. The hospital, hastily converted from a barracks, was built near great sewers and cesspools. It was ridden with vermin. The most elementary necessities were lacking. There were not enough beds or blankets, only coarse canvas sheets, no bedroom furniture at all except empty beer-bottles for candlesticks, hardly any basins, towels, soap, brooms, trays, plates, knives, forks, spoons, fuel, scissors, stretchers, splints, bandages, or drugs. When materials did arrive, they were lost in the Turkish Customs House or held up by departmental regulations and War Office red tape. To treatment in such conditions those who were maimed in the

Investment of
Sebastopol

Todleben

War conditions

Hospital conditions
at Scutari

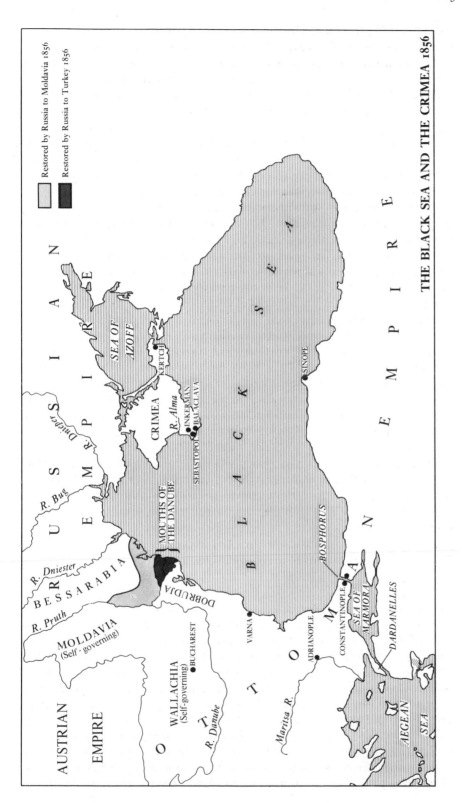

THE BLACK SEA AND THE CRIMEA 1856

Restored by Russia to Moldavia 1856
Restored by Russia to Turkey 1856

AUSTRIAN

EMPIRE

RUSSIAN EMPIRE

R. Dniester
R. Pruth
R. Bug
R. Dnieper

BESSARABIA

MOLDAVIA
(Self-governing)

WALLACHIA
(Self-governing)

BUCHAREST

R. Danube

DOBRUDJA

MOUTHS OF
THE DANUBE

CRIMEA
SEA OF
AZOFF

KERTCH

R. Alma
INKERMAN
BALACLAVA
SEBASTOPOL

SINOPE

B   L   A   C   K   S   E   A

VARNA

Maritsa R.

ADRIANOPLE

CONSTANTINOPLE

BOSPHORUS

SEA OF
MARMORA

DARDANELLES

O   T   T   O   M   A   N   E   M   P   I   R   E

AEGEAN

SEA

Crimea could look forward; and meanwhile the dreary siege of Sebastopol dragged on.

Reorganisation of Allied effort, 1855

Fortunately for the Allies an unofficial observer, W. H. Russell, the correspondent of *The Times*, gave the British public some account of the ghastly mismanagement. An inquiry was started into the conduct of the war. Lord Aberdeen, never an enthusiast for the war, was replaced as Prime Minister by the more vigorous Palmerston, and in the spring of 1855 the Allied army was reorganised. Meanwhile

Florence Nightingale

Florence Nightingale, an Englishwoman from a wealthy family, who had gone out with some volunteer nurses, had transformed the hospital at Scutari. Using money collected by her friends and by *The Times*, she succeeded, against the bitter opposition of many of the regular authorities, in reorganising the nursing, the laundry, the sanitary conditions, the food and the clothing of the wounded. On one occasion when she was visiting the Crimea the chief medical officer even tried to starve her into submission by ordering that no rations should be supplied to her and her nurses, a manoeuvre which the prudent Miss Nightingale forestalled by arriving with a great quantity of provisions! After six months' heroic struggle she succeeded in reducing the death rate of the wounded from forty-four per cent to two per cent. The one lasting result of the Crimean war was the reform in military nursing brought about by this remarkable woman, who gained the reputation of a saint by the ruthless persistence of a demon.

Capture of Sebastopol, September to October 1855

At last, in June 1855, after the Allies had been reinforced by the Piedmontese, the southern part of Sebastopol fell. Even then it took another four months before the whole fortress succumbed, the key to success being the storming of the Malakoff redoubt by the French in September. Palmerston at this stage was for continuing the war and winning a more resounding victory. Eventually, however, Napoleon III made him agree to peace by intimating that if the French continued the war they would do so to liberate Poland and other subject nationalities of Europe – developments so far-reaching that Palmerston quailed at the possibilities involved. The conclusion of peace was helped too by the death of Nicholas and the accession of his son Alexander II, more liberally inclined, with no personal enmity towards the French Emperor and willing to concede most of the points at issue. The most decisive factor of all, however, was that Austria at last decided on action, and issued an ultimatum to Russia based on the Allies' minimum terms. An armistice was then quickly arranged between the powers and one of the most futile of wars was over.

Treaty of Paris, 1856

The Treaty of Paris, which fixed the final terms, gave the Allies most of what they had fought for. Among the most important clauses the Black Sea was neutralised (i.e. both Turkey and Russia were forbidden to have warships on it). The Russian demand for a protectorate over the Balkan Christians was dismissed and a simple promise accepted from the Sultan that he would treat this section of his subjects on an equality with his Mohammedans. In addition, Moldavia and Wallachia, enlarged by southern Bessarabia taken from Russia, were given complete independence, except that Turkish overlordship had to be formally acknowledged, and the same arrangement was made for Serbia. Thus, on paper at least, the Allies had won a considerable victory. In fact, however, none of the objects achieved by the war on which the victors most congratulated themselves had the slightest permanence. The Black Sea clause was repudiated by Russia while France was busy fighting Prussia in 1870. The Sultan showed not the least sign of carrying out his promise about the Christians. Moldavia and Wallachia, it is true, prospered and soon became the Kingdom of Rumania, but that was more or less incidental, as was the development of Serbia – it was not for them that over half a million men had died. The results which really counted were rather apart from the issues both of the war and the peace – results such as Florence Nightingale's reforms and the impetus given to reform, and later revolution, in Russia by the revelation of the Tsardom's inefficiency. If the war did in any sense check the advance of Russia, the check was purely a temporary one. Not the preservation of the power of the Sultan but the formation of new national states in the Balkans was to provide the best barrier against a Russian advance to Constantinople. That, however, was for Britain to discover in the future. Meanwhile the Crimean War had illustrated the truth that war is a risky instrument of policy, liable to produce results which are largely unforeseen.

Temporary nature of the settlement

3. The Balkan Nations to the Congress of Berlin, 1878

The main developments of the next few years in the Eastern Question concerned rather the small Balkan nationalities than the great Powers. In 1862, for example, the Greek king Otto, whose reign had been one long period of misgovernment, had to abdicate, a successor being found in Prince George of Denmark after the throne had been practically hawked round Europe. Britain showed goodwill to the new dynasty by ceding to Greece a British protectorate – the Ionian Isles.[1]

Greece

In Serbia difficulties also occurred with the ruler, partly as a result of a long-standing and bloody feud between two rival families who claimed the throne. The Serbs, after losing their independence in the fourteenth century, had remained under direct Turkish rule until the beginning of the nineteenth century, when a chieftain of peasant origin known as Kara George ('Black George') started a successful rebellion. From 1804 to 1813 the Serbs under Kara George enjoyed practical self-government; but then the Turks, having made peace with the Russians, reasserted their control and drove out Kara George and his main helpers. His place as leader of the national movement was taken by one of the few who remained, Milosh Obrenović, who in turn led a revolt against the Turks and by 1817 re-gained virtual self-government for Serbia. Hearing this, Kara George returned from exile: and when the Turks demanded his body, dead or alive, Milosh obligingly sent along the severed head of his former chief. Under Milosh as ruling prince the country enjoyed administrative independence, but was subject to a Turkish garrison and payment of tribute.

Serbia

Virtual independence of Turkey

In 1839, however, Milosh was forced to abdicate because of his autocratic methods. He was succeeded briefly by two sons in turn, the second of whom, Michael, was deposed in 1842. Russia, the Serbs' 'big brother', who resented the independent policies of the Obrenovićs, had some influence in all this. The new prince was, not surprisingly, a son of Kara George, Alexander Karageorgović. However, he did not please the Serbs, and in 1859 this Karageorgović prince was deposed for Milosh to return, to be followed in due course again by his son Michael.

Obrenović and Karageorgović

---

[1] Corfu and the other six Ionian islands had been taken by France from Venice during the Revolutionary Wars. They were captured by Britain from France during the Napoleonic Wars, and retained as a British protectorate in 1815.

In spite of his military and educational reforms, his promising alliances with other Balkan peoples, and his successes in getting all Turkish troops withdrawn (only the Turkish flag then remaining), Michael Obrenović was murdered in 1868 by Karageorgović assassins. An Obrenović continued on the throne for a while, however, though the deadly rivalry, as we shall see, was by no means over. The nature of this royal gangsterdom is shown by the fact that of the Serbian rulers of the nineteenth century only one was allowed to die in his bed in his native land – and he was insane.

Moldavia and Wallachia –

The two districts of Moldavia and Wallachia, at the mouth of the Danube, had, as we have already seen, received virtual independence at the end of the Crimean War, paying a tribute still to Turkey. As outposts of the Turkish Empire they had constantly been occupied by Russian forces when war threatened between the two powers. They had, however, always shown a strongly national spirit and taken pride in their descent from the old Roman colony of Dacia. Revolutions had occurred, notably in 1848, but little progress was made until in 1856 the powers recognised the provinces' independence with the idea of creating a buffer zone between Turkey and Russia. They were given separate assemblies and forbidden to unite, but this was ingeniously overcome by the two assemblies each choosing the same prince – a development eventually agreed to by Turkey and the powers. The new state of Rumania may be said to date from 1861, when the prince concerned, Alexander I, united the two separate assemblies. This name, however, was not given to it until 1866, when Alexander was forced to abdicate in the usual Balkan fashion. His reign had brought free compulsory education and the liberation of the peasantry, but he had offended too many vested interests. Prince Charles of Hohenzollern then accepted the throne with the blessing of Turkey, which retained a nominal overlordship. He promised to rule by the terms of a new constitution, a very democratic one except in its denial of political rights to the Jewish population. The selection of Prince Charles, a close relative of the King of Prussia, William I, gave the future German Empire a useful ally on the Danube, and Rumania began to revolve in Bismarck's orbit.

– virtual independence, 1856

– union, 1861

– they become 'Rumania', 1866

Montenegro

Of the other Balkan peoples Montenegro, under a separate prince, had for centuries enjoyed the same virtual independence as Serbia, an effort by the Sultan to increase his authority having been defeated by vigorous Montenegrin resistance in 1858. Close relations were pursued with Serbia, and it could be reckoned that if the Sultan ran into any difficulties, Montenegro and Serbia would take the chance to increase their territory and end the last traces of Turkish authority.

Revolts against Turkey

Bosnia and Herzegovina

Serbia and Montenegro support the Bosnians, 1876

Bulgarians also revolt

By 1870 of all the main Balkan peoples only the Bulgarians had yet to taste independence. It was precisely in this quarter that the next acute phase of the Eastern Question developed. In 1875 Bosnia and Herzegovina, two provinces inhabited largely by Serbs but not yet united with Serbia, rose against their Turkish masters. The trouble was the unfavourable position of the Christians, who were excluded from governmental employment, and their heavy taxation by the Turks, who took some two-thirds of the peasants' crops. When the revolt showed signs of establishing itself, Serbia and Montenegro joined in to help their brother Serbs, declaring war against Turkey in 1876. This encouraged a small section of the Bulgarians to revolt simultaneously while the going was good. The Turks, in a fright at being confronted with four sets of foes, now behaved with the utmost

THE DECLINE OF THE OTTOMAN
EMPIRE IN EUROPE 1783–1913

H U N G A R Y

TRANSYLVANIA

R. Save

R. Danube

BESSARABIA
(To Russia 1812)

R. Pruth

R. Bug

nioster

LITTLE
TARTARY
(To Russia 1791)

OCHAKOF

M O L D A V I A

BOSNIA
1878 (Austrian Occ.)
1908 (to Austria)

BELGRADE

R U M A N I A

WALLACHIA
1861   BUCHAREST

1817

To Rumania (1878)

HERZEGOVINA

R. Danube

1833

1878

MONTENEGRO

S E R B I A

PLEVNA
1878

SOFIA

B U L G A R I A

B L A C K

S E A

A L B A N I A

EASTERN RUMELIA
1885

ADRIANOPLE

1913

1913

1913

A D R I A T I C   S E A

1913

M A C E D O N I A

1913

1913

SALONIKA

1913

GALLIPOLI

1913

T U R K E Y

SCUTARI
CONSTANTINOPLE

Bosphorus

SEA OF
MARMORA

CORFU   EPIRUS

G R E E C E

THESSALY
1878

Dardanelles

IONIAN
SEA

A E G E A N   S E A

A N A T O L I A

1830,1832

I O N I A N   I S L A N D S

MOREA

ATHENS

CYCLADES

M E D I T E R R A N E A N   S E A

RHODES
(Italian Occ.1912)

CRETE   1898
,1913

Boundaries of States at
times prior to 1913
Boundaries of States in 1913
Boundary of Turkish Empire in 1783
Boundary of Turkey in Europe 1913
'Big Bulgaria' as proposed in Treaty of San Stefano 1878

ferocity. In one village of Bulgaria, for example, the inhabitants surrendered on a promise that their lives would be spared – only to be slaughtered to a man, or rather to a woman and child. Those who were not butchered like cattle were collected in the school and the church, there to be burned alive as the buildings went up in a flare of petroleum. For two months no one could approach the village, so nauseous was the stench of the five thousand rotting corpses. The news of these massacres startled and shocked the world, though at first the details were imperfectly known.

'The Bulgarian
Atrocities'

Russia takes a hand

It was hardly surprising in the circumstances that Russia decided to intervene, especially since the Serbs were being badly beaten by the Turks. The Powers compelled Turkey to restore the captured Serbian territory, and then demanded that all Christian subjects of the Sultan should enjoy equal treatment with Mohammedans, and that Bulgaria, Bosnia, and Herzegovina should be granted home-rule. The new Sultan, the wily Abdul Hamid II, foiled this, however, by the clever manoeuvre of announcing a constitution for all subjects, complete with a parliament of approved Western type. As no one, not even the British Prime Minister, Disraeli, who was more strongly pro-Turk than anyone, could see the Sultan carrying out this promise, an ultimatum was sent requiring some guarantees and Turkish disarmament. When this was refused, Russia, soon supported by Montenegro, Rumania, and Serbia, to say nothing of the Bulgarian peasants, declared war on Turkey. Before this onslaught the Turks at first wilted. Then, to the surprise and eventually the admiration of Europe, they held up the Russian armies for several months by their heroic defence of Plevna. At last, however, the Russians, with their Cossack troops rivalling the Turks in barbarities, penetrated south as far as Adrianople, and it seemed that by January 1878 nothing could prevent the fall of Constantinople.

Abdul Hamid refuses the powers' demands

Russia, Serbia, etc., fight Turkey, 1877

At the critical moment, however, two other powers had their say. Though the Liberal opposition in Britain under Gladstone and even a section of his own Conservative party by no means agreed with him, Disraeli had all along minimised the extent of the Turkish atrocities in Bulgaria. Now, alarmed at the rapid Russian advance on Constantinople and anxious to cling to Palmerston's traditional policy of preserving the Ottoman Empire, he ordered the British fleet to the Dardanelles. With this force he threatened Russia if she advanced farther. The same sort of attitude was at this point also belatedly taken up by Austria-Hungary, who had ambitions of her own in the Balkans. In 1876 she had concluded a secret agreement with Russia to remain neutral in a Russo-Turkish war if she were allowed to occupy Bosnia and Herzegovina,[1] but if the war went on much longer Russia and Serbia would be so powerful that they might not permit this occupation. Accordingly Austria-Hungary now demanded that an armistice should be signed; and Russia, with her Black Sea fleet not as yet rebuilt after the Crimean war, decided she could not face the combined hostility of Britain, Austria-Hungary and Turkey.

Disraeli and Austria check Russia

Treaty of San Stefano, 1878

The treaty of San Stefano of March 1878, now dictated by the Russians to the Turks, contained clauses to enlarge Serbia and Montenegro and secure their complete independence. Russia herself was to take territory in Asia and regain her lost part of Bessarabia at the mouth of the Danube, which was to be ceded by her unfortunate ally Rumania, who was to get in return a barren strip of Turkish territory. Bosnia and Herzegovina were to be given home-rule. Most important of all were the clauses concerning the Bulgarians. A great new state of Bulgaria was to be set up, including the district of Macedonia, which would cut Turkey off from her remaining possessions in the Balkans. Many Greeks and Serbs, besides the Bulgarians, were to be included in it. It was to be self-governing, but to be 'advised' in its first years by Russia.

The 'big Bulgaria'

The terms of this settlement immediately aroused the hostility of Britain.

---

[1] Austria's excuse for her desire to occupy Bosnia and Herzegovina was the misgovernment there under Turkish rule.

THE DOGS OF WAR.

Bull A 1. "TAKE CARE, MY MAN! IT MIGHT BE AWK'ARD IF YOU WAS TO LET 'EM LOOSE!"

Russia's supposed control of the small Balkan States and Britain's anxiety to preserve Turkey are both well shown here. Cartoon by Tenniel.

Though the British government had gone a certain way with Russia and though the Sultan had made British support difficult by his behaviour, Disraeli was not prepared to see the Ottoman Empire carved up so completely. He objected particularly to the size of the new Bulgaria, for he persisted in regarding it as simply a Russian puppet-state. In this he was supported by the usual anti-Russian feeling in the country, exemplified in the famous song which now swept the music-halls:

> We don't want to fight, but by jingo if we do,
> We've got the men, we've got the ships, we've got the money too

– a song which gave the word 'jingoist,' meaning an aggressive patriot, to the

Disraeli objects to the 'big Bulgaria'

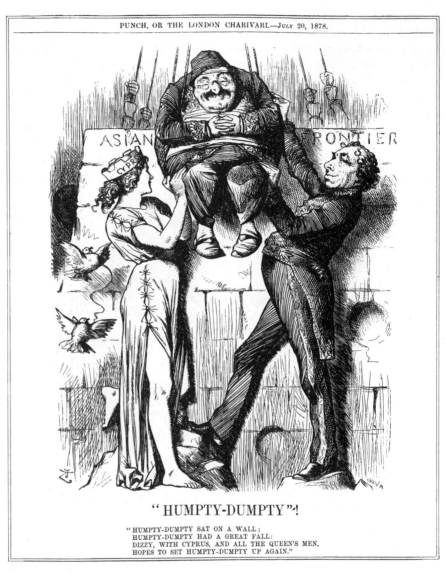

"HUMPTY-DUMPTY"!

"HUMPTY-DUMPTY SAT ON A WALL;
HUMPTY-DUMPTY HAD A GREAT FALL:
DIZZY, WITH CYPRUS, AND ALL THE QUEEN'S MEN,
HOPES TO SET HUMPTY-DUMPTY UP AGAIN."

Thanks to Disraeli, Turkey regains part of the 'big Bulgaria' at the Congress of Berlin. Cartoon by Tenniel.

language. Accordingly Disraeli now threatened Russia with war unless she consented to a revision of the terms of the Treaty of San Stefano by a European Congress. Austria-Hungary supported Britain after receiving a promise that Britain would not object to an Austrian occupation of Bosnia and Herzegovina. Faced with this combination Russia again gave way, and the Powers met at Berlin under Bismarck's 'honest brokerage' to revise the treaty.

The Congress of Berlin was at once Disraeli's greatest success and his greatest failure. Everything went much as Britain wished. Certain of the Russian terms were recognised: the complete independence of Serbia, Montenegro, and Rumania, for example, and the Bessarabia arrangement. The 'big Bulgaria' of

Congress of Berlin,
1878

San·Stefano, however, was drastically reduced. It was in fact trisected, part forming the new state of Bulgaria, part forming a separate district with semi-independence known as Eastern Roumelia, and part being handed back to Turkey. Moreover, when Russia claimed her Asiatic conquests, Disraeli produced a private agreement with the Sultan by which Britain was to receive a lease of Cyprus from Turkey – officially to give Britain a base to protect Turkey in Asia and to watch over Turkey's Christians, actually to offset Russian gains in Asia Minor. This, then, was the price of Britain's aid! Austria-Hungary too, was allowed to occupy Bosnia and Herzegovina and another strip of territory which severed Serbia from Montenegro. The Sultan, of course, promised his usual reforms in connection with his Christian subjects, and Disraeli and Salisbury

The 'big Bulgaria' reduced

Britain takes Cyprus; Austria 'administers' Bosnia and Herzegovina

PUNCH, OR THE LONDON CHARIVARI.—June 15, 1878.

FIGURES FROM A "TRIUMPH."

(A RELIEF—ON THE ROAD TO BERLIN)

Disraeli and Salisbury set off for the Congress of Berlin, whence they returned bringing 'peace with honour!' There is a pun here in 'relief' – a form of sculpture and a relief from the fear of war. Cartoon by Tenniel.

were able to return to Britain in triumph. As far as they could see, Russia had been checked, Turkey strengthened once more, and though some millions of Bulgarians had been restored to the Sultan's rule, there was no danger of further massacres because he had given promises of good behaviour! Britain, too, had acquired a valuable Mediterranean outpost – and all without a war! No wonder Disraeli claimed to have returned bringing 'peace with honour', and no wonder that historians, examining the outcome of the Berlin settlement, have sometimes waxed a little sarcastic at the phrase.

'Peace with honour'

Indeed, if we look ahead from the Berlin settlement, we find that most of Disraeli's work either collapsed rapidly or else contributed to later disaster. Within

Results of the Congress

Bulgaria unites with
Eastern Roumelia

seven years Bulgaria had united with Eastern Roumelia in spite of all the work of the Powers. The Sultan, of course, neglected his promises of reform, and the Armenians were later to suffer the barbarity of systematic massacre – against which Britain's occupation of Cyprus proved no guarantee. Perhaps worst of all, Montenegro and Serbia were bitterly offended by the Austrian occupation of Bosnia and Herzegovina. The occupation of these provinces, with their mainly Serbian population, so inflamed relations between Austria-Hungary and Serbia that in the long run there was bound to be a conflagration. When it came, in July 1914, all Europe was involved in the blaze. Further, it became obvious within a few years that the new Balkan states, with their strongly nationalist feeling, were a far more effective barrier against Russian aggression than a decadent Turkish Empire. Even Salisbury, co-author with Disraeli of the Treaty of Berlin, confessed before long that in supporting Turkey Britain had 'backed the wrong horse'. When a politician admits error we may well agree with him – and meanwhile the Eastern Question remained unanswered.

Increase in Serbian
hostility to Austria –
Hungary

CHAPTER 14
Russia and Poland, 1789–1881

1. To the End of the Reign of Alexander I, 1825

Baffling alike to our ancestors as to ourselves, in the east of Europe – and beyond it – lay the enormous state of Russia. Living almost in a different world from the west of Europe, a world in which, as the century wore on, great literature, music and ballet mingled strangely with tortures, floggings, drunkenness and corruption, Russia had a huge array of problems all her own. Perhaps the main clue to these is simply the size of the country, stretching by the end of the century from the Arctic to the Black Sea, from the Baltic to the Pacific. Indeed, the first fact to remember is that most of Russia is not in Europe at all. The immense difficulty of communication in such circumstances, especially before the development of the railway, inevitably kept Russia in an extremely backward condition compared with states like Britain or France. This, however, did not prevent her pursuing a foreign policy calculated to increase her territory at the expense of Turkey and the Asiatic tribes, and so, in many ways, add to her difficulties.

Unique character of Russia

Though signs of Western influence had appeared before, Russia's real importance in European history dates from the reign of the Tsar Peter the Great. This brutal, intelligent ruffian, nearly seven feet tall, who enjoyed birching a woman or personally carrying out an execution, greatly admired the efficiency of his Western neighbours. His journeys to Europe, in one of which he worked as a shipwright to improve his knowledge of ship-building, are famous. The effect of his policy was to direct Russia's attentions westwards – as in his successful war against Sweden for Baltic supremacy (involving the acquisition of Latvia and Esthonia) and his foundation of St Petersburg ('the Window to the West', known since 1925 as Leningrad). To make sure that this policy survived, he had his own son and heir, who disapproved of it, murdered after unspeakable tortures. Peter was not, however, interested in expansion only towards the West. He repeatedly fought the Turks, without much final success, for a foothold on the Black Sea; and from the Persians he wrested control of territory on the Caspian.

Peter the Great, 1689–1725

Something of Peter's interest in the West was also shown in his policy within Russia. He did not, of course, desire political liberty for his people: what he did desire was to improve the deplorably low standard of Russian material civilisation. With his floggings and killings, his drunkenness and immorality, he was hardly a shining light of culture himself, but he struck hard at certain Russian customs symbolic of the conservative East – the Oriental seclusion of women, the power of the priests, the beards and gowns of the men. Above all, he strove to create the three things which he perceived were the basis of European state-power – a strong army, a strong navy, and an efficient civil service. Industries, too, like iron-production, he encouraged as necessary for military power.

Catherine II (the Great), 1762–96

Reform –

The broad lines of Peter's policies were resumed over thirty years later by Catherine the Great. Before the excesses of the French Revolution alarmed her, she had been disposed to introduce reforms of a Western character. Some advances were made in education and medicine, and a codification of the chaotic Russian laws was contemplated if not achieved. Catherine's German ancestry and French culture brought the Russian upper classes more into touch with European thought generally – she had a notable correspondence with Voltaire, and the philosopher Diderot stayed with her. By the end of the eighteenth century the Russian nobility habitually spoke French among themselves. But the most outstanding feature of her emulation of Peter the Great (apart from the scandal of her private life) was

– and expansion

in her foreign policy. Here, like Peter, she waged successful wars against Sweden (for further Baltic territory) and against Turkey (from whom she took the Crimea). Victory over the Turks established Russia on the Black Sea and gave her ports from which to export the grain grown in her new southern provinces.

The partitions of Poland –

The greatest expansion of Catherine's reign, however, was westward at the expense of Poland. This ancient Kingdom, one of the largest of European states, had since the seventeenth century lapsed into a kind of governmental anarchy. Almost alone of Continental states it had kept its medieval parliament, not, however, as an instrument of liberty but as a battleground of the nobility. With the nobles' privilege of the *liberum veto* and an elective monarchy foreign powers could influence matters in their own interest very easily by bribery. Efficient government was impossible, and the state of Poland, hopelessly weak through internal dissension, was a great temptation to its stronger neighbours.

– 1772

The complete lack of morality which usually marked the foreign policy of the European Powers was shown most nakedly in the partitions of Poland. In three stages within less than twenty-five years a state which had existed for centuries vanished from the map. The first partition between Russia, Prussia, and Austria in 1772 cost Poland two-sevenths of her land and nearly half her population. Not content, Catherine then encouraged the other two Powers to intervene against the French Revolution to keep them occupied while she absorbed some more; and when the Poles, frightened at last into sense, tried in 1791 to make the monarchy hereditary and abolish the *liberum veto*, Catherine launched an invasion. Not to be outdone, the Prussians, who had noted Catherine's movements and avoided being too deeply involved in the French Revolutionary war,

– 1793

then also occupied part of Poland. Thus a second partition, this time between two Powers, took place in 1793. It gave Russia, in addition to the remaining parts of White Russia and part of Lithuania, the whole of the Ukraine.

– 1795

A Polish revolt against their King's acknowledgement of these losses and of Russian suzerainty then gave Catherine the opportunity for further intervention. This was done by agreement with the other powers concerned.[1] In 1795 she gave

[1] See p. 37.

A GREAT RUSSIAN GENERAL: SUVOROV

A life-long soldier ennobled for his many victories, especially against the Turks, Suvorov was dismissed when the erratic tsar Paul I succeeded Catherine the Great. In 1799, at the age of 70, he was recalled to lead the Russian armies against the French in Italy. In co-operation with the Austrians he almost drove them out – but later suffered reverses in Switzerland which led to his new renewed disgrace. A fierce man with a biting wit, he despised court life and comfort, and lived mostly like a private soldier when on campaigns and a peasant when not. He showed no mercy to captured cities, and little to his own troops if heavy losses could bring victory.

Poland the *coup de grâce* by seizing the most valuable section of what remained (Courland and the rest of Lithuania) and leaving Austria and Prussia (who acquired Warsaw) to divide the rest. With most of Poland under her control Russia was now more deeply involved than ever before in Europe.

Paul I, 1796–1801

The Napoleonic wars soon showed the strength of Russia's interest in Europe. As we have seen, Catherine's son Paul had brought Russia into the second coalition (1799) against revolutionary France.[1] His reasons included resentment against Napoleon for occupying Malta, for the Knights of St John had recently made the Tsar their protector. This anti-French policy, however, lasted only a year or so.

'Armed Neutrality'

By 1801 he was leading the 'Armed Neutrality' against the British 'right of search'. This move was unpopular in Russian court circles – but not as unpopular as Paul's many acts of capricious tyranny. Catherine, who had probably not intended him to rule, had kept him isolated on an estate where he was given 2,000 soldiers as a more or less personal force. He had become a maniac for military drilling and discipline, and completely spoiled good ideas (in which he was not lacking) by the punishments he inflicted for failure to carry out his instructions to the letter. 'The garrison of the capital,' writes one historian, 'lived under a kind of parade-ground terror, and it became a common thing for officers to parade with their affairs wound up and with a stock of ready money lest they were sent off the square straight to Siberia.' All this, together with acts like banning the import of books and manuscripts, subjecting the lower clergy, till then exempt, to flogging as a punishment, and enforcing a new and impractical military uniform (which reintroduced pigtails and powder), cost Paul his throne. In 1801 there was a court

Murder of Paul

conspiracy, which his son Alexander almost certainly approved, to dethrone him. It went further than Alexander intended, and resulted in the murder of the Tsar.

Alexander I, 1801–25

Much has already been said about Paul's son Alexander I in connection with the Napoleonic wars, the Congress System, and the career of Metternich.[2] Deeply interested from the first in foreign policy, his natural move was to join Britain in

The Third Coalition, 1805

the third coalition against France. The defeat of the Russians at Austerlitz and Friedland, however, and annoyance at being denied a loan by Britain brought him for a time into the French camp. The Treaty of Tilsit (1807) seemed to promise

Tilsit, 1807

him great advantages – even a domination of Europe shared with Napoleon, with the first instalment for Alexander to be found in Turkey. But since Napoleon did nothing to fulfil this hope and non-industrialised Russia badly needed the cheap British goods excluded by the Treaty of Tilsit, Alexander soon shook off Napoleon's spell. The result was the fatal Moscow campaign and the beginning of the

Moscow campaign, 1812

end for Napoleon. So far the story is well-known. What is less familiar is the extent of Alexander's other wars during this period. By 1815 every neighbour of Russia's except China had felt the weight of her arms, with the result that Alexander's territorial gains – notably Finland from Sweden, Bessarabia from Turkey, Georgia and three other districts from Persia – increased the Russian population by twelve millions. Yet all this time Alexander the conqueror had been at heart Alexander

Expansion of Russia

the liberator, anxious to free mankind from the French, from despotism, from barbarian savagery, from anything except his own shifting and uncertain ideas.

The 'liberal' phase of Alexander's life is usually reckoned to run from his

---

[1] See p. 41.

[2] See pp. 42, 49, 53–4, 61–70, 107.

youth, when he was greatly influenced by his Swiss tutor Laharpe, a disciple of Rousseau, till about 1819, when he succumbed to the views of Metternich. In 1814, for example, on the collapse of Napoleon, he was not at all anxious to shackle France with the old Bourbon monarchy. Instead he wanted Laharpe to design the perfect constitution for the French, a touching instance of the impression a schoolmaster may make on even a Tsar. Again, he allowed Finland, conquered from Sweden in 1808 and recognised as Russian territory by the Vienna treaties, its own separate customs and constitution, and an administration manned almost entirely by Finns.

Alexander's 'liberal' phase

But perhaps the outstanding example of this trend in Alexander's mind was his attitude to Poland. He sincerely desired to restore much of their ancient freedom to the Poles though not to the extent of granting complete independence. His idea was to unite all the Poles in one constitutional monarchy, to be ruled by himself, quite separately from his other possessions; and he was bitterly disappointed when the opposition of Austria, Prussia, and Britain prevented this. The Powers naturally suspected any scheme which gave Russia valuable acquisitions. However he proceeded with the plan in respect of what he had recently acquired of Napoleon's Grand Duchy of Warsaw. This, however, though it included Warsaw itself, amounted to only about one-sixth of the old Polish state.

The 'Kingdom of Poland'

This new Kingdom of Poland was given a constitution in some ways the most liberal in Europe. Freedom from arbitrary arrest, freedom of religion, freedom of the press were all guaranteed, while the right of voting was extended to a far larger class than possessed it at this time in Britain or France. Only Polish citizens could occupy posts in the army and civil service, and the Polish language was to be used for all official purposes. Moreover, in the first few years of the Kingdom a new code of laws was introduced, education was encouraged, the university of Warsaw was founded, Warsaw itself was partly rebuilt, and considerable improvements were made to roads, canals, and the great navigable rivers like the Vistula. The Poles were encouraged in all respects, and notably by the prospect of having Lithuania (which covered a much larger area than the Baltic state of 1918–40) included in their Kingdom. In 1818, when Alexander opened the first Polish Diet, he announced his complete satisfaction with what had been done. 'You have proved yourself equal to the task', he declared to the members, adding that the success of this liberal experiment in Poland encouraged him to extend similar privileges to Russia.

The liberal Polish constitution

There was certainly room for improvement in Russia itself. The reforms of Peter and Catherine (who in some respects had subjected the peasantry still more completely to the nobility) had barely scratched the surface. The root trouble was possibly the institution of serfdom, by which the overwhelming majority of the peasants were 'bound to the soil'. Either they had to supply work-service on the estate to which they belonged or else pay dues in money or kind instead, and they were not allowed to leave their district. The most barbarous part of Russian serfdom was not so much the liability to give labour service (though this was what the peasantry most resented, since they claimed that historically all the land belonged to themselves) as the fact that on the private (as opposed to the Crown) estates the lord had virtually complete power over the bodies and souls of his serfs, for he could easily disregard any laws designed to protect them. They might be made to work in a factory, for example, if the lord should start one, or sent off to the army

Conditions in Russia

Serfdom

if they gave trouble. Or they might be sold: the official price at this time ranged from 22 roubles for a baby boy to 1,000 roubles for a full-grown peasant. Girls were less valuable and changed hands at about two-thirds of this rate. Ghastly punishments, such as confinement in chains or flogging to death with the knout, were frequently ordered by vindictive lords or stewards. Alexander's favourite minister, for example, whose wife had been murdered by a serf in revenge for fiendish torture inflicted on his sister, caused twenty-two innocent but suspected peasants to be flogged to death without trial. Fortunately the position of the Crown serfs, or rather peasants, was better than that of the lords' serfs. Although they were bound to their districts and more or less at the Crown's command, they mostly paid for the occupation of their land in other ways than by direct service and so enjoyed greater freedom. One of their main grievances was the amount of these money dues and of taxation that they were required to pay.

Alexander, in his liberal phase, seemed inclined to do great things for the peasantry. One law allowed landowners to release serfs if they wished – but during half a century less than 400 landowners did wish. Serfdom was, it is true, abolished in one or two of the non-Russian provinces, such as Esthonia and Livonia, and in Russia a proposal to buy out all the private serfs by the Crown was considered. It remained a proposal. Apart from this, two or three of the worst features of serfdom were abolished – families might not be broken up by the sale of individuals (though they could still be sold *en bloc* with the lands), and punishment with the knout was (theoretically) limited to fifteen strokes.

In regard to other reforms in Russia, Alexander contemplated much and achieved little. The finances and the currency of Russia remained in a chaotic state; one-third of the annual expenditure went on the army and one-third of the annual income came from the sale of vodka. Drunkenness and corruption were rife and nothing was done to discourage them. A new army system, that of 'military colonies' was introduced, with the benevolent idea of settling soldiers on the land free of tax, so allowing them to be with their families and to spend part of their time on agriculture. The other idea behind the colonies was that this would be a cheap way of maintaining a large army. The system, however, ended up only by enslaving the local populations in the colonies, for the peasants' sons had to become soldiers and their daughters soldiers' wives.

A proposed codification of the law was no more successful, work on it being abandoned after 1815. Moreover the promised Russian constitution was never forthcoming. For actual reform the country had to be content with the creation of a properly organised State Council, the foundation of several schools and three universities, including that of St Petersburg, a great public library in the capital (stolen, incidentally, from Warsaw), the improvements in serfdom mentioned above, an increase in religious liberty, and minor measures such as abolition of flogging as a punishment for parish priests, and, some years later, for their wives. In general, however, greatly though Alexander's projects exceeded his accomplishments, the first period of his reign was one of hope. In the international sphere we have already seen the idealism which prompted the Holy Alliance of 1815.[1]

Alexander's change from half-hearted liberalism to downright reaction in international affairs has already been noted in connection with the career of Metter-

[1] See p. 65.

Savage punishments

Alexander's reforms

'Military colonies'

A codification proposed

Alexander abandons 'liberalism'

nich.[1] Events such as the Wartburg Festival, the murder of Kotzebue, the assassination of the Duke of Berri, the revolutionary movements in Spain, Naples, and Portugal, and finally two mutinies in his own imperial guards, together with the incessant prompting of Metternich, swung him round. He became convinced that to encourage the liberal spirit further would be to lose all his authority and to invite the fate of his own father, Paul. So the Holy Alliance and the 'Congress System', planned with such good intentions of keeping the peace, became instruments to suppress rebellion, however justified. Intervention by Austria in Italy and by France in Spain met with the Tsar's approval, and only the firm stand of Canning prevented an attempted restoration to the Spanish monarchy of the revolted South American colonies. Even in the Greek War of Independence Alexander was persuaded by Metternich that the Greeks, akin as they were to the Russians in religion, were merely one more set of rebels against their legitimate masters, the Turks.

'Congress System' used for repression

This change of front has sometimes been ascribed to religion. This would seem to be unjust. Alexander first felt deeply the impulses of religion after the delivery from the French during the Moscow Campaign. As he himself put it: 'Through the fire of Moscow my soul has been enlightened . . . I resolved to consecrate myself and my government to God.' An extremely religious Swedish baroness, under whose influence he fell in 1815, confirmed his purpose. The direct effect, however, does not seem to have been repressive, for from this period date the Holy Alliance, which in theory was all love and kindness, the new constitution for Poland, the liberal treatment of the Finns, the proposed Russian constitution, and so on. Nevertheless his religious feelings now prompted him to take more notice of the intolerant Russian upper clergy. By the end of his reign a persecution of all except the Orthodox was beginning.

Alexander's religious beliefs

Just as in foreign affairs Alexander changed to supporting Metternich round about 1819, so his home policy veered correspondingly. Russians were no longer allowed to study abroad; a strict censorship was re-imposed; controversial subjects like economics were withdrawn from the university curriculum. Above all, the Polish constitution, which had promised so much in 1818, was violated in several respects. A censorship was introduced in Poland, and the Tsar deliberately neglected to call the Diet for five years and in any case its debates were to be no longer public. Secret societies were now rigorously suppressed there as in Russia. In Finland similar steps were taken – Russian officials were introduced, the Diet suspended, and a censorship imposed. On all sides the cloudy liberalism of the Tsar was giving way to the clearest reaction.

A stricter régime in Russia

So, in violation of his earlier promises, the Tsar's reign closed. In 1825 he died suddenly, at the age of forty-eight. Undoubtedly his mind had been brilliant and versatile, but it had lacked stability. Either he entertained contradictory notions at one and the same time, or else he succumbed to intense enthusiasms during which he could see only one side of a picture. His fervent Christianity was in flagrant contradiction to his immoral private life and his incessant wars of conquest. His liberal ideas did not accord with his keenly autocratic instincts: he could never harmonise his theories as a man with his interests as a ruler. At one period he could speak of 'the absurd pretensions of absolute power'; at another he could

Alexander's character

[2] See p. 107.

entertain them all. Even in his younger days there was his contradictory foreign policy – first the foe of Napoleon, then his friend, then again his foe. Napoleon, a shrewd judge of men, early remarked that the Tsar's mind 'could not pursue one line of thought'; while Metternich was aware of a brilliant but incomplete personality: 'I never know what part of his mind is missing', he once remarked. An interesting study for the psychologist and a depressing one for the reformer, Alexander has been not inaptly summed up as 'the Russian Hamlet'.

2. From Nicholas I to the Assassination of Alexander II, 1825–81

Nicholas I, 1825–55

The reign of Alexander's brother and successor Nicholas I presents a more consistent picture. A three-week confusion between himself and his older brother about the succession – each at first recognised the other as the new ruler, though the elder had renounced his rights – gave the opportunity, when Nicholas finally proclaimed himself Tsar, for a number of army officers and liberals to attempt a revolution. This had been long contemplated by groups both at St Petersburg and in the south. The idea was not to abolish the Tsardom, but simply to insist on a national parliament and reforms which included reduction of army service, abolition of military colonies, and emancipation of the serfs. When certain regiments in St Petersburg, having sworn allegiance to the older brother, had to swear

The December rising, 1825

allegiance to Nicholas instead, it was not difficult to persuade some 3,000 of the troops to mutiny by demonstrating in favour of 'Constantine and a Constitution' – Constantine being the older brother and a Constitution being (in the opinion of some of the soldiers) Constantine's wife! But when after some hours of indecision Nicholas ordered the use of force, the movement was quickly crushed. Retribution swiftly followed. Apart from 300 or so shot during the fighting, 100 or more were exiled to Siberia and the five ringleaders were hanged. As they were about to die the ropes broke and three of the victims fell to the ground. 'Nothing's well done in Russia, not even hanging', murmured one of them as the noose was readjusted about his neck.

Strict suppression

The effect of this rising of the Decembrists (so called from the revolt having taken place in December) was to determine Nicholas on a strictly anti-liberal policy. A special secret police, previously abolished by Alexander, was re-established to organise ruthless suppression of all liberal views. A chance remark, the possession of a banned book, and a life term in Siberia might be the result. Yet we must remember that Nicholas himself was as conscientious and high-minded a man as many of those so bitterly opposed to him. A ruler of impressive presence and an iron disciplinarian, though kindly in private life, he honestly strove to do his best for his country and for civilisation by maintaining an unquestionable authority. Agitation, disorder, liberalism, these were to him the foes most damaging to peace and good government. He was not blind to the need for reform, and even introduced

A few mild reforms

some measures, such as abolition of punishment by the knout, which would have been admirable had they only been observed. A summary of Russian law was at last compiled. Technical institutes were founded. The currency was reformed. The first Russian factory acts were passed – though not enforced. Above all, the

THE GAMBLERS
A satire by the French artist Gustave Doré from his 'History of Holy Russia'. Russian landowners sometimes gambled for estates; but with these went human souls – the serfs.

emancipation of the nobles' serfs, who with their families made up some forty-five per cent of the Russian population, was – contemplated!

Yet in spite of all this, the government of Russia was an intellectual and social tyranny. The annual expenditure on the army now increased to forty per cent of the budget. Though a number of concessions were made to the state peasants, whose free status was formally confirmed, serfdom on private estates was fully maintained, though after 1833 serfs could no longer be sold in public. Not till 1848 were they given the right to possess chattels. Not surprisingly, there were about twenty revolts by groups of peasants every year of Nicholas's reign. Moreover, serfdom in factories, both state and private, was on the increase. Here again the most brutal conditions often prevailed, with serfs working sixteen or seventeen hours a day even as children, serfs banished to Siberia, and serfs flogged to death, so that the horrors of the English factory system before 1833 were far outdone. Serfs, too, were paid only half the wages of freemen. It was little wonder that Nicholas's reign saw a great growth in strikes, which were soon treated by the government as a serious crime. Serfs even began to commit offences in the hope of being exiled to Siberia, though that involved a terrible march on which many

Factory conditions

Siberia

perished, and – for some – unspeakable conditions in the Siberian mines. Altogether in the reign of Nicholas I about 150,000 of all classes were ordered to Siberia as exiles.

Nicholas's foreign policy

1. Russian expansion in the Balkans and Asia

The foreign policy of Nicholas has already been examined. It had two main objects: Russian expansion and the suppression of liberalism. In her Asiatic expansion Russia acquired another million square miles of territory, mainly in Siberia and central Asia. In Europe Nicholas rapidly intervened to help the Greeks against the Turks and won privileges from the Ottoman Empire by the treaties of Andrianople (1829) and Unkiar-Skelessi (1833).[1] We have seen how he proposed to split up this Empire, even suggesting that Britain should take Egypt. At another period (1833–41) he seems to have been keener on the advance in Asia than the dismemberment of European Turkey. This question of Russian influence in the Balkan Peninsula led on, as we have seen, from a Russo-Turkish conflict to the

Crimean War

disastrous Crimean War.[2] During this Nicholas died, though not before his military and governmental system had been shown up in all its fearful inefficiency.

2. Maintenance of autocracy in Europe:

in the Austrian Empire

in Germany

To uphold autocracy in Europe was an object almost equally important to Nicholas. His despatch of Russian troops to help the Austrians against the Hungarian rebels in 1849 and his pressure on Frederick William IV of Prussia not to accept the crown of a united and liberal Germany from the Frankfurt Assembly, show the extreme importance he attached to suppressing liberalism wherever it might break out. He regarded Britain (where the more prosperous middle classes had been admitted to power by the Reform Act of 1832) and France (where Napoleon III, the man of plebiscites, held sway) as traitors to the cause of European order. Not without justification was Nicholas termed 'the gendarme of Europe'.

His suppression of Polish liberty

To complete the picture of Nicholas's autocratic policy, something must be said of the Polish revolt of 1830. When Nicholas became Tsar in 1825, being hard pressed by the Decembrist conspiracy, he had tried to maintain the loyalty of his outer dominions by certain promises. He had sworn, for example, to uphold the constitutions of Finland and Poland – 'I promise and swear before God to maintain the Act of Constitution'. Nevertheless a censorship was applied in both countries, contrary to the constitution, and Nicholas soon became unpopular. The Poles especially disliked him because he ignored Alexander's promise to include Lithuania in their Kingdom, and even replaced Polish officials there by Russians. The condemnation of a number of leading Poles for complicity in the Decembrist conspiracy also gave offence. Finally, when the French Revolution of 1830 broke out and was quickly followed by the Belgian revolt against Holland, Nicholas prepared for war against France and seemed about to use the Polish army for the

Polish Revolt, 1830–31

purpose. The result was a revolution in Poland itself.

Beginning at the close of 1830, the revolt lasted in all about ten months. The Poles were able to resist for so long because they had been allowed a separate army, and this supported the revolt. The Russian governor, Nicholas's elder brother Constantine, was soon sent packing, and in January 1831 the Polish Diet declared Nicholas dethroned. A Russian invasion of the kingdom then soon began. To divide Polish loyalties Nicholas, who knew that the Polish Diet was considering the long overdue reform of peasant conditions, lightened the burdens of the peasants

[1] See pp. 159–60.
[2] See pp. 91–2, 160–66.

on all estates captured by the advancing Russian armies. This was a shrewd move, because it was the Polish nobles and intellectuals, and not the downtrodden peasants, who had brought about the revolt. A number of fights took place, but in the end there could be only one result. Outside Warsaw, in September 1831, a force of nearly 80,000 Russians beat a Polish army less than half that size, and the Polish capital was compelled to surrender. The remaining Polish forces in the countryside were rounded up or driven into Prussia, where they were disarmed.

Nicholas now set out to punish the Poles for daring to rebel. The old constitution was officially withdrawn: any concessions given by the new one, granted in 1832, were never properly observed. Elections and the Polish Diet were abolished. Most of the leading positions were given to Russians. The Russian language was declared compulsory for governmental purposes, and the Polish universities of Warsaw and Vilna were suppressed. The Polish army was merged into the Russian. For the rest of Nicholas's reign repression and 'Russianisation' continued with extreme severity. Triumphant in maintaining Tsardom intact in Russia, triumphant in crushing the Poles and the Hungarians, triumphant in helping to defeat German liberalism, Nicholas could indeed be regarded as 'the cornerstone of despotism in the world'. Polish constitution withdrawn

It frequently happens that children react violently against the views of their parents. Heirs to autocratic thrones are often liberals – while they are still heirs. Nicholas's son Alexander II was not a liberal, but he was credited with reforming intentions. Naturally the prospect of a Tsar who had constructive ideas aroused a mass of hope and expectations which could never be fulfilled. From one great piece of reform Alexander has gone down to history as the 'Tsar Liberator', a name which might serve for the first few years of his reign. It does not, however, tell the whole story, which was another tragedy of conflicting ideals. Alexander II, 1855–81 'The Liberator'

The reign started promisingly by the granting of pardon to those still undergoing punishment for the December conspiracy of 1825 and the Polish revolt. The Crimean War ended – though not before it had given a terrible blow to Tsardom – and the country could breath again. But the great work of Alexander's early years was the liberation of the serfs, an event which, as he very sensibly said, was better to come from above than below. To achieve this reform, Alexander had to override much opposition from the landowners. By the terms of the edict of emancipation, issued in 1861 after some years' preparation, 'field' serfs on private estates were not only freed but granted a proportion of the estate concerned; domestic serfs were merely freed. Unfortunately the details of the scheme, laid down in a number of measures, were less generous than the broad principle. The land the field serfs got as of right was limited to the amount they had held as serfs – in fact, they usually got anything up to a fifth less than this. Moreover, for this land they had to pay; and even so they did not acquire the freehold, which was vested in the communal organisation of the village – the *mir*. Since most peasants were not in a position to pay their former lords large sums, the state usually met these payments (or four-fifths of them) immediately, and the peasant was obliged to repay the state over a a period of forty-nine years. Often the land the peasant received was too little for him to work effectively; if he wanted more, he had to rent it from his former master by a further money payment or by labour services. All the peasants were also required to give two years' further services before the emancipation took full effect. Meanwhile they could marry freely, and possess chattels; but until they Alexander's early reforms: 1. Edict for emancipation of the serfs, 1861 had met the last payment for their land they were subject to the control of the *mir*, which could stop them leaving the district.

The results of the emancipation of 1861, and of similar legislation in 1866 applying to state-owned serfs, were naturally very great. A desirable reform was

THE YOUNG CZAR COMING INTO HIS PROPERTY.

Alexander II succeeded to his throne in the middle of the Crimean War. Cartoon by Tenniel, 17th March 1855.

certainly accomplished; but with cash and competition replacing service and custom as the basis of their everyday life, many of the former serfs got hopelessly into debt and lost everything. A drift to the towns followed, and this, together with the development of industry as the century wore on, led to a whole range of new problems. Peasant discontent was by no means eradicated, while urban discontent actually increased.

Next in importance in the reforms of Alexander II was the granting of local self-government. By an edict of 1864 special district and provincial assemblies (Zemstva) were set up, the latter being elected from the former. The main duties of a Zemstvo were looking after local transport, crops, education, prisons and hospitals; but it met for only three or four weeks a year, and worked mainly through the local officials it appointed. In 1870 much the same system was applied to the towns, the local council in this case being known as a *duma*. Although Russia lacked a central parliament, all these local councils gave her some experience in the management of public affairs and hastened the demand for a national body.

2. The Zemstva, 1864

Other reforms introduced in Alexander's early years as a ruler included a new legal system with independent judges and trial by jury (though martial law was still retained for political offences), a great extension of education, especially to women, the abolition of military colonies, and the replacement of the long term of military service by a general liability to conscription. On the material side much progress was made through the spread of foreign trade (helped by abolishing many tariffs), the growth of industry, and the building of railways, which had been almost completely neglected under Nicholas I. Nicholas had encouraged road-building but disliked railways, which he thought would 'foster the restless spirit of the age'. When he died only some 650 miles of railway track existed in Russia; but by the end of Alexander's reign the mileage had grown to 14,000.

3. Trial by jury

4. Education

5. Abolition of military colonies

Trade and Railways

Despite all these improvements, the intellectual classes failed to rally to the support of Tsardom. Socialism, often in its extreme forms, began to spread in the towns. A generation of brilliant novelists and dramatists painted remarkable pictures of Russian life and often seemed to show the need to rebuild society from top to bottom. Convinced of the hopelessness of tackling the enormous problems of Russia by the cautious and piecemeal reforms of the Tsar, many people began to adopt one of two attitudes. Either, like many nobles, they drifted aimlessly, aware of an impending crash yet bereft of any will or power to avert it; or else, like many workers, they became avowed revolutionaries. It was the growth in these which made Alexander abandon his reforming intentions and from about 1866 start a thorough-going repression.

Growth of revolutionary spirit

This decision was also prompted by a second revolt in Poland. In spite of certain concessions, such as reopening Warsaw university and reinstating Polish as the official language, Poland still bitterly resented Russian domination. When a Polish body, the Agricultural Society, founded to improve the lot of the peasants, was forcibly dissolved, the Poles began open demonstrations. Firing on the Warsaw crowd produced a counter-crop of terrorism aimed against the Viceroy, and eventually in 1863, after an attempt to conscript trouble-makers, the revolt broke out. It had no chance of victory but was simply an act of national desperation and not even a united one. The suppression was ruthless, though the Polish peasants were rewarded with the freehold of half their land for their failure to support the revolution. The spirit of Poland now seemed to be broken: the Kingdom of Poland was declared to exist no longer and it became a Russian province known as the Vistula Territory. Nevertheless Polish exiles, particularly in friendly France, never lost

Second Polish revolt, 1863

End of Kingdom of Poland

sight of the woes of their country and schemed for the great day when an independent Poland should again arise.

Alexander.II's foreign policy:

Although Alexander in general strove to avoid wars, his reign saw a continuation of historic Russian foreign policy. The advance into Asia was pressed in all directions, often by governors and colonists acting on their own initiative. In the Black Sea – Caucasus area the long-standing struggle against local tribes, successfully concluded, left Russia firmly in possession of the territory (so important later for the oil industry) between the Black Sea and the Caspian. East of the Caspian, Russia took over vast areas of Turkestan, including Bokhara and Samarkand, and used part of the region for cultivating cotton. These advances left Russia with frontiers bordering Persia, Afghanistan and China. Clashing with China over Manchuria, Russia soon stretched out to the Sea of Japan and gained a warm-water port at Vladivostock (1861). Only in Alaska, which she considered too remote and useless to be worth retaining, did Russia anywhere slacken her grip – by selling the province in 1867 to the United States. One result of all this was that Britain, so long suspicious of Russian ambitions in the Balkans, now redoubled her hostility. She felt that Russian ambitions in Persia and Afghanistan might ultimately threaten the north-west frontier of India.

expansion in Asia: British hostility

Russo-Turkish War, 1877

In Europe Russia scored a success when Alexander took advantage of the Franco-Prussian war to announce his intention of reconstructing a Black Sea fleet. Developments in the long-standing Eastern Question led, as we have seen, to the Russo-Turkish war of 1877–78, in which Russia was finally successful, though she had to submit the terms of the treaty of San Stefano to drastic revision at the Congress of Berlin.[1] During the 1860s her relations with Austria-Hungary were very strained, since Austria had refused to help Russia in the Crimean War in spite of the debt she owed Nicholas for his intervention against the Hungarians in 1849. By 1872 friendship seemed restored through the efforts of Bismarck, and the Dreikaiserbund or 'League of Three Emperors' announced the common intention of Austria-Hungary, Prussia, and Russia of maintaining the cause of monarchy in the world. Conflicting Balkan ambitions, however, as shown at the Congress of Berlin, soon widened the gap once more. In spite of Bismarck's success in retaining Russian friendship even after the Dual Alliance of Germany and Austria-Hungary of 1879,[2] it became obvious that Russia and Austria-Hungary could not much longer be yoked together.

Drei Kaiserbund

Alexander II adopts a repressive policy, 1866

At home the turning point in the Tsar's reign probably came in the year 1866, when there was an unsuccessful attempt on his life. Official sympathy with the liberals had already largely disappeared during the Polish rebellion. Now fear and the deadly repression born of fear began to grip the government, and determined its attitude to the 'Populist' movement of the 1860s and 1870s. 'Populism' was not merely a belief in the broad mass of the people, and particularly the peasants, but the belief that the peasants could become the main means of change in a socialist direction through their communal organisation of the village, the *mir*. In what one writer termed 'the mad summer of 1874' thousands of well-disposed intellectuals actually 'went to the people' – they descended on villages, and lived and argued with the peasant folk, trying to urge them forward to their destiny.

Measures against Populists

[1] See pp. 170–72.
[2] See pp. 240–43.

This made very little impression on the peasants, but profoundly shook the government, which soon had hundreds of the missionaries in jail.

Naturally this offended all the progressives, and then the government had still more reason to be afraid. While the liberals and most of the Populists and socialists were peaceful enough, the advocates of revolutionary violence grew on all sides as education progressed. Each school that was founded supplied more of the working class with the means to agitate and plot against the government. Terrorist societies sprang up, some of them consisting of men who dubbed themselves – or were dubbed – Nihilists (literally 'Nothingists'). The Anarchist movement also spread, directed abroad by Bakunin, a romantic figure who had served in the Imperial Guard, taken part in the German revolutions of 1848, been arrested and handed over to the Russian government, and finally escaped from Siberia back to Europe

Growth of revolutionary violence

Nihilism

Anarchism

ASSASSINATION OF ALEXANDER II, 1881
As Alexander II, the 'Tsar Liberator', drove across a bridge into St Petersburg in March 1881, a bomb was hurled at his coach by members of the 'People's Freedom' group. It killed a boy and an escort and wounded another escort. The Tsar alighted to speak to the injured. As he was re-entering his carriage, a second bomb exploded and mortally wounded him. His body was taken away in the sledge on the right.

by way of Japan. Nihilists and Anarchists alike aimed at the abolition of all government, which they had come to consider as evil in itself. It was not till later on, in the closing years of the century, that a more practical and scientific form of revolutionary violence obtained a hold in the form of Marxism.

Violence meets violence

Against this preaching of violence the government was quick to react. Censorship was tightened up, universities strictly supervised, the Zemstva robbed of some of their powers. Everywhere the secret police and the courts-martial were busy. Already in the first twenty years of Alexander's reign over a quarter of a million people had been exiled to Siberia. Still the tide of agitation rose. Generals and governors were murdered. In 1879 five shots missed their destined target, the Tsar. Later in the year three attempts to mine the Tsar's train all failed. In 1880 a mine blew up the Tsar's dining room in the Winter Palace at St Petersburg. The Tsar, unexpectedly delayed, was not in the room, but the explosion killed or wounded sixty-three soldiers.

Assassination of Alexander II, 1881

Alexander's escape did not long profit him. In 1881, ironically enough just as he had signed a paper promising to call a committee to consider the question of granting a constitution, the conspirators at last succeeded. The attempt was thorough enough, for six bombs and two mines were ready to greet Alexander on one of his drives through the streets of the capital. The first bomb, thrown by a youth of nineteen, missed its mark, though it killed several of the Tsar's escort. 'That one?' said Alexander, walking towards the arrested assassin after he had attended to the wounded. 'Why, he's quite nice looking.' A moment or two later the second bomb landed at his feet and blew his legs to pieces. Before the afternoon was out the Tsar was dead.

Alexander III, 1881–94

Fierce repression

The immediate effect of the crime was to divert all general sympathy from the terrorists. The new Tsar, Alexander III, a man of upright but unbending character like Nicholas I, was able to launch a campaign of fierce repression with some success. The societies failed in their avowed object of getting him too, and the police managed to break up the worst of them. Five of the ringleaders in the murder of Alexander II were executed. No steps were taken to carry out the late Tsar's last promise. The Press, the universities, the law courts, the Zemstva were muzzled and dragooned by the government. But though resentment might be stifled except in isolated outbreaks (such as the conspiracy against Alexander III in 1887, for which an elder brother of Lenin, the founder of Soviet Russia, was executed), it existed nevertheless, ready to flare up at the first opportunity.

CHAPTER 15
The Growth of Industrial Europe

1. The Beginnings of Industrialisation (to 1870)

It has often been said that the history of nineteenth-century Europe was shaped by two Revolutions – the French and the Industrial. The French Revolution, short and packed with drama, sent ideas of liberty and equality coursing like strong wine through the veins of Europe – ideas which inspired men for a century or more afterwards to demand a voice in their nation's affairs. But it was the Industrial Revolu-

Two Revolutions

THE PERCY COLLIERY, NORTHUMBERLAND, 1839
Coal was the basis of steam-power, and Britain led the way in large-scale coal-mining. As the mines spread, they created new and grim surroundings – the landscapes of the Industrial Revolution.

tion, protracted and not at all dramatic, which had the even greater result of finally transforming – for good or ill – the pattern of everyday life.

The Industrial Revolution has been defined as the series of changes by which hand craftsmanship in the home or small workshop gave place as the general mode of industry to machine-work in factories. Its birthplace was Britain in the later eighteenth century, and it was first seen in the manufacture of cotton textiles. The early cotton-spinning inventions were often powered by water, and many of the first factories were sited by rushing country streams; but with the perfection of an efficient steam-engine by James Watt in the 1770s, and its application in 1781–82 to produce rotary motion, steam became the great motive-power. Steam could drive heavy machinery in the factories, first for spinning and later for weaving; and steam-pumps, by draining the mines, could win more coal – to make more steam! But machinery could not long survive if made, as some of the earliest was, from wood: the strength, permanence, and precision of iron were needed. So iron, too, smelted since the mid-eighteenth century by coke made from coal and from 1829 by coal directly, became one of the pillars of the Industrial Revolution.

With the invention of the steam locomotive, first used in collieries and in the 1820s perfected by George Stephenson and others, further immense possibilities opened. Soon the Railway Age began. The improved roads of the later eighteenth century with their coaches and carts, the new canals with their horse-drawn barges, faded into the past as the railways took over; goods and people were shuttled about in quantities and at speeds till then undreamed of; the volume of trade doubled and redoubled – and behind everything was King Coal. Textiles, the steam-engine, coal, iron, railways – and soon steamships – these were the foundation of the new industrial Britain.

How swiftly these developments took place in Britain may be seen from one or two comparisons. Complete statistics are not available, but a fair estimate would be that in the fifty years leading up to 1820 the production of cotton textiles was multiplied by about twenty, of coal by two, and of pig-iron by nearly seven.

Britain could not, of course, have become a great industrial power so swiftly had she not already been a considerable commercial one. From her commerce – including in the eighteenth century the lucrative and iniquitous slave-trade based largely on Liverpool – she had built up the capital to invest in other enterprises. Among the many other advantages which enabled her to take the lead in industrialisation were her possession of fairly well-developed systems of banking and insurance as well as her colonies, a merchant marine, and a powerful navy to guard her trade routes. If we add to these Britain's convenient position for world-wide trade, the richness of her resources of coal and iron, the comparative stability of her government, the long years of internal peace that she had enjoyed, and the absence of the internal customs barriers that so restricted trade in most of the continental countries, we see some of the factors which favoured fast industrial development in Britain.

Industrial development and world-wide trade demanded a good supply of labour, and here Britain was probably helped by the fact that her population was steadily rising. For 1760, before industrialisation on any large scale began, the population of Great Britain and Ireland is estimated to have been $11\frac{1}{4}$ million. By 1831, as ascertained by official censuses, it had risen to no less than 24 million. So huge a rise was at once a cause of industrial growth and a result of it: the increased

THE 'GET RICH' STRUGGLE: 'RAILWAY MANIA' IN THE 1840 S
After the successful pioneer schemes of the 1830s railways spread rapidly in Britain during the 1840s and many fortunes were made in the process. This German sketch of 1844 shows British railway company promoters jostling to present their schemes at the Board of Trade.

population helped the industries by providing both labour and a market, while the output of the industries helped to sustain the growing population.

The causes of this growth have been much debated, and the general opinion is that the governing factor was not a rise in the birthrate – for before the spread of artificial birth control in the late nineteenth century most married women produced children as frequently as it was physically possible for them to do so. It is true that during the eighteenth century peopled tended, for a number of reasons, to marry earlier than in the seventeenth century and so their reproductive span was longer. Nevertheless the main cause of the increase in population seems to have been something quite different – a fall in the death rate. But what caused the fall in the death rate? Improved medical knowledge (including vaccination against smallpox), better sanitation, the abandonment of the practice of binding infants in 'swaddling clothes', the long years of internal peace, the growing wealth of the country from trade – these are doubtless some of the reasons. But high on the list must come the increased food supply resulting from the great agricultural improvements of the eighteenth century – the movement usually known as the Agrarian or Agricultural Revolution.

Increased food supply: the Agrarian Revolution in Britain, mid-eighteenth century–c.1820

The Agrarian Revolution was at its height in Britain over the years 1760–1820. Its most striking feature was the transformation of the old open-field regions with their scattered strip holdings into compact, enclosed farms under single ownership. In the process, much common pasture and woodland was enclosed too. Once their holdings were consolidated and enclosed, enterprising owners or tenants could introduce some of the many improved techniques already available. They could substitute turnips, for instance, for the fallow period under which most of the open fields had lain every third year; these both broke up the soil and provided winter food for cattle. And with root-crops for winter food, and the hedges of the new enclosed farms to provide shelter, cattle had no longer to be killed off at Michaelmas; their numbers increased, their quality improved with selective stockbreeding and the ending of the old mingling on the common pasture, and the manure from more beasts brought still greater fertility to the fields. All this, together with new devices such as better ploughs, and seed-drills to replace wasteful 'broadcast' sowing by hand, led to a great increase in the food supply, both grain and meat, and so played its part in producing and sustaining a larger population.[1]

Resulting social problems:

Though the Agrarian and the Industrial Revolutions together helped to sustain an increased population, they also created many social problems. In agriculture, considerable numbers of the poorest classes in the countryside – those who held no strips in the open fields but eked out a precarious living from the common pasture and woods – lost their customary foothold in the village when most of the common was enclosed. Having no legal share in the main lands of the village, they often got no recompense for the loss of customary if unofficial rights. This, together with the fact that many of the new allocations of land were too small to be worked economic-

Landless agricultural labourers

ally as individual units, and were soon sold off to wealthier neighbours, helped to produce a class of landless rural labourers. With wages very low in relation to the high food prices of the years during the French Revolutionary and Napoleonic wars, these men suffered bitterly and in the worst years survived only by humiliating grants of parish poor relief. This particular pattern of events, however, was not to be closely followed either in France, where a large peasant-proprietor class emerged from the Revolution, or in eastern Europe, where the great estates, untouched by modern improvements, long continued to depend on the compulsory labour of serfs.

Urban problems:

It was in the towns, however, that the most glaring social problems arose. This

[1] There are no reliable statistics for the production of grain and livestock over the years 1760–1820 but the increase was very large.

was partly because, with the growth of the population in the eighteenth century, the older towns became more and more overcrowded. More or bigger families crowded into each house, and small dwellings sprang up in the gardens and courtyards of larger ones. The existing local authorities could not cope with this additional burden and in many of the older towns, such as London, York and Bristol, slum areas proliferated. Trouble also arose because the industrial growth in the north and the midlands created virtually new towns at great speed and without any proper control. The small market-town of Manchester, for instance, in 1773 appears to have had a population of 36,000; by 1851 the number had swollen to over 300,000. In the textile districts of Lancashire and in the coal and iron regions of the midlands and the north-east where – apart from London – the biggest concentrations of population were occurring, builders ran up thousands of terraces of cheap houses depressingly uniform in style and sometimes built back-to-back to keep costs to a minimum. The new terraces, the factories and even the fields nearby were soon blackened by the prevailing smoke of industrial neighbourhoods. All the problems of urban areas without proper sanitation or recreational facilities (other than too many pubs) soon appeared: disease, squalor, drunkenness, crime. In time local 'improvement commissions' and elected town councils brought some cleanliness and order to the expanded towns; but half the nineteenth century passed before the worst was over.

THE MERSEY ESTUARY
A characteristic scene in the early industrial age, painted by T. A. Prior. The factories extending the town are beginning to bite into the countryside, and steamships appear among the numerous sailing vessels.

Factory conditions: long hours, harsh discipline, child labour, etc.

The hours and conditions of work during the Industrial Revolution also constituted a grave social problem. The atmosphere in many factories was almost unbearably hot and moist; much dangerous machinery was unfenced; falls and flooding in the mines were commonplace. In addition, competition between firms was keen, not to say cut-throat, and profit-margins were small, with the result that the factory operatives (of whom there was an almost unlimited supply) had to work twelve or fourteen hours a day to keep alive. Their wages were higher than those in agriculture, but still far too low to satisfy ordinary human needs. To supplement their scanty pay, many fathers sent their children into factories at the age of five or even less – and since no long training was necessary, female labour quickly became one of the staples of the whole factory system. In most factories harsh discipline ruled, with fines for the adults and strappings for the children; and many workers wore themselves out in the long hours of keeping pace with the machines. Years of agitation by enlightened individuals, the formation of trade unions (for long forbidden) and – at length – intervention by the government in the form of factory and mines acts, were all required before the lot of the industrial worker became much better.

Increase in British power

Though this book is not in general concerned with events inside Britain, this development has been described for two reasons. The first is that it so increased the wealth and power of Britain that she was able, throughout the nineteenth century, to play a role in European and world affairs out of all proportion to her size. The second is that this kind of development was followed, at some distance in time and of course with important local differences, by similar developments in other European countries. By recalling what happened in Britain we have some clue to the nature of the changes elsewhere.

Belgium

At the time of the French Revolution, the most advanced country in Europe from the point of view of industry, apart from Britain, was France. The long wars under the Republic and Napoleon, however, slowed down her rate of progress. The first country to show signs of matching the pace of the British developments was in fact the new state of Belgium, established in 1830. Her geographical position astride the northern routes from France to Germany, which had caused her territory to be fought over throughout the centuries and earned it the nickname of 'the cockpit of Europe', was a great advantage. So, too, were her fine traditions in cloth-making and iron-work, and the existence of many thriving commercial towns dating from the Middle Ages. Coal-mines, too, were already working in the eighteenth century on what was to become Belgian soil. The government of the new country under King Leopold I, following its severance from Holland, was quick to encourage commercial and industrial growth, and the state took an early lead in sponsoring railways. These began in 1833, and by 1844 a system of trunk lines was complete, covering the main routes to France, Germany, Holland and Britain. After the state had laid down the framework, private companies were encouraged to fill in other lines, until in 1870 the whole system was brought under state control.

Railways

Canals, coal and iron

This development was matched in other ways. Great attention was paid to canals, which continued to play an important part in the transit of goods. Belgian production of coal, centred around Liège, trebled between 1830 and 1860, and as late as 1870 she was still mining more coal than France. Even so, it was not enough for her growing industrial needs – she had to import more from Britain. Equally outstanding was the Belgian production of iron, metal goods (including machinery) and textiles. One family at least of the new industrialists was of British origin – the Cockerills. The father John, a wandering mechanic from Lancashire and reputedly illiterate, established himself at Verviers in 1798 as a manufacturer of textile machinery and imported one of Watt's steam-engines. His son John founded a great iron and machinery works at Seraing which by 1837 boasted four coal pits, two blast furnaces and various rolling-mills. It made locomotives and all kinds of machinery. All told, Belgium, under a free trade policy – geared, like that of Britain, to exporting manufactured goods and becoming partly dependent on imported food – had developed by 1870 into a considerable industrial power. Even so, her output of coal and iron was only a tenth of Britain's.

The next power to experience any considerable industrial development was France – though industry in France never gained the same ascendancy over agri-

France

PARIS BOULEVARD, 1839
A picture taken by Louis Daguerre – the inventor of the daguerrotype, an early type of photograph in which the impression was caught on a silver plate sensitised by iodine. This was the first photo to include a human being – the stationary figure near the kerb having his boots brushed.

culture as it did in Britain and Belgium. Despite – or perhaps because of – French skill in handicrafts, mechanisation was fairly slow to develop. One reason was that for long France had no great supplies of coal. Nearly all her coalfields were small, and one of the biggest – in the Nord and Pas de Calais – was not fully surveyed or greatly worked until 1850. Her output did increase steadily – from $1\frac{3}{4}$ million tons in 1828 to over 5 million tons in 1847 and over 13 million in 1869 – but she still had to import coal to satisfy her slowly growing industries. If France's production of 13 million tons in 1869 is compared with Britain's 107 million tons in the same year, the extent of Britain's lead is clear.

In pig-iron France came a little nearer to matching Britain's output. In 1847, for instance, she produced just over 590,000 tons, while Britain produced 2 million tons. Most of France's production, however, still came from hundreds of small

Insufficiency of coal

Iron

BORING MACHINE IN THE MT CENIS TUNNEL

Between Roman times and the invention of gunpowder there was no progress in the art of tunnelling. In the late eighteenth century tunnels were built to take canals through hills, and in the early nineteenth century tunnelling became commonplace in connection with the mines and railways. The first tunnel through a mountain was the Mt Cenis to link France and Italy by railway. Work began at both ends in 1857 and progressed at nine inches a day until 1861, when machine-drilling was introduced. Even so, it took another ten years to complete the work.

charcoal furnaces in the woodland areas. Some time was to elapse before the coke and coal-smelting methods used, for instance, at the great iron-works at Le Creusot became general. Not surprisingly in these circumstances, when France began to lay down railways during the 1840s she had at first to import the lines from Britain.

France's Railway Age proper began about 1845. The trunk routes, more system- **Railways** atically planned than those of Britain, radiated from Paris into six main areas and were built by a mixture of state and private enterprise. In general, the state provided the land and the roadbed for the lines, and controlled geographical distribution, fares and freight rates, and safety standards. The promoting companies provided the equipment, including rails and rolling-stock, ran the services, and took the profits – if any. Under this system France managed to build nearly 2,000 miles of

THE OPENING OF THE SUEZ CANAL, 1869
The Suez Canal, 100 miles long, was the first great inter-sea canal for large vessels. Its construction cut 1500–2000 miles off the sea passage from western Europe to India. The idea of such a canal was old, but the man who brought it about, largely on French and Egyptian capital, was the Frenchman, Ferdinand de Lesseps. The formal opening in 1869 after ten year's work was followed by a procession of ships, with the Empress Eugénie aboard the leading vessel.

Textiles

route by 1850 (at which time Britain had over 6,000) and nearly 11,000 by 1870. Even at that date, however, the mileage in Britain, a much smaller country, was nearly half as great again.

In the textile industry, too, France advanced, but again in most branches far more slowly than Britain. For cotton-spinning and weaving a factory system developed from the 1820s, and by 1846 there were 10,000 power looms in operation. Britain at this time had about 200,000. The silk industry was well developed, and quadrupled between 1815 and 1850; but production was later hampered by a disease which affected silk-worms. There was also an extensive linen industry, but this was still carried on largely by village weavers and by housewives producing only for the needs of their family. Indeed, in textiles as in most other trades and industries, the small workshop for long continued to be far more characteristic of France than the factory.

PASTEUR IN HIS LABORATORY

From a drawing by Adrien Marie. Louis Pasteur is here shown experimenting to discover a cure for rabies – which he successfully attacked by inoculation in 1885. He had already developed the germ theory, explained the fermentation process, combatted a silk-worm disease which was ruining the French silk industry, and successfully introduced inoculation against anthrax and chicken cholera.

We have seen how Napoleon I had tried to encourage French agriculture, industry and commerce, and how his efforts had been largely nullified by his constant indulgence in war. One future success, however, lay in the introduction of sugar-beet as a substitute for cane-sugar. Under the Restoration the government paid little attention to industry, and under Louis Philippe not a lot more, though canals were built, railways started, and the first factory acts passed. It was not until the reign of Napoleon III that industrial progress became fairly rapid: the Emperor himself was genuinely interested in promoting commerce, as may be seen from the Paris Exhibition of 1855, held in imitation of the Crystal Palace exhibition of 1851, and from his eagerness to conclude commercial treaties (such as the Cobden-Chevalier Treaty of 1860) leading to freer trade with other countries. His big programmes of public works in Paris and elsewhere created much employment, and the acquisition of colonies in Indo-China led to greater French trade with the Far East. All told, during the period of the Second Empire France's foreign trade roughly trebled.

The fact that France's industrial development was slow and patchy did not mean that she escaped the horrors which were the black side of industrialisation in Britain. They merely occurred in fewer places. Until the late nineteenth century the population of France, though not increasing nearly as fast as that of Britain or Germany, was nevertheless steadily growing – a growth aided by improvements in agriculture, notably the elimination of fallow land in favour of root-crops and cultivated meadows of clover, lucerne and sainfoin. Some of this growing population found work in textile factories, foundries or mines, where conditions were just as bad as in Britain. Others concentrated in the big towns, such as Paris and Lyon, which grew greatly in size without providing comparable increases in available work. The result was overcrowding, insanitary conditions, a low standard of living, and widespread discontent among the poorer classes. This expressed itself in the growth of socialism and in at least two bitter clashes in Paris – the 'June Days' of 1848 and the fight of the Communards in 1871.

Social conditions

Fourth in the league of European industrial development by 1870 was Germany. The political disunity of the country held up industrial progress, and the delay would have been greater but for the gradual extension of the Zollverein, or customs union, over most of the German states between 1834 and 1844. Apart from the Zollverein the greatest stimulus to trade during this period was the building of railways. The first, in 1835, was a small railway in Bavaria and the next, in 1839, a line between Leipzig and Dresden. These were partly due to the propaganda of Frederick List, an economist who had returned to Germany following exile to the U.S.A. on account of his political views. The Leipzig–Dresden railway in Saxony was a great success and according to one historian 'In the first year it carried 412,000 people, some lady travellers keeping needles in their mouths to prevent familiarity in the darkness of the single tunnel'. From 1840 construction was fast, and by 1850 the route mileage in Germany was nearly twice that of France and over half of that of Britain. Most of this progress was due to the various state governments, which (with some notable exceptions such as Prussia) built the railways and kept them under state ownership.

Germany

Zollverein

Railways

Thanks to the Zollverein and the railways, Germany was able to make up some leeway during the years 1850–1870. In the first half of the nineteenth century her roads had been poor and her industries mostly in the medieval handicraft tradition,

Coal, iron, textiles

tightly bound by gild regulations. Exceptions had been the production of coal (which considerably exceeded that of France) in Prussian territory (Silesia and the Rhineland – Ruhr area) and of iron in Bohemia, a province of the Austrian Empire. In Hamburg and Bremen there were sugar refineries and various seaport industries; and in Saxony there were a growing number of cotton textile factories (in which children slaved during 'busy times' from 5 a.m. to 8 p.m.). On the whole, however, large-scale enterprises were rare. Production of woollen cloth and linen, for instance, and even the mining of metals, still remained largely peasant industries.

Arms

From about 1850 this picture slowly began to change. The most striking advances, encouraged by developments in banking as well as better communications, were in the production of coal and iron and the growth of the arms industry. The firm of Krupp's, founded at Essen in the Ruhr in 1810, was by 1846 employing no more than 140 people out of the town's population of 8,000; by 1870, after Alfred Krupp had produced highly successful cast-steel guns and weldless steel tyres for railway vehicles, it dominated the town, which had mushroomed to a population of over 50,000. Another famous concern was the Norddeutscher-Lloyd shipping firm of Bremen, founded in 1857. But perhaps the most important development of all, as the basis of electric power and new electrical industries, was the invention in 1866 of the dynamo by Ernst Werner von Siemens, a scientist who had earlier specialised in the development of the electric telegraph.

Siemens' dynamo, 1866

Germany still largely agricultural in 1870

Till 1870, then, Germany remained largely an agricultural country. It had taken the occupation of the Rhineland by the French in the Revolutionary and Napoleonic periods to end many medieval practices and start the general emancipation of the serfs – a process soon followed in Prussia and completed after the revolution of 1848. In western Germany this led to much peasant ownership; but in eastern Germany the tradition of huge estates and dominant landlords (a legacy of the medieval German advance to the east as conquerors) remained strong well into the twentieth century.

Urbanisation in Britain, Germany and France

One way we can perhaps measure the progress of industrialisation in the three countries of Britain, France and Germany is to consider the extent to which their peoples began to live in towns. Towns do not, of course, imply industrialisation: but industrialisation almost inevitably implies the growth of towns. It has been calculated that the date when more people began to live in towns than in the country in Britain was during the 1850s. For Germany, the corresponding date was around 1900. For France, the date has not yet arrived.

Other countries

Outside these three countries and Belgium, industrialisation in 1870 was still in its infancy in Europe. The wealth of Holland depended on agriculture and overseas trade – she still retained an extensive empire in south-east Asia. In Italy progress was largely confined to Piedmont and Genoa, where Cavour's encouragement of roads, railways, port facilities, banking and commerce was beginning to show results. Spain and Portugal had important trading links, particularly with their overseas colonies or ex-colonies, but their industry was small-scale and traditional. The same may be said of the industry of the Austrian Empire, which was centred largely in Bohemia; much more important was the agricultural production of the great Hungarian plains. Sweden among the Scandinavian countries was developing promising metallurgical and engineering industries; the Balkan nations were not touched by large-scale industry of any kind. Switzerland was known for agricultural produce and clocks, but not yet – of course – for electrical goods.

A STEAM-HAMMER ('FRITZ') IN KRUPP'S, 1861
This photo gives an idea of the size and power of some of the machines available by the 1860s. A steam-hammer was devised – on paper – by the Scottish engineer James Nasmyth in 1839. Three years later he was astonished to discover that the French firm of Schneider, at Le Creusot, had built one based on his design.

Finally, what of the twentieth-century industrial giant, Russia? Like the rest of Europe's, Russia's population was increasing. In her case, the increase was very fast – doubling in the first half of the nineteenth century and again in the second. Part of this increase came from territorial expansion. But until nearly the end of the century the increase was not accompanied by much industrialisation. Railways, though begun fairly early, were slow to develop; by 1870 the length of route in enormous Russia was still less than half that in tiny Britain. Her way of life was rural and conservative, and until the 1860s based on serfdom. In St Petersburg, Moscow and Warsaw were a few large factories, mainly for state enterprises in textiles and armaments; but the number of industrial workers was only about one per cent of the population. Not till the 1890s did this position significantly change.

So Britain in 1870 was still virtually unchallenged in her economic supremacy. She still enjoyed much, if not all, of the position she had attained by 1850 – a position in which she had established herself, according to one historian, 'as not

Russia

1870–Britain still supreme

only "the workshop of the world" but also as the shipper, trader and to a large extent the banker of the world'.

2. From 1870 to 1914

The growth of large scale industries in Europe continued rapidly after 1870 despite several periods of trade depression. The countries in which this growth was already strongest – Britain, Belgium, France and Germany – underwent further industrialisation; and many others – such as Austria-Hungary, Sweden and Russia – took their first big steps along the same path. Two states beyond Europe, however – the U.S.A. and Japan – showed an even greater rate of industrial and commercial growth. Just when the output of European industry was rising to heights previously unknown, industrialisation was spreading to the world outside – with results that were eventually to undermine not only the industrial but also the political supremacy of Europe.

Well beyond 1914 coal remained by far the most important source of Europe's industrial energy. It was used for direct heat, as in metal smelting, or for production of steam to drive locomotives, ships and all kinds of machinery. Often it was employed in the form of coal-gas. With the improvement of the dynamo in the 1870s and the invention of Parsons' steam-turbine in 1884, steam raised from coal was also used to generate that most convenient new form of power – electricity.

Outside Europe, a rival to coal as a prime source of energy was now indeed beginning to appear. Mineral oil, which was to surpass coal in this capacity by the mid-twentieth century, became widely available after the sinking of the first oil-well in Pennsylvania in 1859. Pennsylvanian oil, however, like that already available in the 1850s from Austrian Galicia and Rumania, was used mainly for lighting: it enabled paraffin lamps and paraffin wax candles to brighten every home. It was not until the 1870s and 1880s that further wells, in Russia and Ohio – followed by those of Texas in the 1890s – gave oil suitable for raising steam to drive machinery.

In the refined form of petrol, oil also drove the newly-invented internal combustion engines of the 1880s. These engines made possible the motor-car and later the aeroplane. Cars, however, were still a minor means of transport in 1914, and aeroplanes hardly one at all, compared with railways. Oil was by that date also used to fire the furnaces of ships, notably naval vessels and big liners, where speed, space-saving and comparative smokelessness were important. In the U.S.A. and to a lesser degree in the Far East (where discoveries were made in Borneo, Burma, the Dutch East Indies and Japan) oil was by 1914 already used as a source of power in factories and electrical generating stations. Elsewhere, coal still remained King.

The need for coal gave great advantages to the countries which had good natural supplies, and especially therefore at first to Britain, Germany and the U.S.A. In Britain, coal production went up from about 159 million tons a year during 1880–84 to about 274 million tons a year during 1910–14. This was the highest total achieved by any country in Europe. The increase in Britain's coal production, however, was exceeded by that of Germany (which rose from 66 million tons a year in 1880–84 to 247 million tons a year in 1910–14). This again was surpassed in the United States, where coal production rose from about 85 million tons a year in the early 1880s to the huge figure of 474 million tons a year in 1910–14.

Apart from coal, the main basis of heavy industry was iron and steel, with the

Margin notes:

Spread of industrialisation in Europe –

and beyond

Coal the main source of energy

Electricity

Mineral oil: the beginnings

Coal production

Iron

latter now replacing the former in prime importance. In 1880, Britain was producing nearly twice as much pig-iron as the United States, and nearly three times as much as Germany. By 1910, though her own output had gone up, she was producing only about half as much as Germany, and only about a third as much as the United States. Britain's considerable advance, which kept her well ahead of France, was quite overshadowed by that of Germany and America.

Advance of Germany and the U.S.A.

It was during the 1860s that steel first began to overtake iron in industrial use.[1] This was because such inventions as the blast furnace, the Bessemer converter of 1856, and the open-hearth processes of the 1860s readily gave temperatures previously difficult to obtain, and so greatly accelerated production and reduced cost. This steel however was not so strong as that made in the old-fashioned crucibles. Moreover certain classes of iron-ore – those with a high phosphorus content – could not at first be dealt with by these newer processes. It took the Gilchrist-Thomas invention of the 1870s, in which alkali (mainly lime) was both mixed with the metal and used as a lining to the converter, to solve this problem. The phosphorus was absorbed into the alkali and removed as 'basic slag' (which proved to be a useful fertilizer). Henceforth the phosphoric ores came into general commercial use and the universal supremacy of steel was quickly established. This development was of special benefit to Sweden, which has large quantities of phosphoric iron ore in the north. It also helped Germany – which had acquired rich deposits in the orefields of Lorraine, taken from France in 1871.

Steel

Not surprisingly, the production figures of steel tell much the same story as those of coal and iron. Between 1880 and 1910, Britain multiplied her output by five, but Germany by nearly twenty. By 1910 Germany was producing twice as much as Britain. All the other main steel producing countries, too, showed a greater rate of increase than Britain, though with one other big exception they remained well behind her in total output. This exception was the transatlantic giant, the U.S.A., whose output increased from 1·3 million tons in 1880 (the same as Britain's) to no less than 26·5 million tons (over four times that of Britain) in 1910.

Germany and the U.S.A. surpass Britain

The increased production of coal, iron and steel was essential to the development of most other industries. Among the older ones, textiles and shipbuilding continued to expand, while striking advances were made in the new chemical and electrical industries. In all these Germany, among the European powers, was particularly outstanding. In textiles, for instance, she began to produce worsted (combed wool) cloth in large quantities after 1870, at the same time as mechanisation brought about a great growth in her cotton industry. By the beginning of the twentieth century she was a large exporter, with textiles ranking fourth in the value of her exports after iron and steel, machinery, and coal and coke. Similarly in shipbuilding: great new yards were established at Hamburg, Bremen and Stettin, and German output of steam-propelled vessels rose from 100,000 tons in 1870 to 2.3 million tons in 1910.

Other industries:

German progress in textiles

Shipbuilding

In chemical products, too, Germany began to rival Britain, the acknowledged leader. Among these products were soda (by the ammonia–soda process patented

---

[1] Steel is a form of iron which is malleable at certain temperatures, but both hard and resilient in its final state. This is because it retains some of the carbon present in iron ore. In this way it stands midway in its properties between wrought iron (carbon-free, malleable and comparatively soft) and cast iron (high carbon content, hard and brittle).

A NINETEENTH-CENTURY INDUSTRIAL COMPLEX: PART OF KRUPP'S WORKS AT ESSEN
Germany developed industries very rapidly from the 1860s onwards. In iron and steel the greatest firm was Krupp's, which spread over and beyond the town of Essen and drew on the Ruhr mines for coal. The photo shows part of the works around 1880. By 1900, with the rising demand for armaments – one of its main products – Krupp's was employing about 40,000 men.

Chemical products (including synthetic dyes, fertilizers, explosives)

in the 1860s by the Belgian Solvay), chlorine (required for bleaching powder), and sulphuric acid (by a process invented in Britain which replaced the old lead-chamber method). One great use of sulphuric acid was in the production of artificial fertilizers, especially superphosphates: these chemicals, together with other fertilizers like nitrates (imported largely from Chile) and salts of potassium (rich deposits of which were discovered in Germany in the 1870s), greatly stimulated the production of crops and so helped to feed the world's fast-growing population. Other branches of the chemical industry in which Germany excelled were the production of synthetic dye-stuffs, where she soon eclipsed the originator, Britain, and the manufacture of explosives based on nitro-glycerine. The basic inventions here were those of dynamite in 1860, and blasting gelatine a little later by the Swede, Alfred Nobel. Their main counterparts for shells and bullets, Nobel's smokeless propellant ballistite and the British invention cordite, revolutionised armaments towards the close of the nineteenth century.

New electrical industry:

Equally important, both for Germany and for Europe as a whole, was the new electrical industry. The effect of this on everyday life was enormous. By the 1860s arc-lamps, based on a discharge between carbon electrodes, were available for lighthouses, streets, theatres and other public uses; but for electricity to be used generally for lighting in the home required not only the development of a public supply but also the invention of a cheap and practicable carbon filament lamp. This was achieved by the Englishman Swan and the American Edison almost simultaneously at the end of the 1870s. From then on, helped by the German invention of the incandescent gas mantle in the late 1880s, man's age-old battle against the dark was won. Cities became far safer at night, and an immense range of leisure pursuits, both in the home and outside, became possible for the first time in the evening hours.

Lighting

Social effects

Another application of electricity, following the invention of suitable motors, was for traction. An electric railway was first shown at the Berlin exhibition in 1879. Very soon, it became apparent that steam railways could be electrified. This, however, was for a long time less important than the development of cheap street transport in the form of the electric tramcar. Most big European cities converted their tramway systems (originally operated by horses, but sometimes by steam) to electricity during the 1890s and 1900s; and this, with the growth of suburban railways, enabled workers to live well away from their place of employment, and the cities themselves to become even larger.

Electric traction

Communication, already revolutionised before 1870 by the railway and the steamship, was thus advanced still further in the 1890s by the introduction of electric trams and trains (including underground systems in London, Buda-Pest, Paris and other great cities as time went on). To these was added the petrol-driven car, invented in the mid-1880s, and later the motor-bus, while 'safety' bicycles and pneumatic tyres had been available from the late 1880s. For the first time in history man became highly mobile locally without the aid of the horse.

Increased mobility: trams, cars, bicycles

The revolution did not stop there. Other inventions dependent on electricity also enabled man to communicate at a distance. From the 1830s the electric telegraph, carried along wires and later by submarine cables to regions farther and farther afield, already enabled messages to be sent in code; now, in the mid-1870s, the invention of the telephone by Graham Bell in the United States had an immense but incalculable effect on both business and social life. Finally, the development of wireless telegraphy by Marconi and others around the turn of the century, and already used by 1914 for communication between ships and from aircraft, introduced what then seemed the most incredible innovation of all.

Communication at a distance: telegraph, telephone, wireless

In the manufacture associated with these developments, in the making of generating plant, electric (and petrol) motors, cable and wire, electric lamps, telephones and many other things, the United States soon became the leading power. But Germany ran her very close. For 1913, Germany's output of electrical products and equipment is estimated to have been worth about £65 million. For the same date, that of Britain was worth less than half – £30 million – and that of France £7¾ million.

Though Germany made herself the greatest industrial producer in Europe by 1914, at that date she was still well behind Britain in the extent and value of her trade. From about 1870 Britain gradually ceased to be the 'workshop of the world', but she remained the world's main exporter, importer and financier. She was also still the world's main carrier, owning by 1914 about three-sevenths of the world's total tonnage of shipping. (In Europe, Germany came next with about a quarter of

Germany overtakes Britain in production –

but not in commerce

MARCONI AT SIGNAL HILL, NEWFOUNDLAND
In the 1890s Guglielmo Marconi, working on the scientific discoveries of Clerk Maxwell, Hertz and others in relation to electric waves, began to transmit Morse Code signals through space. So, with 'wireless telegraphy', opened a new era in human communication. In December 1901 he was able to pick up in Newfoundland signals transmitted from Cornwall – and here he is with his receiving instruments.

Britain's tonnage, and France third with less than half Germany's). The income earned from abroad by Britain's shipping was very large, as was that brought in by overseas investments and by services like banking and insurance. In all this apparatus of commerce Britain was still the most highly developed country, but during the final quarter of the nineteenth century similar facilities became available on a large scale elsewhere. With the development of communications and the network of commercial institutions – banks, insurance and shipping offices, stock and commodity exchanges, and the like – trade became truly world-wide.

Industrial growth in Russia

It is impossible in this short sketch to trace the industrial progress, considerable though it was, of such countries as Sweden, Austria-Hungary, Italy, and Switzerland, or to consider why development of this kind was much slower in other areas, such as the Balkans, Spain and Portugal. Attention must, however, be drawn to the remarkable industrial growth achieved by Russia, even if it was only a beginning and left her still well down the table of industrial nations. Though there was a good deal of progress after the emancipation of the serfs the real spurt began in the

1890s with the appointment of the railway administrator Sergius Witte as finance minister and the beginning of direct state intervention in key industries. This was greatly helped by French and Belgian loans and by British investment in the new oil industry centred in Baku. Between 1890 and 1914 by such ventures as the great trans-Siberian line Russia doubled the length of her railway system, to give her – what she obviously needed – the longest route mileage of any European power. Between the same dates she also quadrupled her output of coal and achieved an even greater increase in her production of iron ore and steel. Especially notable was the development of the Ukraine into a great industrial as well as grain-producing region. The spur to all this may be seen in the fact that during Witte's period of power from 1892–1903 no less than two-thirds of government expenditure was devoted to industrial expansion. Largely due to this and foreign loans, Russian industry as a whole achieved during the 1890s the fastest growth rate in the world – a rate not to be matched in Russia again until the 1950s.

Sergius Witte

One feature of industrial and commercial growth which became still clearer during the years 1870–1914 was that trade tended to move in cycles of prosperity and depression. A period of three or four years of continuing expansion would lead to over-production in relation to the purchasing power of the consumers, and then a drop in prices to re-attract custom and a laying-off of workers to economise in costs or scale down output to demand. After a while the contracted output would be insufficient to satisfy even the reduced demand, prices would rise, and industry would pick up again. There were about six periods of depression in Western Europe between 1870 and 1914, the severest – what we should call slumps – occurring in 1873–76 and 1893–96. Since they created unemployment, and state help for the unemployed was then almost non-existent, they were naturally marked by acute social unrest.

Trade cycles

This simple trade cycle was, however, often complicated by very important outside factors which affected prices. One of these was the amount of gold – the basis of the world's currency – available: fresh discoveries of gold, as in California and Australia in the mid-nineteenth century, or South Africa in the 1880s, could cause a rise in general prices by making gold itself less valuable (for sellers of goods naturally demand higher prices as money declines in value). Another disturbing factor – frequent in the nineteenth century – could be some great new invention: a new machine might mechanise a particular industry and drive out the hand-workers (as the power-loom had done) or a new substance might under-cut and replace existing articles (plastics and artificial silk were late nineteenth century examples). A third complicating factor could be some new development in transport (the steamship, for example, coupled with the completion of the Suez Canal in 1869) which drastically improved reliability and journey time or opened up some previously inaccessible part of the world. This might both enlarge the demand for European manufactured goods and at the same time make available to Europe such large quantities of food or raw materials from the newly accessible regions as to alter greatly the previous pattern of trade.

Complicating factors:

gold supply

inventions

transport developments

The most striking example of this in the late nineteenth century was the prolonged depression which affected much of Western European agriculture. To the temporary effects of general trade depression in 1873–76 and exceptionally bad harvests in western Europe shortly afterwards, were added the much more important long-term effects of the arrival of food from overseas in vastly increased

Great agricultural depression (1870s–90s)

quantities. The main causes here were the opening up of huge territories such as Argentina, the American and Canadian Middle-West, Australia and New Zealand, thanks in large part to the railway, and the reliable and inexpensive carriage of their food products to western Europe by steamship. In particular the virgin soil of the Middle-West yielded floods of cheap grain – for expensive fertilisers were at first unnecessary – while the invention of refrigeration made it possible for great meat-exporting industries to grow up in Argentina and New Zealand.

Food from abroad

These things combined to expose western European agriculture to competition such as it had never previously experienced. Corn could not be produced as cheaply in Europe as it was pouring in from North America, and much arable land went out of cultivation. The severity of the effect on western European agriculture – the industrial workers of course benefited from cheap food, and subsistence agriculture in eastern Europe was not much affected – varied from country to country. Britain was especially hard hit because unlike France and Germany she maintained her free trade system and declined to set up protective tariffs. Only in the closing years of the nineteenth century, as North American grain became dearer to produce, did British agriculture begin to pick up; and only in the First World War, when home-produced food supplies suddenly became important again, did it really revive. Most other countries, though similarly affected, managed rather better. In the case of Holland and Denmark this was done by specialising in dairy products and exporting these at attractive yet profitable prices.

Growth of population

Among the results of industrial growth and an increased food supply was the ability to sustain larger populations. In Europe the population rose from about 266 million in 1850 to about 460 million in 1914, while at least another 50 million emigrated during this period to North America and elsewhere. Most countries in Europe, including Britain, Germany and Russia showed a large increase – almost a doubling; but in France the increase was small, doubtless because artificial means of birth control became widely practised there earlier than in the rest of Europe.

Urbanisation

Industrialisation and increased population meant continued urban growth. Between 1870 and 1914 almost every country in Europe developed a number of large cities. Britain was the first country in which more people began to live in towns than in rural areas – this had happened already in the 1850s – and by 1914 nearly four-fifths of her people lived in towns. In Germany by the same date the figure was about three-fifths. In France, on the other hand, where agriculture maintained its old high place, rather more people continued to live in the country than in towns. At the far end of the scale, in Russia probably less than one-tenth of the population lived in towns before 1914.

Movements to benefit the masses:

The growth of large-scale industry and the concentration of people in towns, with all the attendant social problems, stimulated movements to improve the lot of the workers. Among these was the trade union movement. In nearly every European country during this period workers succeeded, often against long-sustained opposition by their governments, in establishing trade unions so that they would be in a better position to bargain with their employers. In Britain, full legal recognition of trade unions was achieved by 1871; in France and Spain it followed in the 1880s, in Germany in 1890, in Russia not till 1906. Usually the first unions were of the more skilled and better paid workers. Later, mass unions developed – and with them, the size and severity of strikes.

mass trade unionism

co-operative societies

Together with this went a growth in movements for co-operative production (as

A SCENE FROM ZOLA'S 'GERMINAL'

Emile Zola was a French novelist of the 'realistic' or 'naturalistic' school whose most powerful works dealt with harsh or unpleasant things (e.g. drunkenness and prostitution). In Germinal *he built up an unforgettable picture of an industrial struggle, with a coal-mining community striking against reductions in wages. Zola died in 1902, and in the last three years of his life led the fight to rehabilitate the wrongfully convicted Captain Dreyfus. The picture above comes from an edition of* Germinal *illustrated by the German Käthe Kollwitz (d. 1944), whose tender yet vigorous art dwelt sympathetically on the life of the poor.*

in Danish dairy farming) or distribution (as in the British co-operative societies). At the same time socialist movements of various kinds, aiming at anything from social improvement by state action to the complete abolition of private enterprise, began to spread and gain momentum. In Britain, where most socialists were ready to work through parliamentary democracy, the movement did not become very influential until a number of groups united to form the Labour Party in 1900. On the continent, socialism was already important some years earlier than this. In Germany, despite the hostility of Bismarck, a strong socialist party managed to establish itself during the 1870s; by 1914 it was the largest party in the Reichstag. By the 1890s socialism was also a considerable force in France, Spain and Italy. It also existed in Russia, where – in the absence of any substantial progress towards democracy – it was naturally of a revolutionary kind.

In fact, most socialists on the continent were revolutionary. Mainly believers in the theories of Karl Marx, they held that the wielders of economic (and therefore political) power, the bourgeois industrialists and capitalists who had taken over from the nobility, should themselves be dispossessed by the broad mass of the working people – the proletariat. They did not imagine that this could come about without revolutionary violence. In practice, however, most of the socialist parties

socialism

were willing to work within existing parliamentary systems to get what benefits they could for the workers, at least for the time being. Disagreement between the more and the less revolutionary socialists, however, were often acute; and so were the disagreements between socialists (who wished to seize the state and use its power on behalf of the proletariat) and anarchists (who wished as far as possible to do away with state-power altogether). Such disagreements helped to wreck the fitst attempt at an international socialist organisation – the International Working Men's Association, usually known as 'The First International', founded by Karl Marx in 1864 and dissolved in 1876.

These, then, are some of the general forces to be borne in mind as we follow the course of political events in Europe through the years 1870–1914. During that period Europe was advancing industrially and technologically at a greater rate than ever before – and possibly since. It was a Europe nearly doubling in its population, and changing in some of its north-western (but not yet its south-eastern) regions into a land of city-dwellers. It was a Europe responsible in 1870 for nearly two-thirds of the world's industrial output, a Europe which because of its economic power and technical superiority was able to dominate less-developed continents.

Imperialism

So it was also a Europe which grabbed other territory with ease (as in Africa or Indo-China), adding between 1878 and 1914 $8\frac{1}{2}$ million square miles to its overseas empires. By 1914 Europe, its colonies and its former colonies (such as the U.S.A. and South America) together covered nearly 85 per cent of the world's surface. The Europe of those years was imperialistic Europe in the hey-day of its power.

Industrial advance outside Europe:

Japan

the U.S.A.

At the same time there were countries outside Europe which were steadily growing in strength. Russia, beginning to industrialise, was acquiring vast tracts of land in Asia and turning herself into a world power rather than a purely European one. Japan had emerged from isolation, and she too was taking sudden and dramatic strides along the path to industrialisation – and imperialism. Above all, the United States, having survived her terrible civil war of 1861–65, was progressing industrially at an even faster rate than western Europe. With her population trebling between 1860 and 1910, her huge natural resources, and her vast increase in industrial production (which by 1914 was about 35 per cent of the entire world output) the U.S.A. was set to become the world's super-power. By the 1890s, in terms of output and income per head, she was already the world's richest nation; but in international politics outside the American hemisphere her influence was not yet great. She had a long tradition of avoiding European and colonial entanglements, of isolation in foreign affairs. Though she already had the economic power to exert world-wide pressure on the international scene she did not yet make a systematic attempt to do so. Until 1914 it was still the great European powers who ruled the international roost.

European tensions

Within Europe itself, despite the growing industrial and commercial wealth of the north-western countries, there were tensions which constantly threatened stability. Apart from the pressure of fast-growing populations, the tension between expanding cities and declining countryside, and the sheer pace of technical and social change, there was all the tension arising from demands for greater equality. This mainly took the form of the demand by excluded classes for a vote in a parliamentary democracy, but there was also the more radical demand for a socialist state to abolish the capitalist system of free private enterprise. In the sphere of industrial action, there were widespread strikes – even general strikes – for better

A BALL IN BUDAPEST, 1902
*By the end of the nineteenth century, many manufacturers and businessmen had become
wealthy enough to be 'accepted' by High Society. This picture shows the Emperor
Francis Joseph gracing an industrialists' ball in Budapest.*

pay. And beyond this, there were all the national tensions – between rival industrial
powers, like Germany and Britain, or recent enemies like Germany and France, or
between subject races and rulers in multi-national states like Austria-Hungary
and the Ottoman Empire. From 1870 Europe was progressing, industrially and
socially, at a pace never before known. But explosive forces were there in plenty,
and in 1914 their combustion would spell the end both of the old dynastic Europe
and of the long-standing European predominance in world affairs.

CHAPTER 16

The German Empire and the Third French Republic: Internal History, 1871–1914

1. The Establishment and Internal History of the Third French Republic, 1871–1914

The new Germany

The Franco-Prussian War gave a new shape to the situation in Europe. Thanks to Prussia's victory, the process of Italian unity was completed by the capture of the last of the Pope's dominions. The Empire of Napoleon III, which in 1860 had been the principal power on the Continent, crumbled away; and the Republic which emerged from the ruins was at first provisional and for many years torn by faction and impotent. In place of the supremacy of France there arose that of the new German Empire, strong in the legions of Moltke and the wits of Bismarck. A new European power had been born, and with it a new European culture. Increasingly during the next forty years men thought of Germany not as a land of great musicians and ineffectual philosophers, but as a land of industrialists, scientists, and soldiers. A distinctive German spirit emerged: confident, thorough, efficient, patriotic, and ruthless. The old Prussian military tradition became the tradition of the new Germany, fostered by all the Bismarckian ideas on the use of force.

The new France

Against the powerful new giant in central Europe the infant French Republic appeared at first of pigmy stature. To begin with, it had the greatest difficulty in establishing itself. Between the proclamation of the German Empire at Versailles in January 1871 and the signing of the peace treaty at Frankfurt in the following May France suffered, in the episode of the Paris Commune, one of the most desparate civil conflicts of modern times.

When famished Paris had at last to surrender in January 1871, there was still a party which wanted France to fight on in her unconquered provinces. It disapproved of the idea of an armistice with the Prussians, although Paris had already endured 135 days of siege, and it showed its disapproval by rioting. When the armistice, in spite of this, was concluded, the emergency government formed during the war arranged for a National Assembly to be elected at Bordeaux. The main

National Assembly elected, February 1871

function of this body was to conclude the peace treaty. To the horror of Paris, with its strong republican tradition, the overwhelming majority in this National Assembly proved to be royalist, a fact which arose not from the desire of the provinces for monarchy, but for peace, which was most strongly supported by the monarchists.

The presidency of the assembly was given to the moderate republican Jules

Grévy but the actual direction of affairs as 'executive head' was entrusted to the veteran politician Thiers, who had all along been against the war and who wanted to wind it up as speedily as possible. Though previously an Orléans monarchist he now supported a republic, but an extremely conservative one. The ministry he chose was not notable for any strong working-class sympathies, and this, together with the fact that Thiers was compelled by Bismarck to agree to an official entry into Paris by the Prussian troops, put Paris immediately on bad terms with the new government. Two or three measures passed by the Assembly in March added fuel to the flames. In the first place all back rents owing to landlords, commercial sums due, and the like, which had been suspended during part of the war, were now to be paid up in full with interest – a demand which it was quite impossible for the poorer and indeed many of the middle classes to meet. Secondly, the Assembly decided to move to Versailles, which had unpleasantly royalist associations. Thirdly, the Paris National Guard was to have its war-time pay stopped and to be disarmed, so that Paris could no longer argue with any effect. When Thiers ordered a detachment of French troops to carry out the disarmament, the National Guards in Paris resisted, a fight followed, and Paris was in revolt.

Before March was out, following the example of one or two traditionally revolutionary cities of the south such as Lyon and Marseille, Paris had set up a Commune, or separate town government. The original idea was that by this defiance both the conservative-republican ideas of Thiers and the monarchical ideas of the Assembly could be defeated. Instead of a single government for the whole country under Thiers or a restored Bourbon king, France would consist of independent Communes, attached to one another in a very loose form of federation – an arrangement which would allow Paris full liberty to carry out its own policy. The Paris Commune itself, when elected, proved a mixed body, its ninety-two members ranging from extreme revolutionaries to sober middle-class citizens. It was supported by most of Paris except the wealthy west-end suburbs.

Paris Commune defies the Assembly at Versailles, March 1871

The Assembly at Versailles, however, led by Thiers, determined on rigorous suppression. The other Communes rapidly collapsed, but for two months civil war raged round Paris under the eyes of the contemptuous Prussians, who had the pleasurable spectacle of watching their enemies destroy one another. Failing to take Paris by assault and the fiercest bombardment, Thiers had to ask Bismarck's leave to increase the French army from 80,000 to 150,000 men. Even when, after five weeks' continuous attack, the Assembly's troops at last broke into Paris, they had to fight their way street by street and house by house until they captured the entire city. As the Communards retreated they set fire to important positions, and this, together with the incendiary shells used by the Versailles troops, reduced half Paris to a blazing inferno. When, by 26th May, the last heroic resistance was crushed, the Hôtel de Ville, the Ministry of Finance, the Palais de Justice, the Tuileries, all were smouldering ruins, to say nothing of theatres, stations, barracks, and whole blocks of streets – even Nôtre-Dame was spared only because there was a hospital close by. But the vengeance taken by the victors, sharpened by the Communards' murder of hostages (including the Archbishop of Paris), was perhaps even more terrible than the actual fighting. Paris prisons ran blood, Paris cemeteries burst with the dead, who had their revenge on the living by creating foul pestilences. Altogether more than twice the number of victims claimed by the 1793–94 Terror in two years perished in Paris in one week, either in the assault or the subsequent executions.

Thiers and the Assembly crush the Commune, May 1871

Damage in Paris

It has been estimated that in the episode of the Commune material damage to the extent of £20,000,000 was done, while about 100,000 Parisians suffered imprisonment, exile, transportation or death.

The results:

These disasters appeared on the surface to have very little permanent effect. Thiers had re-established 'order' and had not been stopped from concluding the final peace treaty with the Prussians. The ruined buildings were mostly rebuilt in fairly faithful and entirely dull copies of the originals. There was no longer any

PUNCH, OR THE LONDON CHARIVARI.—September 27, 1873.

"AU REVOIR!"

Germany. "FAREWELL, MADAME, AND IF——"
France. "HA! WE SHALL MEET AGAIN!"

France quickly paid her indemnity after the Franco-Prussian War, and in 1873 the German occupation forces withdrew. Many Frenchmen, however, dreamed of a war of revenge against Prussia, especially for the recovery of Alsace-Lorraine. Cartoon by Tenniel.

point in Cook's running special tours to see the damage – anyway, disappointed British tourists were said to have complained that the ruins were no longer smoking. The Commune seemed like a hideous nightmare, no sooner suffered than ended. But it did have two very important results. In the first place it threw the middle classes very solidly behind the government of Thiers, while many of the new industrial working classes, resentful and embittered, became ardently socialistic. Secondly the struggles of the Paris rebels to organise themselves into a government were examined critically and historically by the communist Karl Marx, who drew from them certain principles in the technique of revolution. Marx's conclusions were later re-examined by the Russian communist Lenin in the early years of the First World War. The history of the Commune thus provided practical lessons for the maker of the great Russian revolution of 1917 – a distant result but nevertheless an important one. Because of this the original Communards have sometimes been confused with communists – a mistake arising not only from the similarity of the name, but from later communist admiration for the 'heroic days' of 1871.

1. Middle classes support Thiers, industrial working class becomes more socialist

2. A lesson in revolution for Marx and Lenin

The first step in the reorganisation of France was obviously to get rid of the Germans. There was an immediate rush to lend money to the government to pay off the indemnity, and the middle classes enjoyed the pleasures of patriotism while receiving an interest of five per cent – a good figure for the time. Within two years the indemnity had been paid off, and France was entirely free from the army of occupation. The country as a whole certainly agreed with the Assembly in hailing Thiers as the 'Liberator of French Territory', though no doubt many of the Paris working classes would have suggested different names.

Liberation of French territory, 1871–73

Next, after the army had been reorganised by introducing compulsory service – the actual call-up was by lot – came the task of framing a permanent scheme of government for France. A republic had existed since the fall of the Empire; and Thiers, since August 1871 officially President of the Republic, strove hard to preserve it. Yet the majority of the Assembly, being royalist, was anxious to abolish the republic, which it regarded as temporary, and set up a monarchy. It thus began to quarrel with Thiers, who resigned in the belief that, being indispensable, he would be rapidly invited back as master of the situation. For once, however, the usually shrewd veteran had miscalculated, and the Assembly appointed instead as President a Royalist, Marshal MacMahon.

Difficulties in establishing the Republic on a permanent basis

President Thiers resigns, 1873

At first, the main difficulty of the Royalists had been that they could not agree on who should be king. When, however, they reached agreement and MacMahon strove to re-introduce the Bourbon monarchy in the person of the Comte de Chambord, the grandson of Charles X, the negotiations broke down on one detail. Chambord, an elderly 'dyed in the wool' aristocrat, refused to accept the *tricolore* and demanded the restoration of the old Bourbon white flag, with its fleur-de-lys. This would never have been accepted by the army or by the middle and lower classes, and MacMahon himself saw that the demand was politically impossible. Chambord, however, refused to sacrifice his principles; and MacMahon then resolved to wait for the death of Chambord, when the next prince in line, the Orleanist Comte de Paris, grandson of Louis Philippe, would have no objection to the banner of the Revolution and Napoleon. To keep the place warm for him, the Assembly voted to confer the Presidency on MacMahon for seven years.

A Royalist President: MacMahon

Chambord's scruples

That the Royalist hopes were eventually cheated was partly due to a few determined Republicans like Gambetta, who did some strenuous electioneering in the provinces, and from 1873 to 1875 secured the return of twenty-six republican candidates in twenty-nine by-elections to the Assembly. Gradually, then, the political complexion of the Assembly changed; and eventually in 1875 the Monarchists had sulkily to agree to the passing of new constitutional laws, the decisive measure which ensured a permanent republic being passed by a majority of only one vote. France was given a parliamentary democracy, with a Chamber of Deputies elected for four years by the vote of all males, a Senate above this with a considerable degree of power, and a President chosen for seven years by Chamber and Senate together. The President could select ministers; but since he could not dissolve the Chamber except with the consent of the Senate, and since the Cabinet was responsible to the Chamber and not to the President, the latter eventually became a kind of figurehead, corresponding to a British constitutional monarch – though this was not originally intended. When MacMahon, supported by a royalist Senate, dissolved a newly elected Chamber in 1877, largely because it was too Republican for his liking, he was taught an emphatic lesson by the return of an even bigger Republican majority. Soon afterwards he resigned to make way for an undoubted, though conservative, Republican – the president of the Chamber of Deputies and former president of the Assembly, Jules Grévy.

The Third French Republic, founded in the hour of defeat over the blood of the Communards and against all the desires of the Monarchists, endured surprisingly well. In spite of frantic party divisions and the First World War, it lasted for sixty-five years – nearly four times as long as any other government since the downfall of the old monarchy in 1791 – until it collapsed under the weight of defeat in 1940. It weathered, too, a number of severe internal crises, notably in the Boulanger affair, the Panama scandal, and the Dreyfus case.

In 1886 General Boulanger, ex-military governor of Tunis and newly appointed Minister of War, began to capture the attention of the French people. His handsome appearance on his black horse, his fiery speeches, his prophecies of a successful war of revenge and the recovery of Alsace-Lorraine, his attacks on the new constitution, his concern for the welfare of the troops, all powerfully affected certain sections of the people. Among these were men both of the right and of the left, with the result that his colleagues soon became alarmed at his popularity. In May 1887 they dropped him from the ministry, only for his reputation to increase still further with the decline of that of Grévy, whose son-in-law was found to be selling honours within the presidential gift. The government then, in March 1888, forced Boulanger from the army. With the support of many sections of the public, from royalists and Bonapartists to unemployed workers, he then started putting his name forward as candidate in any constituency where there was a vacancy; and constituency after constituency showed its approval by electing him. The climax came with a great victory in Paris in January 1889, and excited crowds urging him on to the Elysée, the Presidential palace. Obviously the General was aiming at a *coup d'état* and a dictatorship, but in fact he feared to take the final step. At length the divided Republicans plucked up their courage and determined to charge Boulanger with treason. At this the gorgeous bubble collapsed – the General's flight to Brussels and suicide two years later on the grave of his mistress showed that he was not of the stuff of which real dictators are made.

The 'Panama Scandal', which burst in the year 1892, was only noteworthy in that it provided the enemies of the Republic with a powerful weapon. The success

A DECIDED PREFERENCE.

FRANCE (*surveying herself in a Looking-glass*). " AFTER ALL, THIS STILL SUITS ME BEST, AND I MEAN TO WEAR IT."

France decides that she is definitely republican. Cartoon in Punch, *27th October 1877.*

of the Suez Canal, planned by the great Frenchman Ferdinand de Lesseps, had encouraged the idea of a similar project through the Isthmus of Panama. The scheme, as we know, has proved of the greatest service – the Panama Canal was eventually built by the U.S.A. between 1904 and 1913 – but as undertaken by de Lesseps it collapsed disastrously. A company was successfully floated in 1880, with de Lesseps as president, but after several years' work it went bankrupt in 1889. The elderly de Lesseps himself, a cousin of the ex-Empress Eugénie, and since the opening of the Suez Canal loaded with honours, ended his career in disgrace. Not only was the technical planning in some places faulty – such as allowing insufficiently for the tropical floods of the Chagres River – but on investigation in 1892 it it became clear that an amazing amount of extravagance, fraud, bribery, and even blackmail had taken place. The worst feature was that many deputies and senators were rightly thought to have accepted bribes to advance the project – one ex-minister was actually convicted – with the result that the enemies of the régime in France could talk of 'Republican corruption'. De Lesseps was condemned to five years' imprisonment (a sentence afterwards annulled) and thousands of French investors lost their money. It was a nasty blow, and it caused many French electors to vote socialist at the next elections. The Republic, however, survived.

The Dreyfus case, 1894–1906:

The Boulanger episode and the Panama scandal were peace and quiet compared with the 'Dreyfus case', which distracted the French nation from 1894 to 1906. In 1894 Captain Alfred Dreyfus, a wealthy Jewish officer from Alsace, was con-demned by closed court-martial to a life sentence on Devil's Island for selling military secrets to the Germans. The case rested on one half of an undated and unsigned document extracted from a waste-paper basket in the German embassy and said to be in Dreyfus's writing – a matter on which there was not agreement.

conviction of Dreyfus, 1894

His race and personal unpopularity, however, told against him. The nature of the trial and Dreyfus's sustained protestations of innocence led his relatives and a few others to try to re-open the case, but for long without success. However, the fact that leakages of information still went on, though Dreyfus was now on Devil's Island, proved suspicious. In 1897 another officer, a notoriously extravagant but

Esterhazy accused – and acquitted, 1897

well-connected major named Esterhazy, was accused, thanks to the work of Colonel Picquart, a newly-appointed head of French military intelligence who dared to risk the hostility of his colleagues by questioning the previous verdict. But all Picquart got for his pains was a posting to a danger area in Tunisia; and the new court-martial took only three minutes to acquit Esterhazy.

Zola's campaign, 1898

At this point, in January 1888, the great French novelist Emile Zola entered the scene. He wrote a remarkable open letter, published in the Press, to the President of the Republic. He began almost every paragraph with the words *J'accuse*; and his specific charges were directed not only at Esterhazy but at the Minister of War and other military chiefs, whom he accused of suppressing the truth, and at three handwriting experts whom he accused (if they were not insane) of fraud. He finished by inviting prosecution for libel – which he got, together with a sentence of one year's imprisonment. This he avoided by going abroad. Round about the same

dismissal of Picquart

time the military authorities further victimised Picquart by dismissing him from the service for 'professional faults' – i.e. failure to stay quiet when required.

the two camps

By this time the public uproar was stupendous. Half France was clamouring that a great injustice had been done to Dreyfus: the other half held that to say this was to attack the honour of the army, which had sentenced him. Though there were some curious cross-currents of opinion, the strongest supporters of Dreyfus tended to be the convinced republicans and the intellectuals, while on the other side were those who yearned for the older France – the monarchists, the clericals, the upper class elements who still occupied many of the higher posts in the army. Many of Dreyfus's opponents were actuated by crude anti-Semitism, which was becoming stronger as Jews took an increasing part in high finance: and in this critics of capitalism on the left sometimes joined hands with clericals on the right. One or two viciously anti-Semitic newspapers had made their appearance, and the con-troversy waxed hot and bitter. Private as well as public life was affected. Long-standing friendships were severed, scores of duels fought.

Before 1898 was out a vital new development occurred. A prosecution was launched against Picquart, now a civilian, in a civil court. A Colonel Henry, who had worked throughout in the Intelligence Office and replaced Picquart as its head, found himself expected to provide evidence for this prosecution, and did so; but the court came to the conclusion that one of his documents was a forgery. He was detained, and that night committed suicide. It appeared that he had concocted a whole series of forgeries in an attempt to sustain the verdict against Dreyfus. At this, Esterhazy fled abroad, later to make admissions. Justice, it seemed, was at last about to triumph. The Minister of War who had upheld the forgeries as genuine was forced to resign; and Dreyfus, white-haired and broken, was brought back from Devil's Island to be given a fresh trial.

suicide of Colonel Henry: flight of Esterhazy, 1898

At this new court-martial the military authorities, still unable to see that the 'honour of the army' was best maintained by justice rather than by blind loyalty, once more behaved with incredible stupidity and meanness. Instead of acquitting Dreyfus they now found him 'guilty with extenuating circumstances', and condemned him to ten years imprisonment. With fine illogicality, they coupled with this a recommendation to mercy. The President of the Republic, advised by his newly elected 'ministry of republic defence',[1] then promptly intervened to pardon the prisoner. This really settled the matter, but the echoes and passions still lingered. The struggle to uphold the honour of Dreyfus against that of the military leaders went on, and at last in 1906 a retrial was granted before the Appeal Court. In this, fresh documents completely cleared the character of the Jew, 'whose only crime was his birth', and the verdict of 1899 was quashed. This did not prevent Dreyfus being shot and wounded two years later by an anti-Semitic journalist. Altogether, the whole 'affaire Dreyfus', was a most unsavoury business. Yet curiously enough its effect in the end was to strengthen the Republic: for it brought closer together the radicals and most of the socialists, the Republic's firmest friends, and it discredited the clericals, the monarchists and their supporters in the army, the Republic's bitterest enemies.

retrial of Dreyfus: guilty but pardoned, 1899

civil re-trial, 1906: Dreyfus cleared

anti-republicans discredited.

The Boulanger crisis, the Panama scandal and the Dreyfus case were three highlights in the domestic history of the Third Republic between 1871 and 1914. There were, however, many other developments which were less spectacular but equally important. Among these were the laws passed 1881–1884 giving complete liberty of the press and public meeting, permission to those exiled or transported after the Commune to return, freedom to join trade unions, and the establishment of free compulsory education. Round about the same time the influence of the Church was also greatly reduced by the expulsion of the Jesuits and other orders unauthorised in France, and by a ban on religious education in the time-table of all schools run by the public authorities. These measures were the work of ministries of convinced republicans in which the leading figures were moderates like Gambetta (who had dropped some of his old radicalism) and Jules Ferry – a group now called Opportunists, since they sought to put into effect only those radical reforms which commanded widespread support. Opportunist ministries were also responsible during the 1890s for passing further laws to regulate female and child labour, to enforce safety measures in mines and factories, and to provide 'cheap and sanitary dwellings' for working men.

Reforms, 1881–84

The 'Opportunist' ministries

Radical ministries

Other important reforming measures were passed by the predominantly radical

[1] See p. 222.

The Waldeck-
Rousseau reforms

ministries of 1899 to 1905. From 1899 to 1902 the premier was Pierre Waldeck-Rousseau, a highly able and respected republican who had helped to legalise trade unions in 1884. A moderate, he formed what he called a 'government of republican defence' to combat the anti-republican forces – in, for example, the army and the Church – which had shown their strength during the Dreyfus case. Most of his colleagues were radicals but his cabinet included for the first time a socialist in Alexandre Millerand, who was made Minister of Commerce. Millerand was responsible for some important laws, notably a Public Health Act and limitation of the working day to nine and a half hours. Apart from this the cabinet was determined first to see justice done in the Dreyfus case – which it did by advising a pardon for Dreyfus after his second trial – and then to crush the political power of the clericals. It saw in them, acting with the militarists, the greatest danger to the Republic. Accordingly, Waldeck-Rousseau was responsible for a law by which schools run by religious orders were closed unless the associations were approved by the government. His intention was that approval should not be unduly difficult

Anti-clerical legislation:
Combes

End of Concordat:
separation of Church
and State, 1905

to obtain; but under his more fanatical successor as prime minister, Emile Combes, such approvals were systematically refused. The papacy reacted to this by abandoning its recent efforts to reconcile or 'rally' French Catholics to the Republic; and Combes then went on to urge the cancellation of Napoleon's Concordat of 1802 by which Catholicism enjoyed an official position and privileges in France. This was done under his successor in 1905, and Church and State became completely separated. The necessary legislation was largely the work of Aristide Briand, another socialist prepared to work with a radical ministry.

Clemenceau and
Briand

Among the radicals who held the premiership between 1905 and 1914 was Georges Clemenceau, who had long been active in politics both as a Deputy and as a newspaper owner. Sitting on the far left of the Chamber, he was a virulent critic who had helped to bring down many ministries; and his journals (in one of which Zola published his famous letter) had played a leading part in upholding Dreyfus and demanding anti-clerical legislation. As premier from 1906 to 1909, however, he had little chance to effect reforms because he was far more involved in dealing with strikes. His use of troops to break these lost him socialist support; but his successor, the socialist Briand, heading another radical-socialist coalition, found himself obliged to resort to the same tactics to deal with an attempted General Strike in 1910. It was Briand, moreover, who defeated a railway strike by calling up the strikers to the colours, so putting them under military discipline.

Strikes

As a background to these events we must remember that, despite the generally depressed economic conditions from the mid-1870s to the mid-1890s, and the scourge of phylloxera which ruined the vineyards, great commercial and industrial development had been taking place in France.[1] Railways, harbours, canals, coal-mines, land improvement, steamship services all made great progress. The wealth of the country increased sharply, possibly aided by the new colonial policy which began in the 1880s. Nevertheless, in spite of the reforms mentioned above, social conditions remained bad – France was still in 1914 a long way behind both Britain and Germany in measures to benefit the poorer classes. Old-age pensions, for example, were frequently proposed by Millerand, but when finally approved in 1910 were so hedged about with restrictions as to be of little social value. Similarly there

Financial and industrial
development

[1] See also pp. 197–201.

were many proposals for an income tax, a necessary preliminary if important schemes of social welfare were to be financed: but it was not until 1914 that such a tax was actually approved. Facts like this led the more extreme socialist leaders, like Guesde and Jaurès, to disapprove of others like Millerand and Briand working in harness with radicals. Thus, although the Republic was undoubtedly strengthened by the admission of the moderate socialists to office, the problem of the extreme socialists, Communists, and syndicalists (those who aimed at a take-over by the *syndicats*, or trade unions) remained. These held that no worthwhile reform could be achieved except by violence, either in the form of strikes or revolutionary civil war. By 1914 they were a far greater danger to the liberal-democratic French Republic than were its old opponents, the monarchists and the clericals.

One other problem, too, in this period beset the statesmen of France. Unlike that of many other countries of Europe her birth-rate began to fall. Her population remained at around forty millions while the new German Empire crept up to sixty-five millions. Her leaders became uncomfortably aware that to every eight Frenchmen there were thirteen Germans – which leads us to the sphere of military and foreign policy, soon to be examined in connection with Germany.

2. Bismarck and his Successors in the German Empire, 1871–1914

The newly founded German Empire, though not so beset by problems as the Third French Republic, nevertheless experienced certain difficulties. Against these, however, two powerful factors worked in its favour: unlike the French Republic it had been founded in victory, not defeat, and above all it was guided by a statesman of the quality of Bismarck. Since the powers of the parliamentary institutions of the new Empire (Reichstag and Bundesrat) corresponded closely with those of the North German Confederation of 1867, Bismarck as the Imperial Chancellor could exercise control with direct responsibility only to the Emperor – whom he knew how to manage. With so skilled a pilot at the helm, Germany was likely to weather the storms better than her rival France. All the same, Bismarck ran into various difficulties. Leaving aside for the moment foreign affairs, which were always his major interest, let us see how Bismarck tackled his two greatest problems at home – the Roman Catholic Church and socialism.

The trouble with the Roman Catholic Church started in 1870, when the Vatican, anxious to safeguard the Pope's spiritual power following the loss of the Church's territories to the new Italian State, proclaimed the dogma of Papal Infallibility. This declared that the Pope, when officially defining what doctrines concerning faith or morals should be held by the Church, was by divine assistance infallible and his decisions therefore unalterable. As six years beforehand Pope Pius IX had issued a statement known as the Syllabus of Errors in which he had condemned 'progress, liberalism, and civilisation as lately introduced', this was important. In the same document he had denied the right of the state to control the Church and education, and repudiated any obligation by Catholic countries to grant religious toleration or complete freedom of speech; while in earlier communications he had already attacked socialism and liberal secret societies. Some leading Catholics in Germany (and elsewhere) accordingly refused to accept the decree of Infallibility, and in Germany a group broke away to form what were called the Old Catholics.

An important question then arose. If the Vatican excommunicated, for example, university professors of theology who declined to accept the decree, was the government of the state concerned (religious regulations in Germany were largely a matter for the individual states, not the Empire itself) to support the Papacy (by suspending the professors from their posts) or the objecting professors? If the government supported the Vatican, German education would be controlled by the Church, since those who objected to any doctrine could be excommunicated and dismissed. In a country where Protestants outnumbered Catholics by nearly two to one, Bismarck could not readily allow this; and as a Protestant himself he also feared that German Catholics might line up with Catholics of other nationalities (for example, Polish, French or Austrian) against the interests of the new German Empire. He therefore opposed the Papal claims strongly. This made him fall foul of the majority of the German Catholics, who supported the Pope in the matter, and who to defend their cause formed a political party known as the Centre.

Bismarck opposes papal claims

'Centre' party formed, 1871

The Centre Party straight away began to occupy an important position in the new Reichstag, where it vigorously criticised Bismarck. It was not long before he determined to crush these 'clericals'. The main battlefield was the most important state, Prussia. He encouraged the passage through the Prussian parliament of the

BISMARCK v. PIUS IX
A cartoon published in 1875 in the German satirical magazine Kladderadatsch *during the* Kulturkampf. *Bismarck's pieces (i.e. his weapons) include Germania (i.e. German nationalism), the Press, and the laws against the monasteries; a number of the Pope's pawns are already 'interned'. Pius IX's pieces are labelled interdicts, encyclicals, and the Syllabus of Errors (see p. 223).*

'May Laws' of 1873, by which, in conjunction with other measures passed between 1872 and 1876, priests were forbidden to inspect schools, and their education, appointment and activities were completely controlled by the Prussian State. In addition he was able, over Germany as a whole, to secure the expulsion of the Jesuits and some other orders, as well as the establishment of civil marriage. When the Catholics objected, thousands of them, including bishops and archbishops, were imprisoned – at one point every Prussian bishop was in prison or had fled abroad, and a quarter of the Prussian parishes were without an approved priest. The issue quickly broadened into a struggle of Catholic doctrine in all forms against the new doctrine of the complete power of the State – hence the title *Kulturkampf* ('civilisation-struggle') by which it is usually known. Slowly the Centre party gained in numbers, while all Bismarck's imprisonings and bullyings could not suppress the opposition of the Church.

The 'May Laws' in Prussia

Persecution of Catholics

Ultimately Bismarck saw that he was hopelessly antagonising a third of the Empire. By 1878 the foreign situation, too, was dangerous and Bismarck's mind was turning to an alliance with a Catholic power – Austria-Hungary. In the Reichstag his most powerful supporters in recent years, the National Liberals, were mostly against his policy of protective tariffs to ward off the agricultural depression (and decrease his financial dependence on parliament). Moreover, the rise of the socialists was giving him food for thought. So the 'Iron Chancellor', helped by the accession in 1878 of a more amenable Pope (Leo XIII), for the first time bent a little and began to call off the campaign against the Catholics. Most of the Centre party then reciprocated by supporting Bismarck over tariffs. Finally in 1887 a bill was passed in Prussia which gave back to the Church much of its old independence and power over its own members, including appointments, though civil marriage and state inspection of schools were retained and the Jesuits were still excluded. Even so, Bismarck yielded so cleverly that the Pope, besides himself sacrificing some points, actually instructed the Centre to vote with Bismarck in the Reichstag for a controversial Army Act. For once the Chancellor had strayed rather out of his depth; but he had managed to get back to dry land and even to bring with him a valuable catch in the form of support from the Centre.

Bismarck relaxes the *Kulturkampf*

The socialist problem was one which Bismarck never solved. With the rapid industrial development of Germany unhealthy factories and dwellings, long hours, low pay, and other unpleasant features were increasingly apparent. Already in 1848, as we have seen, the Germans Marx and Engels in their *Communist Manifesto* had called on the 'Workers of the World' to unite in throwing off their chains. Socialism in France, too, had played an important part from about 1828 onwards. The central idea of the socialists was that so long as individuals were allowed to own land, railways, banks, factories, and the like, the masses would always be poor. This was because the object of the owners or employers would naturally be to make as much profit as possible, which meant paying the employees the lowest possible wage for the greatest possible amount of work. If, on the other hand, socialists argued, the private control of such important things were abolished, and state ownership substituted, then there would be no employer to take the profit except the state – of which the worker was a part. Thus the socialist programme was first to see that the masses got their due share in political power by securing the vote, and secondly to see that the state, once it came under control by the masses, should take over the land and run the key industries for the common benefit. Some

2. Socialism

The socialist programme

Marxist Socialism. (Communism)

socialists thought this could be done gradually and peacefully; others, however, then mostly called Social Democrats but now known as Communists, and of whom Marx was the founder, believed that the employers would never surrender their power through anything short of revolution. It thus became, according to the Social Democrats, the duty of the employees ('the workers') to advance their cause at suitable moments by 'direct action' – i.e. strikes and civil war.[1]

Against such ideas Bismarck inevitably set himself. Even the milder forms of socialism were detestable to him. As an aristocrat, a conservative, and a great landowner, he had at first resented the claims of the educated middle classes to a voice in government, and in the early 1860s had clashed head-on with the liberals. How much more would he resent surrendering power to the often illiterate working classes, and giving them control over all the economic resouces of the country! When, after a period of organisation, the German Social Democratic Party (which proclaimed the need for violence but mostly acted as a peaceful party in parliament, so showing that the two types of socialism were not yet rigidly distinct) obtained half a million votes at the Reichstag election of 1877, Bismarck became alarmed. The international situation was threatening, and he wanted no sources of disloyalty within Germany. In 1878 he accordingly began a fierce campaign against the Social Democrats with the express object of crushing the whole movement. 'Now for the pigsticking', he is reported to have said. Despite the misgivings of the liberals, a law against the dangerous activities of the Social Democrats went through the Reichstag. Offending socialist papers were suppressed, many clubs broken up and meetings stopped, and some of the leaders banished. Two of the few Social Democrat members of the Reichstag who dared to attend a session were all but handed over to the police. Nevertheless it was still possible for a Social Democrat to take part in political activity and to stand for the Reichstag, even if his meetings had to be licensed in advance. The persecution, though vigorous by late nineteenth-century standards, was as nothing compared with that inflicted on their opponents by Hitler's National Socialists in Germany in the 1930s or by the Social Democrats ('Communists') themselves on their opponents in Russia after 1917.

Bismarck persecutes the Social Democrats, 1878

Bismarck's other weapon – social insurance schemes (v. sickness, accident, old age)

Yet in spite of all the power of the state, Bismarck failed to crush socialism. Too intelligent to rely on purely negative means, he also tried a more positive approach by sponsoring what we should call 'welfare legislation'. His policy has been described as introducing small doses of socialism by the state in the hope of warding off a major attack – rather as vaccination injects a mild germ into the system to forestall something more violent. At all events, he succeeded in passing between 1883 and 1889 three welfare measures of great importance based on the principle of compulsory insurance. The first, in 1883, was for compulsory insurance against sickness by all industrial workers, the worker paying two-thirds of the weekly contribution and the employer one-third. This scheme was later extended to many other classes of worker. The second scheme, approved in 1884, was an accident

---

[1] See also p. 234. The name 'Communist,' despite the *Communist Manifesto* of 1848, did not come into general use until the 1920s after the success of the Russian Bolshevik revolution of 1917. In the latter part of the nineteenth century most socialists called themselves either socialists or Social Democrats, irrespective of whether they believed or not in the need for violence. In 1918 the victorious Bolshevik ('majority') wing of the Russian Social Democratic Party renamed itself the Russian Communist Party and thereafter its followers in all lands have called themselves Communists.

insurance scheme to which employers had to contribute for nearly all their workers, except the higher paid. The third, passed in 1889, was for pensions in old age or incapacity. This applied to most of the lower paid workers, and was based on weekly contributions of one half by the employer and one half by the employee, with the state making an addition to the actual pension. None of this provision was very generous, but as a national policy to help the worker in ill-health and old age it was unique at the time in Europe, and well ahead of legislation in Britain.

The socialists, however, were not appeased. They saw no real socialism in what they mockingly called this 'State Socialism' of Bismarck's, and they found their efforts to secure further social reforms (such as limitation of hours, fixed minimum wages and increased powers for the trade unions) all frustrated by the Chancellor. So they kept up their attacks on Bismarck, and his attempts to weaken and silence them failed. By 1890 the Social Democrats polled nearly one and a half million votes, and with the relaxation of persecution following the retirement of the Chancellor in the same year, the figure rapidly mounted until 1914, when it was four and a quarter millions. By that time the Social Democrats were the strongest single party in the Reichstag. The battle against the socialists was far from being one of Bismarck's victories.[1]

But the Social Democrats survive

Bismarck's difficulty in subduing first the Catholics and then the socialists did not, however, prevent substantial progress being made in the organisation of the Empire. Within five or six years of the ceremony at Versailles, a common currency and banking system had been established, together with a postal system for the whole Empire except Bavaria, which had its own. Railways, though not state owned, were constructed and co-ordinated in the state interest. New codes of commercial, civil, criminal, and military law were framed. And, above all, industry and trade flourished, so that Germany soon became, like Britain, one of the 'workshops of the world' – a development which again had its effect on foreign policy.[2]

Progress in the German Empire

Before we pass on to foreign policy, one other important step taken by Bismarck must be noted. Late in 1878 he decided to abandon the existing trade policy of the German Empire, based on progress towards free trade, and to substitute instead protective tariffs. The charge was taken, he maintained, purely in the interests of German industries, since free trade, an ideal 'worthy of the honourable German capacity for dreaming', could never lead to prosperity in a world of competing nations. Protection certainly made sense as a weapon against the depressions of the 1870s and particularly the great agricultural depression which afflicted most of western Europe till the 1890s.[3] Indeed Bismarck's tariffs may well have furthered Germany's huge industrial advance in the late nineteenth century. But what Bismarck did not emphasise was that protective tariffs would ensure for the government a permanent and probably rising revenue from customs duties very little of which was under the control of the Reichstag or the various state governments. Under free trade direct taxes were necessary, which gave the state legislatures an important weapon, as their annual consent to them was necessary under the constitution. Under protection, however, customs tariffs would be voted by the

Abandonment of free trade, 1879

---

[1] For the resignation of Bismarck and his relations with the Emperors Frederick and William II, see pp. 228–29.

[2] For Germany's industrial development 1870–1914 see pp. 204–10.

[1] See pp. 209–10.

Reichstag for a term of years and would make much direct taxation unnecessary, thereby robbing the state legislatures of the opportunity of exercising annually their financial power. Thus in changing the economic system of the country, as he did by introducing – in 1879 – tariffs against many foreign manufacturers as well as foreign corn, Bismarck was also dealing a shrewd blow to the power of the state parliaments and even the Reichstag itself.

The last of German Liberalism

This move also put the last nail in the coffin of the old Liberal party based on parliamentary government and free trade. The party had already split into National Liberals (those who came round to support of Bismarck in the 1860s) and Progressives. Now, over the protective tariffs, the National Liberals themselves split, some supporting Bismarck and others voting with the Progressives and the Social Democrats against him. Bismarck was adept at killing two – or three – birds with one stone; and that his old allies the National Liberals were broken by his tariff policy worried him not at all. Henceforth he would rely for support in the Reichstag on a majority built mainly round the Conservatives and the Centre, the latter reconciled since the abandonment of the *Kulturkampf*.

Death of William I, 1888

In 1890, to his intense surprise, the elderly and remarkably successful Chancellor found himself forced into resignation. The chain of events which led to this had begun in 1888, when the old Emperor William I at last died aged ninety. It was his support, since the power vested in the Emperor was so great, that had enabled Bismarck to overcome all opposition. With his limited intelligence and strong sense of honour, the Emperor's first instincts had in fact been against nearly all Bismarck's outstanding strokes of policy – the defiance of the liberals in 1862, the lenient peace with Austria in 1866, the assumption of the Imperial title in 1871, the Austrian alliance in 1879. But Bismarck had known how to manage him and bring him round to his own viewpoint; a firm partnership had sprung up, and the old Emperor's attitude appears in the single word with which he greeted one of Bismarck's offers of resignation (a customary and powerful weapon) – 'Never'.

Frederick, 1888

Unfortunately William's son and successor, Frederick, came to the throne in the grip of a mortal disease, a cancer of the throat. Within three months this brought him, too, to the grave. History sometimes turns dramatically on the lives of a few individuals. Frederick, though a great German patriot, had as Crown Prince shown himself liberally inclined. Married to Queen Victoria's eldest daughter, he had developed a more constitutional idea of kingship than his father. The carrying out of his ideas must have spelled ruin to much that Bismarck had stood for. When death took him so soon, the last hopes of a liberal Germany disappeared and a great load vanished from Bismarck's mind.

William II, 1888–1918

Frederick was in turn succeeded by his son William II, a brilliantly versatile though unstable young man of twenty-eight. The new monarch, who had been carefully trained in the Bismarckian principles, announced his intention of following the aged Chancellor's policy, and concentrating not on the traditions of his father but on those of his grandfather. Nothing could have been more welcome to Bismarck, who now saw himself as secure in his Chancellorship to the end of his days. Yet within two years, to the amazement of Europe and the consternation of his own countrymen, the young and inexperienced William had parted with the statesman who had made the German Empire. The differences had rapidly become acute. The headstrong Emperor longed to carry out his own ideas, which were opposed by the Chancellor. At home, Bismarck wanted to continue persecuting

Disputes with Bismarck about:

1. Treatment of the Socialists

DROPPING THE PILOT.

Punch's *most famous political cartoon – William II and Bismarck part company. Both of them, strangely enough, liked this representation. Cartoon by Tenniel, 29th March 1890.*

the socialists, whereas the Emperor wished to reconcile them. In Europe the Emperor apparently preferred to assure Austria-Hungary of Germany's friendship in all circumstances and let Russia go hang. Bismarck's policy of keeping a foot in both camps and strictly limiting Germany's obligations to Austria-Hungary was far too complicated for his successors. Austria-Hungary and Germany must control the Balkans between them, thought the Emperor, and that left little room for friendship with Russia.[1] Finally, on the vexed question of acquiring colonies the Emperor insisted on immediate German expansion and the construction of a fleet which could hold its own against any other – a policy Bismarck had largely avoided, since it would inevitably antagonise Britain. Bismarck therefore reminded the Emperor of the rule that the Chancellor alone was entitled to present advice to the

2. Russia's friendship

3. The 'Big Fleet' question

[1] For the foreign and colonial policy of Imperial Germany in this period see Chapter 18.

crown – whereupon William demanded that Bismarck should advise him to alter the rule! The Chancellor, horrified at the idea of being reduced to the level of other ministers, replied that he 'could never serve on his knees'. Pressed to tender his resignation, he at last did so. The veteran pilot was dropped.

Bismarck resigns, 1890

Germany under Bismarck's successors, 1890–1914

It is not necessary to describe the domestic policies of Bismarck's successors as Imperial Chancellor before 1914 – Caprivi, Hohenlohe, Bulow and Bethman-Holweg. They were all overshadowed in the public eye by the flamboyant young Emperor. Germany continued to grow in industrial wealth and in military – and soon naval – power, and to present a model to Europe in the way of welfare legislation, municipal enterprise, and public education. It also remained, for all the universal suffrage and the increasing public support for the socialists (now relieved of the laws against them), a state with many autocratic features. The predominance of Prussia and the Prussian army tradition, and the fact that the Imperial ministers were responsible not to the Reichstag but to the Emperor, kept Germany well short of being a fully constitutional state on the lines of Britain or France. And this, as we shall see, had unfortunate effects on German foreign policy, and on the peace of the world.

CHAPTER 17
The Russian Empire: Internal History, 1881–1914

Alexander III, son and successor of the murdered 'Tsar Liberator' Alexander II, kept firm control over his subjects. This was not felt to be oppressive by the vast majority, who were not in the habit of blaming their poverty on their ruler. Traditional in their beliefs, they still looked on the Tsar as their Protector and Father. But by this time there were also, as we have already seen, certain groups who had begun to regard the Tsardom as a tyranny. Some of these opponents were liberal-minded noblemen with a belief in free speech and parliamentary institutions, but many more were middle-class intellectuals, the product of the new schools and universities. Feeling themselves well qualified to criticise and advise the government, they were intensely frustrated by the absence of any national assembly and by the restrictions on free speech and writing.

Besides critics of this sort, who even if they formed secret societies were essentially groups of individuals, there were also much larger groups who now increasingly felt the Tsardom heavy upon them. These were the religious minorities (like the Jews and the Protestants) and the subject nationalities of the Russian Empire (such as the Poles and the Baltic peoples). But the Tsars, of course, in no way thought of themselves as oppressors. Both Alexander III and Nicholas II regarded themselves as bound by sacred oath and duty to maintain the full power of the Tsardom and to use it for the general good. Moreover Alexander III thought that the concessions made by his father had actually promoted the growth of opposition and terrorism; and in clamping down on revolutionary activity he was for several years fully supported by the mass of the country.

A giant of a man who could bend a horseshoe with his bare hands, Alexander III has sometimes been called the 'Peasant Tsar'. Honourable and straightforward, brusque, shy and simple, he venerated the older traditions of Russia and was determined not to see these weakened by western doctrines like liberalism or socialism. 'Autocracy, Orthodoxy and Nationalism' were his ideals, as they were those of Nicholas I; and almost his first action as a ruler was to cancel his father's edict, signed on the eve of the assassination, approving the setting up of a representative commission to confer with the government about constitutional reforms. Under the influence of his old tutor Pobedonostzev, chairman of the governing council of the Russian Orthodox Church and soon Alexander's main adviser, the censorship was extended, martial law made easier to apply, the independence

Alexander III, 1881–94

His critics:

– individuals

– religious and national minorities

A 'Russian' policy

Strengthening of the autocracy

of the universities restricted, and the powers of the local councils – the Zemstva and town dumas – reduced. The popular or peasant element in the Zemstva was also lessened in favour of the upper classes. In the countryside, new leading officials known as 'land captains' were appointed from the nobility and entrusted with many powers exercised in the previous reign by the local Zemstva or the elected justices of the peace.

Persecution of Jews

These restrictions were as nothing, however, compared with the actions taken by Alexander's government against the religious and national minorities. The treatment of the five million Jews was sheer persecution. The Jews were already confined to a 'Pale' of settlement in the south and west. Now they were barred from settling in rural districts, deprived of voting rights for the local councils, and subjected to a quota system for entrance to high schools and universities. No Jew could practise at the Bar, no Jewish doctor be employed by a public authority, no Jewish soldier become an officer. Worse still, when local mobs, driven by hatred, or more frequently greed, set on a Jewish community in a *pogrom* – a Russian word for 'destruction', usually involving massacre as well as burning and looting – the Russian police all too often proved to be participants rather than protectors. Such attacks were particularly frequent and vicious early in the reign, the excuse being that one of the killers of Alexander II had been a Jewish girl.

The government's anti-Jewish attitude was based on religion rather than race: a Jew could avoid disabilities by accepting the Orthodox Christian faith. Russia's Jewish problem would be solved, Pobedonostzev had declared, when one-third of the Jews had emigrated, one-third had been converted, and one-third had been assimilated or had disappeared. In the case of the national minorities, the hostility was to the nationality itself: in Alexander's eyes non-Russians could only be satisfactory subjects if they spoke and acted like Russians. Accordingly in Poland the government forbade any Pole or Roman Catholic to hold an official position and banned the teaching of Polish in schools. Even Polish literature was studied from Russian translations. Similarly in the Baltic provinces it banned the use in schools of the German language spoken by the ruling class, and in the Ukraine and White Russia it prohibited the teaching of the native tongues and enforced the use of Russian. It also sought to apply, less rigorously, similar policies in the Armenian and central Asiatic regions; while in Finland it made knowledge of Russian compulsory for public-servants and set up a censorship over Finnish newspapers. Everywhere Alexander's object was 'Russification'. So far as possible, the outlying provinces with all their different peoples and traditions must be assimilated to Russia in language, institutions and faith. Such a policy, while intelligible in someone wishing to make a strong, centralised, unified and subservient state, was bound to create immense opposition.

Actions against the minority peoples: (Poles, Ukrainians, etc.)

'Russification'

Peasant and factory reforms: N. K. Bunge (1881–87)

Nevertheless Alexander III's reign also saw a number of reforms, mainly aimed at easing the lot of the peasant. Most of these were the work of Alexander's reforming finance minister N. K. Bunge, who also secured factory laws appointing inspectors and forbidding child labour. The chief measures to help the peasants were the abolition of the poll-tax, the scaling down of the redemption payments dating from the Emancipation, and the creation of a Peasants' Bank to help with the purchase of more land. Control of peasant movements, too, was somewhat relaxed, to make migration to other parts of Russia easier.

Despite such reforms Russian agriculture remained stagnant and in the bad seasons of 1891–92 there was severe famine. Industry, on the contrary, flourished as never before. Something has already been said of the remarkable spurt made by Russia in the 1890s with the help of foreign loans, and of how Alexander's Minister of Communications and later of Finance, Sergius Witte, involved the state directly in the building of great new railways (such as the Trans-Siberian), and in the financing of industry.[1] Witte, whose period of power dated from 1892, came in on a rising tide. During the 1880s Russia's production of coal increased by nearly fifty per cent, of iron by a hundred per cent and of oil by eight hundred per cent – starting, of course, from very low figures.

Industrial progress: S. Witte

Another notable feature of Alexander's reign was his peaceful foreign policy. Though this did not stop the steady Russian advance into central Asia, it kept Russia from adventures in the Balkans and from pressing too hard against Afghanistan. In his relations with the great powers Alexander came to distrust Germany, who had chosen as her closest partner Austria-Hungary – a country with which Russia had several possible points of conflict. This led Alexander to develop ties with France – ties marked by loans and by the Franco-Russian alliance of 1892.[2]

Alexander's foreign policy

Franco-Russian Alliance, 1892

It was accordingly to a Russia which was still being ruled as an autocracy, which was in a period of fast industrial growth, and which was already allied with France, that Alexander III's son Nicholas II succeeded in 1894.

The reign of Nicholas II was one of almost unrelieved disaster. It began, as it ended, in tragedy. At his coronation festivities an open-air gathering for the Moscow people dissolved into chaos as the crowds rushed for the free beer, and hundreds of people were crushed to death.

Nicholas II, 1894–1917

Agitation in Russia, for some years quietened through revulsion against Alexander II's murder, was by 1894 again growing vigorous. The great industrial expansion of the 1880s and 1890s was producing alarming problems. The population of the towns was fast increasing – in the final twelve years of the nineteenth century it grew by no less than a third – and great factories were springing up, often with as many as five thousand workers. The vilest conditions were common in these and the overcrowded towns generally – in 1885, when a factory act was being prepared, people were found working eighteen hours a day, while child labour down to three years of age in some cases still persisted in spite of an earlier prohibition. So Russia, though still in her industrial infancy, showed in her towns the very worst features of a developed industrialism – overcrowding, slums, appalling factory conditions. The combination of discontented urban workers with the penniless university students so common in Russia, produced a formidable revolutionary movement.

Bad urban conditions

Nicholas II himself was the last man who should have inherited the task of solving Russia's overwhelming problems. His intelligence was no more remarkable than that of his father, and he had neither Alexander III's powerful physique nor his iron will. Without the brains or determination to run effectively a village, let alone a state the size of Russia, he was still resolved to rule as a complete autocrat. Even his virtues, such as a religious and loving nature and personal kindness to his

Character of Nicholas II

[1] See pp. 208–9.

[2] The formation of this is described in the next chapter.

family, were those most unfitted to his job. His extremely narrow outlook saw everything in Russia in terms of loyalty to himself: since he knew the honesty of his own intentions, nothing could be good which did not begin by complete devotion to the Tsar. But to reformers and revolutionaries, nothing could be good unless it began by complete devotion to the needs of Russia's downtrodden peasantry and proletariat – a devotion expressing itself in scientific plans for social improvement, not merely in kindly thought or words. Between these two attitudes little compromise was possible.

To the demand for a parliament from those, such as the liberals of the Zemstva, who still hoped for peaceful reform, Nicholas II consistently turned a deaf ear. Such ideas, he announced, were but 'senseless dreams'. This unyielding attitude only produced more supporters of revolutionary violence. In 1898 the Russian Social Democrat Party was founded – to be almost instantly pounced on by the police – and, in 1900, the Social Revolutionary Party. The latter was a mixture of many left-wing groups, including Marxists, but with a strong belief in socialist progress through the Russian village communes.

The Social Democrats were all Marxists, but also contained many shades of left-wing opinion, for different elements in Marx's writings were emphasised by different people. At the second party congress of the Russian Social Democrats in 1903, held in Brussels and hastily moved to London to escape the attentions of the Belgian police, these divisions became very clear. The question which caused the greatest dissension among the forty-three delegates was whether the party should consist purely of devoted workers, or whether it should admit passive members, encourage subscriptions from vaguely interested persons, and so on. The difference was between a party which would be a hundred per cent fighting organisation of professional revolutionaries, and one which would be a far looser body, more dependent on public opinion and unable to make great demands on its members. The advocates of the more aggressive organisation were led by a revolutionary barrister and strike-leader who had served a sentence of four years imprisonment and exile. By name originally Vladimir Ilyich Ulyanov, he was now known as Lenin. His policy was not immediately approved but his followers gained a majority of seats on the party executive, and henceforth he and his supporters were known as Bolsheviks ('Majority Men'), since they had won a majority at this Congress. The advocates of a looser party organisation became termed Mensheviks ('Minority Men'). By 1905 the two groups were holding separate congresses and by 1911 they had formally separated, the Bolsheviks to promote the revolution as soon as possible, the Mensheviks to see first what reforms could be achieved by gentler means.

To the thorough-going Marxist the working classes had two weapons. The final one was armed rebellion, but before that the strike might do much. Mainly through spontaneous discontent, but partly through Marxist propaganda, a wave of strikes now overwhelmed Russia. A strike in 1895–96 in the nineteen St Petersburg cotton factories, encouraged among others by Lenin, had wrung from the Government an important concession: in the following year, on Witte's advice, a factory act was passed which limited hours to eleven and a half a day. This success bred other strikes with demands which became more political, such as freedom of speech and a constituent assembly. In 1904 a big strike among the Baku oilworkers, with these as well as industrial aims, led to troops discharging volleys into the

Social Revolutionary Party, 1900

Social Democrat Party, 1898

Lenin

The Social Democrats begin to split, 1903: Bolsheviks and Mensheviks

Strikes

crowd, and the workmen in revenge firing the oil-wells 'as candles for their dead'.

As though the government had not enough enemies, about 1903 there began a new persecution of the Jews. Alexander III, a great Jew-hater, had issued, as we have already seen, severe laws restricting Jewish political and social rights; and in 1881–82 scores of *pogroms*, or massacres of Jews, had been perpetrated by mobs jealous of their wealth or resentful of their activities. Such *pogroms* were now deliberately encouraged by the Tsarist police. The aim was twofold. For the higher authorities involved, it was to provide in the Jews an enemy who might divert the poor from attacks on the government itself. For the police lower down the scale, it was to line their own pockets, for they often threatened to unleash *pogroms* in order to wring 'protection-money' from the local Jews. One result may perhaps be seen in the extraordinarily high percentage of Jews in the later leadership not only of the Russian revolutionary groups but of extreme left-wing parties in many other countries.

Anti-Semitism

Not content with incurring the opposition of liberals, socialists, and Jews in Russia, the government of Nicholas II now added to its already stupendous difficulties by arousing hostility elsewhere. The Baltic provinces of Estonia and Livonia were subjected to a continuing campaign of the 'Russianisation' begun under Alexander III. So, too, despite one or two gestures of conciliation, were the unhappy provinces inhabited by the Poles. Above all, Finland was now gagged by the introduction of a stricter censorship and a Russian police. In spite of the oaths of successive Tsars, including Nicholas himself, illegal changes were made in the Finnish constitution, and all protests by the Finns, including a petition of half a million people, were ignored. Not surprisingly, in 1904 the Russian Governor-General of Finland was assassinated.

Repression in the subject provinces

The crowning folly of Nicholas and his ministers at this time, however, was to become involved in a war with Japan. This followed not surprisingly from Russia's constant advance across Asia. Perhaps the best pointer to her expansion in this direction may be seen in the building between the years 1891–1901 of the main stretches of the great Trans-Siberian railway. The natural destination of this enormous line was beyond Siberia to the recently founded (1860) Pacific coast port of Vladivostock; but the difficulties of the ground were such that a route going through Russian territory to this port was not completed till 1916. Meanwhile, by arrangements with the helpless Chinese, the Russians were allowed to build another and much more easily constructed line – the Chinese Eastern Railway – to Vladivostock across the Chinese province of Manchuria. This was completed by 1903, with a branch line south. The construction of these railways naturally encouraged Russian ambitions in Manchuria and its neighbour Korea, where they came violently into collision with those of Japan, also determined to batten on the decaying Chinese Empire.

Quarrel with Japan

The Trans-Siberian railway, 1891

Russian railway building in Manchuria; Chinese Eastern Railway, 1903

Russia's ambitions in Manchuria and Korea

Japan was at this time an infant among the powers. It was only recently that she had been awakened from medievalism and enforced isolation from the rest of the world. In 1854 a small American naval force under Commodore Perry had compelled her to open her ports to foreign trade, after which the Japanese, realising that artillery was a decisive argument, had set themselves to adopt Western 'civilisation'. From a land of kimonos and lotus-blossom Japan rapidly became a land of factories and machine guns – a development which might have made the American commodore pause had he foreseen it. Extending her imitation of the West to foreign ventures, Japan by 1895 had successfully challenged China for domination over the weak kingdom of Korea, just south of Manchuria. Korea, previously under Chinese suzerainty, was now declared to be independent; but the Japanese remained virtually in control. The cessions made by China after the war included the island of Formosa and Port Arthur, a warm-water port and fortress at the base of the small Liaotung peninsula west of the Korean peninsula.

It was at this stage that Russia intervened. She had long coveted Port Arthur, for unlike Vladivostock, her most southerly port on the Pacific, it was free from ice all the year round. With a view eventually to getting it herself, she now in concert with France and Germany forced Japan to restore it to China. The Japanese meekly obeyed – and increased their armaments. To their fury three years later Russia herself secured a lease of Port Arthur from China – more or less at the same time as Britain, France and Germany helped themselves to other Chinese ports. War feeling now ran high in Japan and increased when Russia, using the excuse of the Chinese 'Boxer' rising against foreigners in 1900, occupied Manchuria. The last straw came in 1903 with Russian commercial penetration, government-sponsored, of Korea. By this time the Japanese had strengthened themselves by an alliance with Britain to ensure Britain's neutrality if one power were at war with Japan or her active help if Japan had to face two powers. So in 1904, after she had vainly demanded the withdrawal from Manchuria and Korea of Russian troops and influence, Japan challenged Russia by a sudden attack at Port Arthur. As in 1941 with her assault on Pearl Harbour, she struck before any declaration of war.

The Japanese action was rather like David challenging Goliath. The result, too, was the same. The Russian Pacific fleet was largely crippled by the first surprise blow of the Japanese under Admiral Togo, and its later attempts at sallies from Port Arthur led only to further defeats. Meanwhile the Japanese also besieged Port Arthur from the landward side and after a lengthy struggle finally took it. Beaten in Manchuria at the great battle of Mukden, the Russians then pinned their last hope on the arrival of their Baltic fleet in Chinese waters. It had been ordered east in October 1904, had nearly caused war with Britain by firing on fishing-trawlers off the Dogger Bank in mistake for hostile torpedo-boats, and had proceeded slowly round the world by way of Madagascar and Singapore. After eight months it at length appeared off Korea. All the world had followed its progress. And within an hour of meeting Togo near the island of Tsushima between Korea and Japan, it almost ceased to exist: only four of its twenty-seven ships survived to reach Vladivostock. The Russians had suffered one of the most humiliating naval defeats on record, and a treaty was soon made (Treaty of Portsmouth, U.S.A., 1905) by which they had to evacuate Manchuria, give up Port Arthur and the surrounding peninsula to Japan, and recognise Japanese influence as predominant in Korea.

The effect of all this on Russia was profound. Once more, as in the Crimea campaign, war had exposed the complete inefficiency of the Tsardom. Even before the final Russian defeats the demand for a parliament, backed everywhere by strikes, grew irresistible. On a Sunday afternoon in January 1905, two or three weeks after the loss of Port Arthur, huge contingents of strikers and their families, brought together by a young priest, Father Gapon, tried to converge on the Winter Palace Square in St Petersburg. Gapon was the organiser of a workers'

The Winter Palace, Petrograd (St Petersburg) in 1922.

union approved (and supervised) by the police; and the aim of the meeting was to present a petition to the Tsar requesting not merely an eight hour day but political concessions such as a free press and a constitutional assembly. The crowds were unarmed, and some carried ikons or portraits of the Tsar and sang hymns as they marched in from the suburbs. But the Tsar was not in residence and his ministers had made no preparations to receive the deputation except to station soldiers in the square and in the streets leading to it. The result was a series of confrontations, including one in the square itself, in which the crowds refused to turn back or disperse – some knelt down in the snow – and the soldiers then opened fire. Presumably the orders to fire were given either to discourage future demonstrations or from fear of this one. Some of the volleys were even aimed at children in their vantage points in trees. Officially the dead numbered ninety-two, with several hundred wounded, but the real figures were probably much higher. Gapon escaped to denounce the killings and the Tsar – but to be sentenced to death and, it seems, executed later by Social Revolutionaries as a traitor to the revolutionary cause.

'Bloody Sunday'

The massacre of 'Bloody Sunday' raised popular fury to fever-point. Peasants attacked local landlords, strikes broke out, soldiers and sailors mutinied, and finally, just after the conclusion of peace, came virtually a general strike. Industrial and agricultural workers, railways and telegraph operators, even the children in the elementary schools struck. Faced with such a movement Nicholas II could only give in, though with great reluctance. On the advice of Witte, by far his ablest minister, who had succeeded in obtaining very favourable terms from the Japanese, he made large concessions. During the earlier days of the mass movements he had promised to summon a Duma, or parliament. This had not yet met, nor would it have been of much use in establishing democracy, since the franchise would have been very limited and the new body purely consultative. Now Nicholas agreed to widen the franchise, to entrust the Duma with real law-making activities, and to allow certain personal rights such as freedom of meeting and association. The general strike was called off, but the slackening of the censorship only meant an increase in revolutionary propaganda. Outrages and strikes continued, and brutal repression began once more. In certain districts where peasants had got out of hand whole villages were shelled and the ringleaders buried alive.

A general strike

Nicholas's October Manifesto, 1905: extra privileges for proposed Duma

238

The first Duma, 1906

In 1906 the first Duma met. Any hopes that a period of real reform was about to begin were soon dispelled. The Duma was not for the most part an extremist body – the Bolsheviks, for example, had boycotted it on the ground that it was a sham. Every reform asked for by the Duma, however, was refused; all the previous concessions were hedged about with restrictions; and within three months, after the Tsar had dismissed Witte, it was dissolved. By now only the liberals retained much faith in a constitution or a Duma granted by the Tsar. For their part, the working classes organised instead their own town, factory, or village councils, known as 'soviets', and determined that sooner or later these soviets should develop into a democratic government. In this movement a name of great importance for the future soon emerged – Trotsky. By now the Tsar's government had put practically the whole country under martial law, and the death pentaly was inflicted for a mere insult to an official. Between 1905 and 1908 some 4,000 people were executed – though it is fair to say that at least this number of officials were assassinated – while in 1906 alone over 40,000 were banished to Siberia without trial.

The soviets

Trotsky

Stolypin, 1906–11

Much of the drive behind this wave of repression came from the Tsar's new 'strong man' chief minister, Peter Stolypin. Stolypin's policy, however, was constructive as well as repressive. From 1906 concessions were made to the desire of the peasants for greater freedom in selling, dividing, and leaving their land. In fact, under the guidance of Stolypin the government began to break up the old communal system by allowing the peasantry to take over their lands from the *mir* under certain conditions and become completely independent proprietors. By 1914 nearly a half of them had done so. Had their lands been large enough or their cultivation more efficient, the peasants might well have become, as the government now hoped, a strong barrier against revolution.

The second Duma, 1907

In 1907, in accordance with his announced concessions, Nicholas called a second Duma. It proved, however, as little to the Tsar's liking as the first, in spite of strong governmental pressure at the elections. Over a quarter of the members returned had at some time been sentenced for revolutionary activity. It is not surprising that this body, too, was dissolved within three months – when it declined to hand over some Social Democratic members for trial on charges of subversive activity. Before the third Duma met, the basis of voting was altered, fewer representatives being given to Poland, and more power in voting being extended to wealthy businessmen and large landlords. In consequence this Duma was quieter and survived rather impotently its full term.

The third Duma, 1908–12

Agitation recedes

So the Tsarist régime, despite the humiliation of the Russo-Japanese war and the shock of the strikes and revolutionary movements of 1905–06, still survived. By concessions and repression it came through its difficulties, so that in the next few years the tide of agitation receded, despite episodes such as the assassination of Stolypin in 1911. The growing industrialisation, for all its problems, brought greater economic strength; and in the countryside the wealthier peasants at least were more content. Meanwhile, however, the storm clouds were gathering over Europe. The great powers, including Russia, had built up what amounted to a rival system of alliances – as the next chapter will describe. In 1914 those alliances were put to the test in what became the First World War. Three years of fighting on a grand scale, of heroic victories, disastrous defeats and colossal losses, were more than the Tsardom could finally stand. In 1917, overcome by the forces of war-weariness and revolution, it crumbled into ruin – and history.

The First World War – the death-blow to the Tsardom

CHAPTER 18
Bismarck's Foreign Policy and the Framing of the European Alliances, 1871–1907

Much as Bismarck was concerned with developments in Germany, his main interest after 1871 was still in foreign affairs. The German Empire had been built largely by his skill in diplomacy, and by that same skill he expected to preserve it.

The central problem was the attitude of France. It can be argued that Bismarck in 1871 made a fatal mistake by annexing Alsace and Lorraine and so perpetuating France's enmity. This was an injury that France intended neither to forgive nor to forget: she kept the statue in Paris representing the town of Strasbourg permanently draped in black! The resources of the two territories in coal and iron, however, and above all their strategical value for the defence of south-west Germany against a new French attack, meant so much to Germany that Bismarck resolved to risk the undying hostility of France and take them. In so deciding he reckoned on three things. The first was that France would take many years to recover from the Franco-Prussian War. The second was that he could use the bogey of a French war of revenge to make the Reichstag maintain a high level of German armaments. And the third was that his diplomatic genius could keep France 'isolated' – i.e. without any important ally.

The first calculation was soon upset by the swiftness of France's recovery. The £200,000,000 was paid off in two years, the army of occupation had to be withdrawn, the Republic was established as a permanency, and France seemed to be pulling herself together again. Bismarck was furious at the speed of all this (though he supported the establishment of a republic, which he thought would have more difficulty in finding allies than a monarchy). Accordingly in 1875, when France had begun to reorganise her army and increase her armaments, Bismarck indirectly threatened war – not in so many words, but in the form of hostile articles 'inspired' in newspapers. He was certainly not the man to shrink from hitting an opponent as yet imperfectly on his – or her – feet. Nevertheless his object was probably only to bully France into abandoning her arms programme. In this, for once, he was unsuccessful, as both Britain and Russia reacted sharply against the apparent threat to France. They would not allow the balance of power to be completely upset by the annihilation or further weakening of France; and a visit to Berlin by the Tsar and a letter to the Emperor William from Queen Victoria clinched the matter. Bismarck found himself dealing with three powers, not one – and just as he knew the moment for attack, so he also knew the moment for retreat (and denial).

France

Bismarck's calculations in 1871

France's rapid recovery

Bismarck's indirect threats, 1875

Britain and Russia intervene

The attitude of Russia over this incident disappointed Bismarck. Friendship with Russia had always been a mainspring of his policy. He had made it easy for the Russians to suppress the Polish revolt in 1863 and had been rewarded when the Russians remained neutral in the Franco-Prussian war. Immediately following that, in negotiations and meetings in 1872 and 1873, he had brought together the heads of the three great Empires – Germany, Russia and Austria-Hungary – in a pact usually known as the *Dreikaiserbund* (League of the Three Emperors) based on general friendship and consultation between the three powers. All three were conservatively-inclined monarchies, and all three had a common interest in opposing such ventures as Karl Marx's 'International' of working men (which they agreed to denounce). Bismarck also hoped, however, that this league of monarchical friendship, though somewhat vague, would form a common bond against republican France (which was one reason why he wanted France to remain a republic). Now, after Russia's behaviour in 1875, it was clear that the policy of the three empires was very far from identical, and that the sentimental ties of the *Dreikaiserbund* might not count for much.

So indeed it proved a year or two later when the Eastern question entered one of its acute phases.[1] It will be remembered that in 1877 after the Russian defeat of Turkey, Disraeli, being at length assured of the support of Austria-Hungary, by a

Dreikaiserbund of
1873 weakened

Congress of Berlin,
1878

The Dual Alliance of 1879 – Germany and Austria join together, while Russia courts France, and Britain and Italy feel out of it. Cartoon by Tenniel.

PUNCH, OR THE LONDON CHARIVARI.—October 4, 1879.

THE GAME OF THE DAY.

Bismarck. "COME, ANDRASSY, WE KNOW EACH OTHER'S 'FORM.' YOU AND I TOGETHER AGAINST THE LOT!!"
Russia (to France). "I THINK, MADAME, *WE* MIGHT BE A MATCH FOR THEM!"
France. "THANKS! I PREFER TO SIT OUT AT PRESENT!"   England (to Italy). "NOBODY ASKS *US!!*"

[1] For details of this crisis see pp. 170–72.

threat of war compelled Russia to present the treaty of San Stefano to a Congress of European powers for revision. That Congress met, as we have seen, at Berlin in 1878, where Bismarck played the part of 'honest broker' between Russia, Britain, and Austria-Hungary. At the Congress of Berlin Bismarck saw clearly that Russian and Austrian ambitions in the new Balkan states might well be incompatible, and that he might have to choose between Germany's two friends.

Clash between Russian and Austrian interests

Bismarck's choice fell on Austria-Hungary. He had at least three motives, quite apart from the fact that the Austrian core of the Hapsburg empire was German and that Russia was aggrieved by Germany's failure to support her at the Congress. Possibly his main motive was that an alliance with Russia would confront Germany with the hostility of Britain, a power profoundly anti-Russian. Secondly, he knew that he could control Austria-Hungary and be the predominant partner in that alliance, whereas the position would be much more doubtful with Russia. Thirdly, the support of Austria-Hungary would leave open the Danube, the main trade route to the Mediterranean, and allow Germany considerable influence in south-eastern Europe. These three considerations and the fear of seeing Russia in control of Constantinople more than outweighed the danger of a hostile power on Germany's eastern boundary. Moreover, though he was now choosing an Austrian alliance Bismarck had no intention of being involved in war with Russia if he could possibly help it. The upshot was that in 1879 Germany and Austria-Hungary concluded what became known as the Dual Alliance, an arrangement by which each party undertook to help the other in the event of an attack by Russia, or to keep neutral in the event of an attack by any other power (France, for example). This, though purely 'defensive' in form, gave Bismarck everything he wanted, for he knew how to make a German war of aggression appear the reverse, while if Austria-Hungary tried one for her own ends he could disown her. So the Dual Alliance was concluded, and its existence soon publicised – though not its exact terms, which remained secret until 1888. Continually renewed, it remained for the period preceding the First World War the firmest feature in the diplomatic world.

Bismarck chooses Austria-Hungary

Dual Alliance, 1879 (Germany and Austria-Hungary)

Bismarck had not abandoned hopes of patching up his relationship with Russia, nor was he content with merely one ally. The Dual Alliance ensured that if war came again with France, Austria-Hungary would be neutral once more, as in 1870. But there was another power in Europe now, and on France's borders – Italy. Accordingly Bismarck drew Italy into his network. His technique was characteristic. He secretly encouraged French ambitions in North Africa, mainly to 'divert' her from scheming to recover Alsace-Lorraine but also to bring her into collision with Italy, who had ambitions (and some 20,000 settlers) in the Tunis area. Moreover French expansion in North Africa would not improve French relations with Britain. In 1881 the French, reluctant to see an Italian colony established on the borders of French Algeria, took Bismarck's hint and occupied Tunis. This threw Italy into the arms of Germany. The following year she joined the two powers of the Dual Alliance in a separate Triple Alliance. The terms of the understanding were again defensive, Italy having no obligation to support an aggressive policy on the part of Germany and Austria-Hungary. If she were attacked by France, however, she would have the help of the other two powers; and if France attacked Germany, Italy would come to the latter's aid. Altogether Bismarck scored a considerable success in binding Italy to his system, for though her armed forces were not very strong she had a valuable friendship with Great

Bismarck 'diverts' France from Alsace-Lorraine

French occupy Tunis, 1881

Triple Alliance, 1882 (Germany, Austria-Hungary, Italy)

SNUBBED!

Mossoo (*aside*). "HA!—WITH MY HATED RIVAL! WHY WAS I SO RUDE TO HER?!"

Italy, offended by the French occupation of Tunis, joins the Dual Alliance. Cartoon by Tenniel.

Treaties of Triple Alliance powers with Rumania, 1883–88

Britain. Shortly afterwards he extended the network still further by including Rumania, which between 1883 and 1888 signed separate defensive treaties with all the Triple Alliance powers.

So Bismarck now had Austria-Hungary, Italy and Rumania as allies, and Great Britain not only friendly with Italy but on bad terms with France over North Africa – for the French occupation of Tunis was soon followed in 1882 by the British occupation of Egypt. The only danger of trouble for the Triple Alliance was if France, otherwise completely isolated, should come to an agreement with Russia. This danger, however, Bismarck had already skilfully forestalled, partly by playing on the natural objections of the Tsar to the most democratic country in Europe, and partly by persuading Russia and Austria-Hungary to revive the old *Dreikaiserbund*, this time in the form of a much more precise treaty. This was done in 1881, and the general arrangement then concluded – that none of the three powers would help a fourth power (France, for example) if war broke out between that power and any one of them – was renewed in 1884. So the possibility of a Franco-Russian alliance seemed to be banished, France had no friend in Europe, and Bismarck's work was complete. It only remained to keep it so.

Dreikaiserbund Treaty of 1881 guards against Russia supporting France

About this time Bismarck's whole conception of foreign policy began to be challenged at home by a movement which demanded colonies for Germany. Bismarck thought of Germany as a European power dominating the Continent; the Colonial school hoped rather for a Germany which would be a world power. It stressed the importance of colonies as sources of raw materials, markets for manufactured goods, creators of valuable positions for young men and outlets for surplus population. In this it linked up with the growing European movement known as imperialism – the belief that the acquisition of colonies would not merely be economically or strategically beneficial to the European power concerned, but would also be economically and culturally beneficial to the native peoples taken over. (In view of the strength of European arms and industry, the native peoples of course had no choice in the matter). Bismarck himself thought rather of the dangers of a colonial policy – how it would call for a big navy, and how that would inevitably bring Germany into rivalry with Great Britain. And once Great Britain was on bad terms with Germany, France would be no longer 'isolated'. She would have as her ally the greatest and richest empire in the world.

The Colonial Question:

Imperialism

Bismarck's fears of a colonial policy

These dangers, however, did not weigh with Germany as much as Bismarck would have wished. Germans, conscious of their new strength, were resentful when they saw Britain, with her great white dominions, her Indian Empire, her innumerable points of vantage from Gibraltar to Hong Kong, also picking up much of Africa. The Zulu War, the acquisition of Bechuanaland and Rhodesia, the pressure against the Boer republics, the occupation of Egypt, the advances in east and west Africa, all infuriated Germans who longed for similar movements of their own. Even the despised France was quietly building up the second greatest colonial empire. To Algeria (settled in the reign of Louis Philippe) and her protectorates in Indo-China (initiated under the Second Empire and extended in 1884–85), she had added Tunis, whence she began to advance over the Sahara and Western Sudan. Little Belgium, too, was building up a valuable source of tropical products in the Congo: while Portugal and Holland still retained much, and Spain a little, of their old overseas empires. And all the time Russia was pressing relentlessly into the Caucasus and central Asia. So, not surprisingly, the German demand for colonies grew. It was exactly the kind of clamour most difficult for Bismarck to resist – a demand inspired not by liberalism but by patriotism. Reluctantly the old statesman, who later described himself as 'no colonial man', had to shift his ground and set about acquiring enough colonies at least to keep the Germans quiet.

Britain, France and Russia still expand

Bismarck has to follow suit

In 1884 Germany accordingly entered, as a late-starter, the fast-developing competition for Africa. She made off with the districts known as South-West Africa, the Cameroons, and Togoland. In 1885 she followed this by securing leases of extensive areas in East Africa – the beginnings of her colony of German East

German colonies in Africa, 1884–85

"MOSÉ IN EGITTO!!!"

A notable coup *in the struggle for colonial influence was Disraeli's acquisition of the Suez Canal shares held by the Khedive of Egypt. Here the title of a famous opera by Rossini is used to signify the presence of Disraeli and Britain in Egypt. Cartoon by Tenniel, 11th December 1875.*

Africa (Tanganyika). Within a few years a million square miles of territory went to Germany without her so much as fighting a battle for them. It was a good beginning, but she was still a long way behind.

In entering the colonial sphere, Germany at first suffered no bad effects apart from some minor quarrels with Britain. These and similar troubles between other Powers led to an international Colonial Congress being held at Berlin to lay down rules for the future. The most important of these was that the Powers would recognise 'effective occupation' as a title to possession. With this assurance, the 'scramble for Africa' could then get going in earnest.

Since France was at loggerheads with Italy over Tunis, Britain at loggerheads with France over Egypt, and Russia at loggerheads with Britain over the Balkans

Colonial Congress at
Berlin, 1884–85

and the Far East, Germany seemed at first in a very favourable position. Her alliances gave her valuable friends, while her rivals' objections to one another were greater than their common objection to Germany. Bismarck was like a clever juggler who could keep five very costly plates – Austria-Hungary, Italy, Russia, France and Britain – spinning through the air. The plates were always in some danger of being smashed and of injuring the juggler in the process, but Bismarck's skill was such that the disaster never occurred. Consequently he earned much applause and enriched the employer for whom he worked. But sooner or later that employer had to give way to another – and what if the new employer himself should fancy his powers as a juggler (though he was quite an amateur) and want to try his own hand with the plates?

This in fact was what occurred. We have seen how the old Emperor William I at last died in 1888, how his successor Frederick died the same year, and how Frederick's young and headstrong son then became Emperor as William II. We have also seen how William II parted with Bismarck in 1890, largely over domestic issues.[1] Within a few years the new Emperor, successive Chancellors and the force of events brought about all the developments Bismarck had feared. Already during his own period of office he had found the task of keeping friendly with both Austria-Hungary and Russia extremely difficult. To maintain the friendship with Russia he had concluded in 1887, when the renewed *Dreikaiserbund* Treaty ran out, another agreement known as the Reinsurance Treaty. By this Russia and Germany promised to remain neutral if either went to war with a third power – except if Russia attacked Austria-Hungary or Germany attacked France. Now, freed from Bismarck's control, the young Emperor followed other advice and allowed the Reinsurance Treaty to lapse. He did this because he was anxious to see Germany, not Russia, dominant at Constantinople, and because this would inevitably lead to trouble with Russia. His new advisers, being doubtful whether Russia would prove a reliable friend, at first inclined more to friendship with Britain – with whom, in 1890, Germany made an agreement. By this she received Heligoland, which had been in British hands since the Napoleonic wars, in return for recognising a British protectorate over the territories of the Sultan of Zanzibar.

All this had a rapid effect on France and Russia. Germany, with Austria-Hungary and Italy already as firm allies, seemed to be stretching out the hand of friendship to Britain. France had for long been 'isolated': now Russia seemed to be isolated too. What more natural than that the two isolated powers should join together to end their isolation? The process did not take long. Even before Bismarck's fall the publication of the Dual Alliance with Austria-Hungary had made Russia suspect the sincerity of Germany's friendship, and further doubts had come when she found it hard to raise loans in the Berlin money market. Now, in view of the German Emperor's overtures to Britain, his refusal to renew the Reinsurance Treaty, and the renewal of the Triple Alliance in 1891, she began to feel certain of Germany's unreliability. By contrast, she found France eager to cultivate her friendship – and fully prepared to raise big loans for her in Paris. So the two countries came together, in spite of the vast differences between Russian Tsardom and French democracy. By two or three stages a firm defensive military agreement was reached, the main feature being that each would come to the other's help if

Bismarck's success

Bismarck's final efforts at friendship with Russia: Reinsurance Treaty, 1887

New German policy under William II: Reinsurance Treaty lapses, 1890 Anglo-German agreement, 1890

Franco-Russian approaches

---

[1] See pp. 228–30.

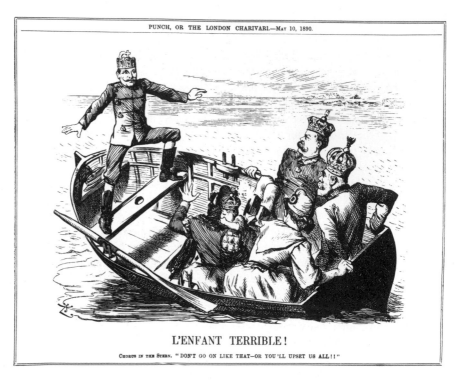

L'ENFANT TERRIBLE!

CHORUS IN THE STERN. "DON'T GO ON LIKE THAT—OR YOU'LL UPSET US ALL!!"

Kaiser William II's indiscretions were notorious. Cartoon by Tenniel.

Dual Alliance (of France and Russia), 1892, 1894

attacked by Germany. This was signed in 1892, and confirmed in 1894. So the Dual Alliance of France and Russia at length stood opposed to the Triple Alliance of Germany, Austria-Hungary and Italy. Bismarck's haunting fear, 'the war on two fronts' – against France and Russia simultaneously – loomed nearer.

As yet, Britain still stood apart. In the early 1890s she was certainly no nearer the Franco-Russian camp than she was to the Triple Alliance. Indeed, in coming together, France and Russia were conscious of their rivalries with Britain as well **Britain and France still on bad terms** as Germany, for bad feeling persisted between Britain and France over Africa and between Britain and Russia over the Near and the Far East. For some years, in fact, the relations between France and Britain grew worse rather than better. France bitterly resented the British occupation of Egypt, while Britain objected to France's protectorate in Tunis and her obvious designs on Morocco. Then, in **'Fashoda Incident', 1898** the 'Fashoda incident', a crisis blazed up over the Sudan. To counter the British occupation of Egypt the French had decided to control, if they could, the Upper Nile. One of their expeditions, led by Major Marchand with a handful of Frenchmen, spent two years of hardship winning its way across Africa from the Congo. Marchand at length reached the Upper Nile and planted the tricolore at Fashoda, a small village on the river. A few days later Britain's General Kitchener arrived on the scene following his defeat of the native Sudanese forces at Omdurman (1898), and found British control of the all-important Nile contested by a few individuals and the French flag. The matter was referred to the respective governments and for a time it seemed that the two countries were on the verge of war.

FOOTBATH IN ASIA

Colonial rivalry between Britain and Russia as seen in an Austrian cartoon of 1894. The two Powers grasp hands and share a footbath marked Asia – i.e. they pretend to tolerate each other's presence in the Far East. But behind their backs they hold cudgels ready for use against each other.

Finally, however, France climbed down and acknowledged British control of the Upper Nile. Delcassé, the new French Foreign Minister, shrewdly calculated that British friendship might be more valuable to France than Fashoda or half a million square miles of the Sudan.

It took some years for Britain to realise her need for friendship with France. For a time she seemed to be turning to Germany. The latter, however, increasingly jealous of British colonial and naval power, contemptuous of British liberalism, and fearful of being drawn into a clash between Britain and Russia, rebuffed Joseph Chamberlain's friendly overtures. Gradually Britain's outlook began to change. The hostility of almost every country in Europe during the Boer War was one factor – particularly that of Germany, whose Emperor had already in 1896 sent a telegram congratulating Kruger on repelling the Jameson Raid. Then there was the retirement from the post of foreign secretary of Britain's foremost expert in foreign affairs, Lord Salisbury – a statesman whose policy has been described (not quite accurately) as one of 'splendid isolation'. Any splendour which isolation held for Britain was now becoming less and less visible with each fresh cloud on the horizon. The passing of the old Queen, too, and the accession of Edward VII made some difference. Victoria had been pro-German, whereas Edward not only intensely disliked his nephew, the Emperor William II, but had a passionate fondness, understandable in view of his upbringing, for France and the French.

The main factor, however, in swinging Britain against Germany was the increasing clamour in that country for a big navy and colonial empire. In 1895

Germany rejects Britain's overtures, 1898–1900

Britain moves from 'isolation'

German Navy Laws,
1898 and 1900

the Kiel Canal connecting the Baltic and the North Sea was opened, essential if Germany were to become a major naval power. In 1898 and again in 1900 the Reichstag approved Navy Bills which laid the foundation of a great German battle-fleet – the dream of Admiral von Tirpitz, by this time in charge of the German admiralty. Germany was already the strongest European power on land. It was not likely that Britain, whose navy had ruled supreme since the Napoleonic wars, would welcome a powerful rival in her own sphere of the sea.

Anglo-Japanese
alliance, 1902

In 1902 Britain took her first step away from isolation. She made an unexpected alliance with Japan, whose rapid westernisation was the wonder, and not yet the dismay, of the world. Its declared object was to safeguard the independence of China and Korea – which meant, among other things, discouraging Germany, Russia and France from further 'pickings' in the Far East. By its provision for neutrality if either signatory became involved in war in the Far East (or for active help if the war was with two or more powers), the Anglo-Japanese treaty made it possible for Japan to attack Russia, as she shortly did, without fear of outside interference. It also enabled Britain to keep more of her naval forces in Europe, in case of trouble with Germany.

Anglo-French or
Dual *Entente*, 1904

In 1904 the next and much more decisive step for Britain followed: the *Entente Cordiale* with France. The *Entente*, for which Delcassé worked with great skill, was

THE FORCE BEHIND JAPAN
A Russian cartoon on the attitude of Britain and the U.S.A. in the looming quarrel with Japan (c. 1902). Japan threatens Russia, and a delighted Britain makes only pretended and ineffectual moves to restrain her.

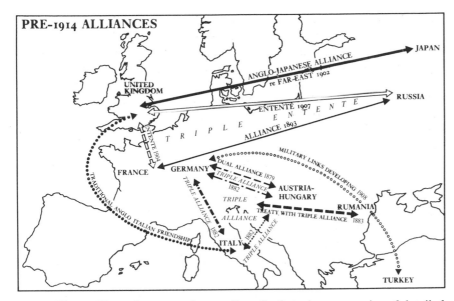

PRE-1914 ALLIANCES

not a military alliance but an understanding. In form it was a series of detailed agreements about zones of Anglo-French dissension, notably in North Africa. Here the terms were the obvious ones – that France recognised Britain's predominant position and interests in Egypt, while Britain recognised France's claim to a similar position (which she had not yet achieved) in Morocco. But although so limited in form, the *Entente* was two years later followed by the first military discussions between the staffs of the British and French armed forces about how to deal with Germany, should that become necessary. Though the *Entente* was not an alliance in name, it soon became something rather like it in fact. At any rate Germany was offended by it, both because it seemed to shut her out of Morocco and because it announced some kind of Franco-British partnership.

Egypt for Britain, Morocco for France

The Germans were not long in reacting to the new agreement. In March 1905, while Russia was in turmoil at home and fighting Japan abroad, Germany seized the opportunity to put pressure on France. William II was sent by his ministers to Tangier, in Morocco, where he made a speech emphasising Germany's interests there and the importance of maintaining the Sultan's independence. Germany then went on to demand the calling of an international conference to review the whole question of Morocco; and the French, in view of their Russian ally's troubles, felt obliged to agree, despite the urgings of Delcassé, who resigned in protest. The conference duly met in 1906 in Algeçiras, in Spain, but Germany got little backing for her views except from Austria-Hungary. Though they accepted that the future of Morocco was of international concern, and recognised trading rights for all and a special zone of influence for Spain, the French were able to emerge from the conference with a valuable gain – the acknowledged right to intervene as necessary to maintain order in the greater part of Morocco. This in effect meant the right to control its government. One fact which encouraged them during the negotiations was that, a few days after the conference opened, the British foreign secretary agreed to contacts between the British and French military staffs.

William II's visit to Tangier, 1905

Algeçiras Conference, 1906

With the *Entente* not only concluded but having survived its first test, France then set about ironing out the differences between her two friends, Britain

British agreement with Russia on Persia, 1907

and Russia. The main trouble, the conflicting aims of the two countries in the Middle East – Britain's Far Eastern worries had been ended by Japan's defeat of Russia in 1904–5 – was soon solved. In addition to forswearing expansion on the northern borders of India (in Afghanistan and Tibet) the Russians agreed to limit their sphere of influence in Persia to its northern part. Britain's influence was declared to be predominant in the south, and a neutral 'buffer' zone was left between. (This was called an arrangement to secure the 'independence of Persia'!) With Russian expansion in the direction of India and in the Far East checked, there remained only the historic question of the Russian advance in the Balkans. To this, however, Britain had ceased to attach so much importance, for the Balkan nations had shown their independence of Russia. And if Russia did get to Constantinople it would be no worse than having Germany in control there, the latest ambition of William II. So the rifts between Britain and Russia were healed, and the Dual *Entente* became extended into the Triple *Entente* of France, Britain and Russia.

Triple *Entente* (1907) faces Triple Alliance

By 1907 there was thus at last a substantial counterweight to the German-Austrian-Italian combination. Alongside, and possibly against, the Triple Alliance, now stood the Triple *Entente*. Bismarck, dead by 1898 after eight years' bitter criticism of his successors, might well have turned in his grave at so dangerous a development for Germany.

CHAPTER 19
The Balkans and the Approach to the First World War

1. The Increasing International Tension. North Africa and the Arms Race, 1907–14

By the end of the nineteenth century the tide of nationalism was everywhere in full flood. Two new major powers, Germany and Italy, had been born. Belgium had broken away from Holland, and Norway was on the point of severing the last ties with Sweden. The Ottoman Empire in Europe had largely dissolved into its component national fragments – Greece, Serbia, Rumania, Bulgaria. There still existed, however, parts of Europe where national feeling had been unable to assert itself against a ruling race. Greeks and Bulgars in Macedonia, the region restored to the Ottoman Empire by Disraeli in 1878, dreamed of the day of liberation from the Turks. Poles, Finns, Latvians consistently aimed at securing freedom from their Russian masters. Above all, in Austria-Hungary several suppressed nationalities bitterly resented their subjection. They regarded the Dual Monarchy as an Austrian device to buy the friendship of the Magyars at the expense of the Czechs, Poles, Ruthenes, Serbs, Croats, Rumanians and Slovenes. From one or other of these dissatisfied peoples there was sooner or later bound to be trouble.

It is clear that national feeling, when denied self-expression in the form of independence, has been a frequent cause of war. It is also clear that even when nations have succeeded in winning their freedom, wars are not less likely to occur. Desire for freedom for one's own nation does not necessarily imply recognition of the rights of other nations. In fact, the historical tendency has been the reverse. The greatest age of national feeling in Europe proved to be also the greatest age of overseas colonisation, involving the subjection of coloured peoples to European ones. Similarly, strong nations patriotically pursuing their own national policies inevitably clashed with one another. Though there were the beginnings of a code of international law in eighteenth- and nineteenth-century Europe there was no international authority to enforce it. In the state of world organisation before 1914 wars were bound to occur, either because nations were not free enough or else because they were too free.

The power of national feeling was amply demonstrated in the years immediately preceding 1914. As we have seen, by 1907 the Triple *Entente* of Britain, France, and Russia had emerged as a counterpoise to the Triple Alliance of Germany,

Nationalism—

unsatisfied in Macedonia, Poland, Baltic provinces, Austria-Hungary

Nationalism as a cause of war

International law, but no force to make it respected

Austria-Hungary and Italy. In the search for national security and in pursuit of their territorial ambitions the European powers had formed themselves into two groups, which became progressively more and more heavily armed and mutually antagonistic. The policies of these groups soon clashed in various parts of the world, and from 1906 a series of 'incidents' disturbed the international atmosphere. The two regions over which the storm-clouds gathered heaviest were North Africa and the Balkans.

The North African question produced two crises within five years. It will be remembered that Germany had objected to France's designs on Morocco, had secured an international conference at Algeçiras, and had there failed to prevent the French from gaining a major share of control over the Moroccan police – the first step towards general French control over the whole country.[1] Germany, however, was not yet prepared to see Morocco swallowed up by France. When, in 1911, following a revolt there, the French despatched an army into Morocco 'to help the Sultan keep order', the Germans sent a gunboat, the *Panther*, and later a cruiser, the *Berlin*, to Agadir harbour to protect German interests. This was a violation of the Algeçiras agreement, by which France and Spain were alone entitled to policing rights. Britain took a very serious view of the situation, fearing that the Germans were seeking to acquire an Atlantic naval base. Lloyd George, then the Chancellor of the Exchequer in Asquith's government, in a speech at a Mansion House banquet practically threatened war if British interests in the matter were treated as of no account. The result was that Germany, not prepared to push matters to this length over an issue of minor importance to her, withdrew and agreed to the establishment of a French protectorate over Morocco. As 'compensation' she obtained some territory in the French Congo just north of the Cameroons, but this could not disguise the fact that the *Entente* had again scored a notable success.

The list of powers interested in the troubles of North Africa, however, did not stop at Britain, France and Germany – or even Spain, now given her own part of Morocco opposite Gibraltar. Italy was desperately anxious to fill her pockets and vindicate her claim to be a major power by acquiring colonies. We have seen how the French occupation of Tunis, on which Italy had herself cast longing glances, had been partly responsible for the Italian entry into the Austro-German camp. Frustrated over Tunis, the Italians planned to absorb Abyssinia. They succeeded in overrunning two coastal strips by the Red Sea (Eritrea in 1885 and Italian Somaliland in 1892), but their larger object came to grief when the Abyssinians, catching an invading Italian army in hopelessly inferior numbers, won a crushing victory at Adowa (1896). The result of this battle was that Abyssinia continued to be ruled by Abyssinians – a state of affairs so outrageous to Italian dignity that revenge had eventually to be sought, and obtained, in 1935.

Unsuccessful by 1900 in picking up anything worth mentioning, the Italians next developed ambitions in connection with Tripoli, the last remaining part of the Ottoman Empire in North Africa. It consisted largely of desert and Italy had no quarrel with Turkey, but these were minor matters to a country eager for colonies. In 1911, taking advantage of the general commotion caused by the Agadir crisis and of certain restrictions on foreign trade introduced by the new nationalist

Marginal notes:

'Tangier Incident', 1905, and Algeçiras Conference, 1906

'Agadir crisis', 1911

Germany climbs down: French protectorate over Morocco, 1912

Italy also interested in Africa:

Abyssinian campaign

Adowa, 1896

Italo-Turkish War gives Tripoli to Italy, 1911-12

[1] See p. 299.

AFRICA 1914

- British Control (with dates of acquisition)
- French Control
- German Control
- Belgian Control
- Portuguese Control
- Italian Control
- Spanish Control
- Independent

movement in the Ottoman Empire, Italy declared war on Turkey. As the Turkish navy was not strong enough to afford Tripoli any effective relief, the Italians were able to capture the province and its neighbour Cyrenaica from the Sultan within a year.[1] This action had results of importance in European politics. The Triple Alliance was shaken, partly because Germany had herself begun to covet Tripoli and partly because Italy had attacked Turkey, by this time a centre of German patronage and commercial development. So in the seven years from 1905 to 1912, North African affairs brought about two threats of European wars, greater ill-feeling among the powers, armed conflict between Turkey and Italy, a strengthening of the Triple *Entente* and a weakening of the Triple Alliance.

Italy drifting from Germany

The increasing international tension arising from North Africa and other colonial disputes and from difficulties in the Balkans was soon reflected in a European arms race. This danger had already weighed sufficiently with Tsar Nicholas II – largely for economic reasons – for him to initiate a Conference at the Hague in 1899. Here Russia suggested a five-year halt in arms increases, but no positive

The arms race: Hague Conference, 1899

[1] The two provinces together were later known as Libya.

proposal of this kind was accepted. The lead in rejection came from Germany, who pointed out that Russia could increase her military effectiveness merely by building more railways. Progress was however made in revising the 'laws' of war and framing rules for the 'humanisation' of warfare, for example, in the treatment of wounded soldiers and prisoners, and the prohibition of soft-nosed bullets and asphyxiating gases. A very important advance was the setting up of a Tribunal at the Hague to which countries could appeal for arbitration in a dispute.

In the next few years many minor quarrels, such as the Dogger Bank incident, were submitted to the Hague Tribunal. As the nations, however declined to refer to it matters of 'national honour,' 'independence' and 'vital interest,' wars were just as liable as ever to occur. A second Hague Conference in 1907 got little further. A few additions were made to the list of things inadmissible in warfare, and the machinery of the Hague Tribunal was improved, but no agreement was reached on the main issue of disarmament, where again Germany showed strong opposition. When Britain expressed a willingness to stabilise naval armaments at existing levels, Germany made it clear that she regarded this merely as a device to keep the German navy permanently inferior – which indeed in many ways it was.

Europe's progress to destruction now continued apace. In 1906, with the launching of Britain's 'Dreadnought', the first of a class of 'all big gun' battleships, a new standard was set in naval armaments. Admiral Sir John Fisher, First Sea Lord at the British Admiralty from 1903 to 1910, calculated that it would take the Germans some years to follow, since to use Dreadnoughts effectively they would first have to enlarge the Kiel Canal. His conviction that war between Britain and Germany was but a short way ahead was so strong that he actually prophesied a date – October 1914 – for the beginning of hostilities. Further, he even suggested to King Edward in 1908 that Britain should 'Copenhagen' the German fleet – i.e. demand that it should be handed over, and on refusal, annihilate it, in the same way as the Danish fleet had been destroyed in 1807! Since war was bound to come, he argued, it might as well come while Britain still held the superiority – why wait for the Germans to catch up?

Fisher's advice was not accepted, but there were many, both in Britain and Germany, who thought on similar lines, and who made the chances of maintaining peace even fainter. The fact too that Fisher was one of the British representatives at the Hague disarmament conference in 1899 helps to explain why disarmament conferences then, as so often since, were all conference and no disarmament. In any case, the Germans, following the policy of Tirpitz and the Kaiser, were not slow to take the next step. The Kiel Canal was widened and deepened, dreadnought-type battleships were constructed, new navy bills were passed for big increases in the fleet. Between 1909 and 1912 Germany laid down nine Dreadnoughts. Britain consequently laid down eighteen. The exceptionally heavy armour and short range of the German vessels indicated that they were destined for use not far from home, rather than for the distant preservation of colonial connections. The British countered by concentrating eighty per cent of their fleet in the North Sea, and by arranging with France that she should look after the Mediterranean. The arrangement stated that there was no alliance between the two countries; but clearly things were moving that way.

On the military side the arms contest proceeded with equal fury. The German army was enlarged and trained to the highest degree of efficiency, while the French

Hague Tribunal

Second Hague Conference, 1907

Naval competition: 'Dreadnoughts'

Fisher

Anglo-French naval arrangements, 1912

Military competition

and the Russians increased the length of conscript service with the colours. Very soon, by calling up trained reservists, Germany and France would each be in a position to put about 3½ million men into the field, and Russia about 4 million. Even Britain under her Secretary for War, Lord Haldane, organised a small but efficient Expeditionary Force which could be readily mobilised for service on the continent or elsewhere, coupled with a new non-regular Territorial Army not limited to home defence. Once started, it was almost impossible to slow down the arms race. On each side there was a complete lack of trust in the other's intentions; on each side national pride refused to budge from a position once taken up; and on each side a big vested interest in the war industry was being created in the form of people, ranging from arms manufacturers and shareholders to newspaper proprietors, who profited financially from a state of international tension.

In Germany, a country always liable to be misled by the power of ideas, certain circles, taking their lead from the historian Treitschke or some of the army chiefs, preached not only the inevitability but the desirability of war. The theories of Darwin on evolution and the 'survival of the fittest' were perverted to mean that war, the highest form of struggle, is the supreme test of the human race, and that by eliminating the unfittest nations and giving greater power to the fittest, it advances the cause of civilisation. The Germans from 1864 to 1871 had been so successful in warfare that they regarded future victory as certain. Then, with victory achieved, the German *Kultur* of science, strength and state supremacy could displace the decadent civilisation of France, based on liberty and literature, and that of Britain, based on comfort and cricket.

German 'militarism'

These ideas, however, were by no means universally held, nor was there general recognition of the trend of international affairs. German naval commanders might toast 'The Day', German university professors might proclaim absurd theories, the Kaiser might rattle his sabre, Fisher might strain at the leash, French and British generals might make military arrangements together, Austrian and Russian foreign ministers might plan diplomatic coups in the Balkans – but the great European public went on blind to the increasing menace of war. Foreign policy, even in a democracy like Britain's, was always shrouded in mystery – several members of Asquith's cabinet were unaware until the last moment of how far the Prime Minister and his Foreign Secretary, Sir Edward Grey, had committed Britain to France. Ordinary British people, though, and especially those connected with the sea, resented the new German naval claims. Businessmen resented the loss of trade to German firms, which were undercutting British goods particularly in South America. Everyone resented the Kaiser's speeches. But very few people realised what combustible material surrounded them or what calamity would befall them were it to take fire. Even if a war did come, war was traditionally a matter for the army and navy, while the rest stayed at home and enjoyed the accounts in the newspapers over breakfast. Thus, in a curious mixture of the accidental, the unconscious and the deliberate, Europe approached disaster. In truth, it mattered little how much the masses were aware that all Europe had become a powder magazine liable to explode at any moment. The fact of the powder magazine remained. It could have gone off over the North African incidents, though before 1911 the average man had never even heard of Agadir. And now in 1914, though the average man did not know Sarajevo from the Sahara, the catastrophe was to come all the same from the Balkans.

The public largely unaware of developments

Europe a powder magazine

2. The Balkans, 1878–1914. The Guns go off

The fact that most of the subject races of the Turks had gained independence during the nineteenth century had not brought lasting peace to south-eastern Europe. As we have seen, by 1878 Greece, Serbia, Montenegro, Rumania and Bulgaria had all been formed from the Ottoman Empire. At the end of the century, however, the Greeks and Bulgars of Macedonia and the Albanians were still under Turkish rule. The districts of Bosnia and Herzegovina, too, containing a million Serbs, while nominally still under Turkish sovereignty, had been administered since 1878 by Austria-Hungary. Trouble might easily arise from these unliberated districts. Further, the formation of four or five new states had merely multiplied the conflicting national policies in the Balkans. No state was satisfied with its existing boundaries, while to most of them revolution and fighting came almost as second nature.

The history of south-eastern Europe from the Congress of Berlin to the First World War is neither simple nor edifying. It would be fruitless to attempt to follow it in detail. Beyond the Balkan peninsular to the north-east, Rumania (whose ruler proclaimed himself a king in 1881) experienced a less violent history than the actual Balkan states. The main disturbances arose either from peasant revolts against bad economic conditions or from the traditional Rumanian persecution of Jews. Until 1908 the main incidents which affected her southern neighbour Bulgaria were the expulsion of Russian 'advisers', the union with East Roumelia (1885) in spite of the Treaty of Berlin, a war with Serbia (1885), and the kidnapping and deposition of the first Bulgarian prince (1886). In Serbia restless intrigue among politicians and the army led to the brutal crime of 1903, when a number of conspirators broke into the royal palace, tracked the Obrenović king and his queen in the dark to their hiding-place in a cupboard, murdered them as they sheltered in each other's arms and threw their outraged bodies out of a window. The '*coup*' was completed by a 'purge' of other opponents, after which a Karageorgović naturally ascended the throne. Of the other Christian countries, Greece went to war with Turkey in 1897 about the future of Crete and Macedonia, but was badly beaten inside three weeks.

In the Turkish Empire itself the main excitement was caused by the hideous misgovernment of Abdul Hamid II. Following unrest among his Armenian subjects in Asia Minor, he organised extensive massacres of that unfortunate Christian race. These were carried out by the Armenians' fierce Mohammedan neighbours, the Kurds, with the help of Turkish troops. Abdul Hamid, not surprisingly, became known in Britain as 'The Great Assassin' and in France as 'The Red Sultan'. In six weeks alone of the year 1895 over 30,000 Armenians were butchered. In the following year the order was given to attack the Armenian quarter in Constantinople, and 6,000 were slaughtered in two days. The whole appalling episode seemed to illustrate the grim jest that while Christianity provides martyrs, Mohammedanism creates them. The Powers, of course, protested, but to little avail.

These events were regarded as standard Balkan activity and had little effect on the main stream of European history. 1908, however, saw some momentous changes which led directly to general warfare. In that year a revolution, known as the 'Young Turk' movement, broke out in the Ottoman Empire. The conspirators aimed at imitating the methods and efficiency of the West in a fervently nationalist attempt to check the rapid decline of Turkish power. They demanded a parliament and a modern constitution, and to strengthen Turkey were prepared to allow Christian subjects equal privileges with Mohammedans. Fostered in Paris by exiles, the movement in 1908 transferred to Macedonia, where it was officially proclaimed. Sympathetic Turkish regiments prepared to advance and instal the leaders in Constantinople. Finding himself without support, Abdul Hamid agreed to restore the constitution which had been momentarily in force in 1876. The censorship was relaxed, over 80,000 exiles returned, the different subject races seemed closer than brothers, and liberals all over Europe rejoiced.

Within two or three months the picture began to look different. Taking instant advantage of the natural disorganisation at Constantinople, Bulgaria proclaimed herself freed from the last shreds of her dependence on Turkey and elevated her prince into a tsar, or king. Austria-Hungary annexed unconditionally the Turkish provinces she was administering, Bosnia and Herzegovina. Crete proclaimed itself united with Greece. Serbia and Montenegro demanded a rectification of their frontiers. In face of these events the 'Young Turks' naturally lost their desire to improve the lot of Turkey's Christian subjects, especially when the Christians began to demand not reform but independence. When Abdul Hamid tried to restore autocracy he was deposed, but the Young Turks soon had additional reason to concentrate on their nationalist rather than on their democratic aims. In 1911 the problems of Turkey tempted the Italians to seize Tripoli quite wantonly from her. And before this difficulty was over, Turkey in 1912 suddenly found herself confronted by a union of the Balkan powers, who momentarily put aside their mutual hatreds for the purpose of despoiling the Ottoman Empire.

Bulgaria fully independent

Austria-Hungary annexes Bosnia and Herzegovina. Crete unites with Greece. Italy takes Tripoli

This 'Balkan League' was largely the work of an astute Greek politician, Venizelos. It found its opportunity to attack Turkey in the fact that the Young Turks had now, like their older brethren, begun persecuting Christians in Macedonia. Disunited in home affairs and with the Italian attack barely over, the Turks could do nothing against the combined onslaught of Greece, Serbia, Bulgaria and Montenegro. The allies soon overran different parts of Macedonia and made other conquests. In 1913 a peace conference met at London, and by the treaty then concluded Greece acquired Crete, Salonika and South Macedonia, Serbia was rewarded with North and Central Macedonia, and the Bulgarians received Thrace and a stretch of the Aegean coast. Since much of Macedonia, which was inhabited largely by Bulgars, went to Serbia by this treaty, Bulgaria could not be satisfied with the division of the spoils. The Serbs, in fact, although they had actually conquered a large section of Macedonia, had intended most of it to go to Bulgaria, while they themselves took Albania, with its valuable sea-coast. Austria-Hungary, however, had insisted that Albania should be independent, partly to stop Serbia reaching the coast and becoming too powerful and partly because Albania was inhabited not by Serbs but by Albanians. Thereupon Serbia, denied her desired coastland, had insisted on retaining the parts of Macedonia she had conquered.

The 'Balkan League'

First Balkan war, 1912 (v. Turks)

Spoils shared: Bulgaria dissatisfied

The Bulgarians now in a fatal moment allowed themselves to be prompted by the wishes of Austria-Hungary, and pressed their grievance to the point of attacking Serbia and Greece. Within a year a second Balkan war thus broke out. Montenegro supported Serbia, and when matters began to go badly for Bulgaria, the

Second Balkan war, 1913 (v. Bulgarians)

THE UNTRUSTWORTHY FIREMEN AT THE BALKAN BLAZE

A Kladderadatsch *cartoon of 1912 giving a German view of the First Balkan War. The firemen John Bull and Ivan (Britain and Russia) are meant to be dousing the flames but instead maliciously pour petrol on them.*

Rumanians and the Turks joined in against her as well. Bulgaria was now fighting against five powers. She was, not surprisingly overwhelmed, and at the resulting Treaty of Bucharest (1913) lost much of what she had gained in the first war. Turkey got back Adrianople, Serbia and Greece were confirmed in their possession of Macedonia, and Rumania gained from Bulgaria some valuable territory on the Black Sea – the Dobrudja.

Results of Balkan wars

    Though none of the great Powers had been involved, the results of these two Balkan wars were profound. In the first place Turkey was now at last reduced in Europe to regions racially Turkish. Secondly, all the Balkan powers obviously

1. Turkey drastically reduced

regarded the Treaty of Bucharest as something to be consigned to the wastepaper basket at the first opportune moment. None of them saw the settlement as permanent; all were ready for another war before long; and in particular Bulgaria nursed grievances against Serbia and Greece. Thirdly, the great gains made by Serbia filled her with confidence and inspired her with the ambition to unite all remaining Serbs in the Balkans under her rule. In particular she was brought even more sharply into collision with Austria-Hungary, partly because that country had taken the lead in denying her Albania, partly because Austria and Hungary between them ruled about six million Serbs and Croats, including the million Serbs of Bosnia and Herzegovina.

It was this last fact which led on directly to the First World War. In Serbia a great agitation for the acquisition of Bosnia and Herzegovina was launched. The Serbs within these two districts grew extremely troublesome to their Austro-Hungarian masters. The temper of those in charge of Austro-Hungarian military and foreign policy grew short. They began to dream of a campaign which would annihilate this increasingly dangerous Balkan race, confirm Austria-Hungary in her possession of the two Serbian provinces, and remove the barrier which stretched across the Austro-Hungarian path to the Aegean Sea. In 1913 Austria-Hungary sounded Italy on the possibility of a war with Serbia, only to receive the reply that Italy would not support aggression. But if one member of the Triple Alliance was doubtful, there was no hesitation about the other. The Kaiser more than once assured Austrian statesmen that they would have Germany's backing if matters came to a conflict. Further, Austria-Hungary might rely on Turkey, a natural enemy of Serbia, and now, since the beginning of the Berlin to Baghdad Railway and the appointment of General Liman von Sanders to reorganise the Turkish army, increasingly under German commercial and military control. Austria-Hungary waited for the opportunity which Serbian agitation was sure to present.

The opportunity duly occurred on 28th June, 1914. On that day the Austrian Crown Prince Franz Ferdinand and his wife were driving through the streets of Sarajevo, capital of Bosnia, when they were assassinated by a local Serb. The murderer had come straight from a meeting of an anti-Austrian society in the Serbian capital, Belgrade. There was actually no evidence to show that the Serbian government had any hand in the affair – indeed, there is some reason to believe that the Austrian government hoped an incident might take place, for the Crown Prince's political views were unwelcome to them and they knew the danger of Sarajevo on a Serbian festival day. For nearly a month nothing much seemed to come of the crime – the Austrians made their investigations and public excitement cooled down. But behind the scenes preparations for war were progressing, as Austria-Hungary received Germany's final 'blank cheque,' or permission to deal with Serbia as she pleased.

Suddenly, on 23rd July Austria-Hungary launched an ultimatum at Serbia, demanding acceptance within forty-eight hours. The terms were framed in the hope of a refusal. Not only was Serbia to suppress all anti-Austrian activity and dismiss all Serbian officials to whom Austria-Hungary objected, but Austrians were to enter Serbia to investigate Serbian complicity in the murder and to supervise the suppression of the anti-Austrian societies. Serbia's reply, in fact, was extremely conciliatory. She agreed to the first two demands, and offered to submit the third to arbitration by the Hague Tribunal. Had she accepted the last point it would have meant almost the loss of her independence. Even the Kaiser

Austria–Hungary
declares war on Serbia,
28 July

thought the reply was satisfactory, and urged moderation, but Austria–Hungary was not to be baulked at the last moment. On 28th July she declared war on Serbia.

Within a week the whole of Europe was ablaze. Britain, France, and Russia had been warned by Germany not to interfere. But Russia especially was not willing to see a fellow Slav country crushed by a vastly stronger opponent while Germany held the ring. Russia too had Balkan ambitions of her own, and here was a chance to pursue them. Accordingly on 30th July Nicholas II ordered general mobilisation of the Russian armies. Germany now chose to regard this as a threat to her, resisted all the efforts of Grey to refer matters to a conference, and despatched two ultimatums. One demanded of Russia that she should stop her mobilisation. The other insisted that France should give clear guarantees of her neutrality. When neither country heeded these threats, Germany declared war, first on Russia (1st August) and then on France (3rd August).

Russia mobilises:
German ultimatums

Germany declares war
on Russia (1 August)
and France (3 August)

There remained one doubtful factor – Britain. Grey had made great efforts in the final fortnight to avoid the catastrophe, but it had come. What was Britain to do? She had no military alliance with France, but she had an 'understanding', had concerted plans in case of war, and had arranged that the French fleet should be predominantly in the Mediterranean. Could she now allow Germany to enter the Channel with her High Seas Fleet and attack the French coasts? Asquith's Cabinet wavered, while French politicians indignantly demanded whether the word 'honour' should be expunged from the English language. Ultimately, on 2nd August, before Germany had actually declared war on France, but when it was obvious that war would come, a majority of the British cabinet decided to give at

Limited British support
for France

any rate limited support to France.[1] But some of their own colleagues disagreed violently. How would the country as a whole react? Would the House of Commons toe the line obediently, or would the government be rejected as having committed Britain to war unnecessarily, and collapse ignominiously? Fortunately for the future of the Allies, fortunately for the unity of Britain, fortunately for the peace of mind of the Cabinet, fortunately in fact for everyone except the Belgians and their own cause, the Germans had long since decided to invade France by way of the easiest route. On 2nd August they moved into Luxemburg, and on 3rd August into Belgium.

Belgian neutrality and
its importance for
Britain

By the Treaty of London of 1839 both Britain and Prussia, as she then was, had promised to guarantee Belgian neutrality. If Germany violated it now she would put herself hopelessly in the wrong with every section of British opinion. When the British Ambassador in Berlin stated what Britain's attitude to such an action would be, the German Chancellor inquired whether Britain would plunge into war for the sake of 'a scrap of paper'.[2] But a Belgium under German control meant more than tearing up a 'scrap of paper' to Britain – it meant the danger of a great hostile naval power within easy distance of her shores. For centuries Britain had made the freedom of Belgium from control by a major naval power the main point of her foreign policy. For that she had aided the Dutch against the Spaniards in Elizabeth's reign, had fought France in the war of the Spanish Succession, and later in the Revolutionary and Napoleonic wars, and had prevented a French prince ascending

---

[1] By promising to protect French Channel ports and shipping if the German fleet entered the Channel.

[2] This translation caused much ill-feeling at the time. The actual German words would have been more accurately rendered as 'a piece of paper' – which is less offensive, but means the same.

BRAVO, BELGIUM!

The typical British attitude in 1914. 'Gallant little Belgium' defies the German bully. Cartoon by F. H. Townsend, 12th August 1914.

the Belgian throne after the revolution of 1830. For that Gladstone in 1870 had warned the Prussians against invading France through Belgium, and had seen that Prussia took the more difficult route through Alsace. Now, on 4th August, after the Belgians had appealed for help in repelling Germany, Britain sent her ultimatum demanding that Belgian neutrality be respected. On the afternoon of the same day she learnt that the Germans had penetrated farther into Belgium, and when midnight came with no satisfactory reply, Britain had in effect declared war against Germany. The Conservative opposition, the Irish party, the Socialists all lined up behind the Liberal government. The militarists of Germany were violating the sanctity of treaties – it all put the Allies so magnificently in the right. As the statesmen made their decisions and European youth on both sides rushed unhesitatingly to sacrifice itself in the cause of patriotism and the right, few can have realised that before the hideous conflict could end 40 million men would be killed or wounded.

British ultimatum

Britain declares war on Germany (4 August)

And all from an assassination in an obscure town in the Balkans – or so it appeared! But, in fact, although we may apportion 'war-guilt,' deciding that Austria-Hungary was certainly the main criminal, Germany and then Russia perhaps next in degree of culpability, the more we study the origins of the war the more clearly the general truth emerges that no state was entirely free from blame. All were part of the same system. All had their national policies and ambitions which could not but clash fatally some day. All frankly recognised the fact by piling up arms and preparing alliances in readiness for the conflict. Few really wanted war; but none was prepared to abandon the objects which made war almost inevitable. The spark happened to come from Sarajevo, but it might have come from anywhere. The result would doubtless have been the same. The powder magazine was there all the time.

War almost inevitable in the European system of 1914

CHAPTER 20

The First World War and the Peace Treaties

1. The First World War, 1914–18

Nature of the First World War

The war which began in August 1914 was a new experience in human history. It was a struggle until then unparalleled in the forces involved – the number of warring states, the size of the armies, the deadliness of the weapons, the colossal expenditure of life and money. Other conflicts had lasted longer and by their savagery or prolongation had inflicted greater suffering on some unhappy land – notably Germany in the Thirty Years' War (1618–48) – but no armed struggle can previously have caused such widespread human agony as the four years' war which followed the murder of Franz Ferdinand. The whole of the British Empire in India and Canada, for example, was acquired with a loss in men less than that reported in a single British advance of two miles on the Western Front in 1917. At the battle of Plassey in 1757, which settled the fate of much of India, the British lost less than a hundred men; during the Somme offensive in 1916, which settled nothing, they lost (in killed, wounded and missing) nearly half a million. The result of such a slaughter was to strip the glamour from war and reveal it for what it is – an appalling catastrophe.

Initial German advance –

In this short space it is impossible to give more than the barest outline of the conflict. On the Western Front it began with a tremendous German drive through Belgium and Luxemburg which by-passed the resistance of the Belgians or sent them reeling back. Meanwhile the French, besides trying to hold this attack as it crossed the River Meuse into France, launched an offensive of their own into Alsace-Lorraine. It failed immediately and at huge cost. The strategy of the Germans, based on a plan devised years earlier by General Schlieffen (Chief of the German General Staff, 1891–1906), was to concentrate an overwhelming proportion of their forces in the west, knock out France, and then turn east to deal with Russia. Only by striking through Belgium, rather than at the heavily defended Franco-German frontier, could they hope to crush France with the necessary speed: 'We can be at Paris within a fortnight', said the Kaiser, and his words almost came true. German superiority in numbers, organisation, training and equipment carried all before it. The small but well-trained British Expeditionary Force under Sir John French, brought out to France and stationed on the left of the French armies, moved forward to Mons, in Belgium, only to be instantly forced back; the French armies on their right fared no better; and by the beginning of September, a month after the outbreak of war, the Germans were less than fifty miles from Paris. The French Government fled to Bordeaux for safety.

At the critical moment, however, the situation was saved by skill, luck and German mistakes. The Germans decided to by-pass Paris on the east and actually succeeded in crossing the River Marne; but in dealing with two French counter-attacks – one from Paris on the German right and the other farther east – the Germans allowed a big gap to open between their two advancing armies on the right. Into this gap the British, who had retreated from Mons to the Marne to maintain contact with the French, were directed to advance by the French Commander-in-Chief, Joffre. As they moved forward, the Germans on either side came in danger of being outflanked; and to prevent this the German High Command pulled the whole German force back across the Marne to form a line farther north. This proved to be one of the decisive moments of the war. The initial German attack had become disrupted, and was stemmed.

– stemmed at the Battle of the Marne, September 1914

After the French had recovered a little of their territory north of the Marne, the Germans dug themselves into their positions by means of an elaborate trench system protected by machine-gun posts and barriers of barbed wire. The Allies quickly followed suit. Each side then tried to outflank the other farther north near the Channel shore and the British clashed bloodily with the enemy around Ypres. Little progress was made, the digging in continued, and soon the lines of opposing trenches stretched from the Belgian coast to the Alps. The war on the Western

Trench warfare sets in

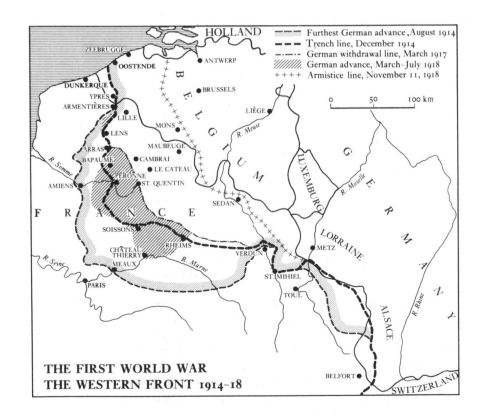

THE FIRST WORLD WAR
THE WESTERN FRONT 1914–18

Furthest German advance, August 1914
Trench line, December 1914
German withdrawal line, March 1917
German advance, March–July 1918
Armistice line, November 11, 1918

OVER THE TOP: BRITISH TROOPS IN ACTION
The dreaded moment in the Western Front fighting – up from the trench and 'over the top' for an infantry attack.

Front settled into a dreary struggle to smash the opposing forces and their entrenchments by gunfire and so open the way for an advance. To the bewilderment of many commanders, the attacking infantry could rarely capture more than a few hundred yards without appalling casualties, and they could never clear the way for the cavalry to 'go through'.

The other fronts:

Russians stopped at Tannenberg, August 1914

Turkey joins Germany and Austria-Hungary, November 1914

Meanwhile in the east the Russians, to relieve the pressure on France, had launched a premature invasion of Germany. This fulfilled its purpose in that the Germans weakened their advancing forces in the west in order to deal with it. But at Tannenberg in East Prussia the Russians were overwhelmingly defeated at the end of August by Hindenburg, an elderly general recalled from retirement for his knowledge of local conditions, and Ludendorff, his chief of staff, one of the few generals in the war whose tactics might be termed brilliant. Another decisive battle had been fought and from then on German territory was free of Russian troops. Austria-Hungary, however, began to suffer defeat both by the Russians in her province of Galicia – she had invaded Russian Poland but been driven back – and by the Serbs, whose territory she had also invaded. Nevertheless Austria-Hungary and Germany received a useful reinforcement when Turkey, for long

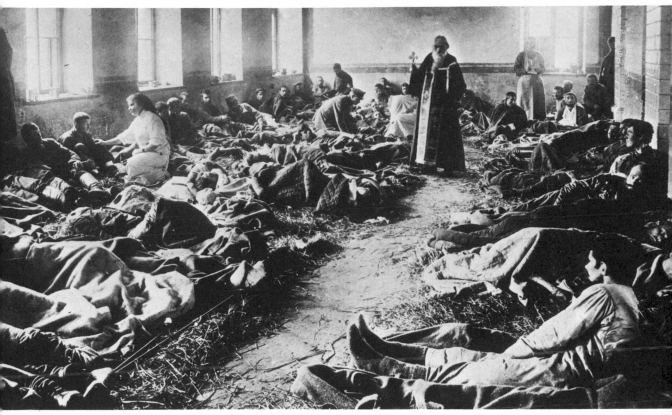

TENDING THE RUSSIAN WOUNDED
*Before the revolutionary government of 1917 took them out of the war, the Russians
suffered enormous losses. Huge reserves of manpower proved to be no substitute for
proper equipment and supplies.*

under German influence, came in on their side in November. This put Serbia,
between Austria-Hungary and Turkey, in mortal danger.

The deadlock on the Western Front and the danger of Serbia made the British
cabinet resolve to extend its strategy. An 'Eastern school' grew up which maintained
that the best way to win the war was first to knock out the Turks and then smash
the Hapsburg Empire. Once the Dardanelles and Bosphorus were freed from
Turkish control, support could be sent through them to Russia. Germany and
Austria-Hungary would thus become exposed not only to attack from the south,
but also to renewed Russian pressure from the east. This strategy was powerfully
advocated by Lloyd George, the Chancellor of the Exchequer, and Winston
Churchill, the First Lord of the Admiralty, who had ensured that the Fleet was
completely ready at the outbreak of war. Naturally, however, the generals on the
Western Front bitterly opposed the diversion of troops to objectives outside
France, where the position was never too secure.

The first attempt at such a plan was an unsupported effort by British and French
vessels to force the Dardanelles in March 1915. Then in April came a gallant
landing by British and 'Anzac' (Australia and New Zealand Army Corps) forces

The 'Easterners'

The Dardanelles and
Gallipoli, 1915

on the Gallipoli peninsula, with the intention of seizing the Dardanelles by an advance overland. Neither venture succeeded: the Dardanelles was too well mined (and the project too well advertised), and at Gallipoli the initial landings were not followed up with vigour. The Turks on the hills above the beaches held out, trench warfare set in attended by dreadful heat and plagues of flies, and finally the expedition had to be evacuated. This was done with great efficiency and no loss at the close of 1915. Meanwhile, to appease Russia's suspicions of British operations in this quarter and to sustain her zeal for the war, the British and French had agreed that with an Allied victory Russia should acquire Constantinople.

German successes against Russia

Bulgaria joins Germany, September 1915

In 1915 the Germans, held up in the west, temporarily reversed their 1914 policy and drove eastwards against Russia. A series of brilliant successes not only carried them through Poland and Lithuania but in September also brought Bulgaria into the war on their side. The Bulgarian king, Ferdinand, 'the Fox of the Balkans', had long been waiting to see which way the cat would jump. Now, with Bulgaria joining them, the Central Powers could – and did – easily overrun Serbia. The only crumb of comfort for the Allies this year, apart from some minor but expensive gains in France, was that in the spring they successfully tempted Italy into the war on their side by an offer of the two Austrian districts of the Trentino (the south Tyrol) and Trieste (on the Adriatic). The Italians (who had refused to support Germany and Austria-Hungary in 1914 on the grounds that the war was one of aggression and that they had no obligation to fight against Britain) had always regarded these districts as 'unredeemed Italy'. In fact, however, many of the inhabitants of the Trentino were German, and the bargain to transfer them to Italy, and to give her north Dalmatia and territory in Asia Minor as well, showed how far from their proclaimed ideals Britain and France were being driven by the necessities of war. The effect of Italian intervention was to engage a large Austrian army in the Alps which divide the two countries.

Italy joins the Allies, May 1915

Reorganisation of Allied war effort

The lack of success of the Allies thus far naturally brought about changes of command. In the field Joffre retained his position till December 1916, but Sir John French had been displaced by Haig a year earlier. In political direction the British, like the French, began to forget party differences and by 1915 formed a National Coalition, at the head of which the energetic Lloyd George by the end of 1916 took the place of the more cultured but less efficient Asquith. Huge new armies were created: three million men volunteered in Britain before conscription was introduced in 1916. New weapons emerged: the Germans, for example, began in 1915 to use poison gas contrary to international treaty. Aeroplanes, at first used for reconnaisance, then as fighters (for shooting each other down), soon turned also to bombing. They attacked not only military objectives but transport and industrial targets (and therefore incidentally civilian populations), a process begun by the German Zeppelin airships, which proved too bulky to defend themselves.[1]

New weapons: gas, Zeppelins, aeroplanes, tanks

In 1916, too, the tank, (an invention cold-shouldered by the War Office for some time and developed largely through the foresight of Winston Churchill at the Admiralty!), was first tried out. Little use, however, was made of tanks as yet, for they were not at first very reliable and the Allied generals had still to learn how to employ them effectively.

---

[1] The German airships were popularly called Zeppelins after their designer, Count Zeppelin. They attacked targets in England between 1915 and 1918.

WAR IN THE AIR
The new dimension in warfare. Reconnaissance, air fighting, bombing – as the war proceeded, these tasks called forth specialist aircraft. Here, in an air combat of 1917 depicted by the artist Norman Arnold, the famous British fighter 'ace' Albert Ball engages the enemy.

WOMEN MUNITION WORKERS, 1918
During the 1914–18 War, women became employed on a far wider range of tasks than ever before. These women are shell-case machiners at Woolwich Arsenal.

BRITISH TANKS MOVING FORWARD NEAR ST QUENTIN, SEPTEMBER 1918
The caterpillar-tracked armoured vehicles known as tanks could move across the broken country of the Western Front and survive against rifle and machine-gun fire. Introduced in a small way by the British in 1916, they were a major factor in the final Allied counter-attacks and breakthrough of 1918. These tanks carry 'cribs' to help them to cross trenches.

Verdun and the Somme, 1916

On the Western Front in 1916 the main features, apart from the new weapons, were some protracted and terrible battles. In these the French held the Germans at bay throughout the first half of the year near Verdun, and the British and French for most of the second half of the year attacked by the River Somme. On 1st July, the first day of the Somme offensive, the British suffered 57,000 casualties, of whom 19,000 were killed. By November the casualties of all nations as a result of the Somme campaign numbered over one million.

Brusilov's offensive, June 1916

Rumania joins the Allies, August 1916, but is soon overrun

Meanwhile in the east, after heavy Russian losses against the Germans in Poland, another Russian force farther south under General Brusilov made a surprise attack on the Austro-Hungarian armies and for a time carried all before it. The success of Brusilov's offensive, which netted some 250,000 prisoners, had an important result. It tempted the Rumanians to enter the war on the Allied side in the hope of wresting Transylvania from Austria-Hungary. The Russian recovery was momentary, however. Rumania was soon overrun, and its wheat and some of its oil wells (others were damaged by Allied sabotage) were at the disposal of the Central Powers.

Naval warfare

1916 also saw the one big naval battle of the war. In the early months of the war three or four German warships had given trouble in distant waters until they were rounded up; and towards the end of 1914 the German Pacific squadron had enjoyed a success against British vessels off Coronel (Chile) before being annihilated at the battle of the Falkland Islands. But, apart from a little raiding by minor forces, the German High Seas Fleet had not emerged from its harbour at Kiel to challenge the Royal Navy. Equally, although the Royal Navy patrolled the seas and enforced a blockade on the enemy, mines off the German coast had kept it well away from the enemy homeland. At the end of May 1916, however, the main German fleet put out into the North Sea in the hope of catching smaller British forces at a disadvantage. But the British could read the German wireless code, and the Germans ran into the hastily summoned full might of the Royal Navy – first the battle-cruisers under Beatty, then the main battleship force under Jellicoe. In the evening of 31st May, and later that night, a series of glancing actions was fought off Jutland, with results which were claimed as a victory on both sides – by the Germans because they inflicted a much greater loss in men and tonnage than they themselves suffered, and by the British because the German High Seas Fleet steamed off home and only once or twice again emerged in force, and then very briefly. Whatever the damage they suffered the British remained in command of the seas, with all the enormous consequences that this entailed: the distant blockade of the enemy (to starve him of food and raw materials), the capture of enemy colonies, the maintenance of communications with the Allied armies and the safeguarding of Britain's vital food supply from overseas.

The inability of Germany to challenge the Royal Navy in open contest had another result of profound importance. The Germans had already been employing their U-boats, or submarines, against Allied and neutral merchant shipping. A U-boat, however, cannot easily 'investigate' a vessel to see if it is hostile or carrying declared contraband. The Germans had therefore begun to adopt a 'sink at sight' policy, but had desisted after neutral protests. Now, in February 1917, they determined to wage unrestricted submarine warfare against all merchant vessels in the war zone of the eastern Atlantic, in the hope of starving Britain into submission. In doing this Germany knew that the U.S.A. would certainly react to the sinking of her vessels by entering the war on the side of the Allies – in fact, some circles in the U.S.A. had wanted to enter the war *against* the Allies because the British had turned back American ships trading with Germany. Sinking vessels, however, was far worse than turning them back. The Germans fully appreciated the likely result of their action, but reckoned to knock out Britain and France before American intervention could become effective.

So the U-boats began unrestricted warfare and in April the U.S.A. duly declared war on Germany.[1] For some months things were extremely awkward for Britain, where food-cards and rationing were later introduced. Ultimately, however, the U-boat menace was defeated by technical devices such as the depth charge, the hydrophone, and above all by using destroyers to convoy groups of merchant

Britain keeps command of seas

Jutland, May 1916

Blockade and mines

Unrestricted U-boat campaign, 1 February, 1917

U.S.A. declares war on Germany, April 1917

[1] Another reason for the USA's entry into the war was the fact that she had made big loans to the Allies which would have been lost by an Allied defeat. A third reason was the famous 'Zimmerman telegram'. Zimmerman, the German foreign minister, sent a telegram in code to the German legation in Mexico suggesting that the Mexicans should be induced, by an offer of German help, to attack the USA and recover New Mexico from her. The British intercepted this telegram, broke the code and suggested to the Americans that they bribe a clerk in the German legation in Mexico City to reveal the text. They did so, and the telegram was published in the American press. The outcry at German interference on the American continent was immense.

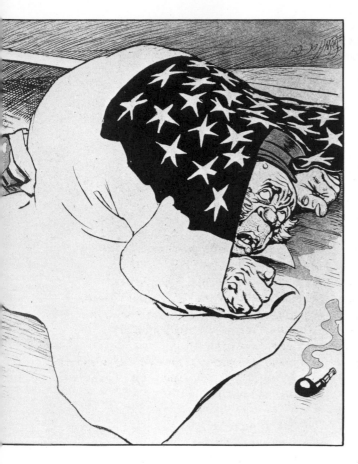

UNDER THE STAR–SPANGLED BANNER!

From Kladderadatsch, *1915. John Bull hides beneath the American flag – i.e. British merchant shipping sails under neutral colours to avoid U-boat attack. Germany advanced this as one of her reasons for starting unrestricted submarine warfare, including sinking neutral vessels on sight.*

THE BATHING SEASON BEGINS – 18TH FEBRUARY 1915

From Kladderadatsch, *over the sub-title 'The German sticklebacks and the pained Master of the Seas'. The Germans declared intensified U-boat warfare – sink at sight Allied or neutral – in February 1915 in a 'war zone' around Britain and northern France. Its results were not as dramatic as anticipated here, and it offended the* U.S.A. *Germany therefore observed restrictions during the latter part of 1915 and for most of 1916; but in February 1917 she began unrestricted U-boat warfare again and on a bigger scale. Within a few weeks, the* U.S.A. *entered the war against her.*

vessels. Some leading officers in the Admiralty were for technical reasons, strongly against introducing the convoy system but its supporters, thanks to powerful intervention by Lloyd George, prevailed. The results were dramatic. In April 1917, before convoy was introduced and before the U.S. naval forces could be fully employed, U-boats sank over 800,000 tons of Allied and neutral merchant shipping. Had such losses continued Germany must have won the war; but thanks to American aid, convoy, and the new technical measures, the crisis was overcome. From mid-1917 to November 1918 losses among ships in convoy to and from British ports amounted to less than one per cent.

The entry of the U.S.A. was soon partly offset by the defection of Russia. Russia's defeats had shown up her government's inefficiency: equipment had not matched man-power, and in some battles thousands of soldiers had no rifle of their own until they could snatch one from a fallen comrade. Without enough industrial output for her mass armies, and geographically badly placed to receive supplies from her allies, Russia had had to rely largely on her inexhaustible resources of man-power. More and more millions were sent to the slaughter, but after 1916 all their valour could not turn the tide. Eventually an immense war-weariness settled on the masses and in March 1917 food riots and strikes broke out in Petrograd.[1] The troops refused to fire on the demonstrators; many members of the Duma, when it was prorogued by the Tsar, would not disperse; and Nicholas II, his influence also undermined by the unpopularity of his wife and her dependence on the disreputable ex-monk Rasputin, was quietly advised by his generals to abdicate. This he did in favour of his brother, the Grand Duke Michael, who declined the position. So, without a blow, the centuries-old Tsardom collapsed. Its place was taken officially by a Provisional Government formed largely from liberal and conservative members of the Duma under Prince Lvov. But equally, if not more powerful was a newly formed soviet, or council, of deputies of workers and soldiers in Petrograd – an organisation which was soon imitated in other towns.

The first Russian revolution, although it destroyed the Tsardom, did not take Russia out of the war. Indeed the Provisional Government was positively welcomed by the Allies, because they thought it would improve the Russian war effort. Moreover the Provisional Government and the Petrograd soviet were able to agree, for a while, on a common programme, including the calling of a constituent assembly, guarantees of freedom of speech and association, an eight-hour working day, independence for Poland, and the more efficient conduct of the war. Very soon, however, a new factor entered. One group of the Russian revolutionaries – the exiled Bolsheviks – called not for a stronger war effort but for peace and a social revolution. The damage that the Bolsheviks would do to Russia's fighting powers was so obvious that the Germans gave facilities to the Bolshevik leader Lenin, who was exiled in Switzerland, to travel across Germany by train with his companions to Russia. They arrived in Petrograd in April 1917 and at once Lenin began to attack the Provisional Government and to put forward his own demands, crystallised in the slogan 'Peace, Bread, Land'. All three items had a powerful appeal in the circumstances of the time. Indeed, the peasants were already putting the third demand into effect by taking over the large estates for themselves.

Within less than three months the propaganda of Lenin, helped by that of Trotsky (who had returned from exile in America, where he had earned his living as a film extra), split the Bolsheviks decisively from the other revolutionary parties.

Russia

The 'February' Revolution, March 1917[2]: Abdication of Nicholas II

Provincial Government and Petrograd soviet

Return of Lenin and Bolshevik leaders, April 1917

[1] The name Petrograd replaced that of St Petersburg in 1914 as being more 'patriotic' ('grad' and 'burg' meaning 'town', but the former being Russian and the latter German.) In 1924 Petrograd was re-named Leningrad.

[2] In 1917 the Russians were still using the Julian calendar, which the rest of Europe had abandoned in the sixteenth–eighteenth centuries. By the Julian calendar the revolution occurred in February 1917.

Provisional
Government
temporarily suppresses
Bolsheviks, June 1917

Kerensky

Following a congress of soviets in June 1917, the Bolsheviks supported an out-break of strikes and riots directed against the Provisional Government; but for the moment the latter was strong enough to crush the revolts, to imprison Trotsky, and to force Lenin to flee across the border into Finland. Reconstructed in a more socialist direction under Alexander Kerensky, a former Social Revolutionary, the Provisional Government then strove with decreasing success to maintain order in the army and the factories and to carry on the war. Meanwhile the Bolsheviks, led by Lenin in Finland, prepared their further revolution. Winning control of the Petrograd and Moscow soviets with a programme calling for peace, a constituent assembly and extensive nationalisation, and helped by the failure of an attempted army *coup* under the commander-in-chief, Kornilov, they were soon able to stage

Bolshevik or 'October' Revolution, November 1917

their own uprising. In November 1917, in an operation directed mainly by Trotsky, rebel soldiers and sailors and factory 'Red Guards' on Bolshevik orders seized the key points in Petrograd and forcibly took over from Kerensky and the Provisional Government. Again the revolution – though not the savage repression of op-ponents which followed – was almost bloodless.

In opposing the Provisional Government, the Bolsheviks had raised the cry of 'All power to the soviets'. It soon became apparent that this meant 'all power to the Bolsheviks within the soviets', which in turn came to mean that only Bolsheviks were permitted to become members of soviets. And when the constituent assembly

Soviet Republic and the Bolshevik dictatorship, January 1918

at last met and its majority turned out to be heavily anti-Bolshevik, Lenin as President of the Council of People's Commissars (i.e. the Bolshevik government) at once dissolved it. So Russia, already declared a republic under Kerensky and now in January 1918 declared to be a 'Republic of Soviets of Workers, Soldiers and Peasant Deputies', lapsed into dictatorship: in theory the dictatorship of a single party, the Bolsheviks or Communists, in practice the dictatorship of the leaders of that party. Naturally, this new régime, though it came to power so easily, was bitterly opposed as its nature became clear. Conservative, liberal, religious and even moderate socialist circles, together with all the manifold defenders of the rights of private property, joined together against it. Soon a civil war developed, in which the anti-Bolshevik forces were aided by the Allied governments. This, and the drastic nature of the new Bolshevik government's decrees – such as confiscating

Chaos and civil war

industries, handing over factories and land to the workers, and abolishing private trading, private property and inheritance – plunged Russia into a chaos from which it took her years to emerge.[1]

Russia out of the war

Meanwhile the Bolsheviks at great cost were at least able to carry out one part of their programme: they took Russia out of the war. An armistice was arranged in December 1917, but peace negotiations took some time to conclude, for with Russia in dissolution the Germans were able to put forward hard terms. After some delay the Bolsheviks, on Lenin's insistence, swallowed them, and in March

Treaty of Brest-Litovsk, March 1918

1918 concluded with Germany the treaty of Brest-Litovsk. By this Russia had to recognise the loss of almost all the territory she had gained in the west since the time of Peter the Great. Georgia, the Ukraine and Finland were to be independent; Poland and the Baltic provinces were to come under the care of Germany and Austria-Hungary; and other territory, including Kars and Batum, was to go to Turkey. Altogether Russia was to lose 62 million people, about a third of her arable

[1] See pp. 285–88.

MAKERS OF THE RUSSIAN REVOLUTION
Lenin speaking in Moscow in 1918. Trotsky (bottom right) watches reactions.

land and factories, and three-quarters of her coal and iron. Most of these areas were not, it is true, inhabited by Russians.

Though the entry of the U.S.A. and the exit of Russia were the main events of 1917, bitter fighting continued in the west. In the spring the British had some success in attacks near Arras and the Canadians captured the important Vimy Ridge, but an offensive launched by the new French commander-in-chief, Nivelle, near the River Aisne caused so many casualties in the French armies that the morale of many of the troops broke. Mutinies occurred, and the commanders were in the greatest difficulties. To allow France to reorganise, the British diverted attention by a sustained offensive near Ypres, directed towards the coast at Ostend (July–November 1917). It relieved the French and killed many Germans, but succeeded in getting only a few miles forward to the ridge at Passchendaele. All attempt at surprise, one of the greatest factors in achieving victory, was abandoned in favour of preceding the attack with tremendous bombardments. Then, over ground

The Western Front, 1917

Nivelle's offensive: French mutinies

'Passchendaele' offensive (Third battle of Ypres) July–November 1917

YPRES, 1917

When the trench line settled down in October 1914, Ypres remained just within the zone defended by the British Expeditionary Force, and only two or three miles from the German lines. The shattered buildings in this hot corner of the Western Front were a familiar sight throughout the war to thousands of British soldiers.

broken by gunfire or later a sea of mud from autumn rains, the British troops were supposed to advance. Hundreds actually drowned in the mire. Altogether the British suffered some 300,000 casualties in this shambles.

The Italian front: Caporetto, October 1917

The story of Allied disaster in 1917 was completed by a deplorable Italian failure against the Austrians. The battle of Caporetto, in which an Italian force trying to capture Trieste was repulsed and pursued, was the nearest thing to a rout since 1914.

The only crumbs of comfort at the end of 1917 for the Allied cause, apart from the improved position at sea, were some striking successes in Near Eastern 'side-shows'. Operations by British and Indian forces had been launched against the Turks in 1915 in Mesopotamia (Iraq), without at first much benefit, but by March 1917 Baghdad had been captured. Meanwhile other British and Anzac forces had successfully defended the Suez Canal and then advanced across Sinai into Palestine. In this area the open ground was suitable for the use of cavalry, and the advance could be aided by operations against the Turkish flank in Arabia.

Allied successes in the Near East, 1917

Here the brilliant work of T. E. Lawrence, scholar turned soldier, was largely responsible for directing a revolt among the Arabs of the desert against their

Turkish masters. Arabia and Palestine saw the beginning of the collapse of the Turkish dominions, and at Christmas 1917 Allenby entered Jerusalem.

Although the Near Eastern campaign continued successfully and the Italians, stiffened by French and British reinforcements, no longer bent before the Austro-German attacks, things nevertheless went badly against the British and French in the spring of 1918. With enormous numbers of troops released from the Russian front Ludendorff now strained every nerve to deliver a knock-out blow in the west. A series of great German offensives began in March. The first attack fell with particular severity on the British Fifth Army at the junction of the British and French forces near the Somme, and for a time carried all before it. With the British and French being driven apart, the danger to the Allies became so great that at last they sank their mutual suspicions and jealousies and consented to the creation of a single Allied command under Foch. The Americans also rushed to send over their first levies to strengthen the bending lines. German attacks in other sectors followed, until by June the Germans were up to their farthest 1914 positions by the Marne, and Paris was once more in danger. Then, as suddenly, the German advances petered out. The Allies held their ground; the Germans, worn out by four years of warfare against superior resources, lacked the reserves to push their effort home. The Americans arrived in increasing numbers. The hopelessness of continuing the struggle against an almost inexhaustible supply of American reinforcements, armaments, and wealth impressed itself on the Germans. In July Foch, whose handling of the reserves during the crisis had been masterly, began to move over to the offensive; and in August Haig followed by opening his counter-attack in the north. This proved to be his best work. Between them the Allied armies, making skilful use of tanks (a weapon neglected by the Germans) forced back the German lines with such rapidity that people could hardly believe the news. By the end of September, when the British stormed the supposedly almost impregnable Hindenburg line, Germany was at the end of her tether – and Ludendorff knew it.

But the German armies still stood on French and Belgian soil and it was not Germany who gave in first. An Anglo-French expedition which had been landed as long ago as 1915 at Salonika, in Greece (who had been practically forced by the Allies to enter the war on their side), at last justified itself. In September 1918 it attacked the Bulgarians, who collapsed almost at once. By the end of September Bulgaria was knocked out of the war and Serbia was being recovered. Then in October Turkey collapsed before the further attacks of Allenby in Syria and the Allied successes in the Balkans. Next the Hapsburg Empire went under, following attacks by the Italians and brilliant propaganda work by the British, who bombed the Austro-Hungarian lines with leaflets promising the various subject nationalities their independence if they deserted the Empire. Czechs, Poles, Slovaks, Croats immediately responded to the offer, and under the combined influence of military defeat, the blockade and disruptive propaganda the Dual Monarchy fell to pieces. The British Department of Propaganda, under the skilled direction of Lord Northcliffe, whose experience as founder and owner of the *Daily Mail* well qualified him for the niceties of the art, thus at the expense of a few thousand pounds and with no loss of life helped to secure results of profound importance.

With her friends all defeated and her own armies fast retreating, Germany had now no alternative but to sue for peace. This she did on the rather favourable basis

Marginal notes:

German offensive in west, March 1918

Unified Allied command

Germans at the Marne again, June 1918

Americans arrive in force

Allied counter-attack, summer–autumn 1918

Salonika force knocks out Bulgaria, September 1918

Turkey gives in, October, 1918

Austria follows, 4 November 1918

Germany asks for peace

276

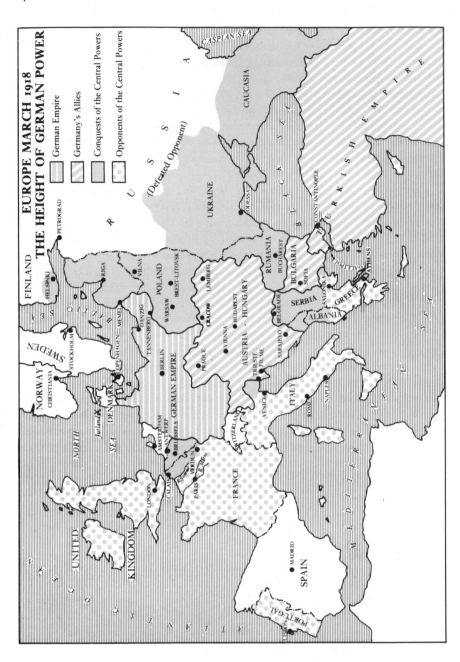

EUROPE MARCH 1918
THE HEIGHT OF GERMAN POWER

German Empire
Germany's Allies
Conquests of the Central Powers
Opponents of the Central Powers

Revolution in
Germany: Flight of
Kaiser, 9 November
1918

Mutiny at Kiel,
3 November 1918

of the 'Fourteen Points' which had been put forward in January 1918 by the American President, Woodrow Wilson. Even so, it needed revolt at home before Germany finally crumbled. On 29th October the German admiralty ordered the German Fleet out to sea from Kiel for a last desperate effort; but the sailors refused to go to certain destruction and mutinied. Other mutinies and strikes followed, and a workers' movement overthrew the King of Bavaria. On 9th November Hindenburg had reluctantly to inform William II that his power was at an end, whereupon the Kaiser and his family made a hurried and undignified exit to

Holland and safety. A German republic was then proclaimed and with inexpressible relief Europe soon learned that it had concluded an armistice with the Western Powers. The armistice came into effect at 11 a.m. on 11th November – a moment long to be remembered.

In considering the reasons for victory and defeat in the conflict we must realise what a task Germany had to face, in spite of her initial advantages and greater freedom from moral restraints. In the end the four Central European Powers were at war with twenty-seven states, including the whole might of the British Empire, India and the Dominions, France and her Empire, Japan, and the U.S.A. With such forces behind them, including Russia in the first years of the war, it would have been a disgrace had the Allies lost. Yet they nearly did lose, through their uninspired military leadership, their imperviousness to new ideas, their disastrous personal differences and lack of co-ordination. In the end the Allies 'muddled through'. The things which counted most were their superiority in manpower (especially with the arrival of the Americans), the almost inexhaustible wealth of the British Empire and the U.S.A., and the control of the seas, which the Royal Navy never lost. The last factor was vitally important. As the years passed, the Allied blockade slowly starved the Central Powers of both food and raw materials. On the other hand the Allied fleets could and did ensure Britain's vital food supply, the transport of troops to convenient centres of operation and the capture of enemy colonies. There was no Trafalgar in this war, but no more than in the Napoleonic war could the struggle have been won without the British Fleet. On Germany's side the great mistakes which cost her the war were the invasion of Belgium and the unrestricted submarine campaign. Both were gambles which came very near to success, but when once the immediate menace was checked both decisions proved fatal. The first offended the moral conscience of the world and united Britain in unremitting opposition. The second reinforced the universal hatred of German militarism and brought about the ultimately decisive intervention of the U.S.A.

Though fighting went on in several places after the German armistice, the 'Great War' (as it was usually called at the time, though afterwards it became the 'World War' and then the 'First World War') was in effect over. Its magnitude and its impact has been well summed up by one historian:

> It had lasted four years and three months, involved thirty sovereign states, overthrown four empires, given birth to seven new nations, taken 10 million lives in the field of battle and perhaps an equal number of non-combatant lives by privation, disease and revolution and wasted incalculable wealth. The civilised world might well believe that it deserved a new era and a millenial peace.[1]

2. The Peace Treaties, 1919–20

Though the carnage had mostly stopped with the armistices of October and November 1918, terms of peace were not at once agreed. For that it was necessary to call a Peace Conference, which met at Paris in January 1919. There it took four months of bargaining and doubtful diplomacy among the Allies before the main

Margin notes:

Armistice with Germany, 11 November 1918

Reasons for Allied victory:
1. Men
2. Wealth and industrial resources
3. Command of the seas

Main German mistakes:
1. Invasion of Belgium
2. Unrestricted submarine campaign

Paris Peace Conference, 1919

---

[1] F P CHAMBERS: *This Age of Conflict*, Harcourt, Brace & Co., N.Y. 1950.

278

THE SANDS RUN OUT.

Mr Punch, like most other people, thought of the defeat of Germany as the defeat of militarism for all time. He seems to have been sadly out in his reckoning. Cartoon by Bernard Partridge, 13th November 1918.

treaties were ready. The delegates from the Central Powers had no share in this discussion, their role being merely to receive the draft treaties, put forward written representations which might or might not be heeded, and then sign on the dotted line.

Treaty of Versailles with Germany, May 1919

At length in May 1919 the treaty with Germany (the Treaty of Versailles) was presented to the German delegation. Their government objected to some of its terms, whereupon the Allies threatened to renew the war unless the treaty was accepted within five days. The German government was quickly reconstructed, and fresh delegates arrived with instructions to sign. They did so on 28th June 1919, in the Hall of Mirrors at Versailles which had witnessed the foundation of the German Empire half a century before. Treaties with Germany's former allies –

Austria, Hungary, Turkey, and Bulgaria – followed in the course of 1919 and 1920, their signature taking place at other palaces in the neighbourhood of Paris.[1]

The peace treaties as a whole entailed a drastic redrawing of the map of central Europe. The work of those who framed it was fantastically difficult. They had to deal with enormous problems, such as the racial complications of central Europe and the Near East, or the best financial settlement obtainable, which they very imperfectly understood. Moreover, they had to work in an atmosphere poisoned by four years of desperate warfare with its inevitable legacy of national hatreds. In general the most liberal attitude to the conquered was taken by Wilson, an idealist to whom detachment was possible in view of his country's greater distance from Europe. The opposite attitude, of stripping Germany of all possible, was exemplified in the veteran Clemenceau, 'the Tiger', who had taken over the French premiership in 1918 and who could never forget what France had suffered not only in 1914 but in 1870. Lloyd George stood between the two, not illiberal himself, but with a constant eye on the fury of British opinion, expressed in the twin cries of 'make Germany pay' and 'hang the Kaiser'.

The settlement produced by compromises between these three men, and between them and others such as the Italian premier Orlando, bore marks of all of them. On the one side there was the application of the 'principle of self-determination' – the release of subject races all over Europe. The Hapsburg Empire had already broken up in the stress of defeat; and by the treaties of St Germain and Trianon the two 'rump' states of Austria and Hungary surviving from the shattered

THE BIG THREE, 1919
Clemenceau, Woodrow Wilson and Lloyd George in Paris during the Peace Conference.

[1] The Treaty of St Germain with Austria, September 1919; Treaty of Neuilly with Bulgaria, November 1919; Treaty of Trianon with Hungary, June 1920. The Treaty of Sèvres with Turkey, August 1920, was repudiated by Kemal's revolutionary forces in Turkey who overthrew the Sultan and finally secured a new treaty with the Allies – the Treaty of Lausanne, July 1923.

Empire, who were treated as its hostile core, acknowledged the position of the breakaway territories. These were the newly functioning republics of Czechoslovakia (which included Bohemia and Moravia) and Yugoslavia (Serbia enlarged by Montenegro, Bosnia-Herzegovina, and the Croats and Slovenes of the former Empire). Czechoslovakia had been set up as the state of the Czechs and Slovaks, Yugoslavia as the state of the south Slavs (the Serbs, Croats and Slovenes). In this process Hungary lost her subject races all round, one of the beneficiaries (Rumania) receiving more former Hungarian territory than was left to Hungary herself. Similarly the new rump state of Austria was limited to the strictly German parts of the old Dual Monarchy, a drastic alteration from the days when Vienna lorded it over thirteen races. She formally ceded territory not only to Czechoslovakia and Yugoslavia, but also to Italy (Trieste, Istria and the Tyrol up to the Brenner Pass). In the east of Europe, where the Treaty of Brest-Litovsk was formally cancelled, the former enemy states had all to recognise the existence of the newly liberated and reconstituted Poland, though its eastern boundaries could not yet be determined. The Poles were soon fighting to extend their territory, and their Bolshevik neighbours were not present at the Peace Conference. Equally, farther east, Turkey recognised the loss of her former Arab provinces such as Iraq, Syria and Palestine.

All these arrangements, like the restoration of Alsace-Lorraine to France, in general conformed to national limits. In this respect the great principle of nationality, constantly enunciated in the nineteenth century, at last received full recognition. Nevertheless it was violated, sometimes inevitably, by the incorporation of foreign minorities in the new states. Three million Hungarians, for example, came under alien rule, and three million Germans were included in Czechoslovakia, besides others in Poland. These decisions made future trouble inevitable. All the same, the subjections to foreign rule – usually made in the interests of strong military frontiers or because the populations were inextricably tangled – though they affected 30 million people in Europe were insignificant compared with those that existed before the war. Furthermore, the treaties usually contained regulations on the fair treatment of minorities which the ruling power was required to observe. A more vital defect, though not one that can be blamed on the treaty-makers, was that the coming into being of so many small states from the ruins of the Hapsburg and Russian empires multiplied economic boundaries, created new tariffs, and made trade more difficult in south-eastern Europe.

In the light of Hitler's subsequent actions in the 1930s, a special interest and importance attaches to the territorial provisions of the Treaty of Versailles affecting Germany. Apart from handing over two small areas (Eupen and Malmédy) to Belgium, and Alsace-Lorraine to France – which the Germans hardly contested – Germany also suffered the temporary loss of the Saarland, the coal-mines of which were to be under French control for a period of fifteen years. Much her most severe loss, however, occurred in the east, where the territories taken by Prussia from Poland in the partitions of the late eighteenth century, including Silesia, had to be restored. Since the new Poland would otherwise have been landlocked, arrangements had to be made for giving her access to the sea. For this purpose the German port of Danzig was declared a free city, and to provide access to it a corridor of land under Polish control, inhabited partly by Poles and partly by Germans, was to run across the former German provinces of Posen and west

Prussia. The effect of this corridor was to sever the most easterly province of Germany, East Prussia, from the rest of the country. All parties in Germany detested this arrangement. Compared with this, the loss of all their colonial territory – over a million square miles – was to most Germans a minor matter.

Though the territorial conditions of the treaties were, if by no means perfect, rather fairer than nearly all previous European treaties, some of the other provisions were extremely stringent. Germany and her satellites had to admit their 'war guilt' and face a bill as large as the Allies could make it with any hope of payment. The figure of the reparations due from Germany could not be calculated at the time and had to be argued about later; meanwhile heavy initial instalments in the form of cash, coal, timber, ships and livestock were required. Germany was in no position to resist these demands, since she had to surrender nearly all her fleet,[1] renounce her air force, abolish conscription, be content with a small professional army, forgo the use of submarines, tanks, heavy artillery and poison gas, and admit an Allied army of occupation into the Rhineland for fifteen years. But she was also in no position to pay, since she had lost her colonies and some of her best industrial districts, notably Silesia (to Poland), Lorraine (to France), and the Saar (to the League of Nations). Payment in goods was not encouraged for the long term since the Allies did not wish, by accepting German commodities, to put their own workers out of employment. Large numbers of intelligent people could see that the financial provisions, when they were eventually settled, would never really work; and in fact they never did. Germany paid a certain amount for some years by first borrowing from the U.S.A. and Britain. Later, as soon as she really began to foot the bill, she found herself unable to do so, and repudiated it.

If the treaties were impracticable financially and imperfect politically, if they carried out to the letter neither the idealistic principles of Wilson's 'Fourteen Points' nor the material bargains of Britain and France with states like Italy, they did at any rate contain one hope for the future in the form of the League of Nations. This, though not his own idea, was Wilson's greatest gift to Europe. More than any other statesman he was impressed with the need to avoid a catastrophe similar to the war which had just ended. Accordingly he insisted that his scheme for a League of Nations should not merely be included in the Treaty of Versailles but that the clauses setting it up should appear as the first part of each peace treaty, and that its machinery should be used to supervise some of the application of the treaties. The new institution was not to be a super-state – national pride would not allow that. It was to be a device to increase international co-operation and avoid war, while leaving each state sovereign in its own affairs. With headquarters situated at Geneva in Switzerland (a traditionally neutral state), its main organs were to be an Assembly, representing each member, and a Council, representing the greater members plus some smaller powers in rotation. The International Court at the Hague was recognised as a valid authority for arbitration. Later an International Labour Organisation was added, for co-operation on problems of health, social conditions, and so on. Initially only the Allied and associated powers and the main neutrals were to form the League; others might be able to join later.

Margin notes:
- Danzig and the Polish Corridor
- Colonial empire
- Financial terms
- Military restrictions
- League of Nations (effective January 1920)
- Its organisation

---

[1] Most of the German Fleet had sailed to Scapa Flow for internment at the armistice. A few days before the signing of the Treaty of Versailles the Fleet's officers scuttled the vessels rather than see them handed over to the Allied navies.

EUROPE AFTER THE FIRST WORLD WAR.
Showing also the pre-war boundaries of Germany,
Austria-Hungary and Russia

The Covenant

The obligations of each member were enshrined in a Covenant. The main promises undertaken in this remarkable document were that members would plan together how to decrease their armaments to the 'lowest point consistent with national safety', guarantee the integrity and independence of other members' territory, submit any international dispute to some form of arbitration or peaceful decision, and take instant action against an agreed aggressor by economic and possibly military means. (The last point was the famous 'Sanctions' clause – Article XVI.) Further, the members promised to publish their treaties, to exchange information on armament programmes, to use their best endeavours to obtain humane labour conditions in their own and other countries, to entrust the League with control of measures against disease, slavery and the opium trade. It will readily be understood why this Covenant, with its aims of peace and a better life and its vision of 'collective security', appealed to many thoughtful people as the one thing which made some of the appalling sacrifice of the war years worth while.

'Collective security'

Unfortunately for those hopes a terrible blow was dealt to the League at its very birth. Wilson, the head of the American Democratic Party, had neglected the American domestic scene from 1917 onwards, and his opponents the Republicans had gained majorities in both houses of Congress in November 1918. In revulsion from the squabblings of Europe and in a desire to return to traditional American policies of non-intervention, they refused to ratify the Treaty of Versailles or take any part in the League. And without the U.S.A. the League was to prove only a shadow of the institution Wilson had intended.

Repudiation of Versailles and the League by U.S.A., January–March 1920

One other innovation was included in the Covenant: the idea of 'mandated territories'. These were districts which had been captured by the Allies, such as the German colonies in Africa or parts of the Turkish Empire in the Near East, but which it was difficult with justice for the conquerors to retain. The war had officially been fought on the Allied side 'to break militarism' and 'to protect the rights of small nations' – even, according to Wilson, 'to make the world safe for democracy'. Clearly, it would not look well to indulge in wholesale annexations in the old imperialist fashion, especially since it was by a promise of future independence that the Arabs had been induced to revolt against the Turks. Equally, South Africa and Australia, for example, after having conquered German colonies, did not want to see them restored to Germany to become once more a menace to their security. Yet the territories were too backward to govern themselves in accordance with standards acceptable to western nations. The solution arrived at was the 'Mandate' system, first suggested by the South African General Smuts, who was one of the fathers of the League itself. By this system the territories were entrusted to a mandatory power, whose duty was to rule with the benefit and in most cases the ultimate independence of the natives in mind, and who had to give an account of its stewardship to the League of Nations.

'Mandates'

On the whole the system scarcely succeeded. The French encountered bitter opposition in their mandate over Syria, and the British mandate and rule over Palestine completely failed to reconcile the Arabs to the establishment of a Jewish 'national home' there.[1] Germany of course regarded the mandatory system as a mere device by which annexation was cloaked in 'morality', though Britain very soon surrendered her mandate over Iraq. The least troublesome mandates proved to be those over the old German colonies in Africa, for these were virtually (and later actually) absorbed by Britain, France and South Africa.

[1] The Balfour Declaration of 1917, made by the British foreign secretary at the time on the prompting of leading Zionists and Jewish Americans, had promised Britain's co-operation in establishing this national home for the Jewish people. The condition was made that nothing should be done 'which may prejudice the civil and religious rights of existing non-Jewish communities in Palestine'.

CHAPTER 21
The Aftermath of War, and the Years of Hope

1. From Chaos to Recovery, 1918–25

Fighting after 1918

Events after 1919 gave little satisfaction to those who dreamed of a new era of peace after 'the war to end war'. For at least five years much of Europe was in a state of turmoil or even armed conflict. In 1919, for instance, there was fighting in Hungary when the advent of a communist government there gave Hungary's neighbours, Rumania and Czechoslovakia, a good opportunity to despoil her of territory – seizures legalised the following year in the Treaty of Tianon. In 1919 too, Italian volunteers under the airman poet d'Annunzio seized the former Hungarian port of Fiume, on the Adriatic (it had a large Italian population) and held it for fifteen months in defiance of the Allies and Yugoslavia.[1]

Hungary, 1919

Fiume, 1919

Ireland, 1919–23

Turmoil and fighting were also rife in Ireland, where the Sinn Fein ('ourselves alone') movement set up an independent republic supported by the volunteer Irish Republican Army, while the British strove to re-establish their authority. This was the time of the Irish 'troubles' (1919–21). It was ended by a treaty partitioning Ireland and giving the southern part self-government within the British Commonwealth as the Irish Free State. Almost immediately a civil war broke out in the Free State (1922–23) between the Irish rebels who had accepted this compromise and those who stuck out for a completely independent republic.

All these were minor affairs compared with the clashes between the Greeks and the Turks, and between the Russian Bolsheviks and their numerous enemies. The first of these conflicts nearly involved Britain in war again with Turkey. The second involved Britain, France and others in actual – and unsuccessful – armed intervention in Russia.

Turkey

Mustapha Kemal's nationalist revolt, 1919

The trouble between the Greeks and the Turks quickly followed Turkey's request for an armistice with the Allies in October 1918. Although the Sultan was willing to meet nearly all the Allied demands, one of his generals was not. Mustapha Kemal, who had earlier distinguished himself in the defence of the Gallipoli peninsula, was sent by the Sultan in 1919 to supervise Turkish disarmament in Anatolia, the mountainous heartland of Asiatic Turkey. But instead of disarming

---

[1] It was then recognised as a Free City, but in 1923 went to Italy as the result of an Italian agreement with Yugoslavia. In 1945 it became part of Yugoslavia.

he recruited, and announced his intention of protecting Turkish independence. He summoned a Turkish National Assembly to meet in Asia Minor; and this appointed an Executive Council, with Kemal as President, to govern in place of the Sultan's inert régime at Constantinople. Kemal, in other words, began a nationalist revolution in Asiatic Turkey and very soon he clashed with the Greeks, who had been authorised by the Allies to annex the Smyrna region (of mixed Turkish and Greek population) in Asia Minor.

Kemal's rising reputation among the Turks soared still higher when details were published of the Treaty of Sèvres concluded between the Sultan and the Allies. The terms were much more severe than most patriotic Turks could readily accept. Kemal, for instance, although ready to give up Turkey's Arabic provinces, was not prepared to see an Allied commission in control around Constantinople or a large part of Turkish Asia Minor split between the Greeks, the Kurds and the Armenians. He announced his intention of resisting such surrenders; and the Allies left the Greeks, already established around Smyrna, to deal with him. For a while they did so with success, nearly penetrating to his fortress of Ankara. But then the tide turned and Kemal drove the Greeks across Asia Minor in a chase which ended at Smyrna in evacuation, a blazing town and wholesale massacre.

Kemal opposes Treaty of Sèvres, 1920

Greeks v. Turks, 1920–22

Kemal was now ready to move from Asia Minor into Europe, to clear the Greeks out of another of their recent acquisitions, the former Turkish territory of eastern Thrace. This meant crossing the Dardanelles, then still under Allied control. At Chanak, on the Asiatic shores of the Dardanelles, the British force was under orders from Lloyd George to stand firm. A clash threatened, but Kemal halted and agreed to negotiate, and war was averted.[1] Tightening his hold on the National Assembly, which had now moved to Constantinople, Kemal then abolished the Sultanate, and concluded with the Allies a revised peace treaty to replace that of Sèvres. The new treaty (of Lausanne, in 1923) preserved for Turkey the whole of Anatolia, as well as Constantinople and eastern Thrace. To prevent trouble from national minorities within the new boundaries, a forcible exchange of populations was arranged, about two million unfortunate Greeks, Turks and Bulgarians being uprooted from their homes.

Chanak Incident with Britain, 1922

Abolition of Sultanate

Treaty of Lausanne, 1923

During these years the troubles of even the Greeks and Turks were small compared with those of the Russians. The victorious Bolsheviks, having bought off the Germans at Brest-Litovsk, had before long to meet opposition from the Allies, the Poles, and large sections of the Russian people. By March 1918 discontent was rising; for though the Bolsheviks had ridden to power on war-weariness and the spontaneous development of revolutionary feeling, there was no general desire in Russia for a single-party dictatorship such as the Bolsheviks – or Communists, as they called themselves after 1919 – were determined to enforce in order to establish a communist society. Still less was there any general enthusiasm for such early Bolshevik measures as the wholesale nationalisation of large-scale enterprises (decreed in June 1918), the confiscation of large estates without compensation, the conscription of labour and private wealth, the banning of private trade, and the requisitioning of grain and other foodstuffs from the peasantry. This attempt to

Russia

Opposition to Bolsheviks, 1918–19

---

[1] Much was due to the tact of the British military leader on the spot, General Harrington. Lloyd George's willingness to defy Kemal to the point of war, though successful, was regarded as reckless by many of his colleagues, and helped to bring about the breakup of his Coalition government.

set up a communist society in a rush, coupled with the legacy of the war, foreign intervention, and the ineptitude of many party nominees chosen to manage mines, factories and railways, produced a chaos such as Russia had never before experienced. Trade and production slumped drastically and scarcities of all kinds developed; such shortages could not be made good from abroad, for the Bolsheviks had ruined external trade by repudiating Russia's debts and confiscating foreign investments. All told, the years 1918–20 were a nightmare for the Russian people. Fanned by intervention from outside, domestic opposition was ceaseless and Russia's new masters met it with increasing ruthlessness. Soon their secret or political police, the Cheka, was far bigger than any similar organisation under the Tsars.[1] Scores of thousands of critics or opponents of the new régime were executed, and hundreds of thousands imprisoned in labour camps.

War communism, 1918–20; dictatorship and terror

Murder of Nicholas II, July 1918

Among the early victims were Nicholas II and his family. For some months they had been held captive in Siberia. Then, in July 1918, they were taken into the basement of the house in which they were lodged at Ekaterinburg, in the Urals, and there murdered. In other circumstances the Bolsheviks might, perhaps, have put Nicholas on trial in their new capital of Moscow. They murdered him in July 1918 because he might otherwise have been rescued – an anti-Bolshevik force was within two days march of Ekaterinburg.

Foreign intervention: the Czech legion

The core of this force was a Czech legion of the old Russian army. It had received permission to join the Allies on the Western Front, travelling by way of Vladivostock. As it moved along the Trans-Siberian railway it fell foul of Bolsheviks who tried to disarm it, and it was joined by Russian groups opposed to the Revolution. Other opposition forces with a foreign nucleus soon became active elsewhere and by mid-1918 'White' armies were operating against the Bolshevik 'Reds' not only in Siberia but also in the south around Odessa, in the Baltic lands, and in the north around Archangel and Murmansk. At these two ports British and French units originally sent out to safeguard supplies and deny the ports to the Germans were soon reinforced in order to co-operate with anti-Bolshevik forces. Such intervention became Allied policy (the U.S.A. and Japan also joined in) not so much because the Allies detested Bolshevism (though they did) as because the Bolsheviks had taken Russia out of the war, and the Allies wanted her back.

'White' armies aided by Britain and France, 1918–20

Russian Civil War, 1918–20

By November 1918, when fighting ceased in France, a fierce civil war was raging in Russia, with anti-Bolshevik forces of many kinds and nationalities operating at different points right across the country. By mid-1919 their efforts, though largely uncoordinated and on the part of the Allies rather half-hearted, had stripped the Bolsheviks of at least one third of their territory. The 'Whites', however, though proclaiming democratic principles, proved no more popular or lenient in their rule than the Bolsheviks, and gradually the latter prevailed. In organising the Red Army Trotsky showed genius as well as ruthlessness, and the combination of military efficiency, terrorism, and a degree of popular support proved decisive. By the end of 1919 the Bolsheviks, despite the general chaos and the collapse of normal civilised existence, were winning through.

Bolshevik success

At this stage they encountered a further enemy in the Poles. The frontier between Russia and Poland had been left undefined at the Paris Peace Conference and the

---

[1] The Soviet political police has been known by different names at different times – first as the Cheka, then as the GPU or OGPU, and nowadays as the KGB.

chaos in Russia tempted the Poles to try to set it as far east as possible. In March 1920 they struck a bargain with the White army in southern Russia and with the Ukrainians – a separate nationality – in Russia, who were anxious to secure independence. The initial joint attacks penetrated deep into Russia, but the onslaught of the Poles aroused Russian patriotism. Former opponents rallied to the Bolsheviks, their Red Army hit back, and soon the Russians were chasing the Poles almost to the approaches to Warsaw. On the Vistula, however, the Poles under General Pilsudski rallied, helped by French supplies and a military mission under Foch's chief of staff, General Weygand; and soon the war was moving east again. In October 1920 the Russians signed a preliminary peace at Riga which gave Poland an eastern frontier far beyond her strict national limits – to the extent of including within her boundaries some four million Russians.[1]

The Poles join in, 1920

Preliminary Peace of Riga, 1920

With the withdrawal of the British from Murmansk and Archangel and the crushing of most of the White forces, only the final scene of the Russian civil war remained to be enacted. The last White commander, General Wrangel, became penned up in the Crimean peninsula with 30,000 men and a large number of refugee noble families and former Tsarist officials. At the end of 1920 French warships rescued most of them. The remainder suffered the ruthless vengeance of the Red Army.

End of Civil War in Crimea, 1920

Still the Russian agony was not over. In February 1921 the naval garrison at Kronstadt, who had earlier been foremost in support of the Bolshevik revolution, mutinied. It was the danger signal which showed Lenin that he must make concessions at home and relax the rigours of 'war communism' and strict communist theory in the interests of immediate improvements in supply. During 1920 the volume of industrial production had fallen to thirteen per cent of that of 1913, while prolonged drought brought about a disastrous crop failure in the great grain areas of the Volga, the Don and the Ukraine. The result of this was an appalling famine in 1921 in these regions which probably, despite much relief from foreign, and particularly American, sources, caused the deaths of a million people. To meet this threatened disaster Lenin, against opposition from Trotsky, resolved to retreat. He decided to substitute a grain tax for grain requisition, to allow a free market to the peasant for his produce, and to tolerate once more the individual holding and working of land. The old channels of trade between town and country were re-opened, and directed or forced labour as a general practice (as opposed to a punishment for opponents) was abolished. By these and similar measures, collectively known as the New Economic Policy, Lenin put the régime's communistic programme into temporary reverse, and in so doing helped to revive Russian production and restore some stability to his tormented country.

Kronstadt Mutiny, 1921

Lenin's New Economic Policy, 1921–24

At the same time Lenin strove to bring about more normal relations between Russia and the outside world. This was made easier by the collapse of intervention. During 1920 and 1921 Russia signed peace treaties with the new Baltic States – Estonia, Latvia and Lithuania – detached from her former Empire, and with her southern neighbours Persia and Turkey; and in 1921 she made her first trade treaty with Britain. Full diplomatic recognition by Britain and France of the communist régime did not follow till 1924. The French were much upset by Russia's repudiation of her huge pre-war debts to France, but by the time of

Anglo-French recognition of Soviet Russia, 1924

---

[1] The recovery of this territory was part of Stalin's bargain with Hitler in August 1939. See pp.

FAMINE IN RUSSIA, 1921–22

In Russia, the aftermath of defeat, revolution, civil war, class conflict and over-hasty socialisation was famine. Here peasants wait for a distribution of bread.

Lenin's death in the same year the new Soviet state was becoming an accepted, if still isolated, part of the world scene.[1]

Italy

Among the other European states which suffered disruption on a large scale, though not warfare, in the years 1919–22 was Italy. Many parts of the country, particularly in the south, were desperately poor, and many of the returned soldiers, stimulated by the Russian revolution, were demanding socialistic reforms such as workers' participation in the control and profits of estates and factories. In parliament there was a profusion of parties, and a constant difficulty in forming stable ministries. To add to this there was general disappointment at what were considered to be the meagre gains of Italy by the peace treaties, and a disillusionment with the recent Italian war effort. In such an atmosphere strikes, sit-ins and lock-outs quickly multiplied, and in turn led to riots, bomb-throwing and bloodshed.

Post-war strife

[1] The state was a complex federation. The first official constitution in July 1918 regularised the Russian Socialist Federated Soviet Republic (RSFSR). With the recovery by the Bolsheviks of former parts of the Empire, in 1922 a wider federation was set up under the title of the Union of Soviet Socialist Republics (USSR). This, the over-all state, consisted of a federation of the RSFSR with six other republics, including the Ukraine.

With governments at Rome apparently incapable of controlling the violence, private armies of supporters of various causes quickly sprang up, distinguishing themselves by their shirts of different colours. Among these the clash was especially violent between the red shirts of the Communists and Socialists and the black shirts of the Fascists. The latter, whose name derived from the ancient Roman *fasces*, or bundle of rods carried round an axe by the lictors as a symbol of power and unity, was a party of 'authority'. Though not lacking in socialistic tendencies, it stood above all for Italian nationalism and state power: it glorified the Italian war effort, and emphasised the need for 'law and order' as opposed to the industrial unrest fomented by the Socialists and Communists. To assert this need, its young black-shirted supporters fought in the streets with cudgels from time to time against their opponents, and developed a special (and revolting) treatment for those who fell into their hands – a large and forcible dose of castor oil. This was especially used to keep opponents from the polling-booths at elections.

The founder of Fascism was Benito Mussolini, the son of a blacksmith. A journalist and former ardent Socialist, several times imprisoned for his activities, Mussolini had first opposed and then supported Italy's entry into the war. In March 1919 he founded his first *fascio* or group, in Milan; and soon similar groups spread throughout the country. By mid-1921 they probably had about 250,000 members, mostly lower middle class but with some industrialists and landowners who saw in Fascism the best defence against Communism. At first only Mussolini and one other Fascist were members of parliament, but at the elections of May 1921, after nearly two years of industrial strife, the Fascist representation rose to thirty-five. Throughout the rest of 1921 and 1922 public order deteriorated still further, with Fascists and Communists clashing nightly in the streets and Fascist gangs driving Socialist mayors and officials out of the town halls. In the absence of effective control by the predominantly Liberal government, in August 1922 the left wing parties staged a general strike. It was broken largely by the Fascists, who captured the strikers' headquarters, seized newspaper offices, broke up the strikers' meetings, and ran the public services.

Events now moved to their climax – the establishment of the Fascists in power. First, Mussolini made plain what had not been so evident before – his determination to preserve the Italian monarchy and safeguard the rights and property of the Church. Then, in October 1922, he struck. He ordered the mobilisation of the Blackshirts, and directed them to march on Rome from their different parts of the country. He himself did not accompany them, but his deputies were successful in their mission. Even before the Fascist threat, King Victor Emmanuel III was willing to appoint Mussolini as Premier, and he now did so. A few hours later Mussolini arrived in the capital by train. He wore a black shirt, with a bowler-hat and spats.

Within a few months, Mussolini's hold on Italy was complete. He called the Blackshirts off the streets, but later enrolled them in a disciplined militia. At first, he included members of other parties in his ministry, for the Fascist party in parliament was small. By 1923 he was able to win a big electoral victory after which he could establish, by legal means, what amounted to a complete one-party dictatorship. Using these immense powers, he not only drove his opponents from Italian political life but also made strenuous efforts to solve Italy's economic problems. These quickly showed success, and with strikes and lock-outs prohibited, order in

Marginal notes:

The Fascists (Blackshirts), 1919

Mussolini (b. 1883)

The Fascists in parliament, 1921

General strike, August 1922

Fascist 'March on Rome', October 1922 Mussolini Premier

Fascist electoral victory and dictatorship, 1923

Improvement in
Italian public order and
economic position

the streets, and the revival of European trade in general, Italy's industrial production and public finances took a sharp turn for the better. Italy, like Russia, though under dictatorship was at last settling down.

Among the great countries which experienced extreme disruption in the years after 1918 was also Germany. She had to suffer not only the losses and penalties imposed by the Treaty of Versailles but also much civil strife and uncertainty about the future.

Germany

The nature of the republic proclaimed just before the armistice in November 1918 was not at first clear. Though most Germans probably desired a parliamentary democracy, there were plenty of extremists who wanted something along soviet lines. Elections were arranged for January 1919, as a step towards drawing up a constitution, but a fortnight beforehand there was an attempted *coup* by the extreme left. The Chancellor, Frederick Ebert, a former saddler, was a moderate

Ebert: moderate
Socialist rule

socialist like most of his ministers. When he decided to eject from the Royal Palace in Berlin some naval revolutionaries from Kiel who were occupying it, he was deserted by the most extreme socialists in his government, who joined the com-

Abortive Communist
coups, 1919

munists outside. The leader of these, Karl Liebknecht, whose group were known as Spartacists,[1] set up a revolutionary committee which called for a general strike and the overthrow of Ebert's government. The Spartacists captured some of the Berlin public buildings, but the government was able to call on some remnants of the old imperial army enrolled in an irregular Free Corps. For a week Spartacists and Free Corps fought it out in Berlin, victory going to the Free Corps – and the government. Among those killed were Liebknecht and his enthusiastic supporter Rosa Luxemburg, who were arrested and then shot 'while trying to escape'. Three months later, extreme left wing groups in Munich tried to set up a virtually independent soviet-type local state. Again Free Corps bands quickly suppressed the revolutionaries.

National Assembly at
Weimar, January 1920

Meanwhile the new National Assembly had met at Weimar. The majority was of the moderate left, and Ebert became provisional President of the Republic. The constitution finally produced in July 1919 gave most of the power to the central government in Berlin, but reserved a little for the various component states of the federation. It set up a liberal democracy based on universal suffrage and propor-

Constitution of the
'Weimar Republic'

tional representation of parties in accordance with votes cast, with guarantees of freedom of speech and assembly and the right to private property. The Chancellor and his ministers would need the support of the Reichstag to remain in office, but the President of the Republic could, if public order were seriously threatened, 'declare the fundamental rights of the citizen wholly or partly in abeyance'.

The 'Kapp Putsch'
(*coup*), March 1920

The first big challenge to this new 'Weimar Republic', came not from the left but from the right. In March 1920 a group of strong nationalists eager to repudiate the Treaty of Versailles, backed by one of the Free Corps from the Baltic, seized key points in Berlin and tried to rule under their leader, Wolfgang Kapp. The government quickly left for Stuttgart and called for a general strike against the rebels. The response from the workers and public servants was so complete that Kapp, who had no support from the regular forces, could not carry on. Within four days he and his henchmen were in flight to Sweden.

The success of the socialist government in quelling at least three revolts in these

[1] From Spartacus, who led a revolt of the slaves in ancient Rome.

years did not secure its return at the next elections in June 1920. The voters thought instead of the humiliations which the government had accepted in the Treaty of Versailles. The socialist vote fell, and the remaining ministries of the Weimar Republic were nearly all coalitions built around the central parties.

Non-socialist governments, 1920 onwards

The greatest problem with which they at first had to deal, and which for long bedevilled European politics, was that of reparations. Germany's total obligations had not been settled at Versailles, though some initial instalments had been arranged. Despite much work on the Reparations Commission (an Allied body) and many meetings with German representatives, it was not until May 1921 that a final figure was determined – £6,600,000,000. At the 1970s value of money, and with our experience of mammoth state expenditure, this does not seem so huge a sum as it did in the 1920s. In any case, it had to be found in one country, Germany, and handed out to others – a very different matter from raising and spending such a sum within the same country. The Germans protested that payment on this scale was impossible, and after meeting their dues for one year asked for a delay. Lloyd George, still at that time the British Prime Minister, might have agreed; but the French Premier, Raymond Poincaré, stood firm. When, amid mounting confusion in Germany's finances and a rapid decline in the value of the mark, Germany fell short in previously agreed deliveries of timber and coal to France, Poincaré took drastic action. In January 1923 he ordered French troops into Germany's great industrial region, the Ruhr. If Germany would not pay willingly, she should be made to pay by force. His action was supported by Belgium and Italy, but not by Britain.

Reparations: total decided, May 1921

Germany's default

French and Belgians invade Ruhr, January 1923

The invasion of the Ruhr threw Germany into almost total chaos. The Germans met it on the spot by passive resistance. They refused to hand over reparations, and refused to co-operate in any way with the occupiers. The French and Belgians for their part were reduced to making wholesale arrests and confiscations. Brawls and shootings became common, but worst of all was the complete collapse of the currency throughout Germany. The already fast-mounting inflation got out of control, and the mark suddenly became almost valueless. At the end of 1922 it had been worth about 500 to the pound. By the close of January 1923 it had fallen to 100,000 to the pound, by April to 500,000, by August to 25,000,000. New notes were issued by over-printing fresh values on the old ones. Prices and wages had to be revised first weekly, then daily, then hourly. At the height of the inflation a man's weekly wages might be almost worthless by the time he got to the shops with them. When one great printing of banknotes was ordered, and the printers took a fortnight to deliver them, the value of the notes, officially amounting to billions of marks, was less than their value as pulped paper.

Collapse of the mark: uncontrolled inflation, 1923

This was an appalling experience for Germany, and particularly for her thrifty middle and upper working classes, whose savings mostly disappeared overnight. Those with land, houses, goods, were all right; and so too were those with debts or mortgages, which could now easily be repaid in worthless currency. But savings in banks or government bonds or shares became worthless. This virtual destruction of Germany's middle class was to cost her dear in stability later.

Loss of middle-class savings

Such conditions could not go on. In August 1923 a new Chancellor, Gustav Stresemann, leader of the moderate right wing People's Party, took over on a policy of stopping the resistance in the Ruhr and trying to collaborate again with the Allies. This policy was continued by his successor shortly afterwards, while

Stresemann

STADT KÖLN SERIE A
GUTSCHEIN ÜBER
EINE
BILLION
MARK

Dieser Gutschein wird von allen städtischen u.anderen öffent=
lichen Kassen in Zahlung genommen. Er verliert seine Gültigkeit
einen Monat nach Aufkündigung in den Kölner Ortsblättern.
Die Stadtgemeinde Köln haftet für die Einlösung.

№ 008566

Köln, 25. Okt. 1923
Der Oberbürgermeister
Adenauer

Umlaufsfähig im ganzen Regierungsbezirk Köln.
Gültig bis zum 1. April 1924.

A BILLION MARK NOTE, 1923

Following the German default in reparation repayments in 1922 and the French occupation of the Ruhr, the German currency collapsed completely. Ordinary coins and banknotes could not cope with astronomically increasing prices. At first, existing notes were overprinted with new, enormously magnified values. Later new notes were printed, like this one issued by the city of Cologne in 1923 for a thousand million marks. In 1914 that sum would have been worth £50,000,000 in the English money of the time. In August 1923 it was worth about £50.

Stresemann himself concentrated on the work of negotiation as Foreign Minister. Little could be done until the mark was stabilised. In October 1923 it stood at 100,000,000,000 to the pound, and was worthless. The following month the new German government issued a new mark – the Rentenmark – backed by the value of the country's land. Each of the new marks was worth one trillion of the old. This drastic operation was painful, but successful. At appalling cost to all those who had lost their savings, German trade and industry could start to revive, and the Reparations Commission be assured of Germany's serious desire to meet her obligations.

A new currency
(Rentenmark),
November 1923

The Stresemann government's decision to cease resistance in the Ruhr went down badly in many quarters in Germany. Attempts were made in the Rhineland and in Saxony and Thuringia to break away from the federal organisation – though with short-lived success. The most dramatic and scatter-brained of the revolutionary movements came from Munich, and brought to notoriety for the first time the name of Adolf Hitler. A number of highly-placed nationalists in Bavaria, including the local army commander and the retired general Ludendorff, had been planning some kind of local *coup*, possibly involving the restoration of the Bavarian royal

Hitler's Munich
putsch, November 1923

family. Hitler was also a fanatical nationalist, but of modest origins: the son of a minor customs official in Austria, he was a would-be artist who had led an impoverished life in Vienna till 1913 and had risen no higher than corporal in the war. His task now was to supply an irregular force to support the revolt. He was able to do this because he had created in 1920, round the nucleus of a tiny organisation he had joined the previous year, what he called the National Socialist German Workers Party, and had been building it up as a semi-military organisation with a section specially trained for marching and street-fighting. This was the *Sturmabteilung* (S.A.) or Storm Section, recruited in part from former Free Corps men, and originally disguised as a 'Gymnastic and Sports Division' of the party.

Hitler's own ideas went far beyond merely establishing a right-wing government in Bavaria or securing greater local independence from Berlin. Indeed he was strongly opposed to Bavarian separatism. What he planned was to use the forthcoming Bavarian insurrection to overthrow the central government in Berlin and establish there a more nationalistic régime with himself as a principal figure. On the evening of 8th November 1923, while the leaders of the Bavarian conspiracy were holding a large meeting in a Munich beer hall and Hitler was among the audience, Hitler's henchman Göring suddenly burst in with a squad of Nazi[1] stormtroopers. After firing his revolver at the ceiling to secure attention, Hitler leapt on to the platform and declared the Bavarian and German governments deposed. In a back room at pistol-point he then appointed the leaders of the Bavarian conspiracy to places in his national government – Ludendorff, hastily summoned, persuaded them to agree – and all then returned to the hall, where Hitler announced the news to the cheering crowd.

The next morning, as soon as they safely could, the Bavarian leaders repudiated their promise to serve with Hitler. In the absence of their support (and regular troops) the *putsch* was doomed. Nevertheless that morning Hitler, Ludendorff and two or three thousand stormtroopers marched into the middle of Munich to try to get the army on their side. A few volleys from the local police sufficed to disperse the members. Hitler, captured later, was given the minimum sentence of five years imprisonment, and released after less than nine months. In jail, where he had considerable freedom, comfort and company, he was able to begin dictating – he was a ceaseless talker – a brief account of his life and an enormously lengthy account of his views entitled *Mein Kampf* ('My struggle'). It later became the Bible of the National Socialist movement.

Hitler's imprisonment: *Mein Kampf*

This episode did not shake the German government in its determination to reach agreement with Germany's former enemies. Though Hitler made a remarkable impression at his trial and to many Germans became a hero, most found him a laughing-stock and were confirmed in their belief that Munich was a centre of crack-pot ideas. Stresemann and his colleagues went on to negotiate with the Reparations Commission an interim but more practicable settlement known as the Dawes Plan (from the American chairman of one of the Committees, General Dawes). It did not set a term to Germany's liability, but arranged for a series of payments over five years rising from about £50,000,000 in the first year to about £127,000,000 in the fifth, which would then become the standard payment. Nearly all the first year's payment would be provided for Germany in the form of a

Reparations: the Dawes Plan, May 1924

[1] NAZI – abbreviation for Nazional Socialist.

loan raised internationally, and at the same time arrangements would be made for a new and permanent German currency, the Reichmark, bearing a stable relation to gold.

This plan by no means met previous French demands, but its acceptance in France was helped by the defeat in May 1924 of the relentless Poincaré in the French Chamber and the formation of a new French government under the moderate radical Edouard Herriot. In Germany the Plan was unpopular, and held

to be too severe. At the elections in May 1924 the nationalist parties accordingly gained, and Hitler's National Socialists were able to secure thirty-two seats. Stresemann and his colleagues still governed, but the Reichstag ratified the Dawes Plan by a majority of only three votes. Nevertheless the greater financial stability deriving from the agreement and the loan helped German trade and industry, already reviving, and at further elections later in the year the moderate parties increased their strength.

Thus fortified, and with the reparations question momentarily dormant, Stresemann was able to take his next step. His objective was to secure an agreement with Germany's former enemies which would give Germany greater military security; she had been virtually disarmed, but the victors, especially France, maintained large armed forces. At the same time he wanted to restore Germany to a

Problem of French security

respected place among the nations. The main problem here was the understandable fear felt by the French of a revival of German military power. To prevent this, the French at the Peace Conference had not only insisted on German disarmament, but had wanted to detach territory from Germany on the left bank of the Rhine. They had been dissuaded by the British and Americans, who allayed France's fears by offering her instead a guarantee of military help in the event of further German aggression. Then the American Congress in 1919–20 had repudiated Wilson's work, and France had been left without her guarantee – for without the Americans the British promise lapsed too. Instead, France had concentrated on building up friendship with the new states ringing Germany and Austria (who were forbidden under the Treaty of Versailles to unite) on the east and south. These were Poland, Czechoslovakia, the enlarged Rumania and Yugoslavia. Under French

Little Entente, 1921

patronage the last three had formed in 1921 a 'Little Entente' to resist any attempt to recover territory by Hungary; and in that year France herself concluded an

French alliances with Poland (1921), Czechoslovakia (1924), Rumania (1926), Yugoslavia (1927)

alliance with Poland. In January 1924 she went on to make an alliance with Czechoslovakia and later made similar agreements with Rumania and Yugoslavia. At the beginning of 1924 the French were thus still completely unreconciled opponents of Germany. They were not merely occupying German territory including the Ruhr and insisting on vast reparation payments, but were also the patrons of a military combination in south-east Europe which Germany regarded as hostile to herself as well as to Hungary.

It was largely due to three outstanding foreign ministers capable of European as well as patriotic views – Stresemann, Aristide Briand and Austen Chamberlain – that French and German fears were simultaneously lessened by a further agreement reached in October 1925. This was the pact negotiated at the Swiss resort of

Locarno Pact, October 1925

Locarno. It consisted of several treaties, of which the most important was one of mutual guarantee in connection with the German-French and German-Belgian frontiers. If Germany violated the French or Belgian frontiers, Britain and Italy would assist France and/or Belgium. If France violated the German frontier,

Britain and Italy would assist Germany. The powers involved also undertook to guarantee the demilitarisation of the German Rhineland, once the Allied occupying forces were withdrawn.

This agreement seemed at the time, at any rate, to offer a new hope for Europe – though the Germans obviously got more out of it than the French, who would probably in any case have been helped by Britain in the event of a German attack. Briand spoke of a 'new era of conciliation, arbitration and peace', and Chamberlain referred to the pact as 'the real dividing line between the years of war and the years of peace'. In harmony with the Locarno spirit, Germany in 1926 applied for, and was granted, membership of the League of Nations. And on the day the pact was formally signed, the Allied armies of occupation began the first stage of their withdrawal from Germany.

Germany joins the League, 1926

So by the end of 1925 the chaos of the post-war years in central, south-eastern and eastern Europe had given place to some sort of order. The domestic turmoil in Italy and Germany had been brought under control; Soviet Russia was slowly securing international recognition; and France and Germany had taken big steps towards reconciliation. Industry was re-adjusting itself to a peace-time footing, trade was stabilising and expanding. Europe breathed with a new hope. The war of 1914–18, it seemed, was at last over.

A new era for Europe?

2. The Years of Hope, 1924–29

The new era of hope for Europe which seemed to open in 1924 lasted very few years. By 1930, much of the world was in the grip of an economic crisis. Three years later Hitler came to power in Germany and the fragile plant of peace quickly wilted.

The five years from 1924 to 1929 were Europe's best since before 1914. Though there was still much poverty, unemployment, internal disturbance (including the British general strike of 1926) and colonial conflict, no European state actually fought another. On the contrary, many treaties of friendship were made and there was constant study at the League of Nations of the best way to ensure peace and disarmament. Agreements involving everybody tended to be nebulous – the Pact of Paris of 1928, for instance, proposed by the American Secretary of State F. W. Kellog and Aristide Briand, 'outlawed' war 'as an instrument of national policy' and was signed by sixty-five states, but provided no actual force for restraining an aggressor. Nevertheless the general European atmosphere was one of increasing amity. This atmosphere was slightly ruffled by a new reparations settlement, the Young Plan of 1930 (which visualised Germany continuing modified annual payments until 1988 !), but was restored by the withdrawal of the last occupying troops from Germany in 1930, five years earlier than the date laid down at Versailles.

Reconciliation in Europe, 1924–29

Pact of Paris, (Briand-Kellogg), 1928

In Germany during these years Stresemann as Foreign Minister continued to be the most important figure. His death in 1929 removed a statesman who, though a strong German nationalist and always working basically for Germany, had also done much for European peace. At home Germany by 1929 was benefiting from her new stable currency. The nation, too, had confidence in the President elected on Ebert's death in 1925 – the seventy-seven-year-old Hindenburg, who reluctantly agreed to stand when the original ballot failed to give any of the seven candidates a clear majority. The election of this aged warrior with his strongly traditional

Germany

President Hindenburg, 1925

outlook and Prussian soldierly virtues, however, was a sign that Germany had not disowned her military heroes, and might be looking back nostalgically to her imperial past. The increasing prosperity, too, rested on foundations which seemed solid enough before 1929 – loans raised largely from wealthy America – but which were to prove all too shaky in the storms that lay ahead.

American loans

The France of these years was also a country which seemed to be winning through to prosperity. During the early post-war years a coalition of the parties of the right and centre known as the *bloc national* had dominated the Chamber. Its ministries under Clemenceau, the former socialist Mitterand, and Poincaré had done their best to wring reparations payments out of Germany and to improve France's security by allying with Poland and by proposing new frontier defences.[1] They also put much effort, successfully, into the restoration of war-shattered north-east France. This was costly, and placed a great strain on France at a time when she had just suffered huge losses in men, material and overseas investments. The French governments of these years, however, were reluctant to face the need for higher taxation; they relied far too much on German reparations (which proved hard to get), on borrowing, and on printing excessive amounts of paper money. By 1924 the face value of the paper money in circulation was six times that in circulation in 1914, without any increase in the supporting gold reserves. With such inflation the franc had become weak, and it grew weaker still under the Radical-Socialist coalition – the *cartel des gauches* – which won the election of 1924. Under the Prime Minister of this coalition, Herriot, France did much to help international reconciliation by withdrawing troops from the Ruhr, accepting the Dawes Plan, and recognising Soviet Russia. Financial difficulties, however, became worse, the budget was unbalanced, and Herriot's government fell in July 1925.

France

Bloc national, 1919–24

War damage restored

Weakness of franc

Cartel des gauches, 1924–25: Herriot premier

There ensued a desperate search for some fresh combination of political forces capable of achieving stability. In the course of twelve months, no less than six different ministries were formed – one, under Herriot in July 1926, lasting only a day. After this fiasco, Poincaré took over in an atmosphere of national emergency at the head of a right and centre coalition. His ministry included five former premiers (among them Herriot) and was drawn from all parties except the Socialists and Communists. Helped by the improvement in international trade, he was able to restore financial stability by such orthodox methods as increasing the taxes, collecting them more efficiently, and reducing expenditure. By the end of 1926 the franc had regained much of its value – from over 240 to the pound it recovered to 120 – and in 1928 Poincaré was able to put France back once more on the gold standard.[2] When Poincaré relinquished office in July 1929, France was more stable and prosperous than at any time since 1914.

Poincaré again, 1926–29

Finance strengthened

While France and Germany in these years remained democracies, Italy under Mussolini became increasingly a dictatorship. The Fascist victory in the elections of 1923 still left opposition parties in the Italian parliament, where one of the

Italy

---

[1] A vast and costly plan for excavated modern defences was devised in the 1920s, approved in 1927–28, and begun in 1929. This was the Maginot Line, so-called after the Minister of War under whom it was begun.

[2] When a country is on the gold standard gold is usually freely available on request at banks in exchange for paper money, and the amount of paper money printed is controlled rigidly, any sum beyond an approved total having to be covered by government reserves of gold. Britain returned to the gold standard (which was general before 1914) in 1925, and went off again in the economic crisis of 1931.

Socialist leaders, Matteotti, was bitingly critical of Mussolini. In June 1924 Matteotti paid for his outspokenness: some Fascists kidnapped and murdered him. The resulting outcry was great and the remaining Socialist deputies seceded from parliament to set up an opposition elsewhere. Mussolini, however, rode the storm. Acting within powers granted him by parliament, he dismissed the non-fascists from his cabinet, removed non-fascists as far as he could from local government, instituted a stricter censorship and a secret police, and disbanded all other political parties. By 1925 he was not even technically responsible to parliament. Prime Minister and President of the Fascist Grand Council, he was the Italian leader, *Il Duce*.

The Matteotti murder, 1924

Mussolini's dictatorship

Mussolini's declared policy was not, of course, simply to extend his own power. Against communist encouragement of class warfare as a means to a new society, he preached the need to unite all classes in service to the existing state. An upholder of private property and differences in wealth and status, he nevertheless believed that the welfare of the individual should be strictly subordinate to that of the nation. These ideas underlay the gradual development of what Fascists called 'the corporate state'. In this, corporations including employers and employed were created for each main industry in place of the old trade unions, together with other corporations representing non-industrial activity and the professions. These corporations were given powers of supervision and arbitration in the activity concerned and by 1928 they were entrusted with the task of nominating most of the candidates for the Italian parliament.

The Corporate State

Mussolini's dictatorship, though greatly restricting freedom, was not exercised with anything like the same cruelty and thoroughness as that which the Communists were already enforcing in Russia, or that which Hitler was later to impose in Germany. It sat, on the whole, fairly lightly on the Italian people, who were quite prepared to accept minor Fascist bullying if it brought an end to incessant strikes and lock-outs, more efficient public services, and greater respect for Italy in the outside world. Moreover, after an early clash with Greece in 1923, when Italy temporarily occupied the Greek island of Corfu, Mussolini in these years did not embark on any military adventures. Instead, he collaborated with the main European powers in such conciliatory developments as the Locarno treaties.

The Corfu Incident, 1923

Mussolini also set out to resolve one great conflict within Italy itself – that between the Italian State and the Roman Catholic Church. From the time when Victor Emmanuel II's forces had occupied Rome in 1870 in defiance of its papal government and made it their capital, successive Popes had refused to emerge from the Vatican or to recognise the loss of the city and their temporal power. After three years of negotiations, Mussolini succeeded in healing this breach. By the Lateran Pacts of 1929 the Vatican at last recognised the rule of the House of Savoy over the whole of Italy, and that Rome should be the capital of the kingdom. In return, Mussolini agreed to compensate the Vatican for the papal losses, to recognise papal sovereignty over an independent neutral territory – the Vatican City – about a mile square in Rome, to acknowledge that Catholicism was the state religion, and to accept a number of other papal requirements including the restriction of divorce and the compulsory teaching of religion in schools. Naturally this was a great satisfaction to millions in a country as Catholic as Italy who had been concerned about some of the earlier anti-religious pronouncements of the Fascists. Together with the greater political stability, the fast increasing industrial prosperity

Lateran Pacts, 1929

and the beginning of a great new programme of public works, it helped to commend Mussolini whole-heartedly to the Italian people.

The general settling-down of Europe between 1924 and 1929 was also seen in Soviet Russia. This was largely because Lenin's New Economic Policy of 1921–22, allowing the peasant once more to sell much of his produce as he wished, was allowed to continue. The peasants regained a direct financial interest in their out-

The N.E.P. continues

put, the food supply greatly improved, and the benefits were felt throughout Russia. At the same time some of the peasants with the larger holdings – the class known as *kulaks*, who were allowed to employ hired labour – naturally grew more prosperous than their less fortunate neighbours and the workers in the towns. This, and the whole idea of private ownership, production and distribution in so important a sphere as agriculture, was an affront to communist theory. The Communist leaders saw the danger of allowing a class to flourish on practices opposed to communism, and become anxious to end these concessions as soon as possible. First, however, they had to settle their own internal struggle for power within the Communist Party.

Power-struggle in the Communist Party

Their struggle had begun before the death of Lenin in 1924 and it continued in a still more intense form afterwards. Though several other leading figures were involved, the main contenders for the mantle of Lenin were Trotsky and Stalin.

Trotsky

Trotsky had been Lenin's chief lieutenant, almost his partner, during the Revolution and the civil war. His brilliant talents as an orator, a writer, a theorist and an organiser were unmatched among the Bolshevik leaders after Lenin's death. But he was no man for half-measures or compromise: he detested the New Economic Policy and had fallen out with Lenin about it, and he was all for trying to establish a communist society rapidly not merely in Russia but everywhere else. Indeed, he did not see how a single communist state could survive in a capitalist world. He had expected war-weary Europe to crumble into communism in 1918, and when it did not he thought Russia should foment communist insurrection in other states as widely as possible. This view was challenged as impracticable while there were still so many problems to be solved inside Russia itself. Several of the leaders opposed Trotsky, but the one who did so most effectively was Josef Stalin.

Stalin (b. 1879)

Stalin – man of *stal*, or steel – was not his real name, but it suited him very well. It was about the sixth he had adopted during a long revolutionary career. Born of peasant stock in Georgia in the Caucasus, he was put to study for the priesthood, but was expelled from his theological college – by his own account for spreading Marxism. In turn teacher and scientific worker, he became an ardent Social Democrat – at first a Menshevik, later a Bolshevik – helped to organise strikes, and suffered imprisonment and exile to Siberia (whence he rapidly escaped). As a tireless, if exceptionally vindictive, party worker he came to Lenin's notice and was on hand in Petrograd to help during the October Revolution. Later he played a prominent part in fighting the Whites during the Civil War. But it was not until 1922, when he became General Secretary of the Communist Party's Central

Stalin's Party position

Committee, that he achieved a position of real power. That he had done so was not at first fully appreciated, partly because Stalin was unspectacular and taciturn – according to Trotsky a 'mediocrity' – but also because the position itself had not been a dominant one. However, with the growth of the Party to some 500,000 members, the banning of all other parties, the discouragement of group controversy within the Party itself, and the extension of Party control over almost all aspects of Russian life, the position of the top administrator became extremely important. Stalin, a born intriguer, knew how to make the most of his opportunities – not least by arranging for other leading members of the Party to undertake tasks in the remoter regions, while he himself remained at the centre of the web in Moscow.

Stalin's triumph over Trotsky, who was not helped by his quarrelsome nature, was achieved in three or four main stages. Early in 1925 Trotsky was forced out of his post as Commissar for War and assigned to lesser duties. At the end of that year Stalin won a battle at the Party Congress against the Trotskyites by securing approval for his policy of 'Socialism in one country', as opposed to Trotsky's policy of 'permanent revolution' involving continuous major efforts to bring about revolutions elsewhere. The following year Trotsky lost his place in the Politburo, the main policy-making committee of the Party. In 1927 he and several followers were actually expelled from the Party; and finally, two years later, he was deported from Russia. Even then, Stalin's fears and enmity persisted, for Trotsky was still active in exile. (The feud was to continue into the '30s, when Stalin had most of Trotsky's real or imaginary supporters in Russia executed, and it ended only in 1940. In that year, when Trotsky was busy in Mexico writing a critical life of Stalin, a Russian visitor secured an interview with him and cleft his skull with an ice-axe.)

Eclipse of Trotsky

Not until this struggle was resolved was Stalin free to proceed with his own policy of first building up 'Socialism in one country'. The basis was laid in work done by the State Planning Commission and in a decision by the Party Congress in 1926 to transform Russia from an agrarian country into an industrial one. 'We are fifty or a hundred years behind the advanced countries', said Stalin later, 'We must make good this lag in ten years. Either we do it or they crush us'. In conformity with this policy the first Five Year Plan was launched in October 1928 with the object of doubling, by 1933, the output of consumer goods, tripling that of heavy industry (coal, iron and steel, oil, machinery) and achieving a six-fold increase in electrical power. But the building up of a massive industrial state on socialist lines did not accord with the progress of agriculture on much more personal and capitalist lines, as was happening under the 1921 New Economic Policy. So the decision was also taken to apply socialism to agriculture – at first by 'persuading' the peasants to merge their holdings and stock into large 'collective' farms which would run without private profit to the cultivators. With this decision Stalin and his colleagues also hoped to modernize Russian agriculture, secure the benefits of large scale farming, and feed at minimum cost the urban workers on whom the burden of the Five Year Plan would fall.

Decision for 'socialism in one country' – (1925)

– and industrialisation (1926)

First Five Year Plan, 1928

Decision to socialise agriculture, 1928

The policy of 'persuasive' collectivisation in agriculture had only a limited success. Some of the poorer peasants agreed to be collectivised, but the better-off with more land – the *Kulaks* – hung back. In May 1929 Stalin and his colleagues accordingly decided to make collective farming compulsory. The stage was now set for an all-out offensive against the main cultivators. In the next three years this was to bring death or exile to millions of Russians, famine or deprivation to millions more. Together with the fierce demands of the Five Year Plan in industry it was to end the illusion, growing over the years 1924–28, that the Soviet leadership was adopting gentler forms of progress.

Compulsory collectivisation, 1929: turmoil in Russia

Though trade and industry picked up almost everywhere in Europe during the years 1924–29, some of the less powerful states found more stability in dictatorship,

Other dictatorships

as in Italy, than in parliamentary democracy. This happened in Poland, where Pilsudski achieved a dominating position in 1926; in Spain, where General Primo de Rivera, backed by King Alphonso XIII, ruled more or less as a dictator from 1923 to 1930; in Portugal, both under General Carmona and then increasingly from 1929 under Dr Salazar; and in Yugoslavia, where King Alexander took dictatorial powers to prevent the break-up of the country into its different national components. All this was a bad omen for democracy in the years that lay ahead, when economic conditions were to be less favourable.

Europe's hopes in 1929

In general, however, after five years of comparative stability Europe approached the 1930s with optimism. Much was still expected of the League of Nations: idealists in Britain, though not many elsewhere, imagined that it had a life and power of its own beyond the changing policies of its members. Much was hoped from the labours, beginning in 1926, of the League's Preparatory Commission for a great Disarmament Conference, to meet when proposals were farther advanced. Problems and misunderstandings among the powers of Europe still abounded as 1929 drew to its close, but at least the fund of goodwill seemed greater than ever.

The 'Great Slump' in U.S.A., October 1929

In October 1929, however, an economic blizzard struck the mainstay of Europe's prosperity, the U.S.A. Within a few months its repercussions were destroying Europe's new-found stability and bringing nearer to power the main cause of the Second World War – Adolf Hitler.

CHAPTER 22
The Nineteen-Thirties and the Road to the Second World War

1. The Great Depression and the Rise of Adolf Hitler, 1929–34

The impact of the Great Slump on Europe, and particularly on Germany, has to be seen against the state of international relations at the time. Though good progress had been made towards reconciliation, the defeated powers of 1918 naturally still harboured grievances. Territorially, the most important were that Hungary longed to recover the Hungarian areas in Rumania and Czechoslovakia, and Germany deeply resented the Polish Corridor and the loss of Danzig. Other grievances included seemingly-endless reparations and the failure of the former Allies to carry out what Germany maintained was an undertaking to disarm.

Continuing grievances in Germany

This last grievance was to some extent a propaganda point on the part of Germany, but the disparity of arms did genuinely strike at her national pride – and, of course, at her chances of rectifying her other grievances by force. There was also the fact that without arms she would be powerless to resist an attack from France or Poland (neither of which in the 1930s had any such intention – but the French had occupied the Ruhr in 1923). These considerations had led Germany in the 1920s to begin a good deal of secret rearmament – for instance, by sending pilots to train on military aircraft in Russia. Nevertheless she was clearly at a disadvantage and the more so because although after 1925–26 she had the benefit of the Locarno guarantee of her western frontiers and membership of the League, she also felt herself surrounded by potential enemies – or at least with states which would resist any changes in the Treaty of Versailles. France still had defensive alliances with Poland and with the members of the 'Little Entente' – Czechoslovakia, Rumania and Yugoslavia.

Germany and disarmament

France's security system

In these circumstances the Germans naturally hoped the former Allies would disarm, as promised, to the 'lowest level consistent with national security' (though ideas of this level could differ widely). During the 1920s Germany repeatedly called on the victors to reduce their arms; but – Britain and the U.S.A. apart – once they had made the initial return to a peacetime establishment they carried out little further disarmament except in the naval sphere. For years the subject was debated while preparations went forward for a great Disarmament Conference. At one of the sessions of the Preparatory Commission the Russian delegate, Litvinov, suggested the disbandment of all armies, navies and air forces. This was

Disarmament Conference, active 1932–33

CHILDREN'S FORCES IN THE U.S.S.R.
All the totalitarian powers had military or semi-military organisations for the training of the young in large numbers. These are young Communists in Russia in 1923.

naturally treated as the propaganda exercise it was. At last, in 1932, the Disarmament Conference really did meet. The American proposal of an all-round cut of one-third was regarded as unfair and impractical, and the experts were left to argue vainly about other schemes. The Conference virtually ended in 1933 but was not formally wound up till 1936. No agreement at all was reached. The subject was in fact enormously complicated, but this was no consolation to Germany.

Such was roughly the position in Europe when, in late 1929 and 1930, the effects of the 'Great Crash' in America began to link up with other factors which were to cause a world-wide depression. The 'Great Crash' itself, beginning with such nightmare events as 'Black Thursday' (24th October 1929) on the New York Stock Exchange was to a large extent a collapse of confidence. Nearly 13 million shares were hastily sold, causing during the month of October a loss of 40,000 million dollars to American investors. In the post-war boom conditions in America, stock values had been pushed up to unrealistic heights – the average rise was about sixty per cent during 1928–29 – not only by professional investors and speculators but by an increasing urge on the part of the general public to 'get in on' the easy profits. The stock market, however, is a very sensitive – perhaps over-sensitive – barometer of outside conditions. Once there are signs that a boom may be ending, sales by investors anxious to dispose of their holdings while the going is still good may start an avalanche of similar sales, and so bring about not just a lowering of

The 'Great Crash' in U.S.A., October 1929

prices but a virtual collapse of the market. In this case, one of the earliest signs was a steady fall in the price of North American grain from 1927 onwards as European agriculture increased in efficiency and as European currencies, returning to the gold standard, became more valuable. Food production – the same became true of meat, coffee, fruit and other foodstuffs produced outside western Europe – was outdistancing the ability of the industrial world to absorb it all. Millions in China, India and elsewhere were starving for lack of food; but they could not afford to buy it, however low the price. American agriculture was over-producing in relation to its possible market, and as a result its prices were falling to a level which would soon spell ruin to the producers. But a decline in agricultural prosperity is not felt in isolation. Poor farmers cease to buy new machinery and household goods, sell their investments, default on their borrowings. A chain-reaction, doubtless also caused by many other factors, sets in. Share prices in a huge array of apparently unrelated concerns may soon be tumbling dramatically downwards.

Agricultural over-production

The effect of the American stock market collapse was felt in Europe only gradually. The first countries to suffer its impact seriously were Germany and Austria during 1930. They had become heavily dependent on American loans to pay their debts and to finance their industrial development and building works. Most of these sums had been lent for short periods; and with American investors hard-hit, they were not renewed. Without the loans, the pace of German industry slackened; workers had to be laid off and unemployment mounted. This meant not only an industrial recession within Germany, but a falling-off of Germany's trade with the rest of the world. And so the repercussions spread as international trade steadily declined and as the standard remedies taken by the various countries to protect their own interests only made matters worse internationally. Such measures, notably the introduction of high protective tariffs and the cutting back of government expenditure, when widely applied had the effect of strangling world trade still further.

Drying up of American foreign loans – effect on Germany

Growth of world economic crisis, 1930–33

The governments in power at the time of the slump nearly all suffered the consequences at the next elections, though it was not especially their fault. In the U.S.A. the era of Republican government, dating from the defeat of Wilson and the Democrats in 1920, ended in 1932 when Franklin D Roosevelt was elected president to put through his 'New Deal' for 'the forgotten man' – the sharply increasing ranks of the poor and the destitute.[1] This involved much greater intervention by the federal government in economic affairs than the Americans had ever before tolerated – intervention in such forms as unemployment relief, federal aid to farmers, and big schemes of public works. In Britain the Labour ministry failed to balance the budget and with unemployment figures at two and three-quarter million had to make way for a National Government. This was quickly compelled to abandon the gold standard (as did most other countries) and to reverse Britain's historic policy of free trade; and was soon faced with almost three million unemployed. One of the few countries in which the government remained undisturbed was Russia, where Stalin's grip was by now complete. At that time Russia was too isolated and self-sufficient to be much affected by the general trade depression. Sympathisers in the West, however, were naturally quick to claim that it was communist planning which brought immunity.

Effect on governments

National Government in Britain, 1931

[1] By 1933 there were sixteen million unemployed in the USA.

GERMANY TRIES THE
HAT FASHIONS
*A cartoon of 1932 by
K. Arnold in the German magazine* Simplicissimus. *The German
caption reads 'Nothing
to wear, but depressed
by the new hat fashions.'
This is a satire on the
political choices available
at the time. Germany is
trying on the steel-helmet
of the Stahl-helm, a
semi-military organisation of the right wing,
and is handling a clerical
hat and the peaked cap
of the Nazi. Other hats
on the stand refer to the
royalists (the crown),
the nationalists (top hat),
and the communists
(with hammer and sickle).*

Germany, 1930–33

    The slump was not the only factor which brought Hitler to power in Germany, but it certainly helped. Weak coalition governments from 1929 onwards found themselves unable to deal with the economic troubles and the mounting unemployment. Social unrest grew, and people began to look to the extremists to straighten things out – to the Nazis with their ardent nationalism and socialistic tendencies, or to the Communists with their vision of world revolution and international socialism. Their respective supporters clashed frequently in the streets.

Nazi gains in 1930 elections

In the elections of 1930, though the Social Democrats won the largest number of seats, the Nazis secured 107 and the Communists 77. The next year the economic recession worsened when one of the biggest Austrian banks, the Credit Anstalt, failed, and a run on the German banks followed. The mark sank rapidly in value, business wilted, and by 1932 the unemployment figures had reached six million. Hitler now challenged Hindenburg in the election for the Presidency. At the second and final stages he polled nearly $13\frac{1}{2}$ million votes as against Hindenburg's $19\frac{1}{4}$ million. Shortly afterwards in the general elections the Nazis won 230 seats. They were now the strongest party in the Reichstag, and Hitler could no longer be denied a share in power.

    It was, however, a miscalculating right-wing politician – Franz von Papen, leader of a small group with industrial and nationalist links – who eased Hitler's way. Von Papen persuaded Hindenburg that he could deal with the situation with Hitler's support and could at the same time keep Hitler under control. This was like trying to ride on the back of a tiger. The aged field-marshal, who had no love for the former corporal, reluctantly sanctioned the experiment. On 30th January

Hitler Chancellor, January 1933

TOTALITARIAN IDEALS: NAZI AND COMMUNIST 'ART' OF THE 1930S
Above left : The Third Reich *Painting by Prof. Richard Klein.*
Above right : Soviet Workers *Statue by Vera Mukhina*
for the Russian pavilion at the 1937 International Exhibition in Paris.

1933 Hitler became Chancellor and von Papen Vice-Chancellor. Only three seats in the cabinet of twelve went to Nazis. The rest went to men of the right who imagined, wrongly, that they would be calling the tune.

The next elections were scheduled for March 1933. Before they could take place the Reichstag went up in flames. The probability is that this was solely the work of the half-mad Dutch communist who was executed for it; but the Nazis maintained it was part of a planned Communist insurrection – there had already been Communist riots in protest against unemployment – while the Communists swore that it was a Nazi trick to discredit them. The Nazis of course played up the crime for all it was worth; and the elections were held in an atmosphere of violence and anti-communist hysteria. The Nazis got forty-four per cent of the votes – more than any other party. They lost no time in pressing home their victory. As soon as the new Reichstag met – with Nazi stormtroopers lining the corridors – it sanctioned the granting of unrestricted powers for four years to Hitler and his new all-Nazi government. Hitler was now complete dictator – or, as he preferred to put it, *Führer* (leader) of Germany. Though his rise had been greatly helped by strong-arm methods against opponents, he had got there – like Mussolini in

Elections, March 1933

Reichstag fire

Enabling Act: Hitler dictator, March 1933

Italy – legally, and because very large numbers of Germans saw in him some kind of saviour. He was, of course, a hypnotic orator, but his appeal went far beyond this. Many Germans who were not at first Nazis were attracted by his personality, or at least by the image of it skilfully put over by his propaganda chief, Josef Goebbels. As he appeared to the public, Hitler was a man utterly without self-interest. Unmarried (though of course fond of children), and despising wealth and show and class distinction, he cared only for Germany. When in due course people joined his movement and marched about their towns or villages in their brown shirts with swastika armbands, they felt a warm glow of purpose and unity. Hitler had 'made them all one', regardless of wealth and class. Rich and poor, employer and employed, all were working together happily for the Fatherland.

Basically, then, Hitler's appeal was to patriotism; and its strength was the greater because it drew on the power not only of love but of hate. The troubles of Germany, Hitler averred, had not been caused by true, patriotic, racially pure Germans. They were the fault, he declared, of internationally-minded socialists and communists whose doctrines stemmed from the Jew Karl Marx, and whose revolutions 'stabbed Germany in the back' in November 1918 while her armies were still undefeated. They were the fault of these same communists who created disorder in the streets and in the factories on orders from Moscow. They were likewise the fault of Britain, France and others who at Versailles had nailed the lie of war guilt on Germany, and under that excuse had kept her disarmed, tried to wring vast sums from her, and torn away her Empire and even parts of the sacred *Reich* itself. They were the fault, too, of the German régime – the Weimar Republic – which had tolerated these restrictions. And above all, Hitler insisted, Germany's woes were without question the fault of the Jews, who had become communist leaders, flooded into Germany in large numbers from eastern Europe, flourished in business by sharp practice at the expense of simple folk, and launched degenerate movements in art and entertainment. If he should come to power, the German people understood, Hitler would suppress the Communist Party, rebuild Germany's might, release her from the shackles of the Versailles treaty, and enhance her racial purity by freeing her from the Jews. He would also sponsor much-needed social reforms and big programmes of public works, and in so doing would cure unemployment. In addition, those who had read *Mein Kampf* and took it seriously – though this was not many – knew that Hitler would also aim to acquire living-space (*lebensraum*) for Germany in the great grainlands of eastern Europe at the expense of the Poles and the Russians. In the circumstances of 1933, this programme looked good enough to forty-four per cent of German voters for them to put Hitler into power. And once he was in power they had no way short of a revolution of getting him out again, even had they wanted to.

This is little evidence that they had any such wish. Hitler's régime was overthrown in 1945 not because the German people withdrew its support but because Germany's enemies had developed overwhelming military strength. Until 1939 his government was a mixture of effiency and persecution apparently quite satisfactory to most Germans, though bitterly resented by a minority, who were not given an opportunity for self-expression. Within a few weeks of receiving dictatorial powers, Hitler dissolved all political parties other than the Nazis: not only communists but socialists, liberals and even conservatives were driven out of official existence. The German trade unions, too, were disbanded and a govern-

Hitler's appeal to patriotism –

– and national hatreds

Hitler's enemies – Jews, Communists, Versailles powers, Weimar régime

Hitler's programme

Hitler's first steps in Germany

suppression

ment-run Labour Front set up instead. No time was lost in launching the campaign against Germany's half-million Jews – at first mainly by business boycotts and exclusion from professions and official positions. Little outcry was raised against all this. The attentions of Nazi Brownshirts and the possibility of a spell in a 'concentration camp' quickly limited opposition to only the boldest spirits. On the more constructive side, Hitler, as he had promised, soon began to restore economic prosperity and reduce unemployment. He did this partly by public works, including big schemes of roadbuilding, but much more by stepping up the pace of Germany's rearmament. This had already been going on secretly for some time, though in a small way. Under Hitler, though the mask of secrecy was not thrown off until 1935, the orders were soon for full steam ahead.

rearmament

Though there was never a rising against Hitler in his first years of power there was an episode in 1934 which he treated as one. Many of the 'old guard' of the s.a. who had joined the Nazi movement in its earlier days still cherished the 'Socialist' part of its title as well as the 'National'. They wished to see Hitler extend his revolution in a socialist direction by taking over great industrial concerns and redistributing wealth. The head of the s.a., Ernst Röhm, a former army officer and a leading henchman of Hitler's since the days of his 1923 *putsch*, shared some of these opinions. He was eager to see the small regular army of 100,000 men and the s.a., now over two million strong, merged into a single military force under his own command. Hitler, on the other hand, knew that socialistic measures would offend industrialists and disorganise industry just when he badly needed an economic revival, and that to impose the s.a. and Röhm on the army would bitterly offend the military chiefs. If he was to re-establish Germany as a power in Europe, he needed the heads of German industry and the German army solidly behind him. Some sort of bargain appears to have been struck between him and the army leaders, as a condition of their further support, that he would tame the s.a. and the ambitious Röhm.

Action against Röhm and the s.a., July 1934

The task was entrusted mainly to Göring as Minister President of Prussia and Himmler as head of the Prussian Gestapo or secret police and commandant of the black-jacketed s.s. (Schutzstaffeln, or rifle squadrons) – at that time an élite branch of the s.a. They arranged the blow for the night of Friday 29th/30th July – 'the night of the long knives', as it came to be called – and the succeeding two days. s.s. squads rounded up and shot Röhm and other s.a. leaders, together with some notabilities thought dangerous to Hitler's leadership. The killings at Munich, Berlin and elsewhere, numbered anything from seventy-seven – the official total – to several hundred. The deed done, Hitler informed the German people that a conspiracy by Röhm and his associates had been foiled, and that the traitors had got their deserts.

A few weeks later the aged President Hindenburg died. Gratified by Hitler's recent death-blow to the ambitions of the s.a., the Army chiefs raised no objection when Hitler added the Presidential powers to his existing ones as Chancellor and rolled the two offices into one. As Head of the State Hitler was now also Supreme Commander of the German Armed Forces, and he promptly exacted from all ranks a personal oath of loyalty to himself. A fortnight later, Hitler invited the German people to approve by plebiscite his assumption of Hindenburg's powers and his new official title of Führer and Reich Chancellor. If the figures were not rigged – and there seems to be no evidence that they were, though doubtless

Death of Hindenburg: Hitler takes over Presidential powers, August 1934 many people voted out of fear – nearly ninety-six per cent of the voters went to the polls, and of these nearly ninety per cent voted 'yes'.

2. The Darkening International Scene, 1931–37

Germany leaves the League, October 1933

While establishing his dictatorship Hitler had not been inactive in foreign affairs. His first big move, in October 1933, was to announce that Germany, tired of the broken promises of her former enemies and the stain on her honour by being denied equality of arms, would forthwith leave the Disarmament Conference and the League of Nations. This decision was promptly endorsed by the German people, over ninety per cent of the voters approving it in a plebiscite and on the same day accepting the list of Nazi candidates (there was no other) for the new Reichstag.

The precedent of Japan

The shock of Germany's departure from Geneva was not, however, the first that the League or the world had suffered that year. The first blow against the new framework of 'collective security' had been struck by the Japanese. Japan, whose overpopulated homelands badly needed new sources of raw materials and outlets for surplus population and commercial investments, was particularly hard hit by

Japanese occupation of Manchuria, 1931

the world slump. In 1931 she began a 'forward' policy in China. She already had a railway concession in the Chinese province of Manchuria and on the pretext of damage to this she soon overran the entire province and set up a puppet state there under the name of Manchukuo. The Chinese resisted; but though China was officially a united country ruled by Chiang Kai-Shek's Kuomintang party, in fact it was a divided one with various regions under the control of communist forces or local war lords, and was far too weak to restrain the Japanese.

League condemnation; Japan gives notice of leaving the League, March 1933

Naturally, one of China's first moves was to appeal to the League of Nations. The League in due course condemned Japan's actions and ordered her to withdraw from Manchuria. But when Japan declined to obey, the great powers who virtually operated the League – Britain, France and to a lesser degree Italy – took no further action. They were all hard hit by the slump, and none of them fancied waging war against a major power so far from their home bases in a cause which was not directly their concern. Meanwhile the Japanese, aggrieved at the condemnation, announced their intention of leaving the League. This was in March 1933, and it set the precedent for Hitler to follow seven months later.

Austria: Hitler's desire for *Anschluss*

In July 1934, barely a month after the 'night of the long knives', the Nazis tried their first external *coup*. Its object was to bring Hitler's homeland, Austria, into the German Reich – to carry out, in other words, that *Anschluss* or union between the two countries which had been forbidden by the Treaty of Versailles, and which even in the watered-down form of a proposed customs-union had been vetoed as recently as 1931. The instrument for this purpose was the Nazi party in Austria, which had grown so strong and troublesome during the depression of 1931–33 that in the latter year it had been banned. Its victorious opponents, the moderate and right wing parties led by the Christian Socialist Engelbert Dollfuss –

Dollfuss acts against Nazis and Socialists

a tiny man less than five feet tall inevitably nicknamed in the British press 'The Pocket Chancellor' – had managed to set up a dictatorship of their own, virtually in self-defence; but as the price of his support from the right Dollfuss had to take action not only against the Nazis but also against the Socialists. In February 1934 his attempt to disarm some of their supporters – private political armies had become rife – led to the shelling of one of their centres, the great block of workers' flats in Vienna known as Karl Marx Hof (House).

After this Dollfuss for a few months ruled unchallenged, with the help of a semi-military force organised on fascist lines. But on 25th July 1934 some of the banned Austrian Nazis, as part of a movement concerted with German Nazis over the border, seized the Vienna radio station and announced that the local Nazi leader had taken over the government. At the same time a group of Nazis in police and army uniforms entered the Chancellery and shot Dollfuss, who died three hours later. The plot, however, was badly devised and risings in the provinces were not properly coordinated. The government, despite the loss of Dollfuss – whose place was soon taken by his friend and colleague Kurt Schuschnigg – kept control, and most of the rebel leaders were rounded up. The Nazi who had actually shot Doll-fuss went to the scaffold shouting 'Heil Hitler!'; but Hitler himself quickly denied any connection with the *coup* when its failure became apparent. Indeed he went on, in a treaty of friendship, to acknowledge Austria's full sovereignty. His tactful behaviour was no doubt partly inspired by the fact that Mussolini had taken the murder of Dollfuss very badly. The Italian dictator at this stage was not prepared to see Austrian independence overthrown and a powerful Germany as his neighbour. He concentrated troops on the Brenner frontier, ready to intervene if Hitler moved into Austria.

Attempted Nazi coup, *July 1934: murder of Dollfuss*

Mussolini ready to protect Austrian independence

In acting to defend Austrian independence, Mussolini was of course very much in line with the policy of Britain and France. These countries had no wish to see Germany grow more powerful; and they were becoming very worried about the increasing evidence of Germany's rearmament. This lay behind France's en-couragement of Soviet Russia to join the League of Nations, which she did in September 1934, and the subsequent five-year pact of mutual assistance between France and the U.S.S.R. (in the event of attack by any European country) signed in May 1935. Further point had been given to this by Hitler's reintroduction of conscription, in defiance of Versailles, the previous March. However, the harmony of interest between Britain, France and Italy, which was seen again in discussions at Stresa, in North Italy in April 1935, was soon to be broken.

United policy on Germany

Franco-Soviet Pact, 1935

Encouraged no doubt by the ease with which Japan got her way over Manchuria, Italy, which had long coveted the only large tract of Africa still ruled by Africans, in October 1935 invaded Abyssinia. Preparations had been going on for many months, and doubtless Mussolini thought that his friends the British and French were prepared to turn a blind eye. This time, however, the powers, partly impelled by public opinion, resolved to do something more than protest. The League invoked Article XVI and economic sanctions were quickly applied against Italy. But the policy was not wholeheartedly pressed, some influential quarters in Britain and France disagreeing with it for fear of weakening the common front against Germany. Indeed after two months of sanctions the French premier, Pierre Laval, and the British foreign secretary, Sir Samuel Hoare, concocted a compro-mise scheme by which Italy would be allowed one large part of Abyssinia (which she was conquering with ease – and poison gas) as an outright possession and another large part as a zone of economic expansion and settlement.

Abyssinian crisis, 1935–36

Sanctions, November 1935

Hoare-Laval plan, December 1935

This plan to despoil Abyssinia with Franco-British approval caused an imme-diate outcry in both countries, and Hoare resigned to make way for a successor strongly identified with support of the League, Anthony Eden. Sanctions there-

Resignation of Hoare: Eden Foreign Secretary

DICTATORS – AND ORATORS: MUSSOLINI AND HITLER

At first Hitler seemed to imitate Mussolini. Later he completely dominated and overshadowed him.

fore continued, but the vital oil sanction was never applied, nor was the Suez Canal closed. Mussolini let it be known that he would regard both actions as tantamount to a declaration of war. The question became one of bluff, and Mussolini, relying on the divisions in his opponents' councils, their growing preoccupation with Hitler and their greater reluctance to cause a general conflict, easily outbluffed Britain and France. In the event, the half-hearted sanctions failed to do anything except infuriate Italy, who regarded the whole campaign against her as selfish hypocrisy since Britain and France had acquired large empires in roughly the same manner. In May 1936 Italy was able to declare the whole of Abyssinia annexed, and the following month sanctions were withdrawn. The hostile atmosphere engendered by this episode persisted, Italy left the League, and from then on Mussolini sought friendship not with Britain and France but with Hitler.

It was in the midst of the Abyssinian crisis that Hitler cleverly brought off his next move. The timing was good, for Britain and France were embroiled with Italy and had moved forces to the Mediterranean area in case of attack there by Mussolini. At this juncture, in March 1936, proclaiming that the new Franco-Soviet treaty was incompatible with Locarno, Hitler ordered the German army into the demilitarised zone of the Rhineland. This was German territory, but for Germany to garrison it was forbidden both under the Treaty of Versailles, which

Italy leaves League: Mussolini moves towards Hitler

German army enters demilitarised Rhineland zone, March 1936

Germany had accepted under duress, and under the Locarno treaties, into which Germany had entered voluntarily. How would the guarantors of Locarno react?

Reaction of the powers

Mussolini, offended about the sanctions applied over Abyssinia, was at odds with Britain and France: he would do nothing. Britain, with members of the public naively observing that the Germans 'were only going into their own back garden', also decided to do nothing – except, of course, protest. The French, more directly concerned and able to intervene on the spot, were in two minds. Had Britain's reaction been stronger, the French Cabinet, which was divided, might have moved their army into the Rhineland to expel the German troops. As it was, all they could agree on was to refer the matter to the League. Had the French marched, their forces would have far outmatched the Germans, and they would have met no opposition: the German commanders were carrying sealed orders to retire if the French intervened. This was Hitler's concession to his army chiefs, who were deeply conscious of Germany's military inferiority and advised against the whole operation. The gamble was Hitler's own, and it paid handsomely.

The entry of the German army into the demilitarised Rhineland proved to be a turning point in the inter-war years. It was the last occasion on which one of Hitler's breaches of Versailles could have been stopped easily. British public opinion at the time would have been aghast at the very idea of war with Germany to prevent her doing what she liked with her own territory; but once the Germans could fortify their frontier with France any attempt to oppose them in future would be infinitely more difficult. Henceforth the French could never enter Germany easily if Hitler should attack France's allies Poland or Czechoslovakia. In March 1936, bloodlessly, Hitler won a great strategic victory.

Bloodless victory for Hitler

From 1936 to 1939 a sustained crisis hung over Europe in the form of the Spanish Civil War. Spain had done well out of neutrality in the 1914–18 war, and for some years had flourished under the semi-dictatorship of General Primo de Rivera. The development of industry and modern communications, however, though affecting only parts of the country, had introduced new labour problems and sources of unrest. To Spain's age-old trouble of separatism (the desire of the different regions, especially Catalonia and the Basque country, for institutions and policies of their own) were now added the newer twentieth-century troubles of strikes and political parties devoted to overthrowing, or at least reshaping, the existing order of things. There was certainly plenty that needed changing, for the Church still had enormous wealth and privileges, and there were appalling contrasts between the riches of many grandee landowners and big industrialists and the extreme poverty of many peasants and urban workers. Republicanism began to flourish, to challenge the hold of Monarchy, Army and Church, the main republican groups at first being liberals and moderate socialists. Together these parties and the Catalonian separatists, though they had little real unity, began to dominate the scene. In 1931 they managed to secure the departure of Alphonso XIII and a big majority in the Cortes, and established a republic.

Spain

Developments, 1914–30

Spanish republic declared, 1931

The Spanish republic, however, after its first burst of reform fared badly. It ran into the world depression, which led to unemployment. Moreover its legislation, such as banning the Jesuit order and church schools, and its measures against the big landlords, while they offended traditional circles, did not go far enough to satisfy the growing number of extremists on the left – communists, syndicalists and anarchists. These adopted wrecking-tactics – strikes, riots, burning churches

Troubles of the republic, 1931–36

– which soon produced a swing to the right among the general public, the creation of a fascist movement known as the *Falange*, and the election in 1933 of a right-wing government. Against this an alliance of the left-wing parties and the Catalans was formed, and many outbreaks (including about four general strikes) were attempted. In 1934 there was a big strike by the coalminers of the Asturias region, which the government put down with troops of the Foreign Legion led by General Franco. In the fighting the city of Oviedo was devastated and more than 3,000 people lost their lives. Such violence by the government helped to produce a swing back to the left, and in February 1936 brought to power a combination of the leftist parties known as the *Frente Popular* (Popular Front).

Popular Front government, 1936

The anti-capitalist and anti-clerical legislation of the Popular Front government, coupled with its failure to prevent strikes, riots, arson, assassinations and the like, soon produced a hardening and consolidation of forces on the right. Under the name of Nationalists, and soon to be led by General Franco, they launched in July 1936 a series of revolts beginning in Morocco but quickly spreading to the mainland.

Franco

These revolts led to a bitter struggle in which the Nationalists (the forces of Franco and the Army, the Church, conservatism and 'Big Business') were ranged against the Republicans (the legal government, the Basques, the Catalans, liberals, socialists, communists and anarchists – among others). By the end of 1936 the Nationalists controlled three-fifths of Spain and had set up their own government under Franco at Burgos, but the Republicans held Madrid, Barcelona and the foremost industrial areas. The fighting was prolonged and fierce, and the reprisals against opponents exceptionally savage by the relatively civilised standards of Europe in those days. Britain and France resolutely tried to maintain a policy of non-intervention from outside, but this was flagrantly broken by Italy and Germany on behalf of Franco, and Russia on behalf of the legitimate government. These three powers were not only manoeuvring for position, but were also using the occasion as a dress rehearsal for a European war by trying out tactics and equipment – German planes, for instance, tried an exercise in obliteration against the Basque township of Guernica. Help from outside also came in the form of volunteers – mainly of left-wing sympathies – recruited into International Brigades, operating with one exception on the Republican side. Russia abandoned intervention first, and this speeded on Franco's final success, though he was also much helped by the violent, not to say murderous, divisions among his opponents.

Spanish Civil War, 1936–39: Nationalists v. Republicans

Anglo-French non-intervention; German, Italian and Russian intervention

The final Republican stronghold, Madrid, fell in March 1939, and Franco then ruled supreme. This was a dangerous result for Britain and France, since he seemed likely to remain in the German and Italian camp. Throughout, the Anglo-French position was extremely delicate, for Britain and France had no wish to intervene, but also no desire to see German and Italian influence permeate Spain. They were, moreover, by 1936 becoming alive to the danger of the German air force which Hitler had so swiftly called into being. Throughout these troubled years, and particularly in the Czechoslovak crisis of 1938, the inferiority of British and French air power to a *Luftwaffe* thought to be expanding at an unparalleled rate, was to be a governing factor in many minds, and to help determine Anglo-French policy along lines of caution.

Fall of Madrid, March 1939: Franco supreme

One of the reasons why Russia ceased to intervene in the Spanish Civil War was that her armed forces at home were in the midst of a savage 'purge'. The origins of

Russia in the 1930s

this go back to the struggle between Stalin and Trotsky and the latter's expulsion from Russia in 1929. As we have seen,[1] Stalin's policy of 'socialism in one country', involving the collectivisation of agriculture and rapid industrialisation by means of the Five Year Plan, had been put into practice. Though the Plan was declared to be successfully fulfilled by 1932 – a year ahead of schedule – and a second Five Year Plan inaugurated, the great industrial advance was achieved only at fearful cost to the Russian people. Big new industrial centres were created in the Caucasus, the Urals and Siberia; roads, canals and railway facilities were built. Oil and coal, iron and steel, the tractors, tanks, aeroplanes and guns came forth in impressive quantities, if not always at first in impressive quality.[2] Housing, clothing, domestic goods and the elementary comforts of life, however, remained desperately short. So, too, did food. The first big drive for collectivisation in 1929–30, as we have seen, was generally resisted and brought about a famine and the loss of perhaps four million lives. After this the pace was slowed down for a year or two but soon resumed, with the result that by 1939 only five per cent of Russian agricultural land remained in the holding of individual peasants. All this, though a remarkable achievement in its ruthless way, provided plenty of grounds for criticism of Stalin's leadership. In a communist country, however, criticism of a leader is dangerous, particularly when the leader is as well entrenched, as determined, as suspicious, and as vengeful as was Stalin.

First Five Year Plan (1928–32)

– and Collectivisation, 1929–39

For those who resisted the collectivisation of their farm and beasts, who grumbled at heavy 'norms' of work in the factory, or who in any way opposed communism or a government decision, there was a standard treatment: confinement in a labour camp. Others were drafted for forced labour not because they were dissidents but simply because they were needed for a given task. All told, it has been estimated that by the late 1930s some 14 million Russians were subject to forced labour and held in camps. Few of these cases concerning ordinary folk came to the attention of the West, but there was another class which did, because the alleged offenders were sometimes well-known and were put on public trial in order to impress others. The first mass trials of this kind were for alleged sabotage of industrial output. They began in 1928, and helped the government to explain away failures to reach target figures in the Five Year Plan. A notorious series occurred in Moscow in 1933, when forty-one technicians of the Metropolitan Vickers Company, including six British subjects, were put on trial and convicted. The Russians were imprisoned, the British expelled.

Forced labour

Sabotage trials, 1928–33

This was mild stuff compared with the 'treason' trials which began in 1934 and went on till 1938. There had already been a purge of party membership in 1933 but the hunt for traitors really got going after the assassination in 1934 of Kirov, one of Stalin's associates in the Politburo. This murder became the signal, or the excuse, for a massive investigation which revealed, so the government said, extensive evidence of treason and counter-revolutionary plots. A wave of arrests followed, and in the course of the next four years countless thousands of the smaller fry, including many lesser officials, were executed by the security police or sent to labour camps. The honour of a set trial in Moscow was reserved mainly for party leaders and army commanders, though the latter were tried in secret.

Treason trials, 1934–38

[1] See pp. 298–99.
[2] By the late 1930s the USSR was producing annually about 133 million tons of coal, 29 million tons of oil, 15 million tons of pig iron, 18 million tons of steel, 200,000 tractors and 200,000 motor vehicles.

Purge of army leaders

In August 1936 such well known former colleagues of Lenin as Zinoviev and Kamenev, besides fourteen others, were accused of working with a foreign power (namely Germany) and Trotsky to overthrow and murder Stalin. They suffered the usual penalty of death. At the beginning of 1937 a further seventeen prominent communists were convicted as Trotskyists and shot. Then came the turn of the military leaders. Marshal Tukhachevsky, Chief of the Red Army, Admiral Orlov, Chief of the Red Navy, and many other senior officers were accused of treason, and followed the same path. Of the eight military judges who condemned them, six were themselves disgraced within eighteen months. Finally in 1938 the victims, accused of conspiring with foreign powers to overthrow Russian socialism and restore capitalism, included the well known editor of *Pravda* Bukharin and the head of the security police, Yagoda, who had faked much of the evidence against the rest and by this time knew too much to be allowed to live. In all it is reckoned that about a fifth of the Communist Party membership was expelled, that about a fifth of the officers of the armed services was arrested and a high proportion of these shot, and that every prominent Bolshevik of the 'old guard' (Lenin's contemporaries) was eliminated except for three. These were Stalin himself, his later foreign minister Molotov, and Trotsky, who was in exile, and whose murder followed in 1940.

Nature of the trials

It was, of course, inconceivable that all these people could have been guilty of the charges levelled against them. Doubtless there was some internal plotting among the higher leaders, because Stalin's leadership had produced grave difficulties and only by a conspiracy could he be removed. The essence of the situation was that Stalin, working through the secret police, was ruthlessly 'liquidating' every possible source and centre of alternative leadership. Not until all possible rivals and all their possible supporters were eliminated could this brutal tyrant rest secure. The puzzling feature to those in the West who read of the trials, however, was that nearly all the main figures – though not the army chiefs – confessed their guilt, and sometimes even confessed to crimes with which they were not charged. Such puzzlement merely displayed an ignorance of the methods employed by the secret police who had custody of the prisoners. Owing to the extensive use of these methods by many totalitarian régimes since then, they have now become well-known. They include repeated interrogation and argument, denial of sleep, administration of drugs and physical torture, all to the point of imminent mental breakdown where death will be a release; and finally, the threat to the victim's friends and family unless he openly admits to guilt.

New Soviet constitution, 1936

These trials made nonsense of the apparent liberality of the new Soviet constitution which Stalin introduced in 1936. This formalised the U.S.S.R. federation of eleven republics, based on a pyramid of soviets or councils from local level upwards. The constitution officially guaranteed personal liberty and the right of the republics to secede, but this aspect of it proved to be merely window-dressing. The reality behind it all was single-party dictatorship ruthlessly exercised by whoever could get control of the party machine.

3. Hitler's March to War: Austria, Czechoslovakia, Poland, 1938–39

The state of affairs revealed by Stalin's purges doubtless persuaded Hitler that for some time to come he had nothing to fear from Russia. In Spain the side he supported was doing well. In Germany his dictatorship was complete, unemployment was falling, the persecution of the Jews was well advanced. With the German armed forces fast increasing, the time seemed ripe to Hitler – never a patient man – to proceed to the next items in his programme. These concerned territories outside Germany. Thus far his only success in this direction, apart from helping Franco, had been a fairly modest one. The Saar territory, detached from Germany in 1919 to be administered for fifteen years by the League of Nations, was in 1935 in accordance with the Versailles Treaty allowed to decide its fate by plebiscite. It was a thoroughly German region and it voted solidly, as expected, for reunion with Germany.

Hitler's foreign programme

Saar to Germany, 1935 (by plebiscite)

Hitler's next external target was much more controversial. High on the Nazi programme had always been the forbidden *Anschluss* or union with Austria. The attempt in 1934, in which Dollfuss was murdered, had misfired and Hitler had denied complicity. Up to the advent of the Nazis Austria had favoured the union of the two countries, but since 1933 opinion there had been deeply divided. By February 1938 Hitler felt ready to settle the matter. He invited the Austrian Chancellor Schuschnigg to Germany for a discussion, and bullied him, under threat of instant invasion, into lifting the ban on the Austrian Nazis, releasing Nazi prisoners, and appointing three Nazi supporters to key posts in his Cabinet. The most important of these appointments was that of Artur Seyss-Inquart, a Nazi of long-standing, as Minister of the Interior. Back in Austria, the shaken Chancellor complied with Hitler's demands, but also arranged to hold a plebiscite on the question of Austrian independence. This was designed to cut the ground from under Hitler's feet by showing that Austria had no wish to merge with Nazi Germany.

Anschluss with Austria

Schuschnigg's plebiscite proposals

On hearing of the projected plebiscite, Hitler at once took action. He spurred the Austrian Nazis into rioting by claiming that the plebiscite would be faked and that Nazis would not be allowed to vote freely. Amid the resulting disorder he then made it clear that his troops would cross the border into Austria to help their fellow Nazis unless Schuschnigg postponed the plebiscite and made way for Seyss-Inquart. Schuschnigg again yielded, but this did not save Austrian independence. On Hitler's instruction Seyss-Inquart called on the Germans to help him suppress the disorders. On the night of 11th/12th March German forces poured across the frontier – Hitler following a few hours later – and by 13th March Austria was declared part of the German Reich. During the following month plebiscites were held in Germany and Austria to endorse Hitler's actions. In Austria the proportion voting in favour of union was declared to be 99.75 per cent.

German ultimatum – dismissal of Schuschnigg

Entry of German army

Austria incorporated in Reich, 13 March 1938

This dramatic *coup* was entirely typical of Hitler in its boldness and treachery. Modern Europe had seen nothing like this overnight swallowing up of an independent state with nearly a thousand years of history behind it. In 1934, Italy had prevented the *Anschluss* by threatening to make the Brenner 'bristle with Italian bayonets'; but in 1938 she was still aggrieved with Britain and France over the sanctions episode. Warned by Hitler just beforehand of what was afoot, Mussolini did not intervene. A startled Europe thus did nothing but protest: in Britain, on the 'why-shouldn't-all-the-Germans-be-allowed-to-get-together' view of things, there was even sympathy for Hitler's action. Meanwhile Hitler – having won another bloodless victory which this time gave him 7 million more subjects,

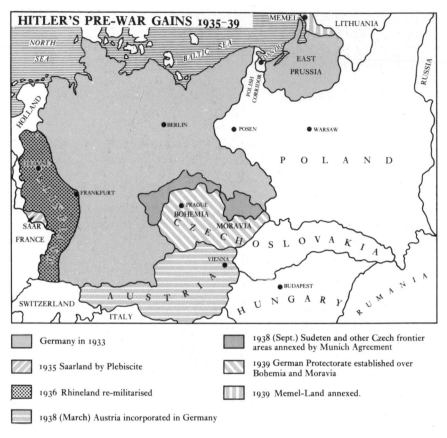

HITLER'S PRE-WAR GAINS 1935–39

NORTH SEA
BALTIC SEA
MEMEL
LITHUANIA
HOLLAND
EAST PRUSSIA
RUSSIA
POLISH CORRIDOR
BERLIN
POSEN
WARSAW
COLOGNE
P O L A N D
FRANKFURT
PRAGUE
BOHEMIA
C Z E MORAVIA
SAAR
FRANCE
C H O S L O V A K I A
VIENNA
SWITZERLAND
A U S T R I A
H U N G A R Y
BUDAPEST
R U M A N I A
ITALY

Germany in 1933

1935 Saarland by Plebiscite

1936 Rhineland re-militarised

1938 (March) Austria incorporated in Germany

1938 (Sept.) Sudeten and other Czech frontier areas annexed by Munich Agreement

1939 German Protectorate established over Bohemia and Moravia

1939 Memel-Land annexed.

extensive territory and a greatly improved strategic position in central Europe – at once began to plan his next *coup*.

Czechoslovakia crisis, May–September 1938

Within a few weeks it became clear that this was to be against Czechoslovakia, a country bitterly hated by Hitler as a Versailles creation where the racially inferior Czechs lorded it over 3 million Germans. These Germans, mostly but not all living in the Sudeten region, had before 1918 been subjects of Austria-Hungary. Hitler's excuse for intervention was that they were persecuted by the dominant Czechs. In point of fact they were among the best treated minority groups in Europe; and the clamour in 1938 by the local Nazis under Konrad Henlein about their oppression was largely made on Hitler's orders. Under the guise of stopping this 'oppression', Hitler's intention was not merely to absorb the Sudeten regions into Germany, but also to break up Czechoslovakia entirely. His motives were not simply racial but strategic; he wanted command of the mountain ranges and mineral wealth of Bohemia, the dismantling of the Czechs' impressive frontier fortifications, the destruction of an outpost of the French 'security' system and the removal of a main obstacle to German expansion eastwards. These motives, however, were by no means fully perceived in Britain, which was still disposed to sympathise with Hitler's declared aim of uniting all Germans within the Reich.

Hitler's motives

Attitude of Britain and France

In face of the rising German press campaign against Czech 'terrorism', Britain and France in the summer of 1938 had to agree what to do at the decisive moment. France had an alliance with Czechoslovakia; Britain had no commitment other

'ON THE GREAT EUROPEAN ROAD'
A Russian cartoon of 1938 giving the Soviet view of the Anglo-French attitude to Germany during the Czechoslovakia crisis. The Nazi thugs (l. to r. Himmler, Hitler, Göring, Göbbels) drive aggressively forward. Two policemen (a very apprehensive E. Daladier, premier of France, and Chamberlain) direct the aggressors away from the road marked 'Western Europe' and down the road marked 'Russia' (C.C.C.P.).

than her general obligations under the Coveneant of the League of Nations to resist aggression. If France aided Czechoslovakia against attack, then by treaty Russia was obliged to support the Czechs. The British and French, however, handled the matter largely without consulting Russia. Their one thought was to avoid war. Finding hints and threats making no impression on Hitler, they put very strong pressure on the Czechs to reach an agreement with Germany – in other words, to give in to Hitler's demands. An important factor in this was the ardent conviction of Neville Chamberlain, Britain's Prime Minister since May 1937, that he could appease Hitler and Mussolini by helping to remedy their grievances – after which, he imagined, the peace of Europe would be secure.

So France, her Cabinet divided and lacking support from Britain for a stronger policy, decided in effect to desert her Czech ally. She asked Chamberlain to get the best terms he could from Hitler for the Czechs. Chamberlain flew to Germany on

Czechs pressed to make concessions

Chamberlain and 'Appeasement'

Chamberlain's flights to Germany, September 1938

15th September, saw – and heard – Hitler, and came back with the view that only a voluntary cession of the Sudetenland by the Czechs could prevent a German attack on Czechoslovakia. During the following week, while Germany stepped up her campaign against Czechoslovakia by spurring Hungary and Poland to demand areas of that country inhabited by Hungarians and Poles, Chamberlain was busy securing French and Czech agreement to the cession. French agreement was of course readily forthcoming; Czech agreement was secured only by an ultimatum that if it were refused, the country would enjoy no further support from Britain and France. On 22nd September a gratified Chamberlain flew off to Germany again to announce to Hitler that he had secured agreement all round on the principle of cession.

Hitler raises his terms

Much to Chamberlain's surprise and indignation, Hitler responded by raising his terms. This was doubtless because the Sudeten question was only a cloak, and his real object was the break-up of Czechoslovakia. He now informed Chamberlain that he was not interested in the Sudeten region being handed over in a few months' time, after joint study of details and disputed areas, but that the main areas as listed by him must be evacuated by the Czechs and occupied by the German army immediately. As a special act of grace to Chamberlain he would put forward the completion date from 28th September to 1st October.

Imminence of war

This seemed an impossible demand for the British and French to force on the Czechs, and instead Britain now gave France her promise of support if France honoured her alliance with the Czechs and hostilities should follow. The British fleet and part of the French army were mobilised, air raid shelter trenches (soon to be heavily water-logged) were hastily dug in the London parks, and the British and French public, in a mood of incredulous horror, came face to face with the probability of war.

At the last moment, however, they were reprieved. It was apparent, even to Hitler, that there was no enthusiasm in Germany for a general war, though an unopposed march into Czechoslovakia would be popular enough. Hitler's generals, too, were frightened of the weakness of Germany's defences in the west, where only about five divisions would be facing about thirty-five of the French.

Mussolini's attitude

And perhaps above all, Mussolini, linked in common policy with Hitler since 1936 on the so-called 'Rome-Berlin Axis', was ill-prepared for war and urged caution on the Führer. So at the last moment, on 28th September, Hitler agreed to a four-power conference of Germany, Italy, France and Britain – the Czechs were excluded on Hitler's insistence and nobody wanted the Russians. With a compromise formula already suggested – that the Germans should begin their occupa-

Munich Conference, 29–30 September 1938

tion of the Sudetenland on Hitler's set date of 1st October, and complete it by stages – the conference, held at Munich on 29th and 30th September, was able to reach agreement on this basis. The date for completion of the occupation was to be 10th October. The areas occupied were to be the predominantly German ones as determined by an international commission, not simply those demanded by Hitler. At the same time France and Britain guaranteed the new frontiers of Czechoslovakia, and Germany and Italy promised to join in the guarantee when the claims of Poland and Hungary on Czechoslovakia had also been met – as they soon were.

Views on the Munich Settlement

On returning to Britain Chamberlain waved aloft at the airport a document bearing Hitler's signature. It formally renounced war as a method of settling differences between their two countries. Chamberlain was later that night rash enough to say that he thought the agreement would give 'peace in our time'. At Westminster he was greeted in the House of Commons with scenes of unprecedented acclamation. Among the British public at large relief from the threat of war following Chamberlain's flights – and concessions – brought the Prime Minister immense popularity. Discordant voices, however, were not lacking in the general shout of praise. According to Winston Churchill the final agreement at Munich was 'a disaster of the first magnitude.' It meant only that 'Herr Hitler had consented to be served his courses one at a time in an orderly fashion instead of snatching his victuals all at once from the table'. Of the whole series of Chamberlain's meetings with Hitler, Churchill said

£1 was demanded at the pistol's point. When it was given, . . . £2 was demanded at the pistol's point. Finally the Dictator consented to take £1. 17s. 6d. and the rest in promises of goodwill for the future . . . .

Up to this point it was still possible, if optimistic, to believe that Hitler's policy was aimed only at incorporating those of German race into the Reich. To those who still naïvely clung to this theory Hitler's next move, in the spring of 1939, proved a rude shock. The Munich Settlement, it seems, had left him dissatisfied. Not content with having stripped Czechoslovakia of her fortified frontier and many of her industries, he now invaded the Czech sections themselves, occupied Prague and declared the whole state dissolved. Bohemia and Moravia were to be a 'Protectorate' under direct German rule; Slovakia was to be a 'self-governing' district under German supervision; and the third part of the country, Ruthenia, was left to be absorbed by Hungary. Hitler had thus, as he had originally intended in September 1938, broken up Czechoslovakia as the first stage in his policy of eastward expansion. In doing so he had managed to acquire a Czech minority three times as large as the old German minority in Czechoslovakia, the Czech gold reserves, and a great industrial output, to say nothing of hundreds of aeroplanes, tanks and guns and the vital Skoda munitions works.

German break-up of Czechoslovakia (including occupation of Bohemia and Moravia), 15 March 1939

All this was done by a technique similar to that used in acquiring Austria. It included the stimulation of an independence movement in Slovakia, resulting in an 'appeal' to Hitler, and frenzied complaints by the remaining German minority about Czech oppression. As his final move, Hitler received the aged Czech President in Berlin and there gave him four hours to choose whether to oppose a German invasion and see his country utterly destroyed (when Göring threatened to bomb Prague the Czech fainted) or welcome a take-over and trust to Hitler's clemency. A few hours beforehand Chamberlain had pointed out to the House of Commons that with the independence declaration by the Slovaks Czechoslovakia was in a state of disintegration, and therefore that the British guarantee given at Munich could not apply. Bereft of any possible support, the Czechs gave way, and the President 'confidently placed the fate of the Czech people in the hands of the Führer'. Two hours later German troops were roaring across the Czech frontier.

The policy of appeasement now lay in ruins, and the question became one of stopping further German advance. Chamberlain was infuriated at Hitler's violation of pledges given personally to himself, and a revolution occurred in Britain's conduct of foreign affairs. Within a month the British and French governments offered guarantees of help, in case of attack, to Poland, Rumania and

End of 'Appeasement'

Greece – a country under threat from Italy since Mussolini had seized Albania on Good Friday 1939. Britain also concluded a treaty of mutual assistance with Turkey, and together with France strove to include Russia in a great block of states pledged to resist German aggression. The negotiations with Russia dragged on unsuccessfully, however, all through the summer. Socialist circles at the time tended to place the blame on the well-known anti-communist sentiments of the Conservative leaders, but in fact Russia was demanding, as a condition of her adherence, the right to send her troops at need into Poland, Finland, and the small Baltic States. This, though certainly necessary for the effective conduct of war against Germany, could never be accepted by the states concerned, for once they let the Red Army in they would probably never get it out. The crucial question concerned Poland, who was resolutely against admitting Russian forces. Britain and France did not feel they could honourably put much pressure on her, and the chance of building up a strong eastern front was lost.

The guarantees to Poland, Rumania, and Greece, however, still held good, and to give reality to her new determination Britain in April 1939 took the epoch-making step (for her) of introducing conscription. She also greatly speeded up her existing rearmament programmes. Germany countered by making the Rome-Berlin 'axis' into a hard and fast military alliance – the so-called 'Pact of Steel' – and by seeking to extend this system to Japan, Hungary, Yugoslavia and Spain. During April Spain had already joined Germany, Italy and Japan (which had been extending successfully in China since 1937) in the Anti-Comintern Pact, a movement basically directed against Russia.[1] Thus, with the League discredited for its failure to withstand Japan, Italy and Germany, Europe was back to the bad old system of armed groups. All the powers feverishly hurried on their colossal armament programmes, in which the 'axis' powers had snatched a valuable lead, and which made the preparations for 1914 seem like child's play. It was a method of seeking security which had been tried before, all too thoroughly, and which usually ended in war. It was to do so again.

As the summer of 1939 wore on, it became apparent that Germany was about to direct her next blow against Poland. Poles and Germans had long viewed each other with hostility, but Hitler's government had actually concluded a non-aggression pact with Poland as one of its first steps in foreign policy. This Hitler repudiated in March 1939, shortly before seizing Memel (which was, however, genuinely German) from Lithuania. Flushed with his recent successes and gambling on the kind of resistance from Britain and France which these powers had shown over Czechoslovakia, Hitler now determined not only to settle two long-standing grievances in his own favour, but also to win for Germany a huge 'living-space' in the Polish and Russian Ukraine. Naturally it was the settlement of grievances which appeared as Germany's public aim. She had never accepted willingly either the status of Danzig (populated largely by Germans) as a Free City, in which the Poles had certain guaranteed rights, or the existence of the Polish 'Corridor', cutting off East Prussia from the main body of the Reich. Had Hitler not revealed his true objectives by the occupation of Prague in the spring, some compromise might have been attempted. As it was, the Poles and the whole of Europe knew

---

[1] The Comintern was the Communist International organisation at Moscow – a wing of the Soviet government devoted to spreading communism abroad.

RENDEZ-VOUS

Hitler and Stalin, their long-standing and fundamental antagonism momentarily ended by the Nazi-Soviet pact of August 1939, meet across the dead body of Poland and exchange courtesies. Cartoon by David Low, September 1939.

every step in the well-worn Nazi technique by heart: a demand, an 'atrocity' campaign alleging ill-treatment of German minorities, an 'appeal' by the German minorities for Hitler's protection, more demands, every concession offered by the victim used to extort a further one, and finally the entry of the German army, with not only the disputed territory but the whole country at its mercy. In face of a shrieking German press campaign the Poles kept their temper and their determination, trusting to their own bravery and the help of their western friends – though this indeed, owing to Poland's geographical situation, could not be direct or of immediate effect. They announced their willingness to negotiate, but not under threat of force. Europe held its breath and trembled.

On 21st August the world knew the die was cast. The papers of that day contained the news of the Russo-German non-aggression pact, which was formally signed in Moscow two days later. Russia, while still negotiating with Britain and France, had 'sold out' to the Nazis – the secret terms of the pact including German recognition of a special Russian interest in eastern Poland, Bessarabia, Finland and the Baltic States apart from Lithuania. In the case of eastern Poland and the Baltic States, this would amount to an actual take-over. Doubtless another Russian motive apart from expansion was to avoid trouble with Germany until the Red Army was better equipped and the disorganisation following the recent 'purges' had been righted. Russia probably also calculated on a lengthy war in which the great 'capitalist' powers of Germany, France and Britain would exhaust each other.

Russo-German non-aggression pact, August 1939

Equally, Hitler was prepared to buy off Russia while he dealt with Poland, and possibly with Britain and France – with the thought always in his mind that he could then turn to the final squaring of accounts with Russia.

This cynical bargain on the part of the Nazis and the Russian Communists, who had previously been at daggers drawn, astounded public opinion everywhere. But Ribbentrop, Hitler's sinister foreign minister, was mistaken in his belief that it would frighten Britain and France into betraying Poland, or Poland into abject surrender. On 24th August Britain signed the last formal stages of her alliance with Poland. Hitler and his advisers, however, refused to be swayed from their purpose by the now certain prospect of a European war. The issue was clear, but their new calculation was that, with the Poles irreparably beaten in a few weeks, Britain and France would be glad to withdraw before any further damage was done. In any case, Hitler knew that his policy would eventually lead to another European war, and he preferred to start it while he was still in his full powers. For another week the tension grew. On 31st August Germany communicated to Britain a precise Sixteen-Point Peace Plan, involving the return of Danzig to the Reich, plebiscites in the Corridor, German railways and roads through the Corridor before the plebiscites, and further concessions. Only a few hours later Hitler announced that his 'patience was exhausted', and that the German government, after two days' grace, were now tired of waiting for the arrival of a Polish plenipotentiary who could accept or reject their plan. This announcement to the world was the first time the Poles, who had refused to send a plenipotentiary with *carte blanche*, had officially heard of the Sixteen-Point Plan – a typical example of Nazi perfidy. On 1st September, without further ultimatum or declaration of war, Danzig was proclaimed reunited to the Reich and Germany invaded Poland.

Invasion of Poland, 1 September 1939

At the last moment, once more, Mussolini came forward with a plan for a conference, but this time the Munich technique was not to be repeated. Britain and France demanded that German pressure against Poland should first be slackened, and in face of the German refusal to do anything but go ruthlessly ahead, Italy's peace move failed. For one day, indeed, Britain and France seemed to hesitate: in fact, their decision to help Poland was already made, but France was hoping for a further delay in case Mussolini's negotiations succeeded. Public opinion on all sides, however, and particularly in Britain, clearly indicated that this time there could be no escape – German aggression and the Anglo-French commitments were plain. The opposition parties in Britain and France, except the relatively few Fascists and Communists, were at one with the governments, and the governments at one with the people. On Sunday, 3rd September, Britain and France despatched brief ultimatums to Germany, threatening her with war unless she withdrew from Poland. No reply was received, and by 11.15 a.m. Chamberlain was broadcasting to the British people the news of the tragic breakdown of all his and their hopes. But if gloom was the prevalent mood, if an overwhelming despondency at a second sacrifice within twenty-five years was in the minds of all, there was no lack of determination to see the thing through to its bitter end. With no beating of drums or jingoist parade, but in a sad, sober and steadfast resolution, Britain and France prepared to fight and overthrow the 'evil things' of which Chamberlain had spoken – 'brute force, bad faith, injustice, oppression, and persecution'. It was war again, but never had the British and French peoples fought in a clearer cause, nor against a more dangerous and malignant foe.

European war again

CHAPTER 23
The Second World War, 1939–45

The Poles soon found that bravery was no substitute for tanks and aeroplanes. With their communications paralysed by overwhelming German superiority in the air, they were simply brushed aside by the onrush of the Nazi armoured divisions. On 17th September the Russians, as secretly arranged in the Nazi-Soviet pact a few weeks before, entered eastern Poland; on 27th September the Germans captured Warsaw; and by the end of the month the swastika floated over one half of Poland and the hammer and sickle over the other.

German invasion of Poland

Russian occupation of east Poland

Only by launching an immediate offensive against the Siegfried Line, in the west of Germany, could Britain and France have brought relief to the Poles. But the concentration of the French troops, most of whom were not mechanised, was a slow business; the small British Expeditionary Force had to move across to the Continent; and, except at sea, both Allies were determined to postpone the major clash in the hope of reducing Germany's advantage in armaments. So the brief chance of forcing Hitler to fight on two fronts was lost, and by October the Germans were building up for an attack in the west.

For the next six months matters were surprisingly quiet – so quiet that impatient American journalists dismissed the whole contest as 'phoney'. In point of fact, Hitler, after giving the Allies a chance to recognize his conquest of Poland and meeting with a firm refusal, was preparing to strike in the following spring. The Allies were simply doing what they could – rounding up enemy ships, enforcing a blockade, countering Hitler's magnetic mines, showering German cities with leaflets – to damage Germany without provoking her to violent action. Meanwhile the Russians, anxious to control the seaward approaches to Leningrad, set upon the Finns and after much difficulty took what they wanted – fortunately before Britain and France, indignant at the Russian action, could become embroiled.

The 'Phoney' War, October 1939–April 1940

Russo-Finnish War, November 1939–March 1940

The calm was sharply broken in April 1940. Determined to safeguard his supplies of Scandinavian iron-ore from British interruption, Hitler struck without warning at Denmark and Norway – both unoffending neutrals. Denmark was occupied almost bloodlessly and Norway in a campaign which lasted only two months. With seaborne or airborne troops treacherously descending on all the key Norwegian ports and airfields at the outset, the Germans were able to gain a stranglehold which the Norwegians – who were no stronger for a century's uninterrupted peace – could do little to loosen. Hopelessly handicapped by the

German invasion of Denmark and Norway, April 1940

lack of any major Norwegian port or airfield, Britain and France could give no effective help; and in any case they were bound to preserve their main forces for the forthcoming clash in the west.

Churchill's Coalition in Britain, May 1940

Norway was an unexpected and bitter blow to the Allies – so bitter that it brought down the Chamberlain government in Britain and led to an all-party Coalition under Winston Churchill. But it was nothing to the almost mortal shock which followed. On 10th May 1940 – the day Churchill took office – the German armies at last moved in the west. To by-pass the strongly fortified Maginot Line, covering the Franco-German frontier, the Germans struck at France, as in 1914, through neutral Belgium; and this time they also invaded Holland. Overwhelmed by superior forces and a skilful use of paratroops, Holland succumbed within five days, the unopposed bombing of Rotterdam clinching the matter. The German right flank was secure.

German invasion of Holland, Belgium and France, May 1940

The break-through in the Ardennes

Meanwhile the enemy's strongest punch had been packed into the centre. Employing many tanks and dive-bombers, Hitler's forces struck heavily in the Ardennes – a hilly region where a major offensive had seemed impossible and where the French had stationed the worst equipped of their armies. Quickly forcing the Meuse near Dinant and Sedan, the Germans cut through the French lines with absurd ease. Within a few days they were motoring almost unopposed across France towards the Channel coast. During this time vast French forces remained only slightly engaged in the Maginot Line, while to the north of the German break-through the B.E.F. and the French 1st Army, which had dashed forward into Belgium, were pressed back with almost equal speed.

By 21st May the German penetration had reached the Channel near Abbeville and completely severed the Allied Armies in the north – the B.E.F., the French 1st Army, and the Belgians – from those in the south. The Germans now concentrated on these northern armies, pressing them back from the east while the panzer forces which had carried out the break-through wheeled round along the coast and drove at them from the west. Soon there was only one port open to the northern armies – Dunkirk – and no choice but evacuation or surrender. Exhausted, the Belgians laid down their arms; but thanks to a heroic rearguard action before Dunkirk and strenuous and devoted efforts by the Royal Navy, the Royal Air Force, and large numbers of merchant seamen and amateur yachtsmen, the B.E.F. and most of the French 1st Army were plucked from disaster. Only a hair's-breadth had separated the British army from a *débâcle* unparalleled in its history.

Dunkirk evacuation, 26 May–4 June 1940

After Dunkirk the Germans turned against the French armies to the south – and the few British with them. Sweeping across the Somme and the Seine, they occupied Paris (which was not defended) and split the French forces into helplessly isolated groups. Meanwhile Mussolini's Italy, tempted by the prospect of loot, if not glory, entered the fray against the reeling Allies. Appalled by the utter impotence of her armies against the German tanks and bombers, France now lost all heart for the struggle. Marshal Pétain, the victor of Verdun in 1916, but now old and defeatist, became Premier to make peace, and by 25th June – less than seven weeks from the opening blow – the whole campaign was over. It was typical of Hitler that he made the French receive his armistice terms in the old railway coach at Compiègne where the Germans had had to sign on the dotted line in 1918.

The entry of Italy, June 1940

The collapse of France

The governments of Poland, Norway and Holland, and a provisional Czech government recognised by the British were now carrying on the fight from exile.

ON TO GLORY AND WHATEVER WE CAN GRAB
Mussolini enters the fray against the reeling Allies. Cartoon by Low, June 1940.

Pétain's government, on the other hand, refused to fight on from the French colonies, and preferred to knuckle under to the Germans. Pétain reasoned that France had been offered good terms (the Germans would occupy only northern France and the Atlantic coast, leaving the centre and south 'free', with a capital at Vichy), and that if the great French army could not stop the Germans, a few British divisions would certainly meet with no better success. Some at least of his countrymen disagreed, and a Free French (later called Fighting French) movement was formed in London under General de Gaulle. But as the French government was now ill-disposed towards Britain – it saved French self-respect to blame the disaster on insufficient help from her ally – the British could afford to take no chances with the French fleet, lying intact in north African harbours. When the French refused to hand it over to Britain's safe keeping, the Royal Navy opened fire on the major vessels at Oran and Mers-el-Kebir and put most of them out of action. Naturally this did not improve Anglo-French relations.

    Supported by the Commonwealth (though Eire remained obstinately neutral), Britain had now to face the combined might of Germany and Italy. A second 'peace-offer' from Hitler, demanding recognition of his gains, was as resolutely refused as the first. Then the Nazi dictator was forced to contemplate a task outside the experience even of the German army – the invasion of England. But the German navy had no relish for the job while the Royal Navy remained intact and insisted that the power of the British fleet be 'neutralised' by the German Air Force.

Margin notes:

Pétain's Vichy government

de Gaulle's Free French

British action *v.* French fleet, July 1940

Projected invasion of England

The Luftwaffe could not be sure of doing this, however, or of 'covering' the German vessels and landings until it had gained air superiority over the Channel and southern England. In other words, before England could be invaded, the Germans had first to dispose of the Royal Air Force.

Battle of Britain, August–September 1940

So began the Battle of Britain – an epic struggle which lasted from early August until late September. In an effort to paralyse Britain's carefully devised system of air defence, the German bombers, more and more heavily escorted, shifted from one series of targets to another – first the south coast ports, radar stations and airfields, then the inland airfields, then London itself – but all their efforts failed to break the resistance of the British fighter pilots. At the same time British bombers struck at the build-up of invasion barges in the enemy-held Channel ports. By the end of September, Göring, the Luftwaffe's Commander-in-Chief, was no nearer his objective, and the weather ruled out an invasion later in the year. Hitler could do nothing but postpone the venture until the following spring. And by then he had embraced another project from which he was never to shake free.

'Night Blitz' against Britain, September 1940–May 1941

Though preserved from immediate invasion, Britain was threatened in other ways. Unable to sustain her heavy losses by day, Germany had begun to use her bombers against Britain by night – against ports, arms towns and above all London. The Royal Air Force had been attacking Germany by night since May, though in a smaller way than was possible to the enemy. From September 1940 to May 1941 the Luftwaffe visited London almost nightly, and dozens of other British towns were also badly bombed. The science of night defence was then in its infancy and German losses were small; but the science of night attack was also undeveloped and the bombing was more of an ordeal for the town-dweller than a mortal blow to the British war effort. Exposed to apparently indiscriminate attack, the British

British retaliation

retaliated by going for German 'industrial areas' (which were easier to hit than the individual objectives on which they had previously concentrated), and from then on the civilians of both countries were inescapably in the 'front line'.

American supplies and the U-boat war

To the bombing of British towns Hitler added a determined effort to cut Britain's life-line across the Atlantic. Franklin D. Roosevelt, President of the U.S.A., had early resolved that his country should act as the 'arsenal of democracy'. Soon

Roosevelt

after the outbreak of the war he had secured a modification of his country's Neutrality Act of 1937 to permit belligerents to buy American arms on a 'cash and

'Cash and carry'

carry' basis. This of course worked exclusively in favour of the British and French, whose navies controlled the north Atlantic. Under Roosevelt's skilful guidance and the pressure of events the U.S.A. became increasingly willing not only to supply the goods, but, by the Lease-Lend Act of March 1941, to supply them virtually

Lease-Lend Act, March 1941

free of charge if the transaction was in America's interest. Obviously if this supply proceeded unhindered British resistance would be greatly sustained. Installed by mid-1940 all round the coast of Europe from Narvik to the Bay of Biscay, German aircraft and U-boats were magnificently placed to prey on the transatlantic traffic, and throughout the winter of 1940–41 they took increasing toll of British – and neutral – vessels.

The war in Africa

While Britain battled on alone against Germany in Europe, British and Commonwealth forces in Africa were winning fantastic victories against the Italians. Attacked simultaneously from Libya and Italian East Africa, the ludicrously outnumbered British had at first to give ground everywhere – in Egypt, the Sudan, Kenya and British Somaliland. Then reinforcements began to arrive from South

Africa, Australia and India, while by a bold decision an armoured brigade was sent out to Egypt from England at the very height of the German invasion threat. The result was that General Wavell soon had the Italians on the run. The surrendered outposts in the Sudan and Kenya were recaptured; Italian East Africa was invaded; and in a brilliant advance against an enemy five times as numerous, Wavell's forces pushed the Italians out of Egypt and overran the whole of Cyrenaica (the eastern province of Libya). In this advance Italian casualties amounted to about 150,000 – nearly all prisoners. Those of the British were less than 3000.

British conquest of Cyrenaica, December 1940–February 1941

To defeat in Africa Mussolini had by this time added disgrace in Europe. In October 1940 Hitler occupied Rumania – to safeguard one of his main sources of oil. Whereupon Mussolini in emulation decided to strike at Greece. In view of the small size of the Greek forces, he looked forward to a virtual 'walk-over'. But the Italians, operating from Albania, were held up as soon as their victims had time to rally from the first surprise blow; and within a few weeks the Greeks, helped by the Royal Air Force, were invading Albania. At the same time half of Italy's battleships were crippled by torpedoes (delivered by the British Fleet Air Arm) at Taranto. Disaster, utter and complete, had attended all Mussolini's schemes.

Italian attack on Greece, October 1940

Obviously Hitler could not tolerate the defeat of his ally. At the end of 1940 he sent a strong detachment of the Luftwaffe to Sicily, where it improved considerably on the performance of the Italian air force against the British base of Malta; and in the opening months of 1941 German land and air forces were shipped across to Libya. At the same time the Germans began to infiltrate Bulgaria and prepared to strike at Greece. The British resolved to do what little they could to protect Greece, and hastily sent forces from Egypt across the Mediterranean. They had hardly taken station when the Germans struck. Brushing aside the resistance of Yugoslavia (which at the last moment gallantly overthrew a government prepared to collaborate with Hitler), the Germans poured into Greece and within three weeks had expelled the tiny British force. Fortunately it was nearly all rescued, as at Dunkirk, by the Royal Navy.

German intervention in Africa

German invasion of Yugoslavia and Greece, April 1941

Meanwhile though the Italian fleet had taken another beating at the Battle of Cape Matapan, the Axis had recovered in north Africa. Deprived of the troops despatched to Greece and now called on to face the German Africa Corps under Rommel as well as the Italians, the British forces were driven back from Cyrenaica into Egypt, though Tobruk held out as an isolated fortress. As though this double misfortune was not enough, Nazi sympathisers in Iraq overthrew the Regent and threatened British interests there – fortunately before the Germans could take proper advantage of the move, which was soon crushed. Shortly afterwards British and Free French forces entered and occupied the French mandated territory of Syria, where the Vichy-controlled government had given facilities to Axis aircraft en route for Iraq.

Loss of Cyrenaica, April 1941

Iraqi revolt, May 1941

British and Free French occupation of Syria, June–July 1941

From Greece the Germans jumped to Crete, which they took – with stupendous losses – by airborne invasion. Once more the British force had to be extricated by the Royal Navy. The Navy also defeated a seaborne expedition aimed at the island, but the British ships suffered great damage. Clearly naval vessels could no longer operate effectively in narrow waters within range of a superior air force.

Germans capture Crete, May 1941

The German's occupation of Yugoslavia, Greece and Crete, together with their 'peaceful' domination of Rumania and Bulgaria, cleared Hitler's right flank for his

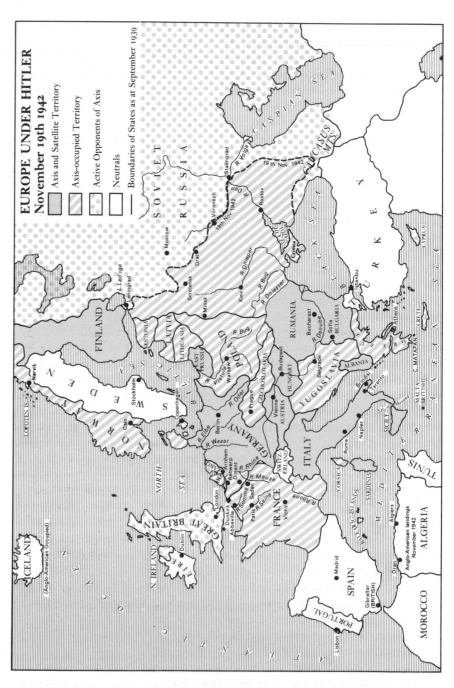

EUROPE UNDER HITLER
November 19th 1942

Axis and Satellite Territory
Axis-occupied Territory
Active Opponents of Axis
Neutrals
Boundaries of States as at September 1939

German invasion of
Russia, June 1941

next, and ultimately fatal, venture. The Nazi-Soviet pact of August 1939 had lessened neither Hitler's hatred of communism nor his determination to expand in the east. With France knocked out and Britain without a foothold on the Continent, the German dictator found the temptation irresistible to turn against Russia. The German General Staff reckoned she could be crushed in eight weeks; the decision was taken in December 1940; and after some months of preparation the blow fell on 22nd June 1941.

Moving forward with a great mass of tanks and using most of their air force in support – it had been transferred from the west, thereby ending the 'blitz' against Britain in any serious form – the Germans overran the Russian-occupied section of Poland and struck deep into Russia. In the north – aided by the Finns – they advanced almost to the suburbs of Leningrad; in the centre they came within a hundred miles of Moscow; in the south they broke right through to the Crimea. But though the casualties ran into millions on both sides, the Germans failed to destroy the Russian armies. Soon the summer and autumn wore away and the plains lay deeply covered in snow; Generals January and February, Russia's traditional allies, were taking over.

Meanwhile the campaign of the Commonwealth forces in Italian East Africa was brought to a victorious conclusion and a new offensive was mounted against the Axis forces in north Africa. For a second time the British overran Cyrenaica, but once more events in other theatres demanded the transfer of some of the British troops, and part of the captured ground had to be given up. This time the diversion was no minor affair, as in Greece, but a major development as decisive for the future of the war as the German invasion of Russia.

Conquest of Italian East Africa (completed November 1941)

Second British conquest of Cyrenaica, November 1941– January 1942

Since 1931 Japan had been absorbing as much of the huge, weak and disunited state of China as she could. Normally the big obstacles to her programme were Britain, France and the U.S.A. All were now occupied elsewhere. Britain was fully engaged in Europe and Africa; France, under the spineless Vichy government, would not fight to retain her colony of Indo-China – a magnificent jumping-off ground for Malaya; and the U.S.A. was pouring her money, arms, and raw materials into Britain and Russia. Only the American Pacific Fleet stood between Japan and her dreams of conquest – a chance which might never occur again. On 7th December 1941, without any declaration of war, Japan struck simultaneously in two opposite directions. To the west her troops, sailing from Indo-China, landed in north-east Malaya and Siam; to the east, in the Hawaiian Islands, her carrier-borne aircraft by one swift, treacherous blow crippled the American Pacific Fleet at Pearl Harbour.

Japanese invasion of Malaya and attack on Pearl Harbour, 7 December 1941

It was now indeed world war. Germany and Italy hastened to support Japan by declaring war on the U.S.A.; and soon the British Commonwealth, Russia, the U.S.A., China and a host of smaller states, including many of the South American republics, were in formal alliance against Germany, Italy, Japan and the more willing of their 'satellites' – Rumania, Bulgaria, Hungary and Finland. Deprived of the protection of the American fleet, the small British forces in the Far East were quite unable to resist the first Japanese onrush. Hong-Kong was an early victim; Malaya was overrun within two months – the vaunted stronghold of Singapore falling with a huge loss in prisoners; resistance in the Netherlands East Indies collapsed; and by May 1942 the Japanese had penetrated through Burma to the gates of India. To the east, the Americans were driven from the Philippines after a heroic struggle, and successive groups of Pacific islands rapidly fell to the enemy. In May 1942, however, a Japanese expedition aimed at Port Moresby, in New Guinea, was repulsed by the American fleet in the Battle of the Coral Sea, and the following month an invasion fleet intended for Midway Island, in the

World war

Japanese capture of Hong-Kong, Malaya, N.E.I., Burma and Pacific Islands, December 1941–May 1942

American victories of Coral Sea and Midway, May–June 1942

PEARL HARBOUR, 8TH DECEMBER, 1941

On Sunday 7th December 1941 the Japanese, without declaring war, struck at the American Pacific Fleet in Pearl Harbour, Hawaii. They used about 350 aircraft, operating from carriers which had sailed from their bases well beforehand. Taken by surprise, the Americans lost about 120 aircraft – nearly all on the ground – and suffered heavy damage to fourteen warships. From then on the war was world-wide.

Central Pacific, was broken up with great losses by American naval aircraft. The period of unchecked Japanese success was over.

Until well into 1942 the initiative remained in the hands of the Axis. The U-boats, preying on vessels near the American coast, enjoyed a fresh wave of success; in Africa Rommel attacked, and carried the Italo-German armies to within sixty miles of Alexandria; in Russia the Germans, taking advantage of the summer conditions, swept forward on the southern front right into the Caucasus. But further north they could not take or by-pass the key town of Stalingrad, on the Volga, though the battle raged until every building was a ruin. Once more the Germans had shot their bolt; and this time the inexhaustible Russians, helped by

Italo-German invasion
of Egypt, summer 1942

Stalingrad,
September–November
1942

Anglo-American supplies and drawing unexpected reserves of strength from arms factories built up or transferred beyond the Urals, were preparing to strike back with redoubled force.

Mid-1942 was thus the high-water mark of Axis success. There were many signs by then that, with good fortune, the Allies could stem the flood. The Japanese, struggling to secure the outposts of Australia, were being held in New Guinea and the Solomons; and in the West an ever-increasing weight of bombs was falling on German soil. The R.A.F. had been steadily attacking since 1940; in May 1942 came the first 'thousand-bomber' raid, against Cologne; and by the summer the United States Air Force was beginning to appear in Europe. Unless Germany could finish off Russia and turn once more against Britain, she would find her foreign conquests mocked by the destruction of her homeland.

The mounting air offensive against Germany

'UNDER THE BROOMSTICK'

A Russian cartoon of 1942. Hitler sweeps up his troops on the French side of the English Channel and sends them off in a direction marked 'To the Russo-German Front'. On the English side of the Channel, Churchill sits comfortably in a chair with his feet up on a paper marked 'Solemn promise to open a Second Front in Europe during 1942' and surveys Hitler's troop movements with satisfaction. (Britain had made no definite promise for 1942: she undertook to study the problem and do all she could.)

The turn of the tide became obvious in the closing months of 1942. In October the British Eighth Army under Montgomery struck at Rommel's forces before El Alamein. After a sharp struggle the enemy cracked. Soon the Italians were being rounded up, while the Germans, who had most of the transport, were being chased right across Libya into Tunisia. To block the enemy retreat and to re-establish control of the Mediterranean, on 7th November the first of the great Anglo-American expeditions under General Eisenhower landed in Morocco and Algeria. French resistance soon collapsed, and aid was given to the Allies. By May 1943 the last of the Axis forces in Africa – over a quarter of a million men – had been cornered in the northern tip of Tunisia between the Allied armies advancing from either side of the Continent. Meanwhile in November 1942 the Russians had begun their winter counter-offensive at Stalingrad and the Germans were being remorselessly pressed back.

By mid-1943 the Allies were definitely winning. On the Russian front, a huge German army had capitulated at Stalingrad; the siege of Leningrad had been raised; the German summer offensive was halted almost at once. At the same time the U-boats were being driven out of the Atlantic as Allied aircraft of increasing range, equipped with radar, reinforced the efforts of the Allied navies. In Germany the great industrial centre of the Ruhr, attacked more accurately with the help of radar devices, was already a scene of devastation, and the main effort of R.A.F. Bomber Command was being switched to German ports. In all the occupied countries of Europe the local 'resistance' movements, sustained by supplies secretly dropped from aircraft, gave the German occupiers increasing trouble.

To crown these developments Anglo-American forces from Africa invaded Sicily. Thanks to the overwhelming air superiority of the Allies a foothold was easily obtained, and the local Italian forces preferred not to put up a serious fight. The Germans, however, held out for five weeks before they escaped across the Straits of Messina to the Italian mainland. Meanwhile Mussolini, overwhelmed by incessant defeat, had been driven from power and imprisoned; and General Badoglio, working closely with the Italian royal family, had taken over the Italian government.

On 3rd September 1943, the Anglo-American forces swept across from Sicily to the mainland. Again it was only the Germans who fought – the new Italian government had secretly negotiated with the Allies to shake off the hated alliance with Hitler, and shortly afterwards came in on the Allied side.

A desperate *coup* by German parachutists soon rescued Mussolini, who set up a rival government in northern Italy. He was now, however, a mere puppet in German hands. Rapidly the Allied armies advanced as far as Naples, but by then the German forces, at first disorganised by the Italian defection, had established a firm hold on northern and central Italy. Aided by the winter weather and the mountainous country, they fought with fanatical determination, and the Allied progress slowed down into a long 'slogging-match' up the Italian peninsula.

Having knocked out their weakest opponent, the British and Americans then perfected their plan for the liberation of north-western Europe. The job was entrusted largely to the victorious team of commanders from the Mediterranean under Eisenhower. Preparations of the utmost thoroughness were made – including two artificial harbours to be towed across the Channel – and on 'D-Day' (6th June 1944) the Anglo-American forces touched down on the beaches of Normandy. By this time the sea-lanes of the Allies were reasonably secure against the U-boats and commerce-raiders; and the Allied air forces, having laid waste the Ruhr, the north German ports and Berlin, besides bringing German production of bombers to a critically low level, had crippled the communications of northern France. This fatally handicapped the Germans' ability to concentrate their troops in the vital area, and gave the Allied armies a chance to make good their footing.

After a few weeks tight struggle, during which the British and Canadians on the left attracted the bulk of the enemy, the Americans on the right broke out from the lodgment area. Threatened by an encircling movement, thousands of Germans were destroyed in trying to get back over the Seine, and in rapid succession the Allies freed northern and western France and swept into Belgium and Holland.

The break-out, August 1944

Meanwhile another Allied army, including the main Fighting French forces, landed in southern France (which had been occupied by the Germans after the north African landings of November 1942), and moved up the Rhône valley towards the Upper Rhine. By September 1944 the Allied armies were across the German frontier in several places, but a bold attempt to leap the Rhine by a parachute operation at Arnhem, in Holland, failed – in part through bad weather, in part through ignorance of the full strength of the German forces near at hand.

Allied landings in southern France, August 1944

Failure at Arnhem, September 1944

UNFINISHED U-BOATS IN SHATTERED HAMBURG, 1945
R.A.F. raids on German ports and industrial towns, although light in 1940 and 1941, began to do serious damage from 1942 onwards. This photo shows unfinished U-boats on the slipways when the town surrendered in 1945.

Soon it became clear that to bring up enough supplies the Allies must open the port of Antwerp – for on Hitler's orders the Germans, even after they had abandoned the rest of the country, clung desperately to the ports, and blew up all installations before surrendering. The island of Walcheren, which guards the Scheldt estuary, was cleared at the beginning of November, and before the end of the month Allied supplies were reaching the front through Antwerp.

The German cause was now obviously doomed. In July 1944 an attempt by a group of German anti-Nazis to blow up Hitler failed to achieve its object, but gave a clear sign that some of the enemy realized the madness of continuing the struggle. The Russians, who had advanced more or less continuously since Stalingrad, had by now eliminated Finland, Bulgaria, and Rumania, penetrated the Baltic States, Hungary, Czechoslovakia and Yugoslavia (where Marshal Tito's resistance forces, aided by Allied aircraft, had for long kept a big German army pinned down), and had reached East Prussia. The German attempt to knock out London by one of Hitler's 'secret weapons' – the V1, or flying bomb – had failed, and the V2, or long-range rocket, promised little more success with the Allied armies overrunning the launching-sites on the Continent. To crown all, Germany's major cities were now masses of rubble, her oil resources (attacked from the air, and doubly weakened by the loss of Rumania) were down to a level which was crippling her whole war machine, and her railways and canals were just beginning to feel the full weight of Allied air power.

Antwerp in use, November 1944

The Russian advance

German V1 and V2 campaign, June 1944– March 1945

Effects of Allied air attack

KNELL
The knell of doom sounds for the German dictator, hammered between the Anglo-American forces on the West and Russians on the East. Cartoon by Low, March 1945.

In December 1944 the Germans in the west made their last effective stroke: a sudden counter-offensive through the Ardennes aimed at Antwerp. It failed, and the effort further weakened the enemy.

German offensive in the Ardennes, December 1944

In the spring of 1945 the Russians completed their conquest of Hungary, liberated Lithuania, and reached the Oder. In March Eisenhower's forces launched their new offensive, and swiftly crossed the Rhine. Irresistibly the Allied armies now converged on the heart of Germany. In the west the Ruhr was encircled and captured, to yield an enormous bag of prisoners; to the south the Russians overran Vienna; in the east they reached the suburbs of Berlin. On 25th April American and Russian forces, approaching from opposite directions, met on the Elbe.

Forces from east and west meet, April 1945

Three days later, with the German armies in Italy about to lay down their arms, Mussolini attempted to flee across the border into Switzerland. He was captured and shot by Italian 'partisan' forces. Hitler did not long survive him, for on 30th April the frenzied German leader, who had refused to leave his bomb-proof underground headquarters in Berlin, in desperation committed suicide.[1] With

The end in Italy: the death of Mussolini

Suicide of Hitler

him perished a number of companions, including Goebbels, the Nazi propaganda minister and one of the world's greatest liars. A few days later Hitler's appointed successor, Admiral Dönitz, accepted the Allied terms of unconditional surrender. On 7th May an armistice was signed at Eisenhower's headquarters at Rheims, and on 8th May German resistance came to an end.

Germany surrenders 8 May 1945

As the Allied armies swept through a Germany where every large town was an appalling tribute to the work of the Allied airmen, they came across the Nazi concentration and extermination camps. The scenes of horror they uncovered there and in Austria and liberated Poland were ample proof, if any were needed, of the sins of the Nazi régime and the complicity of the German people, who for the most part had closed their eyes to its vices and crimes while Hitler's success lasted. Thousands upon thousands of men, women and children imprisoned in the last stages of starvation, disease, filth and every other human misery; thousands subjected to hideous tortures, often for the sheer pleasure of their brutal guards (themselves recruited largely from the criminal classes); merciless floggings and 'beatings-up', finger-nails torn out, lighted cigarettes held against the skin, lengthy exposure to extreme cold or repeated immersion in icy water; millions – literally millions – of foreigners, Jews and opponents of the régime worked to death; millions more Jews and many thousands of elderly or mentally sick Germans exterminated in gas-chambers out of deference to Nazi racial theories – these were but a few of the practices which were revealed beyond any shadow of dispute, and which have made the names of camps like Auschwitz and Mauthausen a grisly and lasting memorial of 'man's inhumanity to man'.

Nazi Concentration and Extermination Camps

With Germany overwhelmed and the Nazi leaders dead or awaiting trial as war criminals, the Allies proceeded to concentrate on Japan. By now the Americans, thanks largely to a generous use of aircraft carriers, had established a firm naval supremacy in Far Eastern waters. The Solomons had been recovered, New Guinea was being cleared up, the islands in the Central Pacific had been recaptured, and the Americans were back in the Philippines. Allied armies had also fought their way back from India to Rangoon. Above all, islands within air striking range of Japan – first Iwo Jima, then Okinawa – were falling into Allied hands. The

The war with Japan

Allied successes, 1943– May 1945

American air attacks on Japan

---

[1] According to the story of those about him. His body was apparently burned.

BELSEN CONCENTRATION CAMP, MAY 1945

As the Allies advanced into Germany and German-occupied territory they overran the Nazi concentration camps and discovered unimaginable horrors. Some had become extermination camps, in which millions of Jews were gassed and cremated. Mass graves of dead bodies, thousands in the last extremities of suffering – everywhere there was evidence of the murder, starvation, neglect and torture of the Jews, foreign workers and anti-Nazis interned there.

The atom bombs, August 6th and 9th, 1945

The end in the Far East, August 14th 1945

Japanese homeland had already suffered severely from American long-range bombers based in China; now it was to feel the weight first of increasing bombardment by traditional means and then of a new and infinitely terrible weapon. On 6th August an American Superfortress dropped an atomic bomb on the port of Hiroshima, devastating four square miles and killing or injuring about 160,000 Japanese men, women and children. On 8th August Russia, thus far neutral in the Far Eastern struggle, declared war on Japan and invaded Manchuria. On 9th August an atomic bomb was dropped on Nagasaki; and on 14th August the Japanese accepted the Allied terms of unconditional surrender. The long nightmare was at last over, even if victory was clouded by the thought of what terrible powers of destruction now lay within the capacity of mankind.

The main reasons for the initial success and later failure of the Axis powers are clear enough. Germany won her early victories because she had a stronger and better equipped army and air force than the opposite combination of Britain, France and Poland, and because of her greater freedom from scruples. The same factors produced Japan's initial successes: the treacherous blow at the American

AFTER THE ATOM BOMB

Hiroshima after the dropping of the first atomic bomb on 6th August 1945. The bomb destroyed three-quarters of the city and killed or fatally injured about 90,000 people.

fleet gained her the temporary command of Far Eastern waters and so enabled her to gather up weakly defended British and Dutch possessions at will. Italy won no honours before her final co-operation with the Allies. Her boastful dictator overlooked the fact that military virtues are not fostered in a non-militaristic people by setting them to fight at the side of a nation traditionally their enemy against those who have always been their friends.

Many factors account for the turn of the tide after the early run of German successes. Britain, protected by a small but highly efficient air force, her unfailing navy, and a twenty mile stretch of water, set a good example of a united people, supported by the Commonwealth overseas, and refusing even to contemplate the possibility of defeat. The Battle of Britain was the first great check to German ambitions. The prolonged and heroic resistance of Russia was the next; unlike western Europe, her vast territory offered room to absorb the first shock of the enemy's attack, and after their early victories the German armies became bogged down in a titanic struggle which wore them out. Equally, the tremendous requirements of the German armies on the Eastern front made it impossible for Germany to maintain her early lead in the air, and so weakened her against the increasing power of the Royal Air Force. This, coupled with the ever-growing strength of the American air force – once Japan had brought the Americans fully into the struggle – tore the industrial heart out of Germany and made possible continued Russian

Reasons for early Axis successes and later failure

resistance and the Anglo-American invasion of Normandy. We must also not overlook the effect of Allied sea superiority – obtained now by air forces as well as navies. Moreover it is obvious that the British Commonwealth, the U.S.A. and the U.S.S.R., once their forces were fully built up, represented a combination of man-power, wealth, raw materials, industrial capacity and scientific skill infinitely more powerful than that of Germany, Italy and Japan – even when Germany ruled nearly all Europe and Japan lorded it over most of the Far East.

Hitler's disastrous
leadership

After the opening phase, the Allies were also fortunate in their leaders. On the Axis side Hitler, rating his opponents very low, at first scored by sheer boldness; but his early success, coupled with pre-war coups like the bloodless occupation of Austria and Czechoslovakia, most of which had been undertaken against the advice of his military commanders, gave him a fatal confidence and prestige. His mixture of ability, will-power, almost mesmeric influence, and utter ruthlessness imposed itself more and more even in purely military details. He brooked no argument, interfered in all directions, and strove to exercise superior and detailed control over all his many armies. The needless attack on Russia was a frightful miscalculation which ruined the whole German cause; and long before the end it became clear that he was ready to drag his country down into complete and utter ruin rather than abandon the power he had so shamefully misused. In the end even large elements among the German people could see him for what he was – a crazy fanatic with the moral code of a gangster.

The Allied leaders

By contrast, the influence of Churchill and Roosevelt was wholly beneficial to their causes. Churchill, though he was not infallible, applied the spur consistently in the right place and by his matchless eloquence inspired the people not only of Britain but of the occupied countries with his own dauntless spirit. Roosevelt, another great orator, picked his way with cat-like skill along the thorny paths of American politics, and brought into the war a nation united if not in admiration of their leader at least in its determination to beat Germany and Japan. The veil – or rather curtain – of deliberate obscurity surrounding Russia makes it impossible to speak in equally positive terms of Stalin, the third great Allied leader; but at least it is clear that in steering Russia triumphantly through the ordeals of 1941 and 1942 he showed iron resolution and consummate skill.

Popular sentiment in
Europe

One other factor must be mentioned. Unlike Napoleon in his early days, Hitler owed none of his success to the welcome of the countries he overran. He was, indeed, aided in most of the occupied territories by local parties fostered along Nazi or Fascist lines, but these represented only a small fraction of their country's population. The sentiment of the common people of Europe, throughout the war, was unquestionably on the Allied side. Hitler's 'New European Order' was never popularly accepted for anything other than the sham it was. In the west the German soldiers on the whole behaved correctly, but the demands of the political authorities for forced labour and the constant fear of the 'knock on the door' from the German secret police made the Nazi régime detested beyond even the normal detestation of a foreign conqueror. In the east, where they came up against less civilized oppon-ents, the German soldiers rapidly descended to the same savage brutality as the German political authorities. In both west and east they left, as a monument to all their tragically misdirected bravery, patriotism and skill, only a general distrust and hatred of Germany – a distrust which would require years of wise and patient effort by Germany's new leaders before it could be overcome.

CHAPTER 24
The Years Since 1945[1]

1. Post-War Europe Takes Shape, 1945–49

Throughout modern history the end of a war has usually been marked by the signing of a peace treaty. After the First World War came a clutch of such treaties – Versailles and the rest – signed in 1919 and 1920. The statesmen of that period were criticised for the length of time they took to conclude these agreements. In comparison with what happened after the Second World War, their work was swiftness itself.

By May 1945 the Allies had defeated Germany, though not yet Japan. They had demanded – successfully – that Germany should surrender unconditionally, and they had made a number of arrangements among themselves. Among these were that a new international organisation, the United Nations Organisation with headquarters in New York, should replace the League of Nations; and while the war against Japan proceeded the arrangements for this were perfected. As with the League, there was to be a General Assembly representing all the nations, and a guiding body – the Security Council of eleven members. On this, Britain, China, France, Russia and the U.S.A. would occupy permanent places. As the task of restraining an aggressor would fall mainly on the great Powers, they were given the dominant voice. Nearly all the real authority was concentrated in the Security Council; and no important decision could be taken unless the five permanent members of this were all agreed. (Much would be heard in the future of this power of veto by any one of the Big Five.)

Within the framework of the United Nations the Allies had agreed to create various subsidiary organisations for dealing with the relief and rehabilitation of war-torn Europe. These got to work from 1943 onwards as Axis-occupied territory was liberated. By 1947 they had saved millions of lives from the effects of famine, disease, the destruction of homes and the general economic breakdown in many of the defeated countries.

Another decision on which the Allies were agreed was that 'war criminals' should be tried and punished. This led among other things to a notable series of trials of the surviving Nazi leaders at Nuremberg before an International Military Tribunal. 'Crimes against peace' and 'crimes against humanity' were considered

Post-war arrangements

United Nations (1st meeting 1946)

Relief and rehabilitation (1943–47)

Trial of German war criminals, 1945–46

---

[1] This chapter does not aim to provide a narrative on the same scale as the rest of the book. To do so would need much more space than is here available. It is included for the sake of interest, to bring the story nearly up to the present day.

Differences between the Allied leaders – Stalin, Churchill, Truman and de Gaulle – became more pointed as soon as Germany was defeated. Cartoon by Low, June 1945.

as well as 'war crimes', and among those executed as a consequence were Ribbentrop, Seyss-Inquart and two of the generals most actively associated with Hitler. Göring cheated the hangman by committing suicide.

Peace treaties with Italy, Rumania, Bulgaria, Hungary, Finland, 1947

The Allies also at a fairly early stage agreed that their foreign ministers should prepare peace treaties with the minor defeated opponents – Italy, Rumania, Hungary, Bulgaria and Finland. Despite fierce wrangling prolonged over two years they actually managed to do this. By treaties signed in 1947 Italy, as a power which had helped the Allies in the later stages of the war, was treated lightly; her main punishments were some mild reparations, the detachment of Trieste, and the loss of her former North African colonies. Among the provisions of the other treaties, Rumania got back Transylvania from Hungary – to make up for the fact that Russia had taken over Bessarabia and other former Rumanian territory. By the treaty with Finland, Russia recovered nearly all that she had taken in 1939–40 and later lost during the German invasion.

American occupation of Japan

On the other side of the world there was the need to settle terms for Japan when her resistance abruptly collapsed in August 1945. It had been decided beforehand by the Allies that she should be reduced to her four main 'home' islands and that she should be 'demilitarised' and 'democratised'. Owing to America's massive part in the victory, President Truman (Roosevelt's successor) was able to claim a similar American predominance in occupying and administering the defeated country. It became the task of the powerful and flamboyant Supreme Commander in the Far East, General MacArthur, to supervise this process, which included

Peace treaty, 1951

rechanneling Japanese industry to peaceful ends and reducing the semi-divine position of the Emperor to that of a constitutional monarch. Japan was given a new system of democracy and trade unions, western-style, and soon – to boost her flagging economy – strong injections of American financial aid. By the time a formal peace treaty was at length signed in 1951 – against the opposition of Russia, who wanted harsher terms – Japan was entering a period of great industrial growth.

The greatest difficulty of the Allies in concluding a post-war settlement centred on Germany and to a lesser extent Austria. Certain broad principles had already been decided before the end of the war. Among the territorial changes, Austria was to be detached from Germany, Russia was to acquire part of East Prussia, and Poland was to be given a western frontier incorporating much former German land – the German inhabitants were expelled – up to the line of the rivers Oder and Neisse. These Polish gains at German expense were to apply until a permanent settlement could be made, and were regarded as compensating Poland for the loss of the eastern regions which Russia had taken in September 1939 and now kept. Besides suffering these losses, Germany was to be 'demilitarised', 'denazified' and purged of her war criminals. She was to be occupied for an indefinite time by the four main Allies who had defeated her – the U.S.A., Russia, Britain and (a late admission) France. Each was to occupy and administer a defined zone; and Berlin, the centre of the Allied Control Commission, was to be similarly divided into sectors, but administered as a whole. Reparations were to be collected by the powers from the areas they occupied. All this, broadly speaking, was duly put into effect when the war ended.

The big difficulty came in agreeing on the future organisation of Germany as a whole. Basically the U.S.A., Britain and France, occupying western Germany, were prepared, once a new liberal democracy had been successfully established, to retire from the scene and leave the Germans to run their own country. The Russians were not. Occupying eastern Germany as far west as the Elbe, their power extended farther into Europe than ever before. They were not prepared to retire until they were sure that this power in some form would endure. They intended, in other words, to ensure that their zone remained dominated, if not by Russian Communists, then by German Communists under Russian control.

All this, and a similar policy quickly followed by the Russians in Rumania and the restored Poland, where their proximity was used to bolster up the local Communist parties and destroy all opposition, was in violation of Stalin's wartime promise of 'free elections' given to Churchill and Roosevelt. It led to the 'Cold War' between Russia and her former allies. This struggle was 'cold' because there was no actual fighting between them; and it was 'war' because it was – and still is, though not quite so obviously – a conflict of the most serious and deadly kind. Behind what Winston Churchill in 1946 called 'the Iron Curtain that has descended across Europe', Soviet Russia by that time controlled a ring of satellite Communist states covering almost every country in south-east Europe. Only in Greece, which the Russians had recognised in 1945 to be within the British sphere of influence rather than their own, were the local Communists beaten. Even so, to foil the attempted Communist bid for power took a civil war, sustained British support to the government from 1944 to 1947, and American support when Attlee's post-war Labour government in Britain tired of this task.

The decision of President Truman in March 1947 to support the Greek govern-

	Germany
	Losses to Russia and Poland
	Occupation zones
	Division in Allied policy keeps Germany divided
	Russian satellite Communist régimes
	The 'Cold War' begins
	The 'Iron Curtain'
	The struggle in Greece
	The Truman Doctrine, 1947

European Recovery
Programme (The
Marshall Plan), 1947

ment financially in its struggle against a Communist movement fostered by Greece's northern neighbours was one of the first clear landmarks in the 'Cold War'. It marked the return of the U.S.A. to an active foreign policy, now directed to preventing the spread of communism. Under the so-called 'Truman Doctrine', first announced in connection with Greece and Turkey, American aid was to become available to any country threatened by external communist aggression. Three months later a more subtle American effort to combat communism was developed in the form of the European Recovery Programme, usually called (after the American Secretary of State at the time) the Marshall Plan. Just as the Americans had taken the foremost part in the immediate relief work in war-torn Europe from 1944 to 1947, so they now proposed to go beyond relief to recovery. American economic aid was to be available for the reconstitution of European industry in victorious and defeated states alike. Though behind it lay the supposition that communism may be bred out of poverty, and that if the poverty were removed the communism might be obviated, the granting of Marshall Aid on the scale which followed was certainly one of the most unselfish national acts in history. Unfortunately, though it would have been freely available to communist as well as democratic Europe, Russia quickly showed hostility and prevented her satellites (most of whom would dearly have liked such help) both from attending the European conference called to discuss it and from receiving any of the grants. Thanks to Marshall Aid, most of

NOSES LEFT!

A Low cartoon of July 1947. The Americans had launched the Marshall Plan to help post-war recovery. The Russian satellites of south-eastern Europe – Poland, Hungary, etc. – would have liked to share in these benefits, but were forbidden to by Russia, here represented by Foreign Minister Molotov.

'THE AMERICAN VOTING MACHINE'
A Russian view of the United Nations in the late 1940s. The sub-title is 'New Discoveries in Mechanisation'. A heavily domineering Uncle Sam presses a knob marked 'Against', and the smaller Powers automatically raise hands in his support. Powers on the front bench (l. to r.) are Luxembourg, Holland, Belgium, France, U.K.

the states of Europe outside the Communist bloc – from Britain and France through neutrals like Switzerland and Sweden to former enemies like Austria and Italy – were given a good start in industrial re-equipment, with the result that the 1950s became a period of unexpected economic prosperity.

Russia's counter to the Truman Doctrine and the Marshall Plan was soon seen. In October 1947 a Communist conference in Warsaw set up the delicately-named Communist Information Bureau, or Cominform, to coordinate the activities of the European Communist Parties – in other words to bring them into line with policy dictated from Moscow. This was an up-to-date version of the old Comintern – which had been dissolved in 1943 when Russia needed help from her allies – and it soon lost one foundation member. Within a few months Yugoslavia, under the Communist wartime guerrilla leader Marshal Tito, showed signs of following its own national policies and was expelled. Unlike the other Communist countries of Europe it had no common frontier with Russia, and so kept its freedom.

Not so fortunate was Czechoslovakia, a direct neighbour of Russia. Like the

The Cominform,
October 1947.

Expulsion of
Yugoslavia, 1948

WHO'S NEXT TO BE LIBERATED FROM FREEDOM?

A Low cartoon of March 1948. To stop eastern Europe looking for aid to the Marshall Plan, Russia tightened her control over the satellite states and imposed a Communist régime on Czechoslovakia, which had until then enjoyed a more democratic Government. In the cartoon, Stalin and Molotov plan the next move.

Communist *coup* in Czechoslovakia, February 1948

other states of eastern Europe liberated by the Red Army, she had begun her new life in 1946 with a coalition government. By the beginning of 1948 she was the only country in eastern Europe still to preserve a mixed ministry of this kind. In all the others the Communist ministers had managed with Russian support to oust their non-Communist colleagues and then organise elections which confirmed them in power. In February 1948 this technique, coupled with the fomentation of strikes and demonstrations, was applied to Czechoslovakia. President Benes, one of the original founders of the state, who had been driven out by Hitler in 1938 and resumed office in 1945, was compelled to accept an almost entirely Communist ministry. Shortly afterwards elections on a one party basis – yes or no – gave it an eighty-nine per cent majority. Benes resigned and his principal colleague Jan Masaryk, son of the country's main founder, committed suicide. From then on Russian control over eastern Europe was complete.

The Berlin Blockade, mid 1948–September 1949

With this weak spot in her protective girdle of satellite states repaired, Russia set out to tighten her hold over east Germany. Her problem here was that within her occupation zone was the city of Berlin, under four-power control. How, short of war, could she get the other three powers out? Her solution was to exert her agreed right, though in the most obstructive ways possible, to search road and rail transport crossing her zone from west Germany into Berlin. By creating intolerable delays she was able in practice to blockade west Berlin (the British, American and French sectors) and so try to create scarcities both for the local population and the Western armed forces which would compel the latter to withdraw. The Western Powers, however, resolutely withstood this move. They organised what came to be called 'the Berlin air lift'. Large numbers of British and American planes, service and civilian, flew by night and day over many months to maintain supplies to the western sectors – and the Russians, desiring success but not war, made no attempt to shoot them down. In all, over a quarter of a million supply flights were made into Berlin during this episode. In the contest of wills and nerve the Western Powers came out on top. They clung to their position in Berlin and after over a year Russia lifted the blockade.

Air lift

A Western success

The following year the gulf between Soviet Russia and her former wartime allies opened still wider. Already in 1948 a group of the western European countries – Britain, France, Holland, Belgium and Luxembourg – had signed a treaty in

Military alliances

'ON A DANGEROUS SWIMMING EXPEDITION'

The official Russian view of N.A.T.O. on its formation in 1949 – and since. Sub-titled 'On the surface – and down below', it shows President Truman of the U.S.A., Winston Churchill and E. Bevin of Britain, R. Schuman of France, P. Spaak of Belgium and others swimming along bearing a banner entitled 'North Atlantic Pact – doubly peaceful and purely defensive'. But beneath the surface they are travelling on a dollar-powered torpedo bearing the words 'Aggression Pact'.

Brussels Treaty, 1948

North Atlantic Treaty, 1949

Brussels pledging mutual support in the event of armed attack in Europe. In 1949 this was now extended by a further defensive alliance embracing not only these and a number of other European states – Italy, Portugal, Norway and Iceland – but also the U.S.A. and Canada. The agreement, for mutual help against aggression in the whole European and north Atlantic area, was termed the North Atlantic Treaty. Its distinctive feature was that it soon became not merely an arrangement to operate in time of war but also an institution – the North Atlantic Treaty Organisation (NATO) existing in peace, with a military headquarters in Paris under a Supreme Commander Europe (a post first held by General Eisenhower). Each member state made a commitment of forces to the common cause, and joint plans were framed and exercises held. From that day to this NATO has been a leading feature in the world scene. On the other side it was paralleled by the various defensive arrangements which Russia already had with her satellites – Albania, Bulgaria, Czechoslovakia, Hungary, Poland and Rumania – and which took more systema-

Warsaw Pact, 1955

tic form later as the Warsaw Treaty Organisation.

The widening gulf between the two camps was also seen in 1949 in their treatment of Germany. Tiring of repeated efforts to reach some kind of agreement with Russia about the unification or long-term future of that country, Britain, France and the U.S.A. decided to sponsor a new German political organisation within their

The Federal Republic (West Germany), 1949

occupation zones. In May 1949 the German Federal Republic was set up, with a capital at Bonn. Though confined in practice to west Germany and west Berlin, it claimed the whole of Germany as it rightful sphere. The Russians soon made an answering move. In October 1949 they established in east Germany the so-called German Democratic Republic. In due course the Federal Republic took its place in the NATO alliance, and the Democratic Republic in the Warsaw Pact Organisa-

The Democratic or 'People's' Republic (East Germany), 1949

tion. But whereas the Federal Republic, though at first under allied supervision, was always allowed and expected to have a mind and a policy of its own, the German Democratic Republic was intended to be – and still largely is – a puppet-state manipulated by Russia.

Mao Tse-tung's 'People's Republic' of China, October 1949

Two further events made 1949 a landmark in the history of the post-war world. In China the Nationalist forces of the official government headed by Chiang Kai-shek, who with American help had maintained the struggle against the Japanese during the Second World War, were themselves repeatedly defeated by Chinese Communist forces under Mao Tse-tung. Mao had the backing of Russia and by October 1949 he was able to proclaim a 'People's Republic' of China under his own direction. Chiang Kai-shek and his Nationalist forces had to retire to the island of Formosa where they still claimed, in the United Nations and elsewhere, to be the true representatives of China. A further huge area of the world's surface had thus come under Communist direction – though events were to prove that Chinese and

Russian atomic bombs, 1949

Russian Communists by no means saw eye to eye.

The second shock to the West in 1949 was the news that Russia had successfully developed an atom bomb. Information conveyed – for reasons of conscience – by scientists employed by Britain had helped her to do so. Previously the huge Russian superiority in land forces in Europe – the Americans having withdrawn and demobilised most of theirs – had been counter-balanced by the American monopoly of atomic weapons. Now, America still had a lead in nuclear technology, but the Russians were reducing it as fast as possible. The future, then, would see a struggle of world-wide setting, with two super-powers developing weapons capable of destroying all their opponents' main centres of population – and Europe's – within a few minutes. In comparison with this cosmic confrontation, the affairs of the individual European states began to seem of minor significance.

2. 'De-colonialisation' and 'Confrontation' outside Europe: Korea, Cuba, Vietnam, Israel

By 1949 it was possible to discern many future strands of development. Among these, at least as far as the Western Powers were concerned, was 'decolonialisation'. The moral argument – the right of the colonies to self-government – was now backed by the fact that the main colonial powers were exhausted from their efforts in the Second World War. In the post-war years many colonies were accordingly able to gain their independence, either by agreement or by force.

'De-colonialisation' – led by Britain

With Britain the method was usually by agreement. Attlee's post-war government set the pattern with the independence granted to India (accompanied by its partition into India and Pakistan) in 1947, and to Burma and Ceylon in 1948. In 1957, after a halt in de-colonialisation under Winston Churchill's second government, Britain extended independence to Malaya and to the Gold Coast (as Ghana). Not many people in 1945 imagined that Britain's African colonies would be considered ripe for self-government within less than fifty years, but the precedent of Ghana was soon widely followed. In Africa Nigeria, Sierra Leone, Tanganyika, Uganda, Kenya, Nyasaland (as Malawi) and Northern Rhodesia (as Zambia), were all granted independence during the early 1960s. Elsewhere during the 1960s the same concession was made to – among many others – Cyprus, Malta, Jamaica and other West Indian Islands, Mauritius, British Guiana (as Guyana) and the main Pacific possessions. Though most of these countries remained in the Commonwealth as independent states, the Commonwealth itself by this development, coupled with the already 'grown up' status of the great dominions of Canada, Australia, New Zealand and South Africa, became a far less powerful organisation than it had been in the past. Far more quickly than she had ever acquired it, Britain in the post-war years quietly divested herself of the British Empire.

Independence of India, 1947

Independence in Africa, 1957 onwards

The Commonwealth

The same process, though with much bloodshed, occurred in the French Empire. From 1946 the French fought to recover their old position in Indo-China, to which they had returned after the Japanese occupation. By 1954 they had had to acknowledge defeat in the north by a communist movement supported from China, and to sponsor independent non-communist states in the south. The new communist state was North Vietnam, the non-communist ones South Vietnam, Laos and Cambodia. As soon as the French retired a further struggle ensued between North and South Vietnam. Equally fierce was the clash in French North Africa. Though the French gave up their old position in Tunisia and Morocco fairly readily in 1956, there was a long and bloody struggle before they acknowledged – under the guidance of General de Gaulle in 1962 – the independence of Algeria. During this bitter conflict they granted independence relatively freely to the other French colonies in Africa, and so maintained good relations with them.

The French Empire

Fighting in Indo-China and Algeria before independence

Nearly all the other colonial powers of Europe, too, relinquished control over their colonies during this period. The former Dutch colonies – the Netherlands East Indies including Java and Sumatra, which had been occupied during the war – achieved independence in 1949 as Indonesia. In 1960 Belgium gave up her

Independence for Dutch and Belgian Colonies

348

Portugal holds on until 1974

territory in the Congo – only for anarchy to follow. United Nations' troops moved in to restore order, but for long had little success. Among the old colonial powers only Portugal seemed unmoved by the new trend, and clung to her long-standing possessions of Angola and Mozambique in Africa. Only after many years of warfare, in 1974, did she finally agree to give them up. In India she lost Goa in 1961, but to an Indian invasion, not by voluntary cession.

The Soviet 'Empire'

In discussing colonies, one other European power must be mentioned. Before the war, Soviet Russia officially possessed no colonies – nor does she now. But in 1945 Russia recovered the old Tsarist non-Russian Baltic provinces – Estonia, Latvia and Lithuania – which had enjoyed independence between the wars. By 1948, she was also fully in control of Poland, Czechoslovakia, Hungary, Rumania, Bulgaria and East Germany. All these territories she not merely dominated politically and militarily but also exploited economically. While the rest of the world was giving up colonies, Soviet Russia, theoretically the arch-enemy of imperialism, was constructing for herself something remarkably like an empire.

The U.S.A. and Russia

If 'de-colonialisation' is one theme of European – and world – history since 1945, another is clearly the clash between the U.S.A. and the western European nations on the one hand, and Soviet Russia and her communist supporters on the

HISTORY DOESN'T REPEAT ITSELF

A Low cartoon of July 1950. The old League of Nations had failed to act with sufficient vigour against aggression in the 1930s. Truman's lead to U.N.O. over Communist North Korea's invasion of South Korea was very different in spirit, and proved successful.

other. The early stages of this conflict have already been mentioned.[1] Since 1949 the world has seen the increasing rivalry of the two super-powers in nuclear weapons – the U.S.A. had the hydrogen bomb by 1952, Russia only a year later – and in the exploration of space. The latter seems peaceful but relies heavily on rocket, radar and other techniques developed primarily for military purposes. It is designed not simply to enlarge mens' knowledge of the universe but also to confer strategic advantages on the exploring power.

The world has also seen since 1949 a series of direct and indirect clashes between these powers involving war or its possibility. First came war in Korea. In this the Communist state of North Korea, supported by Russian arms, drove south in an attempt to take over the non-Communist state of South Korea. The latter, however, was promptly supported by the U.S.A. and on American initiative by the United Nations – who were able to become involved largely because at the time of the decision the Russian representative on the Security Council was not present to exercise a veto. The U.S.A.-U.N.O. intervention checked the invasion and began to

Hydrogen bombs, 1952

Rivalry in nuclear weapons and space exploration

Korean War, 1950–53

[1] See pp. 341–46.

FIGHTING IN KOREA
Fighting in the Korean War was very much on the lines of the Second World War – by infantry, artillery, tanks and aircraft. The Americans, whose prompt action brought in U.N.O. and saved South Korea from being overrun by Communists from the North, refrained from any form of nuclear attack.

MISSILES OFF CUBA, 1962

The most dangerous crisis since 1939–45 arose in 1962 when the Russians, with the co-operation of the new Cuban leader, Fidel Castro, set up rocket-launching sites in Cuba. On the Russian ship photographed above can be seen missiles intended for these sites. At the risk of nuclear war, President Kennedy successfully insisted that these supply ships should turn back short of Cuba.

overrun North Korea, at which stage the Chinese stepped in to support the North Koreans and a stalemate ensued, with Korea divided much as before.

The Cuba Missiles confrontation 1962

In Korea the U.S.A., by Truman's decision to intervene at once, successfully 'contained' or held back Communist aggression. Equally successful was President Kennedy's decision in 1962, taken at the risk of setting off a nuclear war, to turn back Russian ships bearing rocket missiles to Castro's Communist régime in Cuba. These missiles would have been installed too close to the U.S.A. for her comfort. Fortunately for the world the Russians recalled their ships at the critical moment.

The struggle in Vietnam

Much less successful was the American intervention in Vietnam, part of former French Indo-China. President Johnson's intention was to help South Vietnam against persistent attack from an internal communist movement, the Viet Cong, which had been backed in 1964 by an invasion from communist North Vietnam. Once again the communist cause was supported by Russia and China. The Americans expended vast sums and effort in supplying the South, and in bombing North Vietnamese key-points and communications. But despite having more than half a million men in the country they were unable to deal effectively with the Viet Cong. Finally President Nixon pulled the American forces out in 1973 when they were still well short of victory, and when the safety of South Vietnam still remained far from assured. The result was seen in 1975, when the North Vietnamcse, still supplied from outside and ignoring the 'stand-still' arrangements agreed with the Americans, overran the South and extended their communist régime over the whole country. In this case the cost of 'containing' communism in a distant part of the world, alike in money, men and national unity and morale, proved more than the American people was finally willing to bear.

It is not, however, only from the clash of Russia and the East against America and the West, of communism against liberal democracy, that the peace of the world has been threatened since 1945. In the eastern Mediterranean area a series of conflicts has occurred between the new Jewish state of Israel and her Arab neighbours Egypt, Syria and Jordan. These conflicts, it is true, could hardly have taken the form they did without the arms, technical advice and funds supplied to the combatants by their backers outside; but they originated not from the communist *v.* non-communist struggle but from older sources such as land-hunger, nationalism, race and religion.

Internationally, the trouble began from the moment in 1947 when the British, tired of trying to satisfy both the Arab and the Jewish populations of Palestine, decided to abandon their mandate over that country and remit the problem to the United Nations. The Arabs, who had dwelt in Palestine for many hundreds of years and had been liberated from Turkish rule in 1918, had naturally resented the return of the Jews in consequence of the Zionist movement and in particular the

The Arab-Jewish conflict

EUROPE DIVIDED 1949–72

Communist States, Russian–dominated   Other Communist States   States in North Atlantic Treaty Organisation with U.S.A. and Canada during all or most of this time

Pre-war boundary of U.S.S.R.   Post-War boundary of U.S.S.R.

increased numbers of Jewish immigrants following Hitler's persecution in Germany. The Jews had equally naturally resented the restrictions on immigration imposed by the British in order to placate the Arabs, and had begun terrorist action against British rule. The United Nations, after investigating the problem, suggested partition; but this did not seem just or acceptable to the Arabs. Nevertheless the instant the British withdrew, in May 1948, the Jews brought it about by proclaiming their own state of Israel. When the surrounding Arabs reacted by invasion, the Jews beat off their attacks and ended up with more land than the United Nations had proposed. From then on some 900,000 Palestinian Arabs, refugees from the territory taken over by the Jews, lived miserably in camps on the borders of Israel, to provide a lasting source of further hatred and conflict.

This situation, coupled with developments in Egypt, soon created one of the most serious crises since the Second World War. In 1952 a nationalist and reformist movement in Egypt overthrew the corrupt King Farouk and within a year established a republic, soon to be headed by one of the organisers of the *coup*, the dashing and aggressive Colonel Nasser. Nasser sought to make Egypt the centre of a united Arab world, and in so doing supported the cause of the expelled Palestinian Arabs against Israel. He instigated border raids into Israel from Syria and the Egyptian territory of Sinai, prevented Israeli ships using the Suez Canal, and blockaded the Gulf of Akaba through which Red Sea traffic approached Israel's southernmost port. The Israelis decided to settle accounts with him, and their opportunity came in 1956.

In that year Britain by agreement with Egypt withdrew the last of her forces which had occupied some part of that country since 1882. A few weeks later Nasser nationalised the Suez Canal, a waterway which was the subject of international treaties and financed and administered by an international company. His excuse was that the U.S.A. had withdrawn an earlier offer to finance the building of a new dam on the Nile at Aswan, and that he needed revenues from the Canal for this purpose. Britain and France, where most of the Suez Canal shares were held, reacted strongly; and when international condemnation of Nasser's action failed to secure results, they seem to have concerted an attack with Israel. On 29th October 1956 the Israelis invaded Sinai – where they crushed the Egyptians with ease and rapidly reached the Gulf of Akaba. A day later Britain and France, on the plea of preserving the free passage of the Canal, ordered both sides not to fight within ten miles of it. When Israel accepted this, and Egypt as naturally refused, British aircraft from Cyprus the next day attacked the Egyptian Air Force. Five days later – a surprising lapse of time which proved fatal to the Allied scheme – Anglo-French forces landed at Port Said and began to occupy the Canal – which by this time was blocked with sunken ships.

The Anglo-French intervention, despite some defects of timing and planning, could easily have overrun the entire Canal Zone and toppled Nasser. This was probably one of the hopes of the British Prime Minister, Sir Anthony Eden, who had seen the futility of 'appeasing' Hitler and Mussolini in the 1930s and was resolved to deal firmly with future dictators. However, the outcry in the United Nations – where Russia and the U.S.A. for once found themselves in agreement – and among anti-imperialist circles in Britain, was so great at the thought of Britain and France setting on Egypt in the old nineteenth-century great-power fashion, that within a day Eden called off the operation. He did so – just when it was nearing com-

Partition of Palestine:
Israel founded,
May 1948

Arab attack on Israel,
1948–49: Palestine
Arab refugees

Nasser in Egypt

The Suez crisis, 1956

Israel attacks Egypt –

– followed by Britain
and France, October
1956

Anglo-French
withdrawal, November,
1956

plete success – on condition the United Nations would take over. A governing factor in Eden's change of mind seems to have been the shocked anger of President Eisenhower, and an American threat to cut off monetary aid from Britain – an anger shattering to Eden, since veiled hints had been given to American officials and no objection had been received in advance from the President. Following Britain's decision France too withdrew, United Nations troops entered in a peace-keeping role, and Nasser survived. Shortly afterwards Eden, his health seriously affected, resigned. The Canal remained in Egyptian hands, the nearly defeated Nasser was a hero, Israel had won a great victory, and only Britain and France were in disgrace.

The ineffectiveness of this last flick of the British lion's tail prompted Nasser to believe that in time he could not merely revenge himself on Israel but obliterate her. He built up what unity he could between Egypt and Israel's other Arab neighbours, and drew heavily on Russia for military supplies. When the United Nations troops withdrew from Sinai in 1967 he again blockaded Israel's Red Sea approaches and massed tanks ready for offensive action. The Israelis, seeing what was coming, struck first. In the 'Six-Dar War' of June 1967 they first destroyed the bulk of Nasser's air force by a surprise assault, then in a couple of days shattered the Egyptian army in Sinai. Other attacks against the Syrians and the Jordanians proved almost equally successful. In one short week Israel seemed to have settled the issue and ensured her own survival.

Nevertheless the struggle was not over. Border clashes between Israel and her Arab neighbours repeatedly occurred – to flare up into a war again in 1973, when the Israelis were taken by surprise (they were attacked on their sacred Day of Atonement) but quickly recovered. The tragic plight of the Palestinian Arab refugees, by this time more numerous than ever, continued to make any permanent settlement difficult. It was to draw attention to their grievances that their guerrilla leaders began terrorist activity involving the frequent 'hijacking' of aircraft and the kidnapping of ambassadors and other prominent men.

Nasser plans revenge on Israel

Israel's preventive attack: the Six-Day War, June 1967

Continuing bitterness

The 'Yom Kippur' War, October 1973

3. Developments in Russia, Germany and France. The European Movement

There is no space here to refer to domestic affairs in most of the European countries since 1945, but something at least must be said of developments within Russia, Germany and France.

In Russia – which, we must remember, covers not only about half of Europe but also one-third of Asia – one landmark was the death of Stalin in 1953. Until then the main features, apart from the domination over eastern Europe and the development of nuclear weapons, were the restoration of war-damaged Russia with the help of sternly exacted reparations, the completion of the Fourth Five-Year Plan, and the continuation of Stalin's ruthless dictatorship. Much was certainly done. About a quarter of Russia's material goods – houses, factories, bridges, machinery, etc. – had been destroyed in the war, and had to be replaced; and the Five Year Plan operating from 1946 doubled Russia's output in heavy industry and made her the second greatest industrial power in the world. But the cost in repression and denial of human freedoms – freedom to discuss, to disagree, to emigrate, to pursue any line not approved by the Party even in subjects like painting and music – was stupendous. At the time of Stalin's death millions

Russia after 1945

Stalin's dictatorship

Reconstruction, industrial advance and terror

were in forced labour camps and a new 'purge' seemed imminent. Stalin's best known biographer has left a memorable picture of the dictator's final years:

> immured . . . in the Kremlin, refusing over the last twenty-five years of his life to have a look at a Soviet village, refusing to step down into a factory; refusing even to cast a glance at the Army of which he was the Generalissimo; spending his life in a half-real, half-fictitious world of statistics and mendacious propaganda films . . . seeing enemies creeping at him from every nook and cranny . . . pulling the wires behind the great purge trials; personally checking and signing 383 black lists with the names of thousands of doomed Party members – inserting in his own hand passages of praise to his own 'genius' and to his own modesty! . . . into his official adulatory biography . . . .[1]

Russia after Stalin's death

After Stalin's death – which may or may not have been from natural causes – there were two or three years during which the Soviet leadership was popularly described as 'collective'. By 1956, however, an obvious leader had emerged in the person of Nikita Khrushchev, a henchman of Stalin's with particular experience of agriculture. His leadership lasted until 1964, when his colleagues tired of his erratic methods and personality. He was never, however, another dictator. From 1953 onwards there was a determination among the Soviet leaders that no one should achieve an all-powerful position similar to Stalin's, and a readiness to relax some of the more odious features of his tyranny. Stalin's chief of police, Beria, was quickly executed, and millions were released from the forced labour camps – many of which still, however, continued. In 1956 Khrushchev, at the Twentieth Congress of the Russian Communist Party, 'came clean' about many of Stalin's methods and mistakes. From then on the statues and mammoth pictures of the former leader were banished from the public squares and he was no longer officially recognised as the third in the great Communist succession of Marx and Lenin – though in point of fact his place in the trinity seems unassailable.

N. Khrushchev (until 1964)

In conformity with this milder policy, Khrushchev was prepared to advocate 'peaceful co-existence' – in other words, warfare by diplomacy and propaganda only – with the West. As a result there was some lessening of the tension between Russia and the non-communist Powers. Even this moderate 'thaw' was interrupted, however, by incidents such as the Cuban missiles crisis of 1962. He and his colleagues continued, moreover, to maintain Russia's armed might, and even at one time gained a lead over the U.S.A. in the space exploration associated with it. And when the partial easing of the dictatorship in Russia produced movements in the satellite states of eastern Europe to liberalise the governments there, Khrushchev and his successors were just as ready to intervene as Stalin would have been.

Russian intervention in Hungary (1956) and Czechoslovakia (1968)

In 1956, when the Hungarian Communist government showed signs of moving in a more liberal direction and wished to get rid of Russian troops, Russian tanks occupied Budapest and crushed the incipient movement for national freedom. Twelve years later, in 1968, when the Czechoslovak ministers under Dubček began to allow greater liberty of discussion, Czechoslovakia suffered the same fate. The main difference after Stalin in fact was an alteration not so much in policy as in the

---

[1] I DEUTSCHER: *Russia in Transition*, N.Y. 1957, quoted in L. Kochan: *The Making of Modern Russia*, Cape 1962.

TEMPORARY DOWNFALL OF A DEAD DICTATOR, 1956
Khrushchev's less repressive régime in Russia after the death of Stalin mistakenly led the peoples of eastern Europe to believe they would be allowed to set up more liberal governments. The biggest anti-Russian rising was in Hungary (where, above, we see a statue of Stalin overthrown). But Russian tanks soon moved into Budapest to crush the movement and reinstate 'hardline' Communists in the Government.

treatment of those who took a different line from the leadership. Under Stalin's successors it was possible for an important official to lose office without being shot.

A quarter of a century after the setting up of the Federal and the Democratic Republics, Germany was still no nearer to national unity. A casualty of the split between Soviet Russia and the West, German unity must seemingly await the day when that split is healed – presumably by one or the other side triumphing completely. In other respects, Germany's achievement since the war has been remarkable. In West Germany the Chancellorship of the aged Christian Democrat Konrad Adenauer (1949–63) witnessed not only the end of the former bad relationship with France and Britain and the participation of the Federal Republic in NATO and the 'Common Market', but also what has been called 'the German economic miracle'. With much American aid but also by dint of hard work and sound financial policy – the special province of Professor Erhard, who succeeded Adenauer as Chancellor – the shattered towns of West Germany were rebuilt with incredible speed and her industries fully restored. In 1950 there were 15 million unemployed in West Germany; ten years later there was a shortage of labour. Thanks to this unexpected prosperity and the policy of the Western Powers in helping to set West Germany on her feet and withdrawing their forces of occupation at a fairly early

Germany

West Germany
(Federal Republic)
under Adenauer and
Erhard

date (1952), Adenauer and Erhard were able to re-establish parliamentary democracy successfully, and to help live down the memory of the Nazi past.

East Germany (Democratic Republic)

Not nearly so fortunate was East Germany. Stripped of industrial machinery and dominated by the Russians and the East German Communists, the Democratic Republic for many years had a standard of living far below that of the Federal Republic. Because of this and the lack of political and intellectual freedom, there was constant secret emigration into West Germany – despite the barbed wire and machine-gun posts on watchtowers erected along the frontier. Feeling against the Russians and the government mounted, and in 1953 there were widespread strikes and revolts. As a result of these – which were quickly crushed – the Russians dropped their favoured East German politician, W. Ulbricht, and relaxed their demands for reparations.

Risings of 1953

The weak point in the East German barrier was Berlin, where for some years it was possible to pass from the east to the west of the city without too much difficulty. This loophole the East German government under Ulbricht's successor K. Gottwald closed in 1961 by erecting a huge and heavily guarded wall across Berlin. From then on the East Germans, 3 million of whom had escaped to the West since 1945, were effectively prisoners within their own Republic. Forced to concencentrate on improving conditions within their own area instead of escaping from it, they achieved during the later 1960s a gradually rising standard of living. For long West Germany refused to recognise this Communist puppet-state in the East; but in 1972 a new Chancellor, the Socialist Willy Brandt, abandoned this policy and recognised the Democratic Republic in an effort to reduce the tension with Russia. His gesture secured somewhat easier visiting conditions between East and West Germany but little else. And with West Germany's formal acceptance of the split, German unity seemed farther away than ever.

The Berlin Wall, 1961

Brandt's recognition of Democratic Republic, 1972

France

France, like Germany, also showed great powers of recovery in the years after 1945. Her swift and overwhelming defeat in 1940, followed by the German occupation and the split between the 'collaborators' headed by Pétain at Vichy and the 'resisters' headed abroad by de Gaulle, had been shattering experiences. Nevertheless her rapid liberation in 1944, in which de Gaulle's 'Fighting French' and the internal resistance forces had played an honourable if subordinate part, gave her a favourable start for the post-war era. Gaullist officials were able to take over the administration behind the retreating German armies; and well before the war was over, de Gaulle was heading a provisional government in France. The Third Republic having, in effect, died when the Vichy régime was set up in the autumn of 1940, it was necessary to give France a new constitution, and for this purpose an assembly was elected in October 1945. The ministry formed from it under de Gaulle as Premier was a coalition of the most successful parties – the moderate Catholics, the Socialists and the Communists (who had played a big part in the Resistance after Germany attacked Russia). De Gaulle, however, was soon at odds with his Cabinet. In particular, he wanted the new constitution to give greater power to the head of state, the President, to avoid some of the extreme instability of governments that had weakened the Third Republic. Defeated on this, de Gaulle resigned in January 1946 and the task of making the new constitution continued under a Socialist premier.

Provisional government under de Gaulle, 1944–45

His resignation, January 1946

After the first proposals for this constitution had failed to win public acceptance, a second version was approved by a narrow margin in a referendum during October

BUILDING THE BERLIN WALL, 1961

To stop free contact with the western world, the Communist-dominated states of eastern Europe put up barbed wire fences and wooden watchtowers manned by soldiers. These barriers stretched across Europe from the Black Sea to the Baltic. A gap in the system existed in Berlin, the western half of which was under non-Communist control. When the flow of refugees from East to West became too great for the East to tolerate, the East German Government built this wall across Berlin to seal its people in.

1946. So came into being the Fourth Republic – which in its reshufflings of political power proved remarkably like the Third. During its existence war damage was restored, economic life was greatly reinvigorated, and many measures of social reform (such as state insurance schemes) and nationalisation (of coal mining, gas, electricity, and the bigger banks and insurance companies) were carried out.

Among other events in the Fourth Republic's short span of life was a Communist bid for power in 1947–48 spearheaded by widespread strikes. It was defeated by

The Fourth Republic, 1947–58: social reform and nationalisation

Monnet and
economic planning

Schuman and the
Common Market:
E.E.C. formed, 1958

united action on the part of the socialist and centre parties. An important innovation was an economic planning commission under Jean Monnet. With the help
of Marshall Aid from the U.S.A., it had great success in increasing industrial output.
Steps were also taken under two great foreign ministers, Georges Bidault and
Robert Schuman, to develop close economic and defensive links with France's
neighbours, including Germany. On the economic side, these culminated in the
formation of the European Economic Community or Common Market in 1958.
On the military side, in 1949 France joined NATO at its inception, and in 1956 she
took part with Britain in the ill-fated Suez affair.

Loss of Indo-China,
1954

Independence struggle
in Algeria, 1954–62

Apart from the instability of its governments, the greatest weaknesses of the
Fourth Republic were its failure to check inflation (the continued rise in prices
and decline in the value of the currency) and its lack of success in two colonial wars.
The bitter six-year struggle to retain Indo-China was abandoned in 1954, only
for another damaging conflict to open up in Algeria. Here France clung to her
position because Algeria had for long been officially a part of metropolitan France
and contained nearly a million colonists of French descent. Nevertheless a
'national liberation' movement of some 20,000 Algerian Arab rebels, using guerrilla
and terrorist tactics, successfully defied the efforts of a French army numbering
350,000 to suppress it. Governments in Paris came and went without improving
the situation, and at length it became clear that France was tiring of this long and
bloody struggle. A new government came in whose head was prepared to negotiate
with the rebels. At once the French army and colonist leaders, fearing a 'sell-out'
by the civilian authorities, seized power in Algiers. The result, indirectly, was the
downfall of the new government in Paris and the recall to power of General
de Gaulle.

de Gaulle Premier
with special powers,
June 1958

The Fifth Republic,
January 1959:
de Gaulle President,
1959–69

Nationalist policy

The General, convinced that the weakness of various administrations in the
Fourth Republic would end in disaster, had been waiting in the wings for twelve
years for this summons. A Gaullist group claiming to be above party had been
formed, only to become another party; but de Gaulle himself had stood aside from
(and above) the political arena. Now, summoned in the crisis by the President,
he came back as Premier on his own terms. These included the right to govern by
decree for six months and a reform of the constitution to strengthen the power of
the President. The Assembly accepted him, and four months later his new
constitution was ready and approved in a referendum by a four-fifths majority of
the French people. Before the end of the year elections produced a Gaullist
majority for the new Assembly, and de Gaulle himself was elected President.
In January 1959 the new constitution setting up the Fifth Republic came into
force, allowing de Gaulle far greater powers than any previous French President.

De Gaulle, whose supremacy lasted until France tired of his paternalistic
approach, pursued French national interests in a vigorous and independent way.
Under him, France successfully developed atomic weapons of her own and – while
not withdrawing from NATO – declined to have NATO forces stationed in her territory. On the economic side, he encouraged industrial reorganisation and expansion,
and continued to collaborate with fellow members of the European Economic
Community, but vetoed the admission of Britain to this organisation. This was
no doubt because of Britain's continuing Commonwealth interests, and his fear
that with Britain in the Common Market the French leadership would be undermined. In at least one respect his régime, in general highly successful, bitterly

disappointed those whose actions had occasioned his recall to power. He became convinced that Algeria must be given her independence; and when the Army and colonist leaders in Algiers tried another *coup*, this time against him, he suppressed them ruthlessly.

Algerian independence, 1962

Although there was much that was depressing in the Europe of the post-war years – such as the protracted 'cold war', and the loss of freedom in the east European countries – there was also much that was exhilarating. Among the heartening things were the speed of war-damage restoration in every western country except Britain, and the rising tide of prosperity in western Europe during the 1950s and 1960s. The latter was certainly helped by another encouraging feature – the greatly improved economic co-operation between the western nations.

Behind this was the desire on the part of statesmen in several countries for some form of European integration or union which would both improve the standard of living and help to lessen the possibility of international conflict. Some further visualised a European federation, a United States of Europe, strong enough to counterbalance the power of the two giants, Russia and the U.S.A. But while some leaders of the European movement advocated giving up national sovereignty in the interests of peace and progress, most felt that political union was a long-term end for which the way must first be paved by closer economic co-operation.

'The European Movement'

This kind of thinking inspired a number of steps which were taken during the 1940s and 1950s. Perhaps the first was the decision in 1944 of Belgium, the Netherlands and Luxemburg to form a customs union – the 'Benelux' group. Next came the insistence of the Americans, in offering Marshall Aid during 1947, that the European countries should co-operate intelligently in its allocation. From this sprang in 1948 the Organisation for European Economic Co-operation, a body formed to administer Marshall Aid, and one in which the various national representatives learnt to harmonise the needs and demands of their own country with those of others.

The Benelux Customs Union, 1944

Organisation for European Economic Co-operation, 1948

Almost simultaneously came a move on the political side to promote what was virtually a European parliament. The Council of Europe, as it came to be called, was formed in 1949 with headquarters at Strasbourg. It consisted of a Council of Foreign Ministers and an Assembly of representatives from the various western and north-western European parliaments.[1] Its functions, however, have been limited to discussion and recommendation. Few people in any country would as yet be prepared to see it take over the powers of decision vested in the various national parliaments.

Council of Europe, 1949

Two years later came the formation of a very practical organisation, the European Coal and Steel Community. Its first members were France, West Germany, Italy and the Benelux countries; and its object was to form a large area in which there would be no trade restrictions or internal tariff barriers limiting the production and free movement of coal and steel. The conception of the French Foreign Minister Robert Schuman, who as a Lorrainer in 1914 had served in the German Army, it brought the six countries together for this very limited purpose. It was strongly opposed by Britain at the time for fear of losing control over two of her greatest industries. Nevertheless its success was such that its members soon be-

European Coal and Steel Community, 1951

---

[1] It has since been joined by representatives of other non-communist countries, for example Austria, Greece and Turkey.

LOVE-IN OF THE LONDON HIPPIES, 1967
A cartoon of December 1967 by the German, Paul Flora. The British Labour ministers, headed by Harold Wilson and George Brown, serenade General de Gaulle – to admit Britain to the Common Market – but he remains unmoved.

came eager to extend its scope. The result was that in 1957 the same powers agreed to establish a European Economic Community, or Common Market. The Treaty of Rome which defined this agreement provided that the six countries should gradually establish a common market by removing barriers such as quotas and tariffs, and institute instead a common tariff against non-members. After a transitional period of fifteen years, it was intended that there should be unrestricted movement between member countries of goods, services, money and people. At the same time a similar authority to bring about the pooling of resources, financial and technical, for the development of nuclear energy was set up in the form of the European Atomic Energy Commission (Euratom).

European Economic Community (E.E.C.) or Common Market, 1958

Attitude of Britain

One reason why Britain declined to join the Common Market at the outset was the strength of her trading links with the Commonwealth. Appreciative of the value of a large customs area, but reluctant to alter her special arrangements with the Commonwealth countries, Britain proposed an alternative scheme to the E.E.C. This was that there should be a free trade area covering the western European countries, but that each should maintain what tariffs it liked against non-member countries. By such an arrangement, Britain could maintain her policy of preferential tariffs for the Commonwealth. The Common Market countries would not

European Free Trade Association (E.F.T.A.), 1960

accept this idea, but some others did, with the result that in 1960 there came into being the European Free Trade Association of Britain, Norway, Sweden, Denmark, Switzerland, Austria and Portugal. Both the E.E.C. and E.F.T.A. proved their value, but the former commanded by far the greater industrial resources and purchasing power. Britain accordingly underwent a change of heart, and in 1961, in Harold Macmillan's government, applied for membership of the E.E.C. Her application was finally vetoed by France in 1963. After an interval of Labour Government in Britain the new Conservative administration of Edward Heath then tried again in 1970, and this time, after two years' negotiation, she was admitted. So too were most of the other E.F.T.A. countries.

Britain joins the Common Market, 1972

The Common Market has become larger, and potentially more valuable than ever. But it is of course disliked both by those who fear the loss of national sovereignty and by those who wish to see western Europe kept weak so that communism will meet with less resistance. The British Labour Party, which includes followers of both these lines of thought as well as passionate 'Europeans,' found itself divided over the merits of the Common Market. A considerable proportion of the party disliked Britain entering, and wished her to withdraw. When Labour came into office in 1974 it accordingly set out – as a compromise – to 'renegotiate' the terms of Britain's entry, and to submit the final 'stay-in or withdraw' decision to a popular vote. This was duly done in 1975, and the first referendum in British history resulted in an emphatic vote to 'stay in'.

'Renegotiation', 1974

These are a few of the features which have marked European history since 1945. From one aspect, we see sharper division than ever; from another, the stirring, whether in the Communist East or the non-Communist West, to achieve greater integration and co-operation. Alike in east and west the technical progress has been immense. The complexity of life has correspondingly increased, with attendant social problems ranging from urban congestion and environmental pollution to drug-addiction and the growth of violence. One thing, however, is certain. From the time the United States entered the war in 1941 and continued to maintain forces in Europe afterwards, and from the time when Soviet Russia beat back the German invasion and spread westwards, we can no longer think of European history in largely European terms. We can still, of course study the domestic history of the individual European countries; but the history of their relations with each other has become inextricably entangled with the history of the world.

Europe and the World

CONCLUSION
Nationalism, Dictatorship, Democracy

From the French Revolution to the Second World War the two conceptions dominating European politics were, as we have so frequently seen, the ideas of nationalism and democracy. How do they fare to-day?

Nationalism, one of the strongest forces in Europe, but somewhat on the decline

First, nationalism. Obviously it still has a very strong hold on Europe. The peace treaties of 1919, by recognising the break-up of Austria-Hungary and by establishing Poland and the Baltic republics, gave expression to the longing of peoples to be governed by men of their own nationality. It was on the rock of nationalism that the international experiment of the League of Nations came to grief. In countries like Germany and Italy, which emerged from the First World War with grievances, nationalism reached an unheard-of pitch, in part through the hysterical oratory of dictators; and this unbridled nationalism was in turn directly responsible for the Second World War.

It may seem strange, in view of all this, to hold that nationalism – in Europe, but not in less developed parts of the world – has probably attained its zenith and may from now on decline. Those countries which have longest enjoyed national unity and freedom, while still deeply patriotic, are less fervent in their nationalism than before. Britain and France, for example, have voluntarily abandoned nearly all the legal ties which bound their overseas possessions to them, and have long ceased to dream of acquiring further imperial territory. Nationalism is still one of the strongest forces in Europe to-day, but the whole trend of modern civilisation must ultimately work against it. Education, ease of communication, the spread of common standards of culture, the sheer necessity of preserving the peace – all may be factors in speeding the decline of nationalism. The creation of the United Nations to replace the old League, and the movement for union in western Europe are indications of the increasing loss of faith in unadulterated national self- sufficiency.

Democracy between the two World Wars

And what of the other conception, democracy? Here the high-water mark was reached immediately after the First World War, when Germany, Austria, Poland, Czechoslovakia, Yugoslavia, the new Baltic states all gave themselves democratic constitutions, with parliaments, written statements of citizens' rights, and the like. From the French Revolution onwards the peoples of Europe had broadly assumed that the path of democracy was the path of progress. By 1914 of the great powers in Europe, Britain and France were the most democratic, Russia the least, Germany and Austria-Hungary about mid-way, being autocracies with some important concessions to democracy. The fact that Britain, France and Belgium, and later Italy and the U.S.A., all found themselves on the same side in the war of 1914–18 cast a kind of democratic halo round the Allies. Even Tsarist Russia, experimenting with the Duma, was supposed to be coming into line. The sentiment of democracy as well as that of nationalism was deliberately appealed to by the Allies in their propaganda against Turkish rule over Arabs, Austrian rule over Czechs, Slovaks, Poles,

Croats, and so on. When the Allies won, it was natural that new democracies should spring up all over Europe. Even defeated states like Germany became democratic, anxious to repudiate the system which had led them to disaster.

Within a few years, however, the picture began to look different. Most of these countries were lacking in parliamentary experience and tradition. For many of them it did not seem to be a 'natural growth'. Their party system worked badly, mainly because they adopted the idea of proportional representation, which by multiplying parties confused the electorate. (In 1925 in Latvia, for instance, the electors were invited to choose between forty-three parties.) It was usually impossible for one party to obtain a clear majority, so resolute government became rare. Then economic conditions were very difficult in the years after 1918, and became increasingly so in the slump of the early 1930s. Finally, the secure and established powers of the West did little to help some of these infant democracies. Germany, for example, was constantly kept aware of the fact that her republic was founded in defeat by the way in which moderate requests, such as a customs union with Austria, were refused – a mistake for which Britain and France could have kicked themselves when it helped to produce Hitler. For Germany at least, the idea of a democracy became associated with the idea of permanent inferiority to Britain and France.

Failure of democracy in many countries

So nearly everywhere in Europe democracy after 1919 went down before dictatorship. Hitler in Germany, Mussolini in Italy, Kemal in Turkey, Pilsudski in Poland, de Rivera and later Franco in Spain, King Alexander in Yugoslavia, King Carol in Rumania, Metaxas in Greece, Salazar in Portugal, Gömbös in Hungary, Dollfuss, then Schuschnigg in Austria – these at some time between the two world wars exercised almost complete power in their respective countries.

Dictators uppermost in Europe

To this formidable list of dictatorships must also be added that of the Union of Soviet Socialist Republics, in the person first of Lenin, then of Stalin. After the Bolsheviks, in the years following the revolution of 1917, had driven out their foreign enemies and crushed military resistance at home, they still had to 'liquidate' the opposition of most of the upper middle classes. This was done by the traditional means – a gigantic 'terror'. As we have seen, a full socialist policy of state ownership was applied, the opposition of the peasants to having their holdings 'collectivised' being brutally suppressed. Under Stalin, the open, secret, and imaginary supporters of Trotsky were then 'liquidated' as ruthlessly as they themselves had 'liquidated' aristocrats and bourgeois capitalists. Officially the Union of Soviet Socialist Republics in 1936 advanced along the path of democracy by a new constitution giving the secret ballot and greater guarantees of personal liberty. But in fact the Communist either means by democracy something very different from what the non-Communist takes the word to mean or else he adopts it merely as a valuable catchword; for while the Communist Party permits no opposition, looking for true democracy in Russia and the other 'totalitarian' countries would seem to be rather like looking for a needle in a whole collection of haystacks.

U.S.S.R.

Soviet 'democracy'

In considering dictatorship in Europe between the two world wars, two or three points should be remembered. First, the dictatorships did not spring from nothing. They had historic causes – usually defeat in war or social chaos following parliamentary inefficiency and labour troubles, or economic collapse. Communism, the dictatorship of the left, also created, by reaction, Fascism and Nazism, the dictatorships of the right and middle. Secondly, many dictatorships had the consent of the

Causes of dictatorship

overwhelming majority of their people. Plebiscites produced ninety-nine per cent in favour of the dictator, and so on – though naturally many of the figures were 'rigged'. Thirdly, in many cases, the dictators brought, in the short run, considerable materials benefits with them. The only possible justification of the Russian dictatorship is that Lenin and Stalin and Stalin's successors eventually succeeded in raising the standard of living in Russia, poor though it remained compared with that of the West, to a height above that of Tsarist days, while at the same time making Russia one of the most powerful countries on earth. Perhaps the most successful of all dictators was Mustapha Kemal Ataturk. Not only did he rescue his country from real peril and win back territory for it, but he successfully directed the progress of Turkey on European lines. He even sent old men back to school to learn a new alphabet, and abolished the fez, the veil, and the institution of polygamy with hardly a murmur from his hypnotised people.

The drift of Europe to dictatorship and the unrestrained behaviour of the dictators led directly to the Second World War. Far and away the prime cause of the war was Hitler, a nationalist fanatic who determined to create a greater Germany, irrespective of the rights or feelings of Poles, Czechs, or any of the other people unfortunate enough to live on the German borders. Mussolini, for what he would get out of it for Italy, aided and abetted Hitler. Stalin, who might perhaps have prevented the whole ghastly tragedy by closer co-operation with Britain and France, chose instead to purchase temporary immunity and advantage by giving Hitler the green light to go ahead against Poland.

Allied victory in the Second World War overthrew the Nazi and Fascist régimes, and restored, for the time being at least, democratic government in western Europe, in Italy, and – initially under Allied control – in West Germany. Britain, her dominions, and the U.S.A., maintaining intact their liberties and their democratic way of life, by a supreme effort passed back to western Europe the torch of freedom. To that extent democracy once more came out on top. But Russia, by the German attack in 1941, also became involved in the war, contributed greatly to the final victory, and finished up in control of the whole of eastern Europe. And the Russian system is, like the menace against which Britain and America were fighting, a dictatorship – if a dictatorship of a different kind.

Liberal, parliamentary democracy, then – the democracy for which Europe strove throughout the nineteenth century – is still a leading concept in the world. But it is now facing its greatest challenge. For the appeal of communism, with its policy of despoiling the upper and middle classes in the interests of the masses (as decided by the Communist Party leaders), is very great, despite the restrictions on personal freedom and the right of opposition which it entails; and among the poverty-stricken and land-hungry peasantry of Asia it has already made immense advances and may well prove irresistible.

The stage is occupied, then, by a drama on an old theme with a new twist. It is still the struggle for freedom which is being played out, just as it was in the nineteenth century. But this time the protagonists are not autocratic kingship and liberal democracy, but liberal democracy and totalitarian communism. Both concepts attract the ardent devotion of their supporters; both claim to be able to achieve the best life not for the privileged few but for mankind as a whole. In the clash between these two creeds, so dissimilar in means, if not in ultimate ends, will undoubtedly lie much of the history of the rest of this century.

Material improvements

Responsibility of the dictators for the Second World War

Re-establishment of democracy by the Allied victory

Eastern Europe under Russian control

The struggle to-day

Glossary of Political Terms used in the Text

Abdication
Surrender of his ruling position by a king, prince, etc. (Literally 'renouncing'.)

Absolute Monarchy, Absolutism
A system of government in which the monarch or ruler is unchecked by any form of parliament, and in which his own wishes are law.

Amnesty
An act granting forgiveness (literally 'forgetfulness') to political opponents or those who have committed some offence against the law.

Anarchism
The belief that all government is bad, and that the world would run more smoothly if all kings, parliaments, dictators, and the like were abolished. (Literally 'no rule'.)

Anschluss
Proposed union of Austria with Germany between the First and Second World Wars.

Arbitrary Imprisonment
Imprisonment at the will of a ruler without reference to the law. (Literally 'by personal choice'.)

Arbitration
A system of settling disputes, not by fighting but by appointing somebody to arbitrate or 'choose' between the two parties to the dispute.

Aristocracy
Literally 'government by the best' – usually employed in the sense of 'the best' by birth. All those belonging to the 'noble' class.

Autocracy
Absolute rule by one man. (Literally 'rule by oneself'.)

Bolsheviks
Majority group in Russian Social Democratic Party, later known as Communists.

Bonapartism
The support, after the overthrow of Napoleon in 1815, of the claim of some member of his family to rule France.

Bourgeoisie
The middle classes. (Literally, the townsfolk or 'burgesses'.)

Centre

Occupying a position between extreme socialism and extreme conservatism. (See also 'left' and 'right'.) Name of Catholic party formed in Reichstag to resist the 'May Laws' against the Church.

Chartism

Movement in England in the early nineteenth century to demand the six points of 'The People's Charter' – i.e. vote for all men, equal electoral districts, payment of MPs, abolition of property qualification for MPs, secret ballot and annual parliaments.

Clericals

Party in France in the later nineteenth century aiming at increased power for the Catholic Church, and showing a preference for monarchy over republicanism.

Communism

Belief that system of private ownership of land, factories, railways, banks, etc., should be replaced by public ownership. This to be done in two stages:

1. The 'proletariat', by 'direct action' (strikes and revolutions) captures the 'machinery of the state' (army, civil service, police) from the control of the employers, and uses it to dispossess the employers of their property. (The 'dictatorship of the proletariat'.)

2. When the employing class has been eliminated, the machinery of state to be abolished, as the use of force will have become superfluous.

First propounded in systematic form by the Germans Marx and Engels in the *Communist Manifesto* of 1848. It is worth noting that no Communist régime has yet shown any sign of advancing, or desiring to advance, from Stage 1 to Stage 2.

'Congress System'

'System' of settling international disputes by meetings of the great Powers, propounded by Metternich and Castlereagh after the Napoleonic wars. Operative, with little success, from 1815 to about 1823.

Conscription

Liability of all men to serve in the army both in home and overseas campaigns. First introduced by the French revolutionaries, and since imitated by almost all states in Europe.

Conservatism

Belief that existing benefits and institutions should be 'conserved' rather than be endangered by untried innovations, controversial 'reforms' and the like.

Constitution

Document or documents guaranteeing a parliament, fixed laws, freedom of speech or similar privileges. Limitation of the power of a ruler.

Constitutional

Legal, according to the constitution.

Constitutional Monarchy

Monarchy where the king has little power, but is bound by the terms of a constitution to accept parliament's advice.

Convention

Agreement in documentary form. (May also mean 'meeting' or 'custom'; in the sense of a meeting or coming together it was the name of the French Revolutionary assembly in 1792–95).

Coup d'état
Seizure of power.

Deism
Eighteenth-century creed held by many of the philosophers, maintaining a belief in God without recognizing the truth of the claims of the Christian church.

Democracy
Literally 'rule by the people' – system of government in which the masses have some control of policy, usually in the form of electing their representatives to some kind of parliament.

Despotism
Absolute rule.

Dictatorship
System of government in which one man or one group has complete power.

Diet
Assembly or parliament.

Economics
Study of the production and distribution of wealth.

Estates
Divisions or classes. In medieval parliaments the three estates were usually represented separately – first estate clergy, second estate nobility, third estate remainder.

Fascism
System of government in which the executive power (the dictator) has control over the legislative power (the parliament). Creation of Mussolini's in post-1918 Italy, marked by intense nationalism and intolerance of all opposition. Literally from the 'fasces', bundle of rods and axe carried before a Roman magistrate to denote his power of inflicting punishment.

Federation
System whereby many states group together to form a bigger state to which they surrender some, but not all, of their power.

Franchise
The right to vote.

Free Trade
Absence of tariffs or customs duties.

Imperialism
Belief in building up or holding a colonial empire.

Inflation
Increase in supply of paper-money, credit, etc. without corresponding backing in gold, leading inevitably to higher prices because the currency becomes less valuable.

Isolation
Freedom from alliances or commitments.

Laissez-faire
Absence of government action – 'leave things alone'. Belief that trade will flourish best without customs duties, subsidies, factory acts, etc.

Left

Holding extreme 'reformist' views, usually socialism or communism. So called from position of seats in semi-circular French Chamber of Deputies, where the conservatives sit on the right, the moderates in the centre and the socialists on the left.

Legislation

Law-making

Liberal

Used with a capital 'L' for a member of a definite party believing in freedom from government restrictions on trade and liberty, and holding with constitutional rule. With a small 'l' implying similar views, or of a broadly tolerant nature, but not necessarily a member of any Liberal party.

Nationalism

Enthusiasm for the right and might of the nation. Desire to see the nation organised powerfully and free from oppression by other nations.

Nazi (National Socialist)

Member of Hitler's post-1918 party in Germany aiming at dictatorship, control of the wealthy, and persecution of Liberals, Socialists, Communists and Jews. Intense nationalist, believing that 'racial purity' is of the utmost importance.

Nihilism

Russian belief in later nineteenth century that everything was bad, and hence that the only attitude to take up was a completely destructive one. (Literally 'nothingism'.) N.B. – Difference from anarchism, which considered that government alone was responsible for all evil.

Plebiscite

Vote by all citizens on some important issue.

Proletariat

The working masses.

Putsch

Rising. Attempt to seize power.

Radical

Aiming at a large programme of reform. (Literally 'from or to the root'.)

Reactionary

Tending to 'put the clock back': opposed to all reform.

Referendum

A plebiscite: the 'referring of a matter' to the people for decision.

Republic

A state not ruled by a monarch.

Right

Conservative: see 'left'.

Sanctions

Penalties or forms of compulsion which could be inflicted by the League of Nations on a state violating the League Covenant.

Socialism

Belief that the state, not private persons, should control the means of production (land, factories, etc.), distribution (railways, etc.), and exchange (banks, etc.).

Sovereignty

Rule, supreme power.

Suffrage
Right to vote.
Suzerainty
Overlordship. Supremacy over another state which has its own ruler but is not fully independent.
Syndicalism
Belief that the power and wealth of the country should be controlled, not by private persons, but by the working classes organised in trade unions. (French 'syndicat' = trade union.)
Totalitarian
Applied to governments which assume 'total' powers, or attempt to deal with the 'total' range of everyday life – e.g. Fascist or Communist dictatorship.
Ultras
Extreme reactionary party in France in early nineteenth century.
Zollverein
A 'customs union' of German states, headed by Prussia, in the 19th century.

Index